Teachin

Balancing Process and Practice

Teaching Writing

Balancing Process and Product

FIFTH EDITION

Gail E. Tompkins

California State University, Fresno, Emerita

PEARSON

Merrill
Prentice Hall

Upper Saddle River, New Jersey
Columbus, Ohio

Library of Congress Cataloging-in-Publication Data

Tompkins, Gail E.
  Teaching writing : balancing process and product / Gail E. Tompkins. – 5e.
    p. cm.
  Includes bibliographical references (p.   ) and index.
ISBN 0-13-158416-2
  1. English language—Composition and exercises—Study and teaching (Elementary) 2.
Creative writing (Elementary education) I. Title.

LB1576.T66 2008
372.62'3—dc22   2006051566

Vice President and Executive Publisher: Jeffery W. Johnston
Senior Editor: Linda Ashe Bishop
Senior Development Editor: Hope Madden
Senior Production Editor: Mary M. Irvin
Senior Editorial Assistant: Laura Weaver
Design Coordinator: Diane C. Lorenzo
Cover Designer: Jeff Vanik
Cover image: Mary O'Keefe Young
Production Manager: Pamela D. Bennett
Director of Marketing: David Gesell
Marketing Manager: Darcy Betts Prybella
Marketing Coordinator: Brian Mounts

This book was set in Korinna by Carlisle Publishing Services. It was printed and bound by Hamilton Printing
Co. The cover was printed by Phoenix Color Corp.

Pearson Education Ltd.   Pearson Education Australia Pty. Limited
Pearson Education Singapore Pte. Ltd.   Pearson Education North Asia Ltd.
Pearson Education Canada, Ltd.   Pearson Educación de Mexico, S.A. de C.V.
Pearson Education—Japan   Pearson Education Malaysia Pte. Ltd.

10 9 8 7 6 5 4 3 2
ISBN 13: 978-0-13-158416-7
ISBN 10:   0-13-158416-2

For Faith Nitschke

All changes have their melancholy,

but I have glad memories of our collaboration.

Now I wish you "fortune's expensive smile"

as you assume the reins of leadership,

confident that you'll achieve new wonders.

About the Author

Gail E. Tompkins is Professor Emerita at California State University, Fresno, where she directed the San Joaquin Valley Writing Project for many years. She continues to work with teachers in their kindergarten through fourth-grade classrooms and leads staff-development programs on reading, language arts, and writing. In 1998, Dr. Tompkins was inducted into the California Reading Association's Reading Hall of Fame in recognition of her publications and other accomplishments in the field of reading, and in 2000, she received the prestigious Provost's Award for Excellence in Teaching at California State University, Fresno.

Previously, Dr. Tompkins taught at Miami University in Ohio and at the University of Oklahoma, where she received the Regents' Award for Superior Teaching. She was also an elementary teacher in Virginia for 8 years.

Dr. Tompkins is the author of six other books published by Merrill/Prentice Hall: *Literacy for the 21st Century: A Balanced Approach,* 4th ed. (2006); *Language Arts: Patterns of Practice,* 6th ed. (2005); *Language Arts Essentials* (2006); *50 Literacy Strategies,* 2nd ed. (2004); *Literacy for the 21st Century: Teaching Reading and Writing in Prekindergarten Through Grade 4,* 2nd ed. (2007); and *Literacy for the 21st Century: Teaching Reading and Writing in Grades 4 Through 8* (2004).

She is also coeditor of three books written by the Teacher Consultants in the San Joaquin Valley Writing Project and published by Merrill/Prentice Hall: *Sharing the Pen: Interactive Writing With Young Children* (2004), edited with Stephanie Collom; *Teaching Vocabulary: 50 Creative Strategies, Grades K–12* (2004) and *50 Ways to Develop Strategic Writers* (2005), both edited with Cathy Blanchfield.

Preface

Teaching Writing: Balancing Process and Product continues to be the definitive book on how to teach writing, as it is the only text with comprehensive coverage of both process and product. This is because teachers in kindergarten through eighth grade must balance the attention paid to both the process that children use as they write and the quality of their compositions.

Learning to teach writing begins by focusing on the writing process, collaborative learning, reading and writing connections, assessment, writing genres, and writing across the curriculum. In this text, you'll find practical strategies for teaching and assessing writing—with step-by-step directions—accompanied by more than 100 illustrative student samples.

This new edition focuses even more specifically on individual student needs and teacher accountability, with features that not only examine the concerns of struggling writers and English learners, but also look closely at large-scale writing tests.

Process and Product

Part 1, *Process and Product,* focuses on the writing process that children use as they write and on ways to assess children's writing. Readers will learn about the stages in the writing process—prewriting, drafting, revising, editing, and publishing—and how to teach elementary students to use these stages as a recursive cycle when they write during writing workshop, literature focus units, and thematic units. Readers will also learn how to teach children to develop ideas, organize their writing, choose vocabulary, apply stylistic devices, and correct mechanical errors in order to create high-quality compositions.

Writing Genres

Part 2, *Writing Genres,* focuses on eight writing forms:

- journal writing
- letter writing
- biographical writing
- expository writing
- narrative writing
- descriptive writing
- poetry writing
- persuasive writing

Part 2 emphasizes five levels of composition instruction that vary according to how much scaffolding the teacher provides: modeled writing, shared writing, interactive writing, guided writing, and independent writing. Through this sequence, teachers vary the amount of support they provide student writers, and students increasingly assume more responsibility for their own writing.

Special Features for the Fifth Edition

Special features increase the effectiveness of this text and provide support for teachers as they teach writing, encourage children to assume more responsibility for using the writing process, and assess the quality of students' finished products.

Addresses Process and Product

- *Vignettes* beginning each chapter present you with an intimate look at real classrooms engaged in writing.
- *Minilessons* provide specific guidance for teaching essential strategies and skills to young writers.
- *Step by Step* features offer detailed guidance for planning instruction and assessment, organizing learning, and managing classroom writing projects.
- *New!* • The CD-ROM, *Writing Workshop,* packaged with the text gives you specific insight into classroom teaching in a workshop model, illustrating both writing process and product.

Meets Individual Student Needs

- *New!* • *How to Address Struggling Writers' Problems* This detailed analysis explains what issues cause writers to struggle, provides clear examples of the problem, and clarifies the steps to take to help writers overcome their obstacles.
- *Scaffolding English Learners* features pinpoint practical ways to support student writers whose first language is not English.

Planns for Accountability

- *New!* • *Preparing for Writing Tests* This new feature will help you prepare students for high-stakes testing by clearly defining each writing genre, providing prompts to generate a writing sample, and outlining possible pitfalls writers may face when writing in this specific genre.
- *Rubrics* throughout chapters help you address and clarify assessment issues.
- *Instructional Overviews* help you prepare for teaching by addressing the question of what to teach and when.

Supplements

For the Student

Writing Workshop CD-ROM ■ The videos CD-ROM packaged in every text contains videos of four classrooms, each following a master teacher through the activities of writing workshop. Experience the effective instruction that takes place in classroom communities by analyzing the techniques of teachers who integrate mini-lessons and strategy and skill development in writing workshops. Examine, re-examine, and manipulate genuine classroom footage to develop a deep and lasting understanding of highlighted instructional approaches and the ways they are effectively carried out in classrooms. The many learning possibilities include:

- Classroom footage, lesson plans, and quotes from the stakeholders
- A notepad feature, which allows you to take notes
- An Internet button, which facilitaties doing more research on the topics being covered
- The Study Builder and Custom Studies features, which allow you to think through your observations, assess and deepen your understandings, and share your conclusions by creating your own studies

For the Instructor

Instructor Resource Center ■ The Instructor Resource Center at *www.prenhall.com* has print and media resources available in downloadable, digital format—all in one location. As a registered faculty member, you can access and download pass-code protected resource files, course management content, and other premium online content directly to your computer.

Digital resources available for *Teaching Writing: Balancing Process and Product*, Fifth Edition, include:

- A test bank of multiple choice and essay tests
- Chapter-by-chapter materials, including Chapter Objectives, Suggested Readings, Discussion Questions, and In-Class Activities

To access these items online, go to *www.prenhall.com* and click on the Instructor Support button and then go to the Download Supplements section. Here you will be able to log in or complete a one-time registration for a user name and password. If you have any questions regarding this process or the materials available online, please contact your local Prentice Hall sales representative.

Acknowledgments

My heartfelt thanks go to the many people who have encouraged me and provided invaluable assistance as I wrote the first edition of *Teaching Writing: Balancing Process and Product* and revised it for subsequent editions. This text is a reflection of what the teachers and children with whom I have worked in California, in Oklahoma, and across the United States have taught me. It is testimony to their excellence. The teachers featured in the vignettes at the beginning of each chapter deserve special recognition:

Chapter 1: Judy Reeves, Western Hills Elementary School
Chapter 2: Susan Zumwalt, Jackson Elementary School
Chapter 3: Eileen Boland, Tenaya Middle School
Chapter 4: Debbie Meyers, Cyril Elementary School
Chapter 5: Lynnda Wheatley, Briarwood Elementary School
Chapter 6: Whitney Donnelly, Pleasant Valley School
Chapter 7: Carol Ochs, Jackson Elementary School
Chapter 8: Betty Jordan, Western Hills Elementary School
Chapter 9: Tom Garcia, Washington Elementary School
Chapter 10: Deanie Dillen, Putnam City Elementary School
Chapter 11: Kimberly Clark, Aynesworth Elementary School
Chapter 12: Shirley Carson, Wayne Elementary School

Thank you all for welcoming me into your classrooms and permitting me to share stories of your teaching expertise.

I want to express my appreciation to the children whose writing samples appear in this text and to the teachers, administrators, and parents who shared writing samples with me: Kathy Bending, Highland Elementary School, Downers Grove, IL; Linda Besett, Sulphur Elementary School, Sulphur, OK; Gracie Branch, Eisenhower Elementary School, Norman, OK; Juli Carson, Jefferson Elementary School, Norman, OK; Pam Cottom and Jean Griffith, James Griffith Intermediate School, Choctaw, OK; Parthy Ford, Whittier Elementary School, Lawton, OK; Debbie Frankenberg, Purcell, OK; Chuckie Garner, Kennedy Elementary School, Norman, OK; Peggy Givens, Watonga Middle School, Watonga, OK; Teri Gray, James Griffith Intermediate School, Choctaw, OK; Debbie Hamilton, Irving Middle School, Norman, OK; Ernestine Hightower, Whittier Elementary School, Lawton, OK; Merry Kelly, Thomas Oleata School, Atwater, CA; Helen Lawson, Deer Creek School, Oklahoma City, OK; Diane Lewis, Irving Middle School, Norman, OK; Mark Mattingly, Central Junior High School, Lawton, OK; Tissie McClure, Nicoma Park Intermediate School,

Nicoma Park, OK; Gina McCook, Whittier Middle School, Norman, OK; Joyce Mucher, Penryn Elementary School, Penryn, CA: Teresa Ossenkop, Eisenhower Elementary School, Norman, OK; Sandra Pabst, Monroe Elementary School, Norman, OK; Alice Rakitan, Highland Elementary School, Downers Grove, IL; Jelta Reneau, Lincoln Elementary School, Norman, OK; Becky Selle, Bethel School, Shawnee, OK; Linda Shanahan, Nicoma Park Intermediate School, Nicoma Park, OK; Jo Ann Steffen, Nicoma Park Junior High School, Nicoma Park, OK; Cecilia Uyeda, Eaton Elementary School, Fresno, CA; Gail Warmath, Longfellow Middle School, Norman, OK; Vera Willey, Lincoln Elementary School, Norman, OK.

I would like to thank the reviewers of my manuscript for their insights and comments: Debbie East, Indiana University; Marjorie R. Hancock, Kansas State University; Linda Kleemann, Harris-Stowe State College; Michael R. Muise, Wayne State University, and Amy Thornburg, University of North Carolina, Greensboro.

I want to express my sincere appreciation to my editors at Merrill. I offer very special thanks to my editors, Linda Bishop and Hope Madden, for their creative inspiration and nurturing encouragement through this revision of *Teaching Writing*. Thanks, also, to Jeff Johnston, who originally provided the opportunity for me to pursue this project. I appreciate their continuing support of my work.

I also want to thank my production team. Melissa Gruzs has expertly put my manuscript into final form, and I am very grateful for her careful attention to detail. And thanks to Mary Irvin, my production editor, who successfully moved my manuscript through the maze of production details.

I thank each and every one of you for your contributions that have helped me complete this labor of love.

Gail E. Tompkins

Brief Contents

Contents

Special Features

Step by Step

Minilessons

How to Address Struggling Writers' Problems

Preparing for Writing Tests

Teaching Writing

Balancing Process and Product

Chapter 1
Teaching Children to Write

Preview

- The process approach to writing instruction is based on how real writers write.

- The five stages of the writing process are prewriting, drafting, revising, editing, and publishing.

- Teachers support and scaffold children as they learn to write, gradually giving them more and more responsibility.

- The five levels of support are modeled writing, shared writing, interactive writing, guided writing, and independent writing.

Mrs. Reeves Teaches Writing

Mrs. Reeves's multiage primary class is learning about weather, and they use writing as a tool for learning. They begin the unit by making a K-W-L chart. Mrs. Reeves divides the chart into three columns: "K: What We Know," "W: What We Wonder," and "L: What We Learned." Children brainstorm things they already know about weather, and Mrs. Reeves writes them in the *K* column. The list includes "Weather is different in summer and winter," "Lightning is very dangerous," and "You tell the temperature on a thermometer." Then a child asks, "How does it rain?" and Mrs. Reeves writes the question in the *W* column. Other questions about tornadoes and types of clouds are asked, and she adds them to the *W* column. The discussion continues, and other information and questions are added to the *K* and *W* columns. During the unit, children continue to add questions to the *W* column, and as they learn more about weather, they write what they are learning in the *L* column to complete the chart.

Mrs. Reeves also talks with students about the kinds of activities they might pursue during the unit. The children want to keep daily weather calendars, interview a television weather forecaster, do weather experiments, and write an ABC book on weather, as they did on plants earlier in the school year. They also want to keep learning logs, read weather books, make posters about weather, and do self-selected projects. Writing will be an

Independent Writing: Two Learning Log Entries

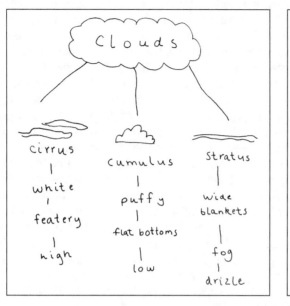

important tool in these activities. Mrs. Reeves uses the children's ideas together with the standards specified by her school district to plan the unit.

Mrs. Reeves prepares a large pocket chart for the word wall; the children will write interesting and unfamiliar words about weather on cards and display them in alphabetized sections on the word wall during the unit. As they write and work on projects, children refer to the word wall. They suggest words, including *tornado, thermometer, hurricane, freezing,* and *thunderstorm,* to be added to the word wall. By the end of the 4-week unit, 50 or more words will have been collected on the word wall.

An assortment of weather books is displayed on a special rack in the classroom library; Mrs. Reeves gives a book talk on each one, briefly mentioning something of interest about the book. Among the books she introduces are *Cloudy With a Chance of Meatballs* (Barrett, 1978), *Hurricanes* (Simon, 2003), *Snowballs* (Ehlert, 1995), *Twisters and Other Terrible Storms* (Osborne & Osborne, 2003), *Weather Forecasting* (Gibbons, 1987), and *Weather Report* (Yolen, 1993), a collection of poems. Children will read one book together as a class and read other books during reading workshop.

Children write about what they read in learning logs. At the beginning of the unit, they make their own logs by compiling 20 sheets of notebook paper and construction paper covers, punching holes, and adding brads. During the unit, children decorate the covers with weather-related illustrations. At the end of the unit, they number the pages and add a table of contents. In their logs, children write, draw pictures, and add charts and other information. Two entries from children's learning logs are presented above. The first entry is a cluster about clouds, and the second is a quickwrite written after Mrs. Reeves read aloud Patricia Polacco's *Thunder Cake* (1990), a story about how a young girl overcame her fear of thunderstorms.

Mrs. Reeves's students use writing as a part of many science activities. One example is when the local television weather forecaster, Mr. Reed, visited the class for an interview. A group of children wrote a letter inviting Mr. Reed to visit the class and answer their questions. Next, the class brainstormed a list of questions to ask him, and Mrs. Reeves listed the questions on a chart. Then each child chose a question to ask and wrote it on an index card. During Mr. Reed's visit, children took turns asking questions and taking notes about his answers. Afterward, children discussed the weather forecaster's visit and decided to make a class book to share what they had learned. Mrs. Reeves demonstrated the procedure for making a page, and then children created their own pages. On each page, a child wrote the question he or she had asked Mr. Reed, along with his answer. They used the writing process to draft, revise, and edit their pages. Because the book was being published and would be shared with parents and other classes, it was important for the children to write in complete sentences and to spell all words correctly. A page from the class book is presented below.

The children used the writing process again to write another class book on weather in an ABC format. They began by hanging a strip of paper beside the word wall and writing the alphabet on it. Then children identified words beginning with each letter on the first list and wrote them on the second list; for example, they wrote *forecasters, flurries,* and *fog* under *F*. As a class, children decided on the page layout featuring the letter highlighted, an illustration, and accompanying text (a sentence or two), and Mrs. Reeves demonstrated how to lay out a page before the children began working on their pages. Then children, individually or in pairs, selected a letter to do. After creating rough drafts of their pages, they met in writing groups to share their drafts and get suggestions on additional information they might include. After they made revisions, Mrs. Reeves met with children for editing. Then children made their final copies on special drawing paper and arranged the pages in alphabetical order. Several children worked together to make the title page and the cover. Mrs. Reeves punched holes in the pages and used ribbon to bind the book. The D page from the class ABC weather book is shown on page 5.

Children also chose individual projects to do that relate to weather. Here are some of their projects:

- Making weather safety posters
- Performing a skit about weather forecasting
- Constructing weather instruments
- Retelling a favorite weather story, such as *Cloudy With a Chance of Meatballs*
- Writing a weather book

Shared Writing: A Page From a Class Interview Book

Guided Writing: A Page From a Class ABC Book

Mrs. Reeves set aside 45-minute chunks of time for children to work on these projects. They worked individually or in small groups, and Mrs. Reeves circulated around the classroom to supervise their work. She met with children briefly in conferences to keep track of their work and to solve problems as needed. After they completed their projects, children shared them with classmates during a special sharing time.

*C*hildren are writers. Notions that they can't write, that they learn to read before learning to write, or that they learn to write letters, words, and sentences before writing longer texts are antiquated. Classroom teachers as well as writing researchers have discovered that even young children communicate through writing, and that they begin writing as they are learning to read or even before they read (Graves, 1994). Writing serves these three purposes:

Children learn how to write. Through experiences with writing, children learn how to write. Informal writing activities, such as clustering and quickwriting, provide opportunities for children to acquire writing fluency. For more formal writing activities, such as stories, reports, and poems, children use the writing process: This is a multistage process through which children gather and organize ideas, write rough drafts, and refine and polish their writing before publishing it.

Children learn about written language. As children learn to write, they discover the uniqueness of written language and the ways in which it differs from oral language and drawing. They develop an appreciation for the interrelations of purpose, audience, and form in writing and learn to consider these three elements as they write. In addition, children learn about the mechanics of writing, including standard spelling and usage, capitalization, and formatting.

Children learn through writing. Writing is a valuable learning tool that has many applications across the curriculum. Children write informally to analyze and synthesize their learning, and they write formally and apply their knowledge when they write books and reports (Halliday, 1980; Indrisano & Paratore, 2005).

Mrs. Reeves's second and third graders exemplified all three components as they used writing during their unit on weather. They learned to write by writing, and they practiced the writing process as they drafted, revised, and edited class books and individual projects. Mrs. Reeves's students learned about written language as they revised and edited their writing when it was to be published. They also used writing as a tool for learning about weather through both informal writing and more formal writing projects.

Frank Smith (1988) reflected that "the first time I explored in detail how children learn to write, I was tempted to conclude that it was, like the flight of bumblebees, a theoretical impossibility" (p. 17). The writing samples in the vignette about Mrs. Reeves's students show that just as bumblebees really do fly, children really do write.

The Writing Process

The writing process is a way of looking at writing instruction in which the emphasis is shifted from children's finished products to what they think and do as they write. James Britton and Janet Emig were two of the first researchers to examine students' writing processes. In her study, Emig (1971) interviewed 12th graders as they wrote, and she studied the writing processes that one teenager used in depth. Several years later, Britton and his colleagues (1975) examined 2,000 essays written by British high school students and found that their writing processes differed according to the type of writing. At the same time, Donald Graves (1975) examined young children's writing and documented that 7-year-olds, like high school students, used a variety of strategies as they wrote.

These early researchers generally divided the writing process into three stages. Britton (1970b) labeled them *conception, incubation,* and *production.* In the conception stage, writers choose topics and decide to write; in the incubation stage, they develop the topic by gathering information; and in the production stage, they write, revise, and edit the composition. Graves (1975) described a similar process of *prewriting, composing,* and *postwriting.* In prewriting, writers choose topics and gather ideas for writing; in the composing stage, they write the composition; and in the postwriting stage, they share their writing.

Linda Flower and John Hayes (1977, 1981; Hayes & Flower, 1986) studied college students' writing and asked students to talk about their thought processes while they composed. They then analyzed students' talk to examine the strategies writers use and developed a model that describes writing as a complex problem-solving process. According to the model, the writing process involves three activities: *planning,* as writers set goals to guide the writing; *translating,* as writers put the plans into writing; and *reviewing,* as writers evaluate and revise the writing. These activities are not linear steps, according to Flower and Hayes, because writers continually monitor their writing and move back and forth among the activities; this monitoring might be considered a fourth component of the writing process. An important finding from their research is that writing is recursive: Using this monitoring mechanism, writers jump back and forth from one activity to another as they write.

Figure 1–1 Key Features of the Writing Process

Stage 1: Prewriting

Choose a topic.
Gather and organize ideas.
Consider the potential audience.
Identify the purpose of the writing.
Choose an appropriate genre.

Stage 2: Drafting

Write a rough draft.
Craft leads to grab readers' attention.
Emphasize content rather than mechanics.

Stage 3: Revising

Share writing in writing groups.
Participate constructively in discussions about classmates' writing.
Make changes to reflect the comments of classmates and the teacher.
Make substantive rather than only minor changes between the first and final drafts.

Stage 4: Editing

Proofread compositions to locate errors.
Correct mechanical errors.

Stage 5: Publishing

Publish writing in an appropriate form.
Share finished writing with an appropriate audience.

Some researchers have examined particular aspects of the writing process. Nancy Sommers (1982, 1994) described writing as a revision process in which writers develop their ideas, not polish their writing. Less experienced writers, according to Sommers, focus on small, word-level changes and error hunting. This emphasis on mechanics rather than content may be due to teachers' behavior. Sondra Perl (1994) examined how the writing process is used in high school and college classrooms and concluded that teachers place excessive importance on mechanical errors. Flower and Hayes found that less successful writers have a limited repertoire of alternatives for solving problems as they write, and Bereiter and Scardamalia (1982) found that even though children participated in writing process activities, they were less capable of monitoring the need to move from one activity to another. Through both expert teaching and extensive writing practice, children can become better at self-monitoring by the time they reach middle school or high school levels.

The five-stage writing process presented in this chapter incorporates activities identified through research. The stages are prewriting, drafting, revising, editing, and publishing, and the key features of each stage are summarized in Figure 1–1. The numbering of the stages does not mean that this writing process is a linear series of discrete activities. Research has shown that the process involves recurring cycles; labeling is only an aid for identifying and discussing writing activities. In the classroom, the stages merge and recur as children write (Barnes, Morgan, & Weinhold, 1997). Moreover, writers personalize the process to meet their own needs and vary it according to the writing assignment.

Stage 1: Prewriting

Prewriting is the getting-ready-to-write stage. The traditional notion that writers have thought out their topic completely is ridiculous: If writers wait for the ideas to be fully developed, they may wait forever. Instead, writers begin tentatively by talking, reading, and writing to see what they know and in what direction they want to go. Pulitzer Prize–winning writer Donald Murray (2004, 2005) calls this stage the discovery of writing: You begin writing to explore what you know and to surprise yourself.

Prewriting has probably been the most neglected stage in the writing process; however, it is as crucial to writers as a warm-up is to athletes. Donald Murray (1982) believes that 70% or more of writing time should be spent in prewriting. During the prewriting stage, writers

- choose a topic;
- consider purpose, audience, and form;
- generate and organize ideas for writing.

Choosing a Topic ■ Sometimes children choose their own topics for writing, and at other times, teachers choose the topics or children and teachers choose topics collaboratively (Chandler-Olcott & Mahar, 2001). More than a quarter century ago, Donald Graves (1976) argued that children should take responsibility for choosing their own writing topics; he called the traditional practice of having teachers choose the topics "writing welfare." When children choose the topics, they become more motivated—even passionate—about writing. Children often keep a writer's notebook (Fletcher, 1996) with ideas, observations, quotations, and other possible writing topics.

It isn't always possible, or even advisable, for children to choose their own topics. Sometimes teachers specify the writing topic for children so that they will learn how to handle new writing tasks, including those they might not choose for themselves. Also, with the current emphasis on district, state, and national writing assessments, it has become increasingly important for children to be able to deal with writing topics regardless of personal interest.

Children also work with teachers and classmates to choose writing topics collaboratively. Chandler-Olcott and Mahar (2001) argue that this may be the most important approach because children learn how to negotiate topics with other writers. These three approaches to topic selection are often used together in thematic units. In the vignette at the beginning of the chapter, for example, the children chose their own topics for their weather projects, they shared responsibility when they interviewed the television weather forecaster, and Mrs. Reeves chose many of the topics that children wrote about in their learning logs.

Considering Purpose ■ As children prepare to write, they need to identify their purpose for writing. Are they writing to entertain? to inform? to persuade? This decision about purpose influences other decisions they make about audience and form. M. A. K. Halliday (1975) identified seven language functions that apply to both oral and written language:

- *Instrumental Language.* Language to satisfy needs, such as in business letters.
- *Regulatory Language.* Language to control the behavior of others, such as in directions and rules.

- *Interactional Language.* Language to establish and maintain social relationships, such as in pen pal letters and dialogue journals.
- *Personal Language.* Language to express personal opinions, such as in learning logs and letters to the editor.
- *Imaginative Language.* Language to express imagination and creativity, such as in stories, poems, and scripts.
- *Heuristic Language.* Language to seek information and to find out about things, such as in learning logs and interviews.
- *Informative Language.* Language to convey information, such as in reports and biographies.

Children write for all of these purposes.

Considering Audience ■ Children may write primarily for themselves, to express and clarify their own ideas and feelings, or they may write for others. Possible audiences include classmates, younger children, parents, foster grandparents, children's authors, and pen pals. Other audiences are more distant and less well known. For example, children may write letters to businesses to request information, write articles to be published in the local newspaper, or submit stories and poems to be published in literary magazines.

Children demonstrate their relationship with the audience in a variety of ways, often by adding parenthetical information or asides. For example, a seventh grader begins "George Mudlumpus and the Mystery of the Golden Spider," his sixth mystery featuring George Mudlumpus, "the detective with the outrageous rates," this way: "I had decided to take my vacation, as you already know from the last story I told you. So, I packed, got my airplane ticket, and got on a 747 jetliner. I was off to San Francisco!" This student feels a close relationship, that of a storyteller, with his unknown audience. He often includes asides in his stories, and George sometimes comments to his readers, "I know! You think I should have recognized that clue!"

When children write for others, teachers are the most common audience. Teachers can assume several roles—trusted adult, a partner in dialogue, and judge (Britton et al., 1975)—and how writers perceive these roles is crucial. In writing to a trusted adult, children feel secure because they can rely on their reader to respond sympathetically. When writing a dialogue with a teacher, children are secure in the teacher's presence and assume that the teacher will be interested in the writing, responding to what has been written, not to how it has been written. Unfortunately, the teacher's most common role is that of judge, but this role is least conducive to good writing. When a teacher acts as a judge, children produce writing only to satisfy the teacher's requirement or to receive a grade.

Considering Form ■ One of the most important considerations is the form or genre the writing will take. A story? A letter? A poem? A journal entry? A writing project could be handled in any one of these ways. As part of a science theme on hermit crabs, for instance, children could write a story about a hermit crab, draw a picture of a hermit crab and label body parts, write an explanation of how hermit crabs obtain shells to live in, or keep a log of observations about hermit crabs living in the classroom. There is an almost endless variety of genres that children's writing may take, but too often the choices are limited to writing stories, poems, and reports. Instead, children need to experiment with a wide variety of writing genres and

Figure 1–2 Six Writing Genres

Genre	Purpose	Activities
Descriptive Writing	Children become careful observers and choose precise language when they use description. They take notice of sensory details and learn to make comparisons (metaphors and similes) in order to make their writing more powerful.	Character sketches Comparisons Descriptive sentences Five-senses poems Found poems Observations
Expository Writing	Children collect and synthesize information for expository writing. This writing is objective, and reports are the most common type of informative writing. Children use expository writing to give directions, sequence steps, compare one thing to another, explain causes and effects, or describe problems and solutions.	Alphabet books Autobiographies Brochures Directions Reports Summaries
Journals and Letters	Children write to themselves and to specific, known audiences in journals and letters. Their writing is personal and often less formal than other genres. They share news, explore new ideas, and record notes. Letters and envelopes require special formatting.	Business letters Courtesy letters Double-entry journals E-mail messages Learning logs Personal journals
Narrative Writing	Children retell familiar stories, develop sequels for stories they have read, write stories called personal narratives about events in their own lives, and create original stories. They incorporate a beginning, middle, and end in the narratives they write.	Original stories Personal narratives Retellings of stories Sequels to stories Scripts of stories
Persuasive Writing	*Persuasion* is winning someone to your viewpoint or cause. The three ways people are persuaded are by appeals to logic, character, and emotion. Children present their position clearly and then support it with examples and evidence.	Advertisements Book reviews Editorials Letters to the editor Persuasive essays Persuasive letters
Poetry Writing	Children experiment with rhyme, alliteration, repetition, and other stylistic devices as they create poems. As children experiment with poetry, they learn that poetic language is vivid and powerful but concise, and they learn that poems can be arranged in different ways on a page.	Acrostic poems Found poems Haiku "I am" poems "I wish . . ." poems Poems for two voices

explore the purposes and formats of these forms. A list of six genres is presented in Figure 1–2. Through reading and writing, children develop a strong sense of these forms and how they are structured. Langer (1985) found that by third grade, children responded in different ways to story- and report-writing assignments: They organized compositions differently and varied the kinds of information and elaboration they used depending on the form. Similarly, Hidi and Hildyard (1983) found that children could differentiate between stories and persuasive essays. Because children are clarifying the distinctions between various writing genres, it is very important that teachers use the correct terminology and not label all children's writing as "stories." Some English learners, however, are not familiar with genres, and they benefit from explicit instruction so that they can "succeed in school and actively participate in the dominant community" (Gibbons 2002, p. 60).

Teaching children to make decisions about purpose, audience, and form is an important component of writing instruction. In each case, children need to know the range of options available to writers. Decisions about these aspects of writing have an impact on each other. For example, if the purpose is to entertain, a form such as a story, poem, or script might be selected. These three forms look very different on a piece of paper: Whereas a story is written in the traditional block format, scripts and poems have unique arrangements on the page. For example, in a script, the character's name appears first and is followed by a colon and then the dialogue. Action and dialogue, rather than description, carry the story line in a script. In contrast, poems have unique formatting considerations; words are used judiciously, and each word and phrase is chosen to convey a maximum amount of information.

Although decisions about purpose, audience, and form may change as children write and revise, writers must begin with at least a tentative understanding as they move into the drafting stage.

Gathering and Organizing Ideas ■ Children gather and organize ideas for writing and the words and sentences to express these ideas in these ways:

- Drawing pictures
- Talking with classmates and the teacher
- Reading stories, informational books, and other texts
- Dramatizing and retelling stories
- Writing
- Making graphic organizers

Graves (2003) calls these activities that children use to activate prior knowledge, gather and organize ideas, and collect words "rehearsal" activities.

Drawing is the way young children gather and organize ideas for writing. Kindergarten and first-grade teachers often notice that children draw before they write. When young children are asked to write before drawing, for example, they explain that they can't write yet because they don't know what to write until they see what they draw. As young children become writers, they use drawing and other symbol systems as they grapple with the uniqueness of writing (Dyson, 1993).

Children use a variety of writing activities to gather and organize ideas before beginning to draft their compositions (daSilva, 2001). They brainstorm words and images, sequence lists of events, cluster main ideas and details, make other charts or diagrams to record ideas, or quickwrite to discover what they know about a topic and what direction their writing might take. Outlining is another form of prewriting, but this traditional prewriting activity is less effective than clustering and not recommended for younger students.

Stage 2: Drafting

Children write and refine their compositions through a series of drafts. During the drafting stage, they focus on getting their ideas down on paper. Because writers do not begin writing with their compositions already fully formed in their minds, they begin with tentative ideas developed through prewriting activities. The drafting stage is the time to pour out ideas, with little concern about spelling, punctuation, and other mechanical errors. Here are the activities in this stage:

- Writing a rough draft
- Writing leads

Writing a Rough Draft ■ Children skip every other line as they write their rough drafts so as to leave adequate space for revising. They use arrows to move sections of text, cross-outs to delete sections, and scissors and tape to cut apart and rearrange text, just as adult writers do. Similarly, children write on only one side of a sheet of paper so that the paper can be cut apart or rearranged. Because word processors are increasingly available in elementary classrooms, revising, with all its shifting and deleting of text, is becoming much easier. However, for children who handwrite their compositions, the wide spacing of lines is crucial. Teachers often make small X's on every other line of young children's papers as a reminder to skip lines as they draft their compositions.

Children label their drafts by writing "Rough Draft" in ink at the top of their papers or by stamping the papers with a "Rough Draft" stamp. This label indicates to the writer, other students, parents, and administrators that the composition is a draft in which emphasis has been placed on content, not mechanics. It also explains why teachers have not graded the paper or marked mechanical errors. Also, if some children who are just learning the writing process plan to make the rough draft their final draft by writing carefully, the label "Rough Draft" at the top of the paper negates this idea and further emphasizes that writing involves more than one stage.

As children draft their compositions, they may need to modify their earlier decisions about purpose, audience, and, especially, the form their writing will take. For example, a composition that began as a story might be transformed into a report, letter, or poem: The new format may allow the child to communicate more effectively. This process of modifying earlier decisions also continues into the revising stage.

📝 How to Address Struggling Writers' Problems

The Problem	Children are too dependent on teacher approval.
What Causes It	Children stick close to the teacher for a variety of reasons. Sometimes they're insecure or fearful of making mistakes. Or, they may not understand what they're expected to do because they didn't pay attention when the directions were given or they don't know how to use the writing process.
How to Solve It	*Quick fix:* Have children work with partners so they can ask questions, check the assignment, get feedback, and share their writing with a classmate before approaching the teacher. Also, teachers may be able to provide enough support for vulnerable students if they check with these children at the beginning of each day's writing time.
	Long-term solution: Teachers should set up a routine for conferencing so that children understand that they will have regular opportunities to get teacher feedback. In addition, teachers can identify several children each week who serve as coaches; children go to these coaches for assistance before interrupting the teacher.
How to Prevent the Problem	Children who are confident writers can work independently, and they understand that they can talk with classmates when they need assistance.

Teachers do not emphasize correct spelling and neatness at this stage. In fact, when teachers point out mechanical errors during the drafting stage, they send a false message to students that mechanical correctness is more important than content (Sommers, 1982). Later, during editing, children clean up mechanical errors and put their composition into a neat, final form.

Writing Leads ■ A composition's lead, or opening sentences, is crucial. Think of the last time you went to a library to choose a book to read. Several titles or book jacket pictures may have caught your eye, but before making your selection, you opened each book and read the first paragraph or two. Which one did you choose? Probably the one that hooked you, or grabbed your attention. The same is true for children's writing: Students who consider audience as they write will want to grab the attention of the audience. Children may use a variety of techniques to appeal to their audience, such as questions, facts, dialogue, brief stories, and problems. Donald Graves (2003) and Lucy Calkins (1994) recommend that students create several leads and try them out on classmates before deciding on one. As students write these leads, they gain valuable knowledge about how to manipulate language and how to vary viewpoint or sequence in their writing.

Stage 3: Revising

Writers clarify and refine ideas in their compositions during the revising stage. Often novice writers terminate the writing process as soon as they complete a rough draft, believing that once their ideas are jotted down, the writing task is complete. In fact, they often see revision as punishment for not having gotten it right in the first place (Heard, 2002). Experienced writers, however, know that they must turn to others for reactions and revise on the basis of these comments. Revision is not just polishing writing; it is meeting the needs of readers by adding, substituting, deleting, and rearranging material. The word *revision* means "seeing again," and in this stage, writers see their compositions again with their classmates and the teacher helping them. Writers

- reread the rough draft;
- share the rough draft in a writing group;
- revise on the basis of feedback received from the writing group.

Because revising is probably the most difficult part of the writing process, teachers often postpone teaching children how to revise; however, even first graders can learn to revise. To get started, children need to know what revising is, why it is important, and how it differs from editing (Saddler, 2003). Franklin (2005) and Overmeyer (2005) recommend that children also learn about the qualities of good writing so that they can recognize some of the differences between good writing and writing that is less effective. Many teachers share anonymous student samples they've saved from previous years or pieces they've written themselves to point out differences and then develop a chart listing the criteria of good writing. Armed with this knowledge, children can begin to spot problems in a piece of writing, and they have the vocabulary to talk about them. Teachers use additional student samples to model revising in minilessons and have children practice revising with partners because it's easier for children to revise someone else's writing. After this instruction and practice, children are ready to begin revising their own writing.

Rereading the Rough Draft ■ Writers are the first to revise their compositions. Some revision occurs during drafting when writers make choices and changes as they write. After finishing the rough draft, writers need to distance themselves from the draft for a day or two and then reread it from a fresh perspective, as a reader might. As they reread, children make changes—adding, substituting, deleting, and moving material—and place question marks by sections that need work. It is these trouble spots that children ask for help with in their writing group.

Writing Groups ■ Children meet in writing groups to share their compositions with small groups of classmates. Writing groups offer the writers choices; give them responses, feelings, and thoughts; show different possibilities in revising; and speed up revising (Mohr, 1984). These groups provide a scaffold, or supportive environment, in which teachers and classmates can talk about plans and strategies for writing and revising (Franklin, 2005).

Writing groups can form spontaneously when several students have completed drafts and are ready to share their compositions, or they can be formal groupings with identified leaders. In some primary classrooms, for example, writing groups may form spontaneously; when students finish writing, they go to sit on an area rug or go to a special table. As soon as a child with writing to share arrives, others who are available to listen and respond to the writing come and join the group. When three or four children have arrived for the writing group, the writer reads the writing and the other children listen and respond to it, offering compliments and relating this piece of writing to their own experiences and writing. Sometimes the teacher joins the listeners on the rug to participate in the writing group; at other times, the children work independently. In other classrooms, writing groups are more formal: Writing groups meet when all children have completed a rough draft and are ready to share their writing with classmates and the teacher. The teacher participates in these groups, providing feedback along with the students. In some classrooms, writing groups may function independently: Four or five children are assigned to each group, and a list of the groups and their members is posted in the classroom. On the list, the teacher puts a star by one child's name, and that child serves as a group leader. Every quarter, the leader changes.

The steps in conducting a writing group are listed in the step-by-step feature on the next page.

Making Revisions ■ As they make revisions, children add words, substitute sentences, delete paragraphs, and move phrases. They cross out, draw arrows, and write in the space they left between the lines of writing when they double-spaced their rough drafts. Children work differently, but they move back and forth into prewriting to gather additional information, into drafting to write a new paragraph, and into revising to replace an often-repeated word (Dix, 2006). Messiness is inevitable, but despite the scribbles, children are usually able to decipher what they have written.

Writers make four kinds of changes as they revise: They add, substitute, delete, and move text from one place to another (Faigley & Witte, 1981). Sometimes their changes involve single words, phrases, sentences, or paragraphs. Children often focus at the word and phrase level and make more additions and substitutions than deletions and moves. Teachers and children can analyze the types of revisions that children make by examining their revised rough drafts. The number and type of revisions are one gauge of children's growth as writers.

Step by Step: Writing Groups

1. **A writer reads.** A group of four or five children take turns reading their compositions aloud. Everyone listens politely, thinking about compliments and suggestions for improvement they will make after the writer has finished reading. Typically, only the writer looks at the composition as it is read, because when classmates and the teacher look at it, they quickly notice mechanical errors even though the emphasis is on content during revising.

2. **Listeners offer compliments.** Group members tell what they liked about the composition. These positive comments should be specific, focusing on strengths. Comments such as "I like the way you wrote 'Monika was as scared as a kindergartner on the first day of school.' That really makes me understand what she was feeling" are much more effective than general "I like it" or "It was good!" comments. Children usually focus on organization, leads, word choice, voice, sequence, dialogue, or theme in their comments.

3. **The writer asks questions.** Writers ask their classmates for assistance on trouble spots or ask questions that reflect more general concerns about how well they are communicating. For example: "I don't have very much information in this part about Betsy Ross's childhood. It's short. What should I do?" Admitting that they need help from their classmates is a major step in learning to revise.

4. **Listeners offer suggestions.** Group members ask about things that are unclear and make revision suggestions. Children are careful to phrase their comments in helpful rather than hurtful ways. For example: "Here you tell why junk food is bad for you. Then you say 'Junk food is fun to eat.' Maybe you could move that to where you tell why junk food is good."

5. **Repeat the process.** Other children in the group share their compositions and repeat the first four steps in the procedure.

6. **Writers plan for revision.** Children each make a commitment about how they will revise their writing after considering their classmates' comments and suggestions. Because children verbalize their revision plans, they are more likely to complete the revision stage.

The minilesson feature on page 16 shows how a seventh-grade teacher drew his students' attention to the types of revisions they were making. For additional ideas for minilessons on revision, check Georgia Heard's *The Revision Toolbox: Teaching Techniques That Work* (2002) and Barry Lane's *Reviser's Toolbox* (1999).

Stage 4: Editing

Editing is putting the piece of writing into its final form. Until this stage, the focus has been primarily on developing the content of the composition; here the focus changes to mechanics, and children "polish" their writing by correcting spelling and other mechanical errors (Parsons, 2001). The goal is to make the writing "optimally readable" (F. Smith, 1994). Writers who write for readers understand that if their compositions are not readable, they have written in vain because their ideas will never be read.

Mechanics refers to the commonly accepted conventions of written standard English; they include capitalization, punctuation, spelling, sentence structure, usage, and formatting considerations specific to poems, scripts, letters, and other writing forms. Using these conventions is a courtesy to those who will read the composition. The most effective way to teach mechanical skills is during the editing stage of the writing process rather than through workbook exercises (Fearn & Farnan, 1998). When editing a composition that will be shared with a genuine audience, children are more interested in using mechanical skills correctly so they can communicate effectively.

MINILESSON

Four Types of Revisions

Mr. Ortiz's seventh-grade language arts students are writing persuasive essays, and because this is an important assignment, he wants them to revise more thoroughly than they sometimes do. The most common type of revision that his students make is single-word substitutions; they might change the word *suggest* to *recommend,* for example. It's easy for Mr. Ortiz to check his students' revisions because they code them in the margin of their papers using these letters: A (additions), S (substitutions), D (deletions), and M (moves). In today's minilesson, his students try other types of revisions using a sample student essay.

1. Introduce the topic

Mr. Ortiz asks his seventh graders to check their persuasive essays to see which types of revisions they're making. The students tally their revisions and report that most of the changes are single-word substitutions.

2. Share examples

Mr. Ortiz presents the first page of a student's three-page, double-spaced, typed essay written the previous year that needs a variety of revisions. He displays it on the overhead and reads it aloud. Together they revise it, and Mr. Ortiz encourages his students to think of revisions other than word substitutions. He points out a sentence in one paragraph that doesn't belong and another paragraph that is out of sequence. In all, the class makes 10 revisions.

3. Provide information

After they finish making revisions, Mr. Ortiz codes each revision in the margin and tallies each type: They made 5 additions, 2 substitutions, 3 deletions, and 1 move on the first page of the essay. Of the 10 revisions, 4 involved single words; the other 6 involved phrases, sentences, and paragraphs.

4. Guide practice

Mr. Ortiz passes out copies of the student's entire essay and asks students to work with partners to revise the rest of the essay. He encourages them to make all four types of revisions. Afterward, students calculate the types of revisions they have marked and share some of them with the class.

5. Assess learning

Mr. Ortiz examines the types of revisions his students make on their persuasive essays. His students also write a reflection about the types of revisions they made and how they improved the quality of their writing through their revision choices.

Figure 1–3 Proofreaders' Marks

Delete		There were cots to sleep on and food to eat on at the shelter.
Insert		Mrs. Kim's cat is the color of carrots.
Indent paragraph		Riots are bad. People can get hurt and buildings can get burned down but good things can happen too. People can learn to be friends.
Capitalize		Daniel and his mom didn't like mrs. Kim or her cat.
Change to lowercase		People were Rioting because they were angry.
Add period		I think Daniel's mom and Mrs. Kim will become friends
Add comma		People hurt other people they steal things and they burn down buildings in a riot.
Add apostrophe		Daniel's cat was named Jasmine.

During the editing stage, writers

- get distance from the composition;
- proofread to locate errors;
- correct errors.

Getting Distance ■ Children are more efficient editors when they set the composition aside for a few days before beginning to edit. After working so closely with the piece of writing during drafting and revising, they are too familiar with it to be able to locate many mechanical errors. After a few days, children are better able to approach editing with a fresh perspective and gather the enthusiasm necessary to finish the writing process by making the paper optimally readable.

Proofreading ■ Children proofread their compositions to locate and mark possible errors. Concentrating on mechanics is difficult because of our natural inclination to read for meaning; even experienced proofreaders often find themselves reading for meaning and overlooking errors that do not inhibit meaning. It is important, therefore, to take time to explain proofreading and to demonstrate how it differs from regular reading.

To demonstrate proofreading, teachers display a piece of student writing on an overhead projector. The teacher reads the composition slowly several times, each time hunting for a particular type of error. During each reading, the teacher softly pronounces each word and touches the word with a pencil or pen to focus attention on it, marking possible errors as they are located. Errors are marked or corrected with special proofreaders' marks. Children enjoy using these marks, the same ones that adult authors and editors use. A list of proofreaders' marks that children can learn and use in editing their writing is presented in Figure 1–3.

Editing checklists also help children focus on particular categories of errors as they proofread their compositions. Teachers can develop these checklists with two to six items appropriate for the children's grade level. A first-grade checklist, for example, might have only two items, one about using a capital letter at the beginning of a sentence and another about putting a period at the end of a sentence. In contrast, a middle-grade checklist might contain items on using commas in a series, indenting paragraphs, capitalizing proper nouns and adjectives, and spelling homonyms correctly. During the school year, teachers revise the checklist to focus attention on skills that have recently been taught. A sample third-grade editing checklist is presented in Figure 1–4. Using this checklist, two writers work together as partners to edit their compositions. First, children proofread their own compositions, searching for errors in each category listed on the checklist, and they check off each item after proofreading. After completing the checklist, children sign their names and trade checklists and compositions; now they become editors and complete each other's checklist. Having the writer and editor sign the checklist helps them to take the activity seriously.

Correcting Errors ■ After children proofread their compositions and locate as many errors as possible, they correct these errors individually or with an editor's assistance. Some errors are easy to correct, some require consulting a dictionary or checking a word wall displayed in the classroom, and others involve instruction from the teacher. It is unrealistic to expect children to locate and correct every mechanical error in their compositions. Not even published books are error free! Once in a while, children may even change a correct spelling or punctuation mark and make it incorrect, but overall, they correct far more errors than they create.

Editing can end after children and their editors correct as many mechanical errors as possible, or children may meet with the teacher in a conference for a final editing.

Figure 1–4 A Third-Grade Editing Checklist

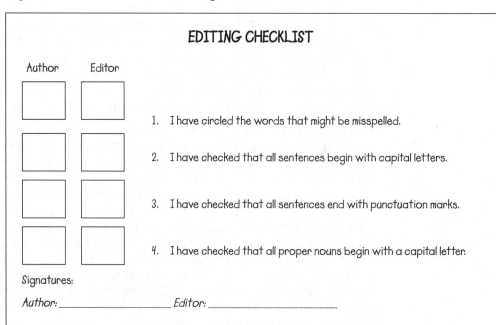

EDITING CHECKLIST

Author   Editor

1. I have circled the words that might be misspelled.

2. I have checked that all sentences begin with capital letters.

3. I have checked that all sentences end with punctuation marks.

4. I have checked that all proper nouns begin with a capital letter.

Signatures:

Author: _____   Editor: _____

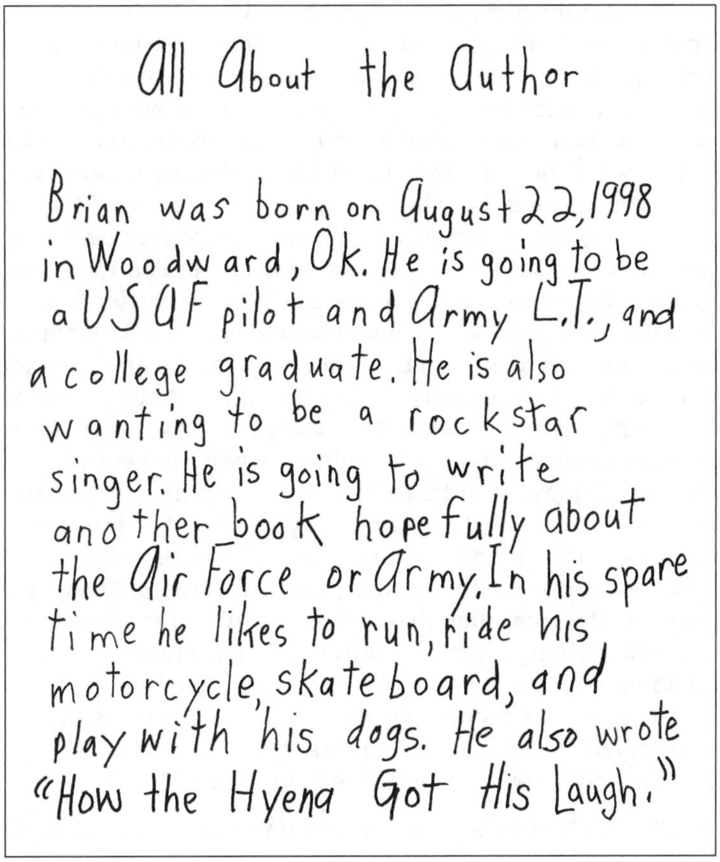

Figure 1–5
Independent Writing: A Child's "All About the Author" Page

> All About the Author
>
> Brian was born on August 22, 1998 in Woodward, Ok. He is going to be a USAF pilot and Army L.T., and a college graduate. He is also wanting to be a rockstar singer. He is going to write another book hopefully about the Air Force or Army. In his spare time he likes to run, ride his motorcycle, skateboard, and play with his dogs. He also wrote "How the Hyena Got His Laugh."

When mechanical correctness is crucial, this conference is important. The teacher proofreads the composition with the child and assists in identifying and correcting the remaining errors, or the teacher makes checkmarks in the margin to note errors that the child corrects independently.

Stage 5: Publishing

In the final stage of the writing process, children publish their writing and share it with an appropriate audience. Publishing is the fun stage in the process; it motivates children to improve their writing because they will be sharing it with a real audience. In fact, Elbow (2002) believes that publishing is the single best way to encourage children to revise and edit their writing.

Children usually recopy a story or other piece of writing into a stapled booklet or hardcover book; these published books are added to the classroom or the school library. Sometimes children form a classroom publishing company and add the company name and the year the book was made to the title page. In addition, children can include an "All About the Author" page with a photograph at the end of their books, similar to the author bio found on the jackets of books written by adult authors. A fifth grader's "All About the Author" page from a collection of poetry he wrote is presented in Figure 1–5; notice that Brian used the third-person pronoun *he* in writing about himself, as in an adult biographical sketch.

One of the most popular ways for children to share their writing with others is by making and binding books. Simple booklets can be made by folding a sheet of paper into quarters like a greeting card; children write the title on the front and have three sides remaining for their compositions. They can also construct booklets by stapling sheets of writing paper together and adding covers made out of construction paper. Sheets of wallpaper cut from old sample books also make good, sturdy covers. These stapled booklets can be cut into various shapes, too. Children can make more sophisticated hardcover books by covering cardboard covers with contact paper, wallpaper samples, or cloth. Pages are sewn or stapled together, and the first and last pages (endpapers) are glued to the cardboard covers to hold the book together.

As they share their writing with real audiences of their classmates, other students, parents, and the community, children come to think of themselves as authors (Rubenstein, 1998). Donald Graves and Jane Hansen (1983) suggest that a good way to help children develop the concept of author is to have a special chair in the classroom designated as the "author's chair." Whenever children read their own books aloud, they sit in that chair. Through sitting in the special author's chair to share their books, children gradually realize that they are authors. Graves and Hansen explain that children first understand that authors are the people who write books; next, they realize that they, too, are authors; finally, children realize that authors make choices when they write, and this awareness grows after experimenting with various writing functions, forms, and audiences.

Children read their writing to classmates, or they share it with larger audiences through hardcover books that are placed in the class or school library, class anthologies, letters, newspaper articles, plays, videotapes, or puppet shows. Ways to share children's writing include the following:

- Sit in an "author's chair" and read the writing aloud in class.
- Submit the piece to writing contests.
- Display the writing on a mobile.
- Contribute to a class anthology.
- Tape-record the writing.
- Submit it to a literary magazine or e-zine.
- Read it at a school assembly.
- Share at a read-around party.
- Share with parents and siblings.
- Produce a videotape of it.
- Display poetry on a "poet-tree."
- Send it to a pen pal.
- Make a hardbound book.
- Display it on a bulletin board.
- Make a big book.
- Share it as a puppet show.
- Read it to children in other classes.

Sharing writing is a social activity, and through sharing, children develop sensitivity to the audience and confidence in themselves as authors. Dyson (1993) advises that when children share writing, teachers consider the social interpretations—children's behavior, teacher's behavior, and interaction between children and the teacher—within the classroom context. Individual children will naturally interpret the sharing event differently. More than just providing the opportunity for children to share writing, teachers need to teach children how to respond to their classmates. Also, teachers themselves model how to respond to children's writing without dominating the sharing.

Supporting Children as They Learn to Write

Teachers support or scaffold children's writing as they demonstrate, guide, and teach, and they vary the amount of support they provide according to their instructional purpose and children's needs. Sometimes teachers model how experienced writers write, or they write along with children. At other times, they carefully guide children as they develop ideas for their writing, record ideas on paper, and proofread to correct errors. Teachers also provide plenty of time for children to write independently, to experiment with writing, and to practice skills they have learned.

Teachers use five levels of support, moving from the highest level to the lowest as children assume more and more of the responsibility for themselves (Cappello, 2005; Fountas & Pinnell, 1996). The five levels of support are modeled writing, shared writing, interactive writing, guided writing, and independent writing (see Figure 1–6). It is not that kindergartners and first graders always have the most support and older students the least; rather, teachers use all five levels because the purpose of the activity, not the activity itself, determines which level of support is used. For instance, when teachers introduce a new writing form or teach a writing strategy or skill, they use demonstrations or modeled writing. The teacher is less actively involved in directing the writing activity in independent writing, but the quality of instruction that children have received is clearest in independent writing because they are applying what they are learning about writing when they write independently.

Gibbons (2002) also advocates a scaffolded approach for teaching English learners. Teachers provide model compositions for children to examine, and then they work together in small groups to create collaborative compositions before writing their own pieces. Through this scaffolding, teachers demonstrate writing strategies, help children expand their knowledge about the craft of writing, and stretch their linguistic capabilities.

Modeled Writing

Teachers demonstrate or model how expert writers write while children observe, and this is the level of the greatest support. Teachers usually decide what they will write and create the text themselves, although they do accept suggestions from children. Then teachers either write on chart paper or use an overhead projector so that all children can see what is being written. Teachers use modeled writing to demonstrate writing workshop procedures, such as how to make small books and how to do new writing forms and formats. Often teachers think aloud or reflect on their writing processes as they write to show children how experienced writers think as they are writing and the types of decisions they make and strategies they use.

Figure 1–6 A Continuum of Teacher Support for Writing

	Modeled Writing	Shared Writing	Interactive Writing	Guided Writing	Independent Writing
What is it?	Teacher writes in front of children, creating the text, doing the writing, and thinking aloud about writing strategies and skills.	Teacher and children create the text together; then the teacher does the actual writing. Children may assist by spelling words.	Teacher and children create the text and share the pen to do the writing. Teacher and children talk about writing conventions.	Teacher presents a structured lesson and supervises as children write. Teacher also teaches a writing procedure, strategy, or skill.	Children use the writing process to write stories, informational books, and other compositions. Teacher monitors children's progress.
Who writes?	Teacher	Teacher	Teacher and children	Children	Children
How much support?	The most: The teacher does both the thinking and the writing.	The teacher and children do the thinking together, but the teacher does the writing.	The teacher and children share the responsibility for doing the thinking and the writing.	The teacher provides the structure, but the children do the thinking and the writing.	The least: The children do both the thinking and the writing.
What size groups?	Whole class Small group	Whole class Small group Buddies Individuals	Whole class Small group Buddies Individuals	Small group Buddies Individuals	Buddies Individuals
Which activities?	Demonstrations	Language Experience Approach K-W-L charts	Predictions Daily news Innovations Letters	Class collaborations Class ABC books Formula poems	Writing centers Writing workshop Writing in journals Letters

Teachers use modeled writing for demonstrations to show how experienced writers write and solve problems as they write. Here are three purposes of modeled writing:

- To demonstrate how to do a new type of writing activity before having children do the activity independently or in small groups
- To demonstrate how to use writing strategies, such as proofreading, monitoring, sentence combining, and revising
- To demonstrate how writing conventions and other skills work

In the vignette at the beginning of the chapter, Mrs. Reeves used modeled writing when she demonstrated how to write a page for the interview book and the ABC weather book. Her purpose in both of these examples was to demonstrate how to do a new type of writing activity.

Shared Writing

In shared writing, the teacher and children work together to compose a text, and the teacher serves as the scribe to record the text for children. As they write, teachers demonstrate how expert writers write while the children observe. They also draw children's attention to letters, words, and conventions of written language. Sometimes teachers write the texts on chart paper so that all children can see what is being written, or they write children's dictation beside drawings or in small books or have individual children each write small parts of the text to put together a class book. Here are three purposes for shared writing:

- To demonstrate how writing works
- To record children's ideas
- To create written texts for the classroom that children could not write independently

The main way that shared writing differs from modeled writing is that the teacher writes the text with input from the children. In modeled writing, the teacher thinks of the text to write and does the actual writing.

Teachers at different grade levels use shared writing in a variety of ways. Primary-grade teachers often write children's dictation on paintings and brainstorm lists of words on the chalkboard, as is shown in the minilesson feature on page 25, whereas upper-grade teachers may take students' dictation when they make K-W-L charts, draw maps and clusters, and write class collaboration poems.

The Language Experience Approach (LEA) is one type of shared writing. It is based on children's language and experiences (Ashton-Warner, 1965). Children dictate words and sentences about their experiences, and the teacher writes the dictation. As they write, teachers model how written language works. The text the class develops becomes the reading material because it has been written with conventional English spelling. Because the language comes from the children themselves and because the content is based on their experiences, they are usually able to read the text easily. The steps in the Language Experience Approach are described in the step-by-step feature on page 24.

The Language Experience Approach is often used to create texts children can read and use as a resource for writing in a social studies or science unit. In the vignette at the beginning of the chapter, Mrs. Reeves used LEA to take children's dictation for the K-W-L chart, to list words on the word wall, and to write questions children wanted to ask the weather forecaster during the interview.

Step by Step: Language Experience Approach

1. **Provide an experience.** Teachers provide an experience or remind children of an experience, to serve as the stimulus for the writing.

2. **Talk about the experience.** Children talk about the experience to clarify and organize ideas and to generate words for their dictation.

3. **Record the dictation.** Teachers write the text that children dictate. They print neatly and spell words correctly, but they preserve children's word choice and syntax. If a child hesitates, the teacher rereads what has been written and encourages the child to continue.

4. **Read the text.** Teachers read the text aloud to remind children of the content and to demonstrate how to read with expression. Next, children read with the teacher, and finally, they read on their own.

5. **Examine the text.** Teachers rewrite the text on sentence strips, and children sequence strips to re-create the text. Teachers also write words from the text on word cards for children to read, and later children add the words they know to their word banks.

EL

Scaffolding English Learners

Too often, teachers think of interactive writing as an activity for young children, but English learners at any grade level learn a great deal when they write with classmates and the teacher. Try working with a small group of children who write a sentence or paragraph together after reading a book or participating in a social studies or science lesson. Children make individual copies in journals as they write the group composition on chart paper.

Interactive Writing

Teachers and children create a text and "share the pen" to write the text on chart paper (Button, Johnson, & Furgerson, 1996). The text is composed by the group, and the teacher guides the children as they write the text word-by-word on chart paper. Children take turns writing known letters and familiar words, adding punctuation marks, and marking spaces between words. The teacher helps children to spell all words correctly and use written language conventions so that the text can be read easily. All children participate in creating and writing the text on the chart paper, and they also write the text on small white boards. After writing, children read and reread the text using shared and independent reading.

Teachers use interactive writing to provide instruction and assistance to children as they are actually writing. It is much like shared writing except that the children are doing much of the actual writing. Here are four purposes of interactive writing:

- To demonstrate how to write words and sentences
- To teach how to use capital letters and punctuation marks
- To demonstrate how to use phonics and spelling patterns to spell words
- To create written texts for the classroom that children could not write independently

When children begin interactive writing in kindergarten, they write the letters to represent the beginning sounds in words and familiar words such as *the, a,* and *is.* The first letters that children write are often the letters in their own names, particularly the first letter. As children learn more about sound-symbol correspondences and spelling patterns, they do more of the writing. They gain valuable experience

Dictating a Sentence

Mrs. Greene regularly writes her kindergartners' dictation on pictures they draw, and most of her students are able to dictate a sentence or two for her to write. However, a small group of students are still learning how to craft a sentence, remember it, and dictate it word-by-word. Today she reviews how to dictate a sentence with a group of five kindergartners.

1. Introduce the topic

"Today I have some photographs of Superman, our pet guinea pig," Mrs. Greene tells the children sitting with her at a kidney-shaped table. She spreads the photos out on the table and says, "Let's choose one to write about." The children choose a photo of their brown-and-white guinea pig munching on a carrot.

2. Share examples

Mrs. Greene and the children brainstorm words about the photo, including *carrot, Superman, guinea pig, eats, crunchy,* and *hungry.* Next, she asks the children to suggest sentences including one or more of the words they brainstormed. For example, Tyrone suggests *Our guinea pig likes to eat a carrot,* and Cassie suggests *Superman eats healthy snacks.* Finally they decide on *Superman eats lots of carrots.*

3. Provide information

The kindergartners repeat the chosen sentence to themselves while Mrs. Greene picks up a pen. She reminds them to dictate the sentence word-by-word to her. The group recites the sentence, emphasizing each of the five words, and then Mrs. Greene writes the sentence as they dictate it again. Afterward, the group reads the sentence aloud, and one child draws a line under each word and counts them.

4. Guide practice

Mrs. Greene glues the photo on the paper with their sentence and suggests that they make a book about Superman using the photos. Each child chooses a photo of Superman, glues it on a sheet of paper, crafts a sentence, and dictates it to Mrs. Greene. Finally, they compile the pages, make a cover, and bind the book. Later, they read the completed book to the class.

5. Assess learning

Mrs. Greene notes each child's ability to craft a sentence and dictate it word-by-word during the fourth step. Three of the children have difficulty remembering and dictating their sentences, so she plans to repeat this minilesson using some pictures she has cut from magazines.

applying the phonics skills and writing the high-frequency words they are learning as they do interactive writing. Figure 1–7 shows a first-grade class chart about insects. Many of the words have lines drawn under each letter; the teacher drew those lines as a spelling aid for children. The dotted letters represent letters that the teacher wrote, and the small squares represent correction tape used to cover mistakes.

Once children are writing words fluently, they can do interactive writing in small groups. Each child in the group uses a particular color pen and takes turns writing letters, letter clusters, and words. They also get used to correcting poorly formed letters and misspelled words with white correction tape. Children also sign their names in color on the page so that the teacher can track which children wrote which words.

Interactive writing can be used as part of literature focus units, in social studies and science thematic units, and for many other purposes, too. Here are some uses:

- Write predictions before reading.
- Write responses after reading.
- Write letters and other messages.
- Make lists.
- Write daily news.
- Rewrite a familiar story.
- Write information or facts.
- Write recipes.
- Make charts, maps, clusters, data charts, and other diagrams.

Figure 1–7 Interactive Writing: A First-Grade Class Writing About Insects

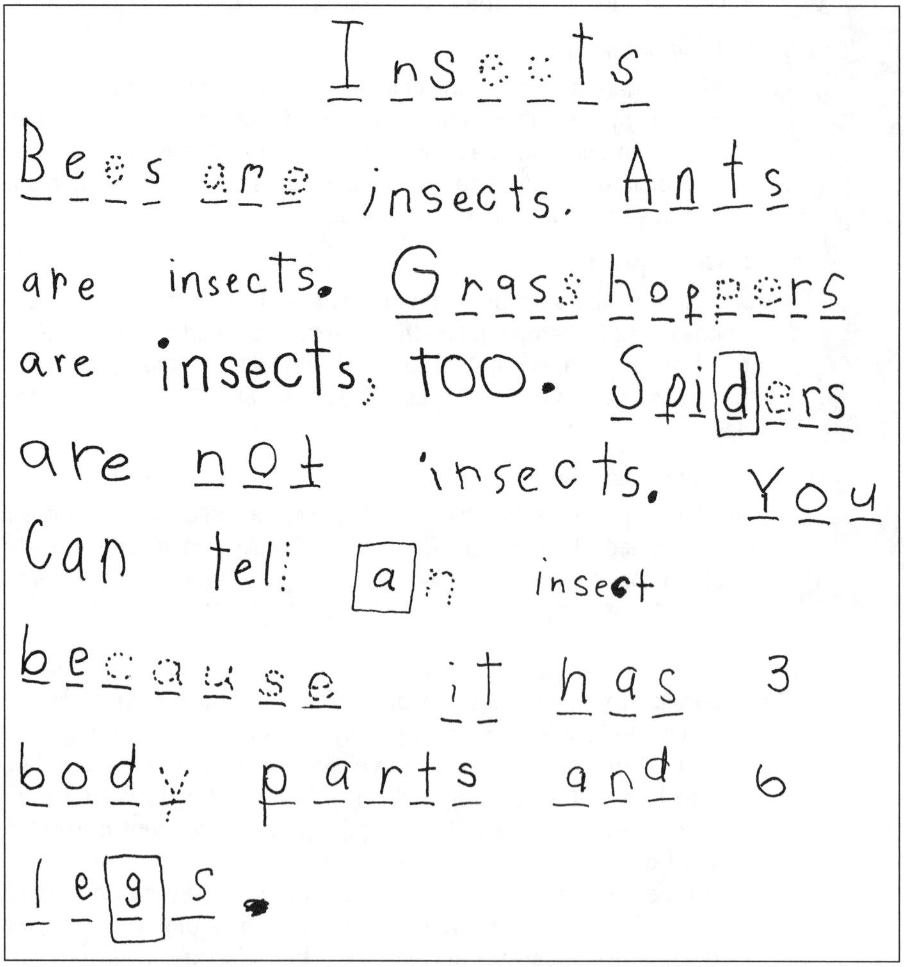

Step by Step: Interactive Writing

1. **Set a purpose.** The teacher presents a stimulus activity or sets a purpose, such as writing the daily news.

2. **Pass out writing supplies.** The teacher distributes white boards and dry-erase pens and erasers so children can write the text individually as it is written on chart paper.

3. **Choose a sentence to write.** Children create a sentence to write and repeat it several times, segmenting it into words. They also count the number of words in the sentence.

4. **Write the first sentence.** Children write the sentence word by word with the teacher's support. They slowly pronounce each word, "stretching" it out. Children take turns writing the letters to spell the word on chart paper. They write the letters using one color pen, and the teacher uses another color to write the parts that children can't spell. Children cover spelling errors and poorly formed letters with white correction tape. After each word is written, one child serves as the "spacer" and uses his or her hand to mark the space between words. Children reread the sentence from the beginning each time a new word is added; when appropriate, the teacher points out capital letters, punctuation marks, and other conventions of print.

5. **Repeat for additional sentences.** The teacher repeats this procedure to write additional sentences to complete the message.

6. **Display the message.** Teachers display the message in the classroom and have children reread it often.

- Create innovations or new versions of a familiar text.
- Write class poems.
- Write words on a word wall.
- Make posters.

Moira McKenzie, a well-known British educator, is credited with developing interactive writing (Fountas & Pinnell, 1996), which she based on Don Holdaway's work in shared reading. Interactive writing incorporates many of the features of LEA, but in interactive writing, children do much of the writing themselves. The steps in interactive writing are described in the step-by-step feature on this page.

Guided Writing

Teachers scaffold or support children's writing during guided writing, but children do the actual writing themselves. Teachers plan structured writing activities and then supervise as children do the writing. For example, when children make pages for a class ABC book (as Mrs. Reeves's class did in the vignette at the beginning of the chapter) or write formula poems, they are doing guided writing because the teacher has set up the writing activity. Teachers also guide the writing when they conference with children as they write, participate in writing groups to help children revise their writing, and proofread with children. With novice writers, teachers use guided writing to help children choose what they want to write, organize their ideas into a sentence, and then transcribe each word onto paper.

Teachers use guided writing to provide instruction and assistance to children while they are actually writing. It is much like guided reading, in which teachers read with small groups of children and provide assistance as it is needed. Here are four purposes of guided writing:

- To scaffold a writing experience so that children can be successful
- To introduce different types of writing activities
- To teach children to use the writing process—in particular, how to revise and edit
- To teach procedures, concepts, strategies, and skills during minilessons

Sometimes guided writing is equated with writing workshop, but children generally use a combination of independent writing and guided writing during writing workshop. The difference is the level of the teacher's support and guidance.

Independent Writing

In independent writing, children do the writing themselves and often use the writing process to write books. They practice the writing strategies and skills they are learning. Often children do independent writing in writing centers and during writing workshop, but they can also use independent writing when they write in reading logs, make posters, and do other types of writing activities. Teachers have children write independently for these six purposes:

- To provide an authentic context for writing practice
- To give children opportunities to choose writing topics and forms
- To gain writing fluency and stamina
- As a tool for learning, such as when children write in reading logs and other types of journals
- To make and publish books
- To document learning in literature focus units and thematic units

Children often write independently, whether they are writing in reading logs, making projects, or writing books during writing workshop. In the vignette at the beginning of the chapter, for example, Mrs. Reeves's students were writing independently when they created projects at the end of their weather unit.

ANSWERING TEACHERS' QUESTIONS ABOUT . . .

Teaching Children to Write

Is the writing process the same thing as writing workshop?

The writing process and writing workshop are related, but they are not the same thing. Writing workshop is a classroom application of the writing process, and it is discussed in Chapter 2, "Writing Workshop."

The writing process is just for older children, isn't it?

No, the writing process is for everyone. Kindergartners and first graders participate in prewriting activities just as older children do, and they share their compositions in writing groups and use the author's chair. At first, young children may write only one draft, but they like hearing compliments about their writing, and before long a suggestion for improvement is intermingled with a series of compliments. For example, a child may say, "I really liked all the facts you told about gerbils, but you didn't say that they are mammals." And the writer responds, "Oh, I forgot. I think I can put it here. Thanks!" With the realization that readers provide worthwhile suggestions and that children need to revise their writing, these youngsters become full-fledged members of the writing process club.

How do you decide when to use modeled, shared, interactive, guided, or independent writing?

The type of support that teachers provide for a writing activity depends on their purpose for the activity. When teachers are introducing a new activity, they often use modeled or shared writing. When they want to focus on conventional spelling and other writing mechanics, they use interactive writing. When teachers want to provide individualized assistance or teach a strategy or skill, they might choose guided writing. And when teachers want children to practice skills they have learned, they have children write independently.

I don't feel comfortable with the writing process. Really, I'm afraid I'll lose control.

A writing process classroom is different from a traditional classroom. There's more noise as children work in groups and move around the classroom for different activities, but this environment stimulates learning because children are actively involved in and are assuming responsibility for their own learning. To ensure that children are learning, teachers can move about the classroom, observing and talking with children as they write, talk, revise, and share their writing. If the noise or movement becomes too great, teachers can stop for a class meeting. At the meeting, they discuss the problem and consider ways to solve it.

To become more comfortable with the writing process approach, teachers might observe in a classroom that is already using the approach. They will observe a teacher who serves as a guide or a facilitator and children who know how to use the writing process and are actively involved in a writing project. In spite of the freedom to talk, move, and work independently, there is discipline and there are techniques for monitoring children's behavior and the work they complete.

Do children use the writing process every time they write?

Children's writing can be divided into formal writing and informal writing. Children use the writing process when they are doing formal writing—stories, reports, poems, and other pieces that they will publish and share with classmates and other audiences.

In contrast, children use informal writing as a tool for learning. When they write journal entries, K-W-L charts, clusters, and other types of informal writing, children don't generally use the writing process for these pieces. You will read more about informal writing in Chapter 5, "Journal Writing."

Chapter 2
Writing Workshop

Preview

> The components of writing workshop are writing, sharing, minilessons, and reading aloud to children.

> The purpose of writing workshop is to provide children with opportunities to use the writing process to create books and other compositions.

> Children can write about self-selected topics or write as part of a literature focus unit or thematic unit.

> Writing workshop and reading workshop are complementary activities.

Mrs. Zumwalt's Writing Workshop

Mrs. Zumwalt's third graders spend an hour and a half in the morning reading and talking about books that are about families, including *Ramona Quimby, Age 8* (Cleary, 1981), *Owl Moon* (Yolen, 1987), *When We Married Gary* (Hines, 1996), *The Relatives Came* (Rylant, 1985), *Grandpa Abe* (Russo, 1996), and *A Chair for My Mother* (Williams, 1982). They call this activity "reading workshop." Later in the day, they spend an hour and a half writing about their own families. They call this activity "writing workshop." Here is Mrs. Zumwalt's schedule for writing workshop:

1:30–1:50	Class meeting
1:50–2:45	Writing
2:45–3:00	Sharing

Mrs. Zumwalt begins with a class meeting. Sometimes they do shared writing and write a class composition together; sometimes she shares information about a favorite author of children's books; and at other times, she models how to write a poem or another writing form, or she teaches minilessons about writing skills and strategies, such as proofreading or writing leads. During the class meeting, Mrs. Zumwalt also does a "status of the class" to check on each child's progress. She calls each child by name, and the child responds by identifying the writing process stage at which he or she is working. This way she can check on how all 23 children are doing within 2 minutes.

Next, the third graders spend almost an hour writing independently and working on their compositions. They work at different stages of the writing process. Some are drawing pictures to illustrate their completed books; others are meeting with Mrs. Zumwalt in a writing group to revise their compositions, for example. Children's desks are arranged in five groups, and Mrs. Zumwalt briefly conferences with children in one group during each writing period and makes notes on a clipboard she carries. She describes the activities children are involved in and records her observations about their progress. An excerpt from a chart she uses for these notes is shown on this page.

Children sign up on the chalkboard when they are ready to meet in revising groups; after four children have signed up, they form a group and meet at a table reserved for revising groups. Sometimes Mrs. Zumwalt joins the group, and at other times, the children meet by themselves. They take turns sharing their drafts and getting feedback on how well they are communicating. The children use the process that Mrs. Zumwalt has taught them.

Mrs. Zumwalt has another sign-up list for children who want to conference with her. She has found it easier than she expected to juggle the activities of third graders working at different writing process stages. Because her students are working independently on their own projects, some are drafting or writing final copies when others need her assistance in writing groups or for proofreading.

The children meet as a class during the last 15 minutes of writing workshop to share their completed compositions. Children sit in the author's chair, a place of honor, to read their published writings to the class. After reading, classmates clap and offer compliments.

An Excerpt From Mrs. Zumwalt's Anecdotal Notes Chart

Child	Notes
Connor	He finished proofing his book about learning to swim. He is doing a good job catching spelling errors. He says he likes using a red pen for editing. He's using quotation marks correctly for dialogue.
Belle	Belle should finish her book about her Mom and stepdad's wedding today or tomorrow. She included lots of details—a very memorable event! She is still capitalizing too many common nouns—needs a minilesson.
Anthony	He's still working on his rough draft about a trip to Yosemite. He's been working on it for almost two weeks. He says he wants to keep working on it, but I wonder. Does he like the topic? Does he know enough about the topic? Should he begin again on a new topic? Should I try shared writing? Check him again tomorrow!
Jason	Jason's revising page 3 of the book about his grandfather. There is too much information on this page. He's trying to reorganize it, but he is unwilling to cut any of it. He's very involved in his tribute to his grandfather. He has a photograph of him to put on the cover. His whole family is involved.
Marilynne	She is writing about a big family picnic last summer at her cousin's farm. In the rough draft she's writing only one sentence on each page so I encouraged her to expand the ideas with more sentences. I asked her to think of three sentences for each page and to say them to herself before she begins writing. Check her again tomorrow!

Sometimes a child offers a suggestion or asks for further information, but writers do not have to go back into their compositions to make additional changes.

As part of their study of families, the children are writing books about a family member. They began by brainstorming a list of questions about families, family histories, and memorable family events. The children interviewed their parents and sometimes their brothers, sisters, and other relatives. These are some of the questions they asked:

What family event do you remember best?
What things did we do when I was a baby?
What was one of your most embarrassing moments?
Did you have any arguments with your parents when you were a child?
Who taught you how to swim?
What do you remember about when you went to elementary school?
What pets did you have?

The third graders also brainstormed lists of their own memories. In a guided writing lesson, Mrs. Zumwalt showed a collection of objects including a dog biscuit, a sports trophy, a postcard, a teddy bear, a camera, a book, a slice of pizza, a bandage, and a package wrapped as a gift. As she shared each object, she asked students to jot down a phrase about a memory that the object brought to mind. She also asked them to list other memories that occurred to them.

Armed with this information, the children sorted through their notes and selected memorable events to write about. They made a cluster about the event to collect and organize information before beginning to write. Some children drew pictures, and others chose a book about a family to use as a model. Other children had more developed ideas in mind and immediately began to write. Mrs. Zumwalt does not try to keep them together, with everyone drafting or revising at the same time. Instead, children prewrite, draft, revise, edit, and publish independently, at their own speed. Some children write two compositions in the time it takes one child to complete one piece, and sometimes they decide to start over after spending a week or two on a topic. Although the students don't work at the same pace, they are all involved in the same type of project.

During the month they spend reading and writing about families, all children are expected to do the prewriting activities and complete at least one book, most likely a personal narrative about a memorable family event or a firsthand biography of a family member. Children can also experiment with other writing forms—a newspaper account of the event, a letter recounting the event, or a poem.

Here is Jason's book about his grandfather, entitled "The Railroad Man":

My grandpap used to work on the railroad. His name was Bert Alan Simpson. He was an old man with white hair but he was nice to everybody. He used to always have gum in his pocket and he gave me some every time I saw him.

He was the engineer on freight trains from Fresno to Portland, and he worked on trains for 35 years. He just loves trains and he knows a lot about them.

When I was little he used to take me to the Fresno Train Station on Saturdays so we could look at the trains. We'd talk to his friends the engineers. I remember Hank and Bill they were his friends. They would let me get up on the engine and let me pretend that I was an engineer too. After we got off the train, we would look at the people getting on the trains and we would watch them pull out. Grandpap said he just loved the sound of trains. "Clackity-clack." He said it was music to his ears.

My Grandpap is dead now. He had a heart attack and he died but every time I see a train I think of him and remember the time we spent together. I have a red railroad handkerchief of his. I guess I love trains too.

Mrs. Zumwalt's Class Rubric

Name _Jason_ Date _10-18_

Book _The Railroad Man_

Rubric for Books About Our Families

Describe the person you are writing about.   1 ② ③

Tell about one or more experiences with lots of details. 1 ② 3

Tell why the person is important to you.   1 2 ③

Use complete sentences.   1 2 ③

Use "good" spelling, capitalization and punctuation. 1 ② ③

Each paragraph represents one page in Jason's book.

Mrs. Zumwalt and her class developed a rubric for assessing the books they wrote about their families. They decided that the rubric should assess these points:

Describe the person you are writing about.
Tell about one or more experiences with lots of details.
Tell why the person is important to you.
Use complete sentences.
Use "good" spelling, capitalization, and punctuation.

Then the class decided to rate each item with 1, 2, or 3 (highest) points, and both Mrs. Zumwalt and the children would score their completed books. The score for the project would be the number circled most often. Jason's completed rubric for his book "The Railroad Man" is shown on this page. Jason scored the rubric first, and he drew a triangle around the numbers to represent his score. Mrs. Zumwalt followed with circles around the numbers for her score.

Mrs. Zumwalt bases the grades that children receive for their work on the accumulated information they present in their writing folders. The children place in their folders their brainstormed lists of memorable events; notes from their interviews of family members; prewriting, drafting, and final copies of compositions; their self-assessment rubric for one book they wrote; and a reflective letter to Mrs. Zumwalt about their writing and work habits during the unit.

Teachers implement the writing process in their classrooms through writing workshop (Dorn & Soffos, 2001). Many teachers use writing workshop to provide an opportunity for children to write on self-selected topics and to work independently, employing the writing process as they work. Other teachers use writing workshop for children to write stories, reports, poems, and other genres as part of literature focus units and thematic units. In the vignette, Mrs. Zumwalt used writing workshop for her third graders to write as part of a unit on families. They worked independently on their writing projects during a regularly scheduled writing time. No matter which way teachers use writing workshop, its great benefit is that children become familiar with the ebb and flow of the writing process and experience the exhilaration that all authors feel as they publish their writing and share it with readers.

The writing workshop approach is an innovative way of implementing the writing process (Calkins, 1994; Fletcher & Portalupi, 2001; Overmeyer, 2005). According to Lucy McCormick Calkins (1986), in this approach, children write about what is vital and real for them. They assume ownership of their learning and choose what and how they will write. At the same time, the teacher's role changes from being a provider of knowledge to serving as a guide. The classroom changes, too; it becomes a community of writers who write and share their writing.

Self-selection, ownership, self-monitoring, feedback, and individualized instruction are the hallmarks of writing workshop (Atwell, 1998). Classrooms are social environments, and children are active participants as they choose the direction their writing will take, consciously monitor their writing processes, and turn to classmates and the teacher for feedback and guidance. These characteristics define the workshop environment, whether students are writing, reading, researching, or spelling (Barnes, Morgan, & Weinhold, 1997; Cohle & Towle, 2001; Rogovin, 2001).

The Components of Writing Workshop

The heart of writing workshop is independent writing, and teachers also add several other components. These four activities are part of writing workshop:

Writing. Children spend 30 to 60 minutes working on writing projects. They use the writing process as they develop and refine their writing, and they conference with classmates and the teacher about their writing.

Sharing. The class gathers together to share their new publications, often during the last 5 to 10 minutes of writing workshop. Children take turns reading their writing aloud to classmates, who respond to the writing and offer compliments.

Minilessons. Teachers provide 15- to 30-minute lessons on writing workshop procedures, information about authors, literary concepts, and writing strategies and skills.

Reading Aloud to Children. Teachers read picture books and chapter books aloud to children to share examples of good writing and to teach children about authors.

It is important to have a clear, simple structure for writing workshop so that children can anticipate the writing activities in which they will be involved. Mrs. Zumwalt had a predictable structure using three components, and other teachers organize their writing workshop in different ways. Figure 2–1 presents four schedules for writing workshop. Teachers decide which components to use according to the other language arts activities going on in the classroom and the time they have available. For example, if teachers read aloud to children every day after lunch, it may not be necessary to include that component in writing workshop. When teachers have only a short period of time available, they can alternate minilessons and sharing or include minilessons in their reading workshop.

Figure 2–1 Four Schedules for Writing Workshop

Ms. Yang's First-Grade Schedule

During the first 90 minutes of the school day, Ms. Yang has her first graders work at literacy centers while she conducts guided reading lessons. After a short recess, children move into writing workshop. Here is her schedule:

10:00–10:15   Reading aloud to children
10:15–10:30   Interactive writing
10:30–11:00   Independent writing
11:00–11:15   Sharing

During interactive writing, Ms. Yang and the children write a sentence together based on the book Ms. Yang read aloud.

Mr. Scott's Third- and Fourth-Grade Schedule

Mr. Scott's students spend the first hour of the school day working in reading and writing workshop. The third and fourth graders alternate between reading and writing projects. Here is his schedule:

8:45–8:50   Status of the class
8:50–9:40   Independent reading or writing
9:40–9:45   Sharing

During the independent writing period, children move through the writing process, and Mr. Scott conferences with individual children as they work.

Mrs. Flores's Fifth-Grade Schedule

Mrs. Flores's fifth graders begin their literacy block with either literature circles, in which students read a book with a small group of classmates, or a literature focus unit, in which everyone reads the same book. During writing workshop, the second half of the literacy block, children spend 75 minutes learning about authors, practicing writing strategies and skills, and writing independently. Here is Mrs. Flores's schedule:

10:30–10:50   Minilesson
10:50–10:55   Status of the class
10:55–11:55   Independent writing
11:55–12:05   Sharing

During the minilesson, Mrs. Flores alternates lessons on authors, spelling and mechanics, and sentence building using sentences from books children are reading.

Ms. Boland's Eighth-Grade Schedule

Ms. Boland teaches writing as part of a 2-hour language arts and social studies block. She alternates reading and writing workshop, depending on the other activities in which students are involved. Here is her schedule:

1:05–1:10   Status of the class
1:10–1:55   Independent writing
1:55–2:05   Sharing

During the sharing period, Ms. Boland asks all students to read aloud a powerful sentence they have written if no one has completed the project.

Writing

Writing is the heart of writing workshop (Fletcher & Portalupi, 2001). Children write independently, usually on topics they've chosen themselves. Sometimes they write in spiral-bound notebooks or on loose sheets of paper that they keep in writing folders. They spend a great deal of time writing rough drafts, and then they take the most promising pieces through the writing process to publication.

Children write about things they know well, often drawing topics from their own lives. When children complain that they don't know what to write about, teachers often help them brainstorm lists of possible topics, including brothers and sisters, holidays, grandparents, pets, friends, and hobbies. Teachers also use trade books as models or "mentor texts" (Overmeyer, 2005) for children's writing. Children incorporate organizational patterns and language structures from favorite stories into the books they're writing.

Of course, encouraging children to choose their own topics is not without some problems. Lee Heffernan (2004) reported that the topics his third graders wrote about were often superficial and without much passion; also, the same topics were recycled again and again. He solved these problems by reading aloud books about social issues, such as *Your Move* (Bunting, 1998), a story about joining a gang, that generated emotional responses and serious conversations about privilege and injustice. As the children's social awareness was heightened, their writing changed, too: They incorporated social themes in the books they wrote. Another potential problem is unacceptable topics: Sometimes children choose violent and offensive topics that make teachers feel uncomfortable. To avoid this problem, teachers establish boundaries about which topics are acceptable.

Teachers often write along with their students, at least for the first five or 10 minutes; in this way, they convey the importance they place on writing. Then they circulate around the classroom as children write, stopping to confer briefly with individual children. The most important thing is that teachers listen to children as they read and talk about their writing.

Fletcher and Portalupi (2001) offer this advice about writing conferences: "Keep these conferences short and punchy. Engage, listen, react as a human being. Find something to celebrate in their writing and point it out to them. Then make your exit" (p. 39). Conferences also provide opportunities for teachers to clarify misconceptions or teach a strategy or skill. The emphasis should be on developing stronger writers, not on fixing a particular piece of writing (Calkins, Hartman, & White, 2005).

Sharing

For the last 5 to 15 minutes of writing workshop, the class gathers together for

---

📝 *How to Address Struggling Writers' Problems*

The Problem	Children don't make constructive revisions.
What Causes It	Children who don't understand the importance of revising often view revising as a time to make cosmetic changes rather than substantive changes.
How to Solve It	*Quick fix:* Require children to make at least two or three revisions, and have them make their revisions with brightly colored pens so that they will stand out. Many children try to hide their revisions because they see them as a sign of failure.
	Long-term solution: Have children participate in writing groups where they provide feedback to classmates about how to revise their rough drafts. At first, children are usually more interested in providing feedback to classmates than in getting feedback about their own writing, but with practice, they learn the importance of making substantive revisions. Teachers also teach and model the types of revision in minilessons, and then they ask children to examine and classify the revisions they make. In addition, teachers can include substantive revision as a requirement on the assessment rubric.
How to Prevent the Problem	When children know how to make revisions and regularly participate in writing groups, they are more likely to make revisions because they want to communicate effectively.

Figure 2–2 Topics for Minilessons

Types	Topics
Writing Workshop Procedures	How to make a graphic organizer
	How to write rough drafts
	How to participate in writing groups
	How to participate in writing conferences
	How to edit with a partner
	How to use writing rubrics
	How to choose pieces for portfolios
Writers' Craft	How to create good lead sentences
	How to show, not tell
	How to use figurative language
	How to use onomatopoeia
	How to use vivid verbs
	How to vary the structure of sentences
	How to create catchy endings
Writing Strategies and Skills	How to generate ideas
	How to ask self-questions
	How to proofread
	How to write dialogue
	How to combine sentences
	How to make a table of contents
	How to use commas

children to share their new publications and make other related announcements; for example, a child who has just finished writing a puppet show script and making puppets may ask for volunteers to help perform the puppet show. Younger children often sit in a circle or gather together on a rug for sharing time, and children take turns sitting in the author's chair to read their compositions. After the reading, classmates clap and offer compliments. They may also make other comments and suggestions, but the focus is on celebrating completed writing projects, not on revising the compositions to make them better (Fletcher & Portalupi, 2001).

Minilessons

Minilessons are focused explanations and demonstrations of writing workshop procedures, writers' craft, and writing strategies and skills (Atwell, 1998; Hoyt, 2000; Ray, 2002). A list of possible topics for minilessons is shown in Figure 2–2. The purpose of minilessons is to highlight the topic, present information about it, and then provide opportunities for guided practice. Worksheets are rarely used in minilessons; instead, children apply the lesson to their own writing. Minilessons can be conducted with the whole class or with small groups of children who need to learn more about a particular topic. They can be taught whenever teachers see a need as they observe children writing on a regular basis to introduce and review topics.

The steps in teaching a minilesson are shown in the step-by-step feature on page 38, and a minilesson on revising is described in the minilesson feature on page 39.

Step by Step: Minilesson

1. **Introduce the topic.** Teachers identify the topic for the minilesson and often write it on chart paper or on the chalkboard; it may be a writing workshop procedure or a writing strategy or skill. After identifying the topic, teachers briefly define the topic or mention its characteristics, and they write this information on the chart paper or on the chalkboard.

2. **Share examples.** Teachers provide examples using children's own writing or books written for children. Then they invite the children to identify other examples and write them on the chart paper or on the chalkboard.

3. **Provide information.** Teachers provide additional information about the topic and how it is used in writing, or they review information presented in the first step. This is the step where teachers clarify misconceptions and contrast the topic with related topics. The teacher may model using the topic in a writing activity or have the students sort examples and nonexamples.

4. **Supervise practice.** Children work in pairs or small groups to practice what they are learning. The teacher circulates around the classroom to provide assistance or review the information that has been presented.

5. **Assess learning.** Teachers monitor children's application of the information they've learned as they participate in writing workshop.

EL

Scaffolding English Learners

The more your English learners read and reread books at their level and listen to others read aloud, the better their writing becomes. Through reading, children learn about English sentence patterns and pick up new vocabulary words that they can incorporate in their writing. These children benefit from opportunities to talk and write about books they are reading; as they make reading-writing connections, their learning is enhanced.

Reading Aloud to Children

Teachers read aloud stories, informational books, and poetry to children every day. Some teachers read aloud during writing workshop, and others schedule this activity during another part of the school day. As the teacher reads aloud, children have the opportunity to enjoy the literary experience and learn about authors and how they write. Teachers also share information about authors and sometimes read and compare several books written by the same author, so that children can examine how that author crafted his or her books or identify the stylistic devices he or she used. This activity also helps children to feel part of a community of writers.

Comparing Writing Workshop to Reading Workshop

Teachers often use writing workshop in conjunction with reading workshop, as Mrs. Zumwalt did in the vignette at the beginning of the chapter. In reading workshop, children have large chunks of time for reading and responding to literature and a choice about what they read (Atwell, 1998; Cohle & Towle, 2001; Serafini, 2001). The components are similar to those of writing workshop, except that the focus is on reading. The components of reading workshop often include the following:

Reading. Children spend 30 to 60 minutes reading and responding to books and other reading materials.

Sharing. The class gathers together to share books children have finished reading and projects they have created.

Minilessons. The teacher spends 15 to 30 minutes teaching brief lessons on reading workshop procedures, information about authors, literary concepts, and reading strategies and skills.

Reading Aloud to Children. The teacher reads aloud high-quality literature that children cannot read themselves to increase their understanding of literature and to provide children with a shared literature experience.

Just as writing workshop fosters independent writing for genuine purposes and authentic audiences, reading workshop fosters independent reading of self-selected books. Teachers often connect the two, and children participate in many of the same types of activities.

Vivid Verbs

Mrs. Hernandez is concerned that her sixth graders use common, familiar words instead of more powerful and precise words that would energize their writing, so she is teaching a series of minilessons on vocabulary. She has introduced the thesaurus and explained the importance of choosing words carefully. Today, she focuses on using vivid verbs.

1. Introduce the topic

"The focus of today's minilesson is on verbs because verbs are often the most powerful words in a sentence. They are the motor that drives the sentence," Mrs. Hernandez explains.

2. Share examples

The teacher passes out copies of two anonymous compositions (written by students the previous year) and asks the children to highlight the verbs as she reads the two compositions aloud. She accentuates each verb as she reads to assist children in identifying them. Then the children read aloud the verbs they highlighted. Verbs in the first composition include *is*, *wanted*, and *thought; annoys*, *startled*, and *crackle* appear in the second composition. The sixth graders quickly notice that the verbs in the first composition are lackluster when compared to those in the second composition.

3. Provide information

Mrs. Hernandez explains that during revision, writers should make sure the verbs they've used are powerful or vivid. Tami asks if they should highlight the verbs in their own writing, and the teacher agrees that it's a good way to check. Then, she continues, if the children find that the verbs aren't vivid, they can substitute better words. Sometimes they can think of these more powerful words themselves, and sometimes they should use a thesaurus to find a better word.

4. Guide practice

Next, Mrs. Hernandez passes out copies of the thesaurus and asks the children to work in pairs to substitute more vivid verbs in the first composition to make the writing more powerful. As the children work, she circulates around the classroom, checking that the synonyms they choose are appropriate ones.

5. Assess learning

As she ends the lesson, Mrs. Hernandez asks the children to highlight at least 10 vivid verbs in the compositions they're working on now, and if they can't find that many, to revise so that they do.

MINILESSON

Implementing Writing Workshop

Teachers begin writing workshop by introducing the writing process and modeling writing workshop procedures. They create a writing workshop environment and arrange the classroom for workshop activities. And teachers continue refining writing workshop as their children grow as writers. Writing workshop isn't easy to implement, but it's worth the effort. Many teachers and parents have reported the positive effects writing workshop has on children's development as writers (Atwell, 1998; Calkins, 1994). One thing that makes writing workshop difficult to implement is that many teachers were not taught this way themselves, and they may not have seen other teachers use writing workshop effectively. Another difficulty is that both children and teachers assume new roles in writing workshop. Children assume more ownership of their work, apply strategies and writing skills, and self-assess their writing. Teachers spend a great deal of their time conferencing with children, working one-on-one or in small groups rather than directing the whole class. These new roles are different for both children and teachers, but with practice, they become comfortable, and most teachers and children could not imagine a school day without writing workshop!

Introducing the Writing Process

Regardless of whether you are teaching first graders or eighth graders, it is crucial to introduce them to the writing process and to help them learn the activities involved in each stage. Teachers begin by explaining the process approach, describing and demonstrating each stage, and guiding children as they develop several brief compositions to experience the writing process. Guidelines for introducing the writing process are presented in Figure 2–3.

Children need to learn the procedures and activities involved in each stage and the terminology associated with the writing process. In particular, they need to learn

Figure 2–3 Guidelines for Introducing the Writing Process

- **Writing Process Terminology**
  Use the names of each stage and related writing terms, including *proofread, leads, revise,* and *author's chair,* when talking about writing.

- **Writing Process Charts**
  Create charts describing each stage of the writing process and display them in the classroom.

- **Demonstrations**
  Model each stage in the writing process and write collaborative compositions with the class to emphasize the activities involved in each stage.

- **Brief Compositions**
  Encourage children to keep their first compositions brief so that they can move through the writing process successfully.

- **Writing Folders**
  Provide writing folders for children to use to hold their prewriting notes, rough drafts, editing checklists, and other papers related to the writing project.

how to make clusters, participate in writing groups, revise, and proofread. Teachers use minilessons to demonstrate each procedure and then provide many opportunities for children to practice each procedure and activity through writing workshop and thematic projects.

Learning the writing process takes time. Children need to work through the entire process again and again until the stages and activities become automatic. Once they understand the writing process, they can manipulate the activities of each stage to meet the demands of particular writing projects and modify the process to accommodate their personal writing styles.

It's a good idea to hang charts outlining the writing process and related activities in the classroom (Tompkins & Zumwalt, 2005). These charts should be developed with children rather than made in advance by the teacher. Two writing process charts developed by third graders are shown in Figure 2–4. The first chart, "Revision," lists the activities involved in the revising stage, and the second chart, "Things to Say in Writing Groups," offers suggestions children can use when they're thinking of comments to make in writing groups.

Class Collaborations ■ One way to demonstrate the writing process is through a class collaboration, shared writing in which children and the teacher write together. Children practice the writing process within a supportive environment, and the teacher reviews concepts and clarifies misconceptions as the group piece is written. Children supply the ideas for writing and offer suggestions for how to tackle common writing problems.

The teacher begins by introducing the idea of writing a group composition and discussing the project. Almost any type of writing project can be written as a class collaboration, including poems, letters, stories, and reports. What's most important is that all children are familiar with the topic and the genre. For example, if children are writing an impassioned letter to the editor of the local newspaper about a community ecological problem, they should be knowledgeable about the problem and about how to write a persuasive letter. Or, if children are writing an innovation (a new version of a familiar text) of *Rosie's Walk* (Hutchins, 1968), they need to be familiar with the story.

Children write the composition together, moving through the prewriting, drafting, revising, editing, and publishing stages of the writing process. They brainstorm ideas, and then children dictate a rough draft, which the teacher writes on chart paper. Or children can take turns doing the writing. The teacher is alert for any misunderstandings children may have about writing or the writing process and, when necessary, reviews concepts and offers suggestions.

Then children and the teacher move on to the revising stage, and the teacher or a child reads the rough draft aloud several times. Next, children make suggestions about how to fine-tune the draft. Some parts may be reworked; others may be deleted or moved. More specific words will be substituted for less specific ones, and redundant words and sentences will be deleted. Also, children may add new parts to the composition. After making the necessary content changes, children proofread the composition, identifying mechanical errors, checking paragraph breaks, and combining sentences as needed. They take turns making changes.

Finally, the composition is published. The teacher or several children copy the completed composition on sheets of chart paper and compile them into a big or regular-size book or copy them on sheets of writing paper and make copies for each child.

Figure 2–4 Writing Process Charts

In another type of collaborative writing, children divide the writing project into small segments, and each child or small group completes one part. If children are writing a report, for example, they divide into small groups, and each group writes one chapter. Or, if the class is writing a retelling of a favorite story, each child or pair of children writes and illustrates one page or chapter of the book. Often the class

Figure 2–5 Shared Writing: An Excerpt From a Fourth-Grade Class Book, "California: The Golden State"

A Tour of San Francisco

Clang! Clang! Clang! go the bells on the cable cars. The cable cars go up and down the hills of San Francisco. Let's take a ride. It's a good way to learn about this city. San Francisco is the third largest city in California and the population is 739,426. It is located on a peninsula next to the Pacific Ocean.

San Francisco is an old city. Spanish missionaries founded it in 1776. The city really began to grow in 1848 with the Gold Rush. It was an important mining supply center. People who made a lot of money came back to live in San Francisco, and they built beautiful homes on Nob Hill. Most of the homes are gone now because of the Great San Francisco Earthquake in 1906.

Our first stop is at Chinatown. There are many people from China that live in San Francisco. Some Chinese people came to America to work in the gold rush and some came to work on the First Transcontinental Railroad that was built in the 1860's. Now some of their great grandchildren live in one area that is called Chinatown. Look on the street signs. You see the names written in Chinese and in English. Do you hear people talking Chinese in the stores and on the street? We can stop and eat Chinese food and buy little gifts that come from China. Did you know there is a fortune cookie factory here, too?

Our second stop is at Fisherman's Wharf. Many, many fishing boats used to dock here. They caught fish in the ocean. Then they came here to sell the fish. Now there are only a few boats but there are good seafood restaurants here. We will walk over to two fun shopping centers. One shopping center is called the Cannery. It used to be a factory that made canned food. That's why it's called the Cannery. The other one is Ghirardelli Square, and it used to be a chocolate factory. You can eat Ghirardelli chocolates at a store there.

Now we will take a boat tour of San Francisco Bay and see the sights. Look straight ahead and you will see the Golden Gate Bridge. It is very tall and you can see the two towers and the cables that hang down to hold the bridge up. It is called a suspension bridge and it is 8,981 feet long. Many people drive across the bridge every day and you can even walk across it. There is a sidewalk. Over here you can see Alcatraz Island. It used to be a military fort and prison. The most dangerous criminals in America used to be put here, but it is closed now.

Thank you for taking this tour. I hope you have learned that San Francisco is a great and interesting city. There is much, much, much more to see and you can take more of our tours. I want you to leave your heart in San Francisco and come back soon. Good bye!

does the first page or chapter together to review the writing process and procedure for the particular writing project, then children work independently on their own parts. Children come back together to revise and edit their writing and finally to compile and publish their writing as a book.

Figure 2–5 presents an excerpt from a class book, "California: The Golden State," written by fourth graders as the culmination of a yearlong study of their state. Children brainstormed topics and divided into pairs and small groups to write the sections. This book is interesting because children wrote the chapters from the viewpoint of Californians in each setting: The chapter about the gold rush was written from a miner's viewpoint, and the chapter on Yosemite National Park was written from naturalist John Muir's viewpoint. The excerpt in Figure 2–5, "A Tour of San Francisco," was written from the viewpoint of a tour guide. This perspective makes the writing more interesting to read and allows students to add personal experiences to the information they present. There is no doubt that these children have visited San Francisco and have been on tours themselves. Children participated in all five stages of the writing process as they prepared the book. As the final step, the chapters were compiled and a cover, title page, dedication, and table of contents were added. Then copies were made for each child.

Writing Centers ■ A writing center is a designated area of the classroom, often a table where writing supplies, including paper, pens and pencils, art supplies, bookmaking materials, and staplers, are stored. Dictionaries, thesauri, computerized spell checkers, and word books are also available. Teachers set up writing centers to provide a supportive environment for small groups of children as they write (Dillon, 2005).

Children come to the writing center to work on writing projects. In kindergarten and first grade, they may write in journals or make books, and the teacher, another adult, or an upper-grade student is often at the center to provide additional guidance to children as they write. Young children work through an abbreviated version of the writing process, gathering and organizing ideas, often by drawing a picture, and then writing words using invented spelling. As the child writes, the teacher often guides the child, helping him or her connect words into sentences, and sounding out the spelling of some words and applying other strategies for spelling other words. After writing, children read their compositions to classmates at the writing center. At other times, children write notes to classmates at the writing center and then "mail" the notes in mailboxes or by tacking them to a "Message Center" board.

Older children participate in a variety of writing activities at writing centers. Often they write books on self-selected topics, but at other times, they work on a writing project as part of a literature focus unit or thematic unit. For example, second graders write letters to Ruby after reading *Ruby Lu, Brave and True* (Look, 2004), and sixth graders make posters with information about a Greek god or goddess while learning about ancient Greece.

Too often, teachers think of writing centers, as well as other types of centers, as a way to organize in primary classrooms, but writing centers can be used effectively at any grade level. One benefit is that as children work in centers, they have support to move through the writing process and share writing. Also, children learn the routines of writing workshop as they work at a writing center. There are benefits for teachers, too. Sometimes teachers are overwhelmed with the idea of "turning their students loose" for writing workshop, and permitting a small group of children to work at a writing center while others are involved in other literacy activities is the first step in implementing writing workshop.

Arranging the Classroom for Writing Workshop

No special classroom arrangement is necessary for writing workshop, but the arrangement of furniture, equipment, and supplies should facilitate workshop activities. Children often sit at desks arranged in small groups so that they can either write independently or collaborate with classmates. One or more tables should be available for student-organized writing groups or teacher-led conferences, and a large, open space is needed for the class to meet for teacher-directed minilessons and to share their writing. An author's chair should be available for child-writers to sit in when they read their published pieces aloud.

Classrooms should be equipped with a bank of computers with word-processing software and printers so that children can produce professional-looking books. Different kinds of paper, writing instruments, and book-making supplies are needed when children are making books by hand, and a class set of red and blue pens are useful for revising and editing activities. A well-stocked, accessible classroom library also supports writing workshop because children use favorite books as models for writing, and they often need to refer to theme-related and reference books while they're writing.

Adapting Writing Workshop for Emergent Writers

Kindergarten and first-grade teachers adapt writing workshop for their young students. The three most important stages in the writing process for emergent writers are prewriting, drafting, and publishing. The revising and editing stages can be added when children begin to see value in revising their writing to make it better, when they have moved from invented spelling toward more conventional spelling, and when they have been introduced to conventional capitalization and punctuation.

Kindergartners and first graders (and older children who are novice writers) can either write single-draft books using invented spelling or write rough draft books that teachers transcribe for them. The choice depends on the purpose for writing and the time and resources that teachers have available.

Young children write single-draft books and spell words inventively according to the phonetic principles they know. They draw a series of pictures in a booklet and write the text to accompany the pictures. Children may be able to read their books, but classmates and the teacher may have difficulty deciphering the words or sentences, which may be strings of letters without any spaces between words. As children become more fluent writers, these books become easier to read.

An excerpt from a child's single-draft book about dinosaurs, which was written with invented spelling, is presented in Figure 2–6. On the page shown in the figure, the child wrote "Baby dinosaurs hatch from eggs." The drawing and the spacing between words make it easier to decipher the child's writing. The emphasis in these books is on encouraging children to be independent writers. Children sit in an author's chair to share their books with classmates, but because they use idiosyncratic invented spelling strategies, the books are not widely read by classmates.

In transcribed books, young children write books that the teacher transcribes into conventional English for the final copy. They draw pictures and write the first draft using invented spelling. Then the teacher (or another adult) prints or types the final copy, changing the invented spelling to conventional spelling and adding appropriate capital letters and punctuation marks. Sometimes teachers type the final copy using a word processor and print out very professional-looking pages. Children bind the pages into a book and make new drawings for each page.

A first grader's transcribed book, "Lisa the Fish," is presented in Figure 2–7. The teacher transcribed the child's invented spelling for the final copy, and then the child added the illustrations. Two pages have been added to the back of the book. Next to the last page is a "Comments" page, where children and parents who read the book write compliments and other comments to the author. The last page is a list of the children in the class; after children read the book or take the book home to read with their parents, they cross off their name.

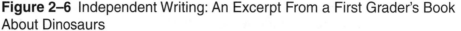

Figure 2–6 Independent Writing: An Excerpt From a First Grader's Book About Dinosaurs

This approach is useful if children place the completed books in the class library for classmates to read or if the books are used as part of the reading program. Making transcribed books is more time-consuming for both children and teachers: Children have to draw the illustrations twice, and sometimes the second set of drawings is not as detailed as the first because they tire or lose interest in the project. Also, teachers spend a lot of time preparing the final copies of the books.

As children's writing becomes more fluent and their spelling approaches conventional forms, they make the transition to the five-stage writing process. Children show their readiness in several ways: If the teacher has been writing the final copy, children may express the desire to do all the writing on both the rough draft and the final copy themselves; or if they have been doing their own writing, they begin to squeeze revisions into their writing. Sometimes children mention how they might change part of a book and ask if they should start over. When children demonstrate an awareness of the need to refine the ideas in their writing and to correct mechanical errors, they are ready to move into the five-stage writing process. It is important that children see value in working through the process; otherwise, revision and editing will seem meaningless to them.

Incorporating Writing Workshop Into Units

Children also use writing workshop in literature focus units and social studies and science thematic units. Children make projects as they apply what they are learning, and many of these projects involve writing. Sometimes children choose their own writing projects related to a particular unit, or they might work on a project chosen by the class. For example, during an author study on Eric Carle, first graders make marbleized paper and use it to illustrate books they are writing. Or, as part of a science unit on insects, fourth graders make models of insects and write an encyclopedia with an entry about each insect. In these two examples, teachers follow a writing workshop format so that the children can use the writing process to develop and refine their compositions.

When children use writing workshop to create projects, teachers set aside a specific period of time for writing. After children read books or are introduced to concepts in social studies and science, they begin work on these writings. If children are working on self-selected projects, teachers usually set aside a period of time each day, perhaps 30 minutes to an hour, for them to create their projects. During this time, children move through the stages of the writing process. Teachers help children identify projects, keep track of their progress, and provide them with information on the various types of activities they've selected. For example, the teacher might explain or model how to write a description to accompany a diorama if a child is making a diorama, or how to format a letter if a child is writing a letter to a favorite author.

If the entire class is working on the same project, the writing proceeds in a more uniform fashion. The teacher works with the children to plan the writing project.

Figure 2–7 Independent Writing: A First Grader's Transcribed Book, "Lisa the Fish"

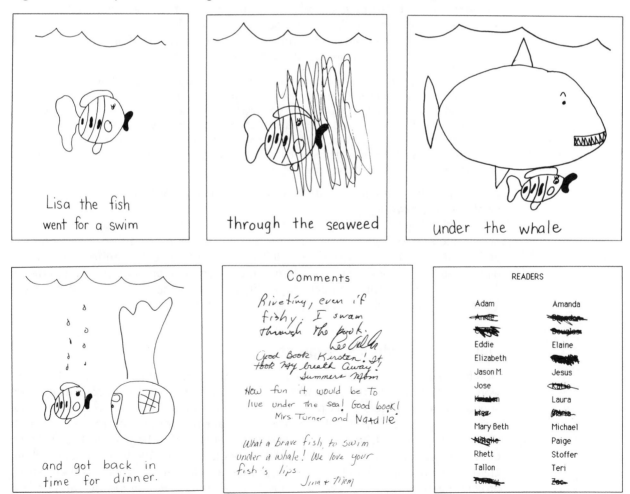

Together they decide on the design of the project and the amount of time allowed for each stage of the writing process. The teacher keeps track of the children's progress and helps them follow the design and keep up with the time schedule. The teacher also guides children as they move from one stage to the next in the writing process.

Writing projects usually span a week or two in which children move through the writing process. The projects usually begin partway through the unit, after children have read related books or learned some big ideas. The preceding activities that are related to the unit serve as prewriting for the project, and children work during the time allocated for the project to create a composition. Writing workshop activities, including sustained writing, sharing, and minilessons, are not delineated, but children and the teacher are involved in these activities nonetheless.

Children use writing to extend learning in literature focus units and social studies or science thematic units. They apply what they are learning by creating poems, reports, posters, and other projects. Sometimes several children work together on a project, but at other times, every student in the class is working on a different project.

Students in a sixth-grade class chose different projects to pursue after reading *Tuck Everlasting* (Babbitt, 1975). One boy decided to put together a story box. He brought a shoebox from home and decorated it with the title, scenes, and characters from the book. Then he collected four items related to the story and placed them in the box: a small bottle of water, Winnie's tombstone made from construction paper, a picture of a Ferris wheel, and small music box. He wrote a paragraph-length composition explaining the book and the items in his box, and glued the final copy of the explanation into the inside of the box top. Here is his explanation:

> *Tuck Everlasting* is an awesome book. The story is about life and how life is like a wheel. The wheel is supposed to keep turning from birth to death. But what happens if the wheel stops? It could if you drank magic water and you stopped getting any older. You would keep on living the same old way year after year after year. You would keep going back to the same old places while the rest of the world lived and died. You would finally learn that the lucky ones are the people who live and love and then grow old and die.

This project demonstrates the depth of understanding that children can develop and display through writing projects.

In an eighth-grade science class, students each wrote picture books about scientific concepts. To develop these picture books, students used the writing process, and because they were publishing their books as picture books, students had an additional step: to break their revised and edited compositions into pages and design illustrations to accompany each page. Figure 2–8 presents an excerpt from one student's picture book about solstices and equinoxes.

Monitoring Children's Progress

Monitoring is an essential component of writing workshop because children are working on different projects and moving through the writing process at different speeds. When teachers don't monitor children's learning, they often feel as though they aren't in control, and children often feel that same loss of control. Teachers use three management strategies to monitor children's work. The first strategy is status of the class (Atwell, 1998). Before children begin to write, the teacher calls roll and children each respond with a word or phrase about their progress on their writing project, such as "Making my final copy," "Clustering," "Ready for a writing group,"

Figure 2–8 Independent Writing: An Excerpt From an Eighth Grader's Picture Book on Solstices and Equinoxes

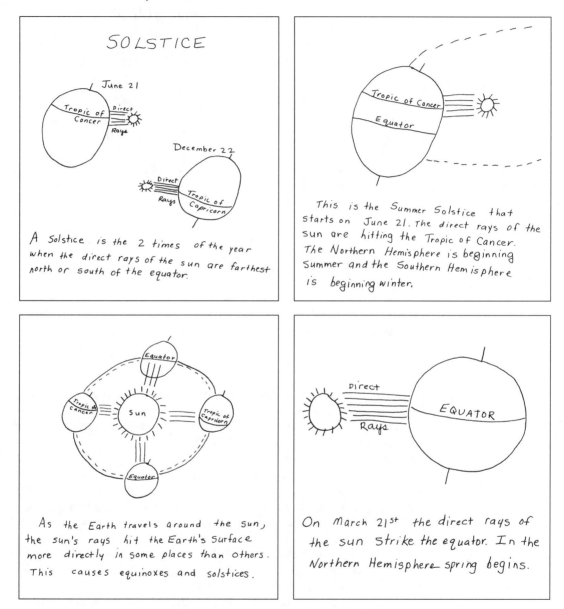

or "I'm still drafting." The teacher writes a word or code number by each child's name on a chart. Many teachers use numbers representing the five stages of the writing process on their charts, as shown in Figure 2–9. Some teachers write status of the class charts on transparencies that they display on an overhead projector, and other teachers make paper charts that they post in the classroom.

Other teachers use variations of the status of the class chart. Some use pocket charts, with a pocket for each of the five stages of the writing process, and children place popsicle sticks with their names printed on them in the pocket for the stage showing their progress. Others have children clip clothespins with their names

Figure 2–9 A Status of the Class Chart

Writing Workshop Chart								
Names	Dates 3/18	3/19	3/20	3/21	3/22	3/25	3/26	3/27
Anthony	4	5	5	5	5	1	1	1 2
Belle	2	2	2 3	2	2	4	5	5
Connor	3	3 1	1	2	2 3	4	5	5
Dina	4 5	5	5	1	1	1	1	2 3
Jason	3	3	4	4	4	5	5 1	1
Eddie	2 3	2	2 4	5	5	1	1 2	2 3
Elizabeth	2	3	3	4	4	4 5	5	1 2
Elsa	1 2	3 4	4 5	5	5	1	2	2

Code:
1 = Prewriting   2 = Drafting   3 = Revising   4 = Editing   5 = Publishing

printed on them onto writing stage coat hangers or onto large circle charts made from pizza cardboards.

The second way that teachers monitor progress is by conferencing with children and making anecdotal notes, as Mrs. Zumwalt did in the vignette at the beginning of the chapter. Many teachers use clipboards with a page for each child, index cards with a card for each child, or charts with boxes for each child. Teachers observe children, read their writing, and talk with them about their progress. They also help children make plans for their work over the next few days and set goals for new writing projects. This conference usually takes 5 minutes or less, and then teachers write notes before moving on to the next child.

Children also keep project checklists listing the stages in the writing process that they mark as they move through them. They keep this checklist in their writing folders along with clusters, drawings, lists, drafts, and other materials related to their project. They compile all of these materials when they finish a project and turn them in to the teacher along with the final copy of their project; these materials document children's use of the writing process.

Ultimately, learning the writing process is far more important than the quality of a child's project. The writing process is a tool that children can use for any project, and learning that process is the most important goal of writing workshop.

ANSWERING TEACHERS' QUESTIONS ABOUT . . .

Writing Workshop

My second graders just aren't mature enough to work independently during writing workshop. What should I do?

Some teachers complain that their students are uninterested in writing, inattentive in writing groups, or irresponsible about completing assignments. The best way to help them become interested in and feel responsible for their writing is to use writing workshop. When children make decisions about their writing, choose topics that are important to them, and share their writing with classmates, their behavior changes.

My fifth graders keep writing about the same tired topics during writing workshop. How can I get them to move on?

Do your students generate lists of possible writing topics? If they don't, they should start lists. Then you can encourage them to choose a new topic from the lists for their next compositions. Or, you might conference with those children who stick to safe and familiar topics and ask them to think of a new topic, and then stay with them while they get started in order to provide support. They may want to talk the idea out with you or need help in brainstorming words about the topic to get started.

Is it better to have children write about anything they want during writing workshop, or to co-ordinate writing workshop with my thematic units?

Neither way is better than the other. They are both effective ways to teach writing, but they serve different purposes. When children choose their own topics during writing workshop, the focus is on helping them to become fluent writers and to have a chance to write about their own lives, experiences, and interests. Through thematic projects, children use writing to learn and to apply what

they are learning. It is important that teachers understand the purpose of each approach and plan activities to fit their goals.

I teach fifth grade. Do you mean that I should set up a writing center?

Sure, you should have several centers in your classroom and provide opportunities for children to work at the centers on a regular basis. Possibilities include a library center, a word work center (with spelling and vocabulary activities), a computer center, a listening center, and, of course, a writing center. Include writing folders, a variety of paper, pens, a dictionary and a thesaurus, and book-making supplies in the center. Arrange materials in each center area and hang signs to label the areas. Explain the centers to children, and then provide time in your daily schedule for them to work at each center as part of their daily assignments, not as busywork for after they finish their regular assignments.

I just don't have time in my daily schedule for writing workshop. What can I do?

Teachers never have enough time in their schedules. Those things you find a way to include are the subjects you value; those that you don't include are not as important to you. Write out your schedule and look for possible time. What can you combine? What might you alternate with writing workshop? Some teachers alternate reading and writing workshop. Other teachers use writing workshop as part of their social studies and science period. Others use writing workshop as the first or last activity of the day. If you really want to include writing workshop, you'll find 30, 45, or even 60 minutes to squeeze it in. And, of course, you should value it. Using the writing process on a daily basis provides lots of writing opportunities and translates into improved learning in reading, writing, and spelling.

Chapter 3
Writing Strategies and Skills

Preview

➤ Strategies are problem-solving behaviors that writers use thoughtfully and consciously.

➤ Skills are information-processing techniques that writers use automatically and unconsciously.

➤ Teachers use minilessons to provide direct instruction about strategies and skills.

➤ Teachers model strategy and skill use and take advantage of teachable moments to explain their use.

Novice Writers Learn Strategies and Skills

Ms. Boland is concerned about a group of seventh graders in her third-period class. During the first month of school, she notices that they avoid writing whenever possible. When they should be writing, several students chat with classmates sitting next to them and joke about each other's compositions. One day during writing workshop, she sees Julian look over at Ruben's writing and ask, "What are you writing about?" He picks up Ruben's paper and reads the first sentence. Then he says, "Oh, that's so stupid, man!" Ruben angrily wads up his paper and tosses it in the trash can. He gets out another sheet of paper but doesn't begin to write, and Julian turns around and repeats the procedure with Alyce.

Ms. Boland notices Houa and Mai at another table. After they write several lines on their papers, they put their pencils down, stretch their arms across the table, and slouch down in their chairs with chins on their chests. They sit quietly like that for 5 minutes or more as Ms. Boland observes them. They seem to be waiting for the class to be over. Ms. Boland approaches Houa and Mai to talk to them about their writing in hopes of getting them back on track. She pulls up her stool and settles onto it. "What are you writing?" she asks. Mai says, "I don't know," and Houa says, "Nothing." Ms. Boland notices that they don't have their writing folders out, so she asks them to get them out. The folders should have various rough drafts and clusters, lists of writing topics, editing checklists, self-assessment charts, and other information sheets, but Houa's and Mai's folders have only a couple of pages, and these are either incomplete or blank! Ms. Boland realizes that she has her work cut out for herself.

The following week, Ms. Boland interrupts writing workshop for the All-School Writing Assessment. All language arts teachers at the school have their students write in response to a prompt at the beginning and again at the end of the school year; this year's topic is "a memorable moment in your life." Students have 60 minutes to write their compositions without any input from their teacher, but they are encouraged to use the writing process to draft and refine their papers. Ms. Boland uses this opportunity to observe her students as they deal with the demands of the assignment. As she expects, this writing assignment is difficult for a small group of her students, including Julian, Ruben, Alyce, Houa, and Mai.

Even though the topic is broad and is something that the teachers hope all students can relate to, these students find it difficult. They begin to write without brainstorming or thinking about how to organize their thoughts. They write hesitantly and stare into space, and they don't reread what they have written to get a running start before beginning to write again. Their writing is brief and not broken into paragraphs. They write four, five, and up to eight sentences, and they don't revise or edit their writing even though they're writing in pencil and both erasers and correction fluid are available. They write single drafts even though Ms. Boland knows that their teachers in previous grades have emphasized the writing process.

These students write about doing something with their best friend, going to a nearby lake with their family, going to the mall with friends, playing soccer, talking on the telephone, or hanging around the apartment complex. As she reads these students' papers, Ms. Boland notices that they write about everyday activities, not more memorable moments.

Mai wrote this composition about talking on the telephone:

> You call Pam at 8:30 and we stay on the phone a long time. You like to talk and she like to talk so you can talk. You talk and your brother say to hang up the phone! And you keep to talking and your brother say hang up! I like to talk to Pam so you talk and talk. Your brother he get real mad and you talk and talk.

It is very interesting that Mai wrote in the second person even though memories are typically written in the first person. Also, she wrote about a habitual activity rather than a specific memory of one special telephone call.

Ruben wrote about playing soccer:

> I play soccer on Saturday and I play at Calwa Field. My team has won many trophies. I play forward and I scored many goals. We play weekend tournaments. It is fun and this is my fifth year to play soccer. My brother plays too and he's a striker.

Ruben also wrote about a habitual activity, but he did write from the first-person viewpoint. Both Mai's and Ruben's writings are very general, lacking details about a specific memory and using simplistic vocabulary and sentence structure.

Ms. Boland and her colleagues score the papers using a 4-point rubric; two teachers read and score each paper so that a total of 8 points is possible. If there's more than one point between the two scores, a third teacher also reads and scores the paper. Most students' papers score a 5 or 6, but Mai's paper scores a 2 and Ruben's a 3.

Ms. Boland decides to interview these five students to learn more about them as writers. She talks to them individually and asks some questions from an interview list that she often has students complete in writing. These questions explore students' understanding of what writers do and what makes good writing. She asks Julian, for example, "What do you do when you start writing?" and he responds, "It's like getting an idea and then it runs down my nerves from my head to my fingers of my hand and then to the pen and onto the paper." "What about your ideas? How do you get them?" Ms. Boland probes. "I don't know. They just come to me," he replies. Julian's answers, like the others', show a lack of organizational skills and no use of writing strategies.

"When you finish writing the first draft of your paper, what do you do?" she asks Alyce. "You mean after I'm done? Well, I turn it in," she replies. "Do you reread it? Do you check it or ask someone in the class to read it for you and give you some ideas?" Ms. Boland explores. "No, when I'm done, well, I'm done," Alyce answers. The other students' responses are similar: They write single-draft papers, they write in isolation from classmates, and they can't articulate any writing strategies that they use.

These students make it very clear that they don't like to write. "No, I don't like to write very much. It's boring and it's hard work" is the universal response to her questions "Do you like to write? Why or why not?" They talk about how their hands hurt when they write, so Ms. Boland asks if they would prefer writing on the computer so that the handwriting demands would be less. They all want to try that, even though they have had little previous computer experience.

"What do you think makes writing good?" Ms. Boland asks Mai, and she answers, "It is long and pretty. That's what makes it good." Ms. Boland then asks, "What about the ideas? Are they important?" "Yes, they are important," Mai responds, but she doesn't seem sure. Then Ms. Boland asks, "So, what's the most important—how the paper looks, or having good ideas?" "Your paper, it should be pretty to be a good paper," Mai responds. Mai and the other students focus on the surface features of writing.

Ms. Boland asks other questions about topics, forms, and audiences for writing. "What topics do you like to write about?" she asks. "I don't know. I just write about stuff," answers Houa. "There are lots of different types of writing, like writing stories, letters, charts, reports, poems, and journals. What kinds do you like best?" she asks next. "I don't know" is the universal response. She also asks, "When you write, who reads your writing?" Ruben looks surprised at her question and says, "You do. You read what I write because you are the teacher. I will put it in a box on your desk and you will read it and give me a grade." "What about other people? Aren't there some other people who read your writing?" Ms. Boland asks. Ruben seems confused and responds, "No. I don't think so." Ms. Boland concludes that the students don't have a repertoire of topics about which to write, that they aren't aware of choices they can make about the form their writing would take, and that the only audience they are aware of is the teacher.

Reflecting on what she has learned about these novice writers, Ms. Boland sets four instructional priorities. Her first priority is to engage them in writing about topics that are important to them. She begins by having them write about their slang and what the words mean, and next they write about their favorite music and compare it to their parents' music. She encourages them to write at the computer and use the spell checker. Her second priority is teaching the students about writing. She does modeled and shared writing lessons and thinks aloud about what writers do as they write collaborative pieces. The students learn the writing process, including how to revise and edit. Her third priority is reading lots of literature to and with these students. They focus on sentences in the books they read and learn to identify examples of figurative language. They manipulate these sentences and write imitation sentences following the structure of the sentence taken from literature. Providing lots of writing opportunities is her fourth goal. Ms. Boland plans lessons using modeled, shared, interactive, guided, and independent writing. She structures their writing so that they apply what they are learning about writing and what writers do as they write.

Ms. Boland collects writing samples each month and finds significant improvements in all five students' writing. First she notices that their sentence length increases and that they use more specific and descriptive words. They make clusters before writing and break their writing into paragraphs according to the sections on their clusters. They gain confidence in themselves as writers and add wordplay to their writing. They also become more aware of their audience because they now volunteer to read a sentence or two aloud in their small group each week. They begin to engage readers by asking questions or adding parenthetical comments directed to the reader, such as "So, do you see what I mean?" By the end of the first semester, these five students are writing first drafts and revising and editing them. They are learning writing strategies and can talk about what they do as writers. They consider options when they write instead of writing whatever comes to mind.

At the end of the school year, Ms. Boland's students participate in the All-School Writing Assessment and write again about a memorable moment. Most students write on different topics, but Ruben writes again about playing soccer. In the fall assessment, he began his paper, "I play soccer on Saturday." Eight months later, he begins his paper this way: "It's easy for me to wake up on Saturday morning! Do you want to know why? It's because Saturday is when I play soccer. Last Saturday we had a great game and I will tell you about it."

Ms. Boland's seventh graders are novice writers. Much like younger, beginning writers, they lack knowledge about the writing process and have few strategies and skills available to use while they are writing. Researchers compared novice and more capable writers and identified these characteristics of capable writers:

- Capable writers vary how they write depending on their purpose for writing and the audience who will read the composition.
- Capable writers use the writing process flexibly.
- Capable writers focus on developing ideas and communicating effectively.
- Capable writers turn to classmates for feedback on how they are communicating.
- Capable writers monitor how well they are communicating in the piece of writing.
- Capable writers use formats and structures for stories, poems, letters, and other texts.
- Capable writers use a variety of strategies and monitor their strategy use.
- Capable writers postpone attention to mechanical correctness until the end of the writing process.
- Capable writers assess writing according to how well they communicate with their audience.

Perhaps the most remarkable difference between capable and less capable writers is that those who are less successful are not strategic. They seem reluctant to use unfamiliar strategies or those that require much effort. They don't seem to be motivated or to expect that they will be successful. These writers don't understand or use all stages of the writing process effectively. They don't monitor their writing.

Figure 3–1 A Comparison of Capable and Novice Writers

Characteristics	Capable Writers	Novice Writers
Audience, purpose, and form	Capable writers vary how they write depending on their purpose for writing and the audience that will read the composition.	Novice writers are unaware of audience, purpose, and form considerations.
Process	Capable writers use the writing process flexibly.	Novice writers move through the writing process in a lockstep, linear approach.
Goal	Capable writers focus on developing ideas and communicating effectively.	Novice writers view writing as putting words on paper.
Peer response	Capable writers turn to classmates for feedback on how they are communicating.	Novice writers are unable to collaborate with classmates.
Self-assessment	Capable writers monitor how well they are communicating in the piece of writing.	Novice writers are unable to assess their own writing.
Genres	Capable writers use formats and structures for stories, poems, letters, and other texts.	Novice writers don't vary how they format or structure writing according to the assignment.
Strategies	Capable writers use a variety of strategies and monitor their strategy use.	Novice writers use few strategies, most often a knowledge-telling strategy.
Editing	Capable writers postpone attention to mechanical correctness until the end of the writing process.	Novice writers are more concerned with mechanics than with ideas.
Quality	Capable writers assess the quality of their writing according to how well they communicate with their audience.	Novice writers assume that longer is better and neater is better.

Or, if they do use strategies, they remain dependent on primitive ones. Novice writers move through the writing process in a lockstep, linear approach. They use a limited number of strategies, most often a "knowledge-telling" strategy in which they list everything they know about a topic with little thought to choosing information to meet the needs of their readers or to organizing the information to put related ideas together (Faigley, Cherry, Jolliffe, & Skinner, 1985; Scardamalia & Bereiter, 1986).

In contrast, capable writers understand the recursive nature of the writing process and turn to classmates for feedback about how well they are communicating. They are more responsive to the needs of the audience that will read their papers and work to organize their papers in a cohesive manner. Figure 3–1 compares capable and novice writers. You will notice that Ms. Boland's students exemplified many of the characteristics of novice writers.

These comparisons have important implications for writing instruction. Because the most significant difference between capable and less capable writers is their strategy use, it's essential that children learn about writing strategies. Collins (1998) states that the goal is to teach novice writers to think strategically about writing: Not only do writers need to know about the strategies, but they need to understand why they're important and how and when to use them.

Strategies and Skills

We all have skills that we use automatically, as well as self-regulated strategies for things that we do well—driving defensively, playing volleyball, training a new pet, or maintaining classroom discipline. We apply skills we have learned unconsciously and solve problems as we think strategically. The strategies we use in these activities are problem-solving mechanisms that involve complex thinking processes. When we are just learning how to drive a car, for example, we learn both skills and strategies. Some of the first skills we learn are how to start the engine, make left turns, and parallel park. With practice, these skills become automatic. Some of the strategies we learn are how to pass another car and how to stay a safe distance behind the car ahead of us. These are strategies, not skills, because drivers must think about speed, visibility, road condition, and other variables in using the strategies. At first, we have only a small repertoire of strategies, and we don't always use them effectively. That's one reason why we take lessons from experienced drivers and practice with their guidance and supervision. These seasoned drivers teach us defensive driving strategies. We learn strategies for driving on interstate highways, on slippery roads, and at night. With practice, we become more successful drivers, able to anticipate driving problems and take defensive actions.

Writing Strategies

Children learn and use strategies for writing (Dean, 2006). Writing strategies are "deliberate thinking procedures writers use to solve problems that they encounter while writing" (Collins, 1998, p. vii). Strategic writers take conscious and deliberate control of the writing process. They select and use appropriate strategies, organize ideas for writing, monitor the development of their compositions, and revise their meaning as they refine their writing (Lewin, 1992; Paris & Jacobs, 1984; Schmitt, 1990). Eight strategies that writers use are described in the following paragraphs and summarized in Figure 3–2.

Generating ■ Children use the generating strategy to gather ideas and words for writing. They consciously think about what they know about a topic and activate their background knowledge. As children think of words and ideas, they brainstorm lists, take notes, and draw pictures to help them remember. Another way children generate ideas is by learning more about a topic. For example, children read articles and books, check information on the Internet, examine artifacts, conduct surveys and experiments, and view films and DVDs. Generating is an especially useful strategy as children prepare to write during the prewriting stage, but writers also use it during the drafting and revising stages.

Organizing ■ Writers need to organize the ideas they've generated so that their writing is easy to comprehend. They make clusters and other diagrams to organize ideas, and they refer to their organizational plans as they write. Organizing is a strategy that children use early in the writing process, but they also use it during the revising stage, especially when they get feedback that their ideas are hard to understand. They way children organize ideas varies depending on whether they're writing stories, informational books, letters, or poetry because each genre has unique organizational patterns. When children write personal narratives, for example, they often organize the events into the beginning, middle, and end, and when they write poems, they use poetic forms.

Figure 3–2 Writing Strategies

Strategy	Explanation	Activities
Generating	Writers brainstorm words, sentences, and ideas for writing, often using their background knowledge or other classroom resources.	Make a list. Draw pictures. Make a data chart. Talk with classmates. Read or reread books. Search the Internet.
Organizing	Writers group, sequence, and prioritize ideas for their compositions.	Cluster ideas. Complete a graphic organizer. Make an outline.
Visualizing	Writers use sensory details to make their writing more vivid.	Add sensory words. Write dialogue. Use metaphors and similes.
Monitoring	Writers coordinate all writing-related activities.	Reread rough drafts. Ask self-questions. Get feedback from classmates.
Playing With Language	Writers incorporate figurative and novel uses of language in their compositions.	Use metaphors and similes. Use idioms. Write alliterations. Create invented words.
Revising	Writers add words and sentences, make substitutions and deletions, and move text around to communicate more effectively.	Reread rough drafts. Participate in a writing group. Use a blue pen to make revisions.
Proofreading	Writers carefully read their writing to identify mechanical errors.	Reread rough drafts. Proofread with a classmate. Use a red pen to edit.
Evaluating	Writers self-assess and value their writing.	Use rubrics. Conference with classmates and the teacher. Write reflections.

Visualizing ■ Writers use the visualizing strategy to make their writing more vivid and bring it to life for the people who read it. They add description, figurative language, and sensory details. Sometimes children brainstorm lists of words related to each of the five senses and then incorporate some of the sensory words into their writing. Adding dialogue is another way that children make their writing more vivid. Children can use the visualizing strategy whenever they're writing, but it's an especially important revising strategy. Children often work to substitute more descriptive words; incorporate metaphors, alliteration, onomatopoeia, and other figurative language; and insert sensory details when they're fine-tuning their writing during the revising stage.

Monitoring ■ Children use the monitoring strategy to coordinate their strategy use. They use this strategy to check on how well their writing is progressing during each stage of the writing process. Once children know what capable writers do and how they work through the writing process, they're alert to potential problems, and when they notice one, they quickly take action to resolve it. It's essential that children recognize potential problems while they're writing and that they have resources available to solve the problems that arise. This cognitive awareness is known as *metacognition*.

Playing With Language ■ Children are often inventive with their use of language, and this playfulness adds both voice and charm to their writing. They use the playing-with-language strategy to incorporate figurative and novel uses of language in their writing. Sometimes children write idioms; add jokes, riddles, and rhymes; and invent new words as they write rough drafts; and at other times, children consciously think of ways to add wordplay as they revise their rough drafts.

Revising ■ Writers use the revising strategy whenever they consciously decide to make content, not mechanical, changes in their writing. Content changes involve adding, deleting, substituting, or moving words, sentences, and paragraphs. The purpose of revising is to make changes to communicate more effectively. Even though this strategy has the same name as the third stage of the writing process, they're not the same thing. Children use the revising strategy throughout the writing process, but most often during prewriting, drafting, and revising: They make changes while they're gathering and organizing ideas during prewriting, and the form of the composition might change, for example, from a letter to a story or an essay. The focus might change, too, as children realize that some ideas are more powerful than others. As children are drafting, they often make revisions. They may think of a better way to phrase a sentence or paragraph and make the changes as they're drafting. The revising strategy is especially important during the revising stage, of course, where the focus is on making changes to communicate more effectively. Children reread their writing, think about ways to make it more effective, and get feedback from classmates and the teacher. Writers need to be flexible, understanding the importance of making revisions to improve the quality of their writing.

Proofreading ■ Writers use the proofreading strategy to identify misspelled words, capitalization and punctuation errors, grammar mistakes, and other mechanical errors in their rough drafts. Proofreading involves a special kind of reading where children attend to the surface features of words rather than the meaning. They often proofread their writing two or three times, each time looking for a different type of error; for example, children might proofread first to locate misspelled words, and then proofread the writing a second time to check for capitalization and punctuation errors. Children usually do proofreading during the editing stage of the writing process, just before they make their final copies in the publishing stage.

Evaluating ■ Children use the evaluating strategy to reflect on their writing and make judgments about it. They use self-assessments, rubrics, and checklists to ask themselves whether their writing says what they want it to say—in other words, whether it is effective. They think about what they have accomplished in this piece of writing and reflect on the writing strategies they have used. As a strategy, evaluating is not teacher's judgment handed down to children; instead, it is children's own thinking about their goals and accomplishments.

The research on capable and less capable writers has focused on differences in how children use strategies. It is noteworthy that all research comparing writers focuses on differences in strategy use, not differences in children's use of skills.

There are many reasons why it is so important that all children become strategic writers. Let's consider five of the most important ones. First, strategies allow children to generate, organize, and elaborate meaning more expertly than they could otherwise. Being strategic is an important characteristic of learning. Second, children learn all sorts of cognitive strategies, including reading, mathematical, and scientific investigation strategies, and the acquisition of writing strategies coincides with this cognitive development. As children learn to reflect on their learning, for example, they learn to reflect on themselves as writers; and as they learn to monitor their learning, they learn to monitor their writing. Many of the cognitive strategies that children learn have direct application to writing. In this way, children's growing awareness about thinking and their writing are mutually supportive.

Third, strategies are cognitive tools that children can use selectively and flexibly. For children to become independent writers, they need to be able to apply these thinking tools. Fourth, writing is a tool for learning across the curriculum, and strategic writing enhances learning in math, social studies, science, and other content areas. Children's competence in writing affects all areas of the curriculum. Fifth, teachers can teach children how to apply writing strategies (Paris, Wasik, & Turner, 1991). Just as driving instructors teach novice drivers about defensive driving, teachers demonstrate and explain strategic writing and provide children with opportunities for guided practice.

The Reading-Writing Connection

Even though these strategies are called "writing strategies," they are the same strategies that children use when they read and use the other language arts (Tompkins, 2006). Let's consider one strategy—organizing. Just as children organize ideas before writing, which facilitates readers' understanding of what they have written, readers organize ideas as they read, and this organization facilitates their comprehension. When children are reading stories, for example, they organize ideas into the beginning, middle, and end, and they understand the roles of foreshadowing, plot development, setting, point of view, and theme. They expect stories to be structured in specific ways, and they use this organization when they retell stories or create new versions.

Children also use the organization of other types of texts to aid in comprehension. When children read informational books, they use expository text structures, and when they read poetry, they recognize and use poetic structures. Children use the organizing strategy when they listen, talk, view, and visually represent. When they view videos, for instance, children organize ideas in much the same way as when they read. When students talk and visually represent, they use the strategy much like they do in writing. As they plan their projects, they use the organizing strategy to structure the information they will present.

Writing Skills

Skills are information-processing techniques that writers use automatically and unconsciously as they construct meaning. Many writing skills focus on words and parts of words, but some require writers to attend to larger chunks of text. For example, writers employ word-level skills such as forming contractions, choosing the appropriate homophone, and capitalizing people's names, and they use sentence-level skills when they punctuate sentences, combine sentences, and write alliterative sentences.

Children learn to use six types of writing skills:

- Structuring skills
- Mechanical skills

- Language skills
- Reference skills
- Handwriting skills
- Computer Skills

Figure 3–3 lists examples of each type of skill. Children use some of these skills, such as spelling skills, almost every time they pick up a pencil to write, but they use other skills only for one type of writing or another. When they write in reading logs, for example, children underline titles of books, and when they write letters, they write dates and use commas after the greeting and the closing. Even though they don't use every skill listed for any particular writing task, capable writers are familiar with most of these skills and can use them automatically whenever they are needed.

Figure 3–3 Skills That Writers Use

Types	Examples
Structuring Skills	Write simple, compound, and complex sentences. Avoid sentence fragments and run-on sentences. Combine sentences. Indent paragraphs. Use Standard English grammar.
Mechanical Skills	Apply spelling rules. Use abbreviations. Indicate dialogue with quotation marks. Use apostrophes in possessives and contractions. Capitalize proper nouns and adjectives.
Language Skills	Create similes and metaphors. Craft sentences with alliteration. Use idioms and slang appropriately. Play with rhyme and other poetic devices. Choose synonyms carefully to express the precise meaning.
Reference Skills	Consult a dictionary and a thesaurus. Locate information in reference books. Create tables of contents. Read and create graphs and tables. Use bibliographic forms.
Handwriting Skills	Hold writing instruments comfortably. Form manuscript letters legibly. Space appropriately between letters, words, sentences, and paragraphs. Form and connect cursive letters legibly. Write fluently.
Computer Skills	Do keyboarding. Type and send e-mail messages. Import illustrations and photos. Verify spellings with spell checkers. Locate information on the Internet.

Structuring Skills ■ Children use structuring or grammar skills as they craft sentences. By the time they come to school, children have developed a sophisticated understanding of syntactic rules—in fact, kindergartners and first graders use most of the sentence structures that adults use (O'Donnell, Griffin, & Norris, 1967), and as they learn to read and write, children learn additional written-language structures (Weaver, 1998).

The focus is on the sentence. Killgallon (1997), Noden (1999), and Anderson (2005) recommend that children examine and manipulate well-crafted sentences taken from books they are reading. Killgallon suggests these four types of sentence work:

Sentence Unscrambling. The teacher selects a sentence from a book children are reading and breaks it apart into phrases. Then children rearrange the phrases to make a sentence and compare the sentence they craft with the original one.

Sentence Imitating. Children write a new sentence that imitates the structure of a sentence taken from a book they are reading.

Sentence Combining. The teacher chooses a sentence from a book children are reading and breaks it into several simple sentences. Then children combine the short sentences to make a more sophisticated sentence. They also compare the sentence they craft with the original sentence.

Sentence Expanding. The teacher selects a sophisticated sentence from a book children are reading and has them expand the nucleus of the sentence into a longer sentence in the author's style. Then children compare their sentence with the original sentence.

Figure 3–4 reviews Killgallon's four types of sentence composing with sample sentences from E. B. White's *Charlotte's Web* (1999).

Teachers also introduce grammar terms as children examine sentences taken from books they are reading. They learn that sentences express a complete thought and that depending on the number of independent and dependent clauses they contain, sentences are classified as simple, compound, complex, and compound-complex. Children search for examples of each sentence type in books they're reading, and they examine the author's sentence structure and explore how the meaning would change if another structure were used. They also learn the terminology for parts of sentences—*dependent clause, prepositional phrase, coordinating conjunction,* for example—as they examine sentences. Anderson (2005) argues that zooming in at the sentence level is valuable because when children examine sentences from the books that they are reading, they will "understand the connections between mechanics, craft, style, and meaning" (p. 19).

Mechanical Skills ■ Spelling, punctuation, and capitalization are the traditional "mechanics" of writing. Children apply spelling patterns, add affixes to root words, use abbreviations, and check spellings in the dictionary as they write words and when they proofread. They focus on these skills during the editing stage of the writing process.

Children learn that capital letters divide sentences and signal important words within sentences (Fearn & Farnan, 1998). Consider how the use of capital letters affects the meaning of these three sentences:

> They were going to the white house for dinner.
> They were going to the White house for dinner.
> They were going to the White House for dinner. (S. Wilde, 1992, p. 18)

Figure 3–4 Killgallon's Four Types of Sentence Composing

Sentence Unscrambling

Children reassemble the parts of a sentence to examine how professional writers structure their sentences. They may duplicate the author's sentence or create an original sentence they like better. The original sentence from E. B. White's *Charlotte's Web* is "A minute later Fern was seated on the floor in the middle of the kitchen with an infant between her knees, teaching it to suck from the bottle" (pp. 6–7). Here are the parts:

in the middle of the kitchen
teaching it to suck from the bottle
a minute later
with an infant between her knees
Fern was seated on the floor

Sentence Imitating

Children create sentences that imitate the structure of a model sentence. The original sentence from *Charlotte's Web* is "Avery noticed the spider web, and coming closer, he saw Charlotte" (p. 71). One group's imitation sentence was "The police officer noticed the car parked at the side of Highway 99, and coming closer, he saw a woman running away from the car and a man racing after her." Another model sentence is "His medal still hung from his neck; by looking out of the corner of his eye he could still see it" (p. 163).

Sentence Combining

Children combine sentences, examine possible combinations, and compare their results with the original sentence. The original sentence from *Charlotte's Web* is "No one had ever had such a friend—so affectionate, so loyal, and so skillful" (p. 173). These are the shorter sentences that children combine:

No one ever had such a friend.
The friend was so affectionate.
The friend was so loyal.
The friend was so skillful.

A more complex sentence that students might practice combining is "For several days and several nights they crawled here and there, up and down, around and about, waving at Wilbur, trailing tiny draglines behind them, and exploring their home" (p. 178).

Sentence Expanding

Children expand an abridged version of a sentence so that the text they add blends in with the rest of the professional writer's sentence. The original sentence from *Charlotte's Web* is "There is no place like home, Wilbur thought, as he placed Charlotte's 514 unborn children carefully in a safe corner" (p. 172). From this original sentence, children expand "There is no place like home . . ." One sixth grader wrote, "There is no place like home, like his home in the barn, cozy and warm straw to sleep on, the delicious smell of manure in the air, Charlotte's egg sac to guard, and his friends Templeton, the goose, and the sheep." The child's sentence differs from the original, but it retains the character of E. B. White's writing style.

Capital letters also express loudness of speech or intensity of emotion because they stand out visually.

Children often begin writing during the preschool years using only capital letters; during kindergarten and first grade, they learn the lowercase forms of letters. They learn to capitalize *I,* the first word in a sentence, and names and other proper nouns and adjectives. Within a few years, the most common problem is overcapitalization, or capitalizing too many words in a sentence. This problem tends to persist into

How to Address Struggling Writers' Problems

The Problem	Writing is difficult to read because of numerous misspelled words.
What Causes It	Children who are poor spellers don't notice the errors in their writing, or they don't realize that correcting errors on their final copies is a courtesy to those who will read their compositions.
How to Solve It	*Quick fix:* During editing, have children work with partners to locate and correct misspelled words. It also helps to have them use red pens during editing. Because they enjoy using red pens, children often spend more time marking and correcting errors. As an alternative, have poor spellers word process their compositions because computer programs usually highlight spelling errors or have spell-check programs children can use. *Long-term solution:* In a series of mini-lessons, teach children how to proofread their rough drafts to locate errors and how to correct spelling errors using a dictionary and other classroom resources. Also, have them practice their editing skills by proofreading and correcting errors in sample compositions.
How to Prevent the Problem	When children share their published writings in authentic ways, they learn the importance of conventional spelling because they want readers to want to read their compositions.

adolescence and even into adulthood because writers have trouble differentiating between common and proper nouns. Too often, children assume that "important" words in the sentence should be capitalized.

It's a common assumption that punctuation marks signal pauses in speech, but punctuation plays a greater role than that (S. Wilde, 1992). Punctuation marks both signal grammatical boundaries and express meaning. Some punctuation marks indicate sentence boundaries; periods, question marks, and exclamation points mark sentence boundaries and indicate whether a sentence makes a statement, asks a question, or expresses an exclamation. In contrast, commas, semicolons, and colons mark grammatical units within sentences.

Quotation marks and apostrophes express meaning within sentences. Quotation marks are used most often to indicate what someone is saying in dialogue, but a more sophisticated use is to express irony, as in *My son "loves" to wash the dishes.* Apostrophes are used in contractions to join two words and in possessive nouns to show relationships. Consider the different meanings of these phrases:

The monkey's howling (and it's running around the cage).
The monkey's howling (annoyed us; we wanted to kill it).
The monkeys' howling (annoyed us; we wanted to kill them).
(We listened all night to) the monkeys howling. (S. Wilde, 1992, p. 18)

Researchers have documented that learning to use punctuation, like spelling and capitalization, is a developmental process. Beginning in the preschool years, children notice punctuation marks and learn to discriminate them from letters (Clay, 1991; Ferreiro & Teberosky, 1982). In kindergarten and first grade, children are formally introduced to the end-of-sentence punctuation marks and learn to use them conventionally about half the time (Cordeiro, Giacobbe, & Cazden, 1983). Many beginning writers use punctuation marks in more idiosyncratic ways, such as between words and at the end of each line of writing, but over time, children's usage becomes more conventional (Hodges, 2000). Edelsky (1983) looked at first- through third-grade bilingual writers and found similar developmental patterns for English learners.

Language Skills ■ Writing involves choosing precise and imaginative language, and children learn language skills to make their writing more interesting. They learn about synonyms and how to use a thesaurus to choose exactly the right word. For example, children learn more precise words for *said,* such as *cried* and *mentioned,* and more descriptive words for *noise,* such as *racket* and *uproar.* They also learn to use these types of figurative language:

Alliteration. Writers use several words that begin with the same sound side by side in a sentence. Third graders wrote silly sentences such as *The king sat in the kitchen with a kangaroo, tying a key on a kite* and included two or three words beginning with the same sound in more serious sentences, such as *The fox with orange fluffy fur trotted out of sight behind the barn.*

Onomatopoeia. Writers use sound words rather than descriptions of sounds to enliven their writing. A fifth grader, for example, wrote *The truck burped and the engine died.*

Personification. Writers attribute human characteristics to inanimate objects and use words that normally refer to people to describe them. Eighth graders wrote *The pigeon tiptoed across the telephone wire* and *The moon winked and then a cloud covered it.*

Similes. Writers create comparisons using *like* or *as* to compare two things. In this example written by a seventh grader, *The jet was as sleek as a porpoise,* the student compares an airplane to an aerodynamic animal.

Metaphors. Writers also create comparisons called *metaphors,* and these comparisons are stronger because *like* or *as* is not used. Compare these two versions of the same idea: *The ballerina was as graceful as a swan* (simile) and *The ballerina was a graceful swan* (metaphor). The metaphor is more powerful than the simile, don't you think? Most children write similes more easily than metaphors, but they can be helped to turn their similes into metaphors during the revising stage of the writing process.

Reference Skills ■ Writers use a variety of reference tools, and children learn about the useful information in dictionaries, thesauri, and other reference books, as well as how to use these resources. Figure 3–5 lists a number of dictionaries and thesauri that have been published specifically for children. Children also learn to use atlases and almanacs, and the Internet is becoming increasingly useful as a reference tool.

They learn reference skills to locate and read information in informational books. The index is probably the most common reference tool, but children also learn to locate information in photos and their captions, charts, figures, maps, and other diagrams.

Handwriting Skills ■ Children develop effective manuscript and cursive handwriting skills so that they can write legibly and fluently. They learn how to form upper- and lowercase letters and how to join cursive letters. Children also develop preferences for using manuscript or cursive writing, and they learn to vary how neat their writing is, depending on whether their purpose is public or private.

The goal is for children to develop legible and fluent handwriting (Farris, 1991). Their handwriting must be legible so that readers can understand what they have written, and fluent so that their writing is not laborious and slow. Here are six elements of legible and fluent handwriting:

Figure 3–5 Reference Books for Children

Dictionaries

American Heritage children's dictionary. (2003). Boston: Houghton Mifflin. (M–U)

Levey, J. S. (2006). *Scholastic first dictionary.* New York: Scholastic. (P)

Merriam Webster children's dictionary. (2005). New York: Dorling Kindersley. (M–U)

Scholastic children's dictionary. (2002). New York. Scholastic. (M–U)

Thesauri

Bollard, J. K. (2006). *Scholastic children's thesaurus.* New York: Scholastic. (M)

Hellweg, P. (2006). *The American Heritage children's thesaurus.* Boston: Houghton Mifflin. (M–U)

Wittles, H. (2001). *A first thesaurus.* Racine, WI: Western. (P–M)

Atlases

Children's night sky atlas. (2004). New York: Dorling Kindersley. (M–U)

Children's world atlas. (2003). New York: Dorling Kindersley. (M–U)

National Geographic world atlas for young explorers. (2003). Washington, DC: National Geographic. (M–U)

Almanacs

Popular science: Almanac for kids. (2004). New York: Popular Science. (M–U)

Time for kids: Almanac. (2006). New York: Time for Kids. (M–U)

World almanac for kids. (2006). New York: World Almanac. (M–U)

Other

Fardon, J. (2005). *Biggest ever book of questions and answers.* New York: Parragon. (M–U)

P = grades K–2, M = grades 3–5, U = grades 6–8

Letter Formation. Letters are formed with specific strokes. Letters in manuscript handwriting are composed of vertical, horizontal, and slanted lines plus circles or parts of circles. Cursive letters are composed of slanted lines, loops, and curved lines. An additional component in cursive handwriting is the connecting stroke used to join letters.

Size and Proportion. Children's handwriting becomes increasingly smaller, and the proportional size of uppercase to lowercase letters increases from 2:1 to 3:1 between first and eighth grades.

Spacing. Children leave adequate space between letters in words and between words in sentences.

Slant. Letters should be consistently parallel. Letters in manuscript handwriting are vertical, and letters in the cursive form slant slightly to the right, or they are vertical or slant slightly to the left for left-handed writers.

Alignment. For proper alignment in both manuscript and cursive handwriting, all letters should be uniform in size and should consistently touch the baseline.

Line Quality. Children should write at a consistent speed and hold their writing instruments correctly and in a relaxed manner to make steady, unwavering lines of even thickness.

Learning to write legibly and fluently is a developmental process, much like learning to spell (Hodges, 2000). Young children move from scribbling to learning to form manuscript letters, and they use them to spell words and sentences. In third grade, children typically learn cursive handwriting and develop greater writing speed. Finally, by the time children reach seventh and eighth grades, they personalize their handwriting by adding distinctive stylistic flourishes.

Computer Skills ■ Computer are valuable tools for writers, and children need to develop the skills to use them effectively. Keyboarding is an essential computer skill, and a variety of "comprehensive" tutorial programs are available to introduce children to keyboarding and teach the home keys and correct fingering on the keyboard. One of the best-known comprehensive programs is Mavis Beacon Teaches Typing® (Learning). Other tutorial programs, such as JumpStart® Typing (Knowledge Adventure), use an arcade game format and are designed to develop children's typing speed.

Keyboarding is important because children who don't know the locations of keys on the keyboard use the hunt-and-peck technique to arduously produce their compositions; too often, children learn bad keyboarding habits that are hard to break later. Many teachers recommend teaching children basic keyboarding skills as soon as they begin to use computers, but others suggest postponing keyboarding instruction until third or fourth grade (Roblyer, 2006). Kahn and Freyd (1990) recommend that young children become familiar with the location of keys and typing conventions as soon as they begin to use word processing programs. They suggest several weeks of brief, whole-class minilessons during which children practice keyboarding using photocopied laminated printouts of the keyboard.

Children learn how to use spell checkers to search their compositions for misspelled words and correct the misspelled words they find. Spell checkers draw children's attention to misspelled words, but they don't recognize incorrect inflectional endings of words or homonym errors. For instance, children may write *their* and spell it correctly, but if the word should be *there*, spell-check software won't catch the error. Thesaurus and grammar programs are also available that allow children to highlight specific problems in their compositions and ask the computer to suggest options, but many writers find them less useful than spell-check programs.

Children learn how to browse the Internet, an almost limitless source of information. They learn how to search for information on particular topics, use "bookmarks" to reach sites that teachers have identified, and import illustrations and graphics into their own writing. It's important that children learn how to use their online time efficiently because they often spend a great deal of time on the Web without accomplishing much writing. Another use of the Internet is for e-mail: Children apply the letter-writing skills they've learned as well as unique e-mail skills as they write and send e-mail notes and letters to classmates, pen pals, the teacher, and the wider community.

Teaching Strategies and Skills

Teachers use both direct and indirect instruction to teach writing strategies and skills (Anderson, 2005; Angelillo, 2002). When teachers teach minilessons and other lessons, they directly and explicitly provide information and guide children as they explore strategies and skills. Also, as part of direct instruction, children apply concepts they are learning in their own writing. In contrast, through indirect instruction, teachers model strategies and skills or implicitly or informally explain them.

All five types of writing provide opportunities for instruction. When teachers do a modeled writing lesson to write a found poem, for example, they demonstrate writing strategies and skills, and when they teach a guided writing lesson to create an innovation on a book, children practice using writing strategies and skills with teacher guidance. Even when children are doing independent writing, they apply the strategies and skills they are learning. When children confer with the teacher during

Figure 3–6 Guidelines for Strategy and Skill Instruction

Minilessons Teach minilessons to introduce and review writing strategies and skills.	**Demonstrations** Model how writers use strategies in the context of authentic writing activities.
Terminology Differentiate between strategies and skills so that children understand that strategies are problem-solving tactics and skills are automatic behaviors that writers use.	**Opportunities** Provide opportunities for children to practice the strategies and skills they are learning in meaningful writing activities.
Explanations Provide step-by-step explanations so that children understand how to use strategies and skills.	**Charts** Post charts that describe strategies and skills in the classroom, and encourage children to refer to them when they're writing.

EL

Scaffolding English Learners

Do grammar and spelling errors in your English learners' compositions jump out at you as you read their writing? If so, you're probably frustrated because as your students learn more about English, they make more errors. It's important to remember that errors are signs of growth. Consider your students' stage of second-language acquisition as you decide which errors to correct and which to teach in minilessons.

independent writing, teachers use teachable moments created when children make comments and ask questions to teach brief lessons.

Through a combination of direct and indirect instruction, children learn when and how to use writing strategies (Duffy & Roehler, 1991). The purpose of instruction is to enhance children's awareness of strategic writing so that they can plan, evaluate, and regulate their own thinking. Rather than teaching isolated skills with fragmented bits of language, stripped of meaning, teachers scaffold and support children's developing writing strategies and skills through interaction with authentic and meaningful texts. As Kucer (1991) explains, "The ability to link classroom-based literacy lessons with real-world, authentic reading and writing experiences is critical if our instruction is to promote literacy development in the children we teach" (p. 532). Guidelines for teaching writing strategies and skills are presented in Figure 3–6.

Ineffective instruction often focuses on isolated skills followed by lots of practice on worksheets. In contrast, effective instruction orients children to the task of constructing meaning from texts and provides a variety of tactics to use during the writing process. In a classic study of two third-grade classes, Calkins (1980) found that the children in the class who learned punctuation marks as a part of editing conferences during writing workshop could define or explain more marks than the children in the other class, who were taught punctuation marks in a more traditional manner with instruction and practice exercises on each punctuation mark. Calkins concluded that a functional approach to teaching the mechanics of writing is more effective than practice exercises. This research documents that children's knowledge of how to use punctuation marks, like other skills, develops from an early awareness through exploration and gradual refinement to increasingly conventional use (S. Wilde, 1992).

Minilessons

Minilessons are 15- to 30-minute direct-instruction lessons designed to help children learn writing skills and become more strategic writers (Atwell, 1998; Hoyt, 2000).

Step by Step: Strategy and Skill Minilessons

1. *Introduce the strategy or skill.* The teacher identifies the strategy or skill and explains why it is useful. The teacher also shares examples of how and when the strategy or skill is used.

2. *Demonstrate it.* The teacher explains the steps and models how to use the strategy or skill in a writing activity.

3. *Provide guided practice.* Children practice the strategy or skill that the teacher demonstrated, with the teacher's guidance and support. The teacher provides feedback to children about how well they are doing. Children make notes about the strategy or skill in their writing notebooks or on a poster to be displayed in the classroom.

4. *Review it.* Children reflect on what they have learned and how they can use their strategy or skill in writing activities. Teachers also often explain how the strategy or skill is used in reading and writing.

5. *Apply it.* Children use the newly learned strategy or skill in new and authentic writing activities. The teacher serves as a coach as children use the strategy or skill in guided writing and independent writing activities.

Teachers focus on one strategy or skill at a time (Davis & Hill, 2003). Sometimes the strategy or skill is taught in a single session, and at other times, the lesson is extended and takes place over several days. In minilessons, children and the teacher focus on a single goal; children are aware of why it is important to learn the strategy or skill, and they are explicitly taught how to use a particular strategy or skill through modeling, explanation, and practice. The steps in a minilesson are shown in the feature on this page. In this five-step minilesson, there is scaffolding and a transfer of responsibility from teacher to children as they apply what they have learned in authentic writing activities (Bergman, 1992; Pearson & Gallagher, 1983).

This minilesson procedure can be adapted to fit whatever strategy or skill is being taught. Teachers often teach minilessons during writing workshop, but they can teach them during other types of writing activities as well. The minilesson on page 70 shows how Ms. Boland uses this five-step procedure to teach her seventh graders about similes. Dudley-Marling (1996), Freppon and Headings (1996), McIntyre (1996), and other researchers have emphasized that direct instruction is important for all children, and especially beneficial for those who are likely to have difficulty becoming capable writers.

Demonstrations and Other Teachable Moments

Teachers demonstrate writing strategies and skills through modeled, shared, and interactive writing. These demonstrations are an important component of writing instruction because children need to watch capable writers as they solve problems during writing. They see teachers organize their writing into paragraphs, stop and reread their writing, check spellings in the dictionary, make revisions, add punctuation marks, and consider alternative ways of crafting a sentence. Guided writing offers other opportunities for informal instruction. As teachers provide structured writing experiences, they observe children as they write and encourage them to use particular writing strategies.

Similes

MINILESSON

Ms. Boland is teaching her seventh graders a series of minilessons on ways to make their writing more powerful during writing workshop, and today her topic is similes. After the minilesson, she encourages the students to apply what they are learning in their writing.

1. Introduce the topic

"Writers often compare one thing to something else," Ms. Boland explains. "If they want to say that an old man is very quiet, for example, they might say that 'the old man is as quiet as a *clam.*'" The students laugh because they don't know that saying, and she explains the meaning. Then she continues, "Or, we might write 'the old man is as quiet as *fog*' because we know how quiet it becomes when the fog rolls in." She writes both sentences on the chalkboard and underlines the similes. She identifies the similes in each sentence and explains that they are called *similes.* Then she steps back and rereads the two sentences and announces that she prefers the "fog" comparison because it's fresher and more clever.

2. Share examples

The students brainstorm a list of other things that are quiet: death, sleep, a mouse, an angry parent, night, a whisper, and a telephone when you don't have any friends. Ms. Boland asks students to try each comparison in "the old man was as quiet as _____ ," and they decide that *sleep* is the most appropriate comparison.

3. Provide information

Ms. Boland and her students make a list of the steps in creating a simile, and the students write them in their writing notebooks.

4. Guide practice

Ms. Boland passes out magazines and asks students to select a picture to use in writing a comparison. Students create similes, making sure to use *like* or *as* in the comparison, and they write them on cards that they attach to the pictures. Then students post their pictures on the classroom wall and take a gallery walk to read each other's work.

5. Assess learning

Several days later during writing workshop, Ms. Boland asks students to examine their writing and share similes they have written. Five students haven't written any similes, so Ms. Boland meets with them as a group for more practice.

Teachers often give impromptu lessons during writing conferences. Teachers answer children's questions, model how to use strategies and skills, provide brief explanations, and encourage children to talk about the strategies they use. For example, during a conference with one of her students, Ms. Boland notices that the student's writing is not divided into paragraphs. She asks the student about paragraphs, and she responds that she really doesn't understand about them. Ms. Boland compares a paragraph to a sandwich, and on a piece of scratch paper she draws a picture of two pieces of bread for the top and bottom of the sandwich and luncheon meat, cheese, and lettuce in between the pieces of bread. She explains that the top piece of bread is the topic sentence; the cheese, meat, and lettuce are the body; and the bottom piece of bread is the closing sentence. Then Ms. Boland and the student break the writing into paragraphs and add topic sentences and closing sentences. The student keeps the picture of the paragraph sandwich, and Ms. Boland notices that she continues to refer to it when she is writing paragraphs several days later.

Ms. Boland's lesson was informal because it was unplanned and occurred in response to a student's question. She explained a concept, made a graphic to represent the concept, and then applied the concept to the student's own writing.

Why Teach Strategies and Skills?

Some teachers argue about whether to teach strategies and skills—and, if they are taught, whether children should learn them inductively or teachers should teach them explicitly. The position in this book is that teachers have the responsibility to teach children how to write, and part of that responsibility is teaching children the strategies and skills that capable writers use. Although it is true that children learn many things inductively through meaningful literacy experiences, instruction is important. The question is not whether to teach strategies and skills, but how and when to teach them (Dudley-Marling & Dippo, 1991; McIntyre & Pressley, 1996).

Freppon (1991) compared the reading achievement of first graders in skills-based and literature-based classrooms and found that the literature group was more successful. Similarly, Reutzel and Hollingsworth (1991) compared children who were taught skills with children who spent an equal amount of time reading books and found that neither group performed better on skill tests. This research suggests that children who do not already know skills and strategies can benefit from instruction, but the instruction must stress application to authentic reading and writing activities.

Carefully planned instruction, however, may be especially important for minority children. Lisa Delpit (1987) cautions that many children who grew up outside the dominant culture are at a disadvantage when certain knowledge, strategies, and skills expected by teachers are not made explicit in their classrooms. Explicitness is crucial because people from different cultures have different sets of understandings. When they teach children from other cultures, teachers often find it difficult to get their meaning across unless they are very explicit (Delpit, 1991). Too often, teachers assume that children make the connection between the strategies and skills they are teaching and the future use of those strategies and skills in writing.

On the other hand, several studies suggest that mainstream and nonmainstream children benefit from the same types of instruction. Lesley Morrow (1992) examined the impact of a literature-based reading program on minority children's reading achievement, and she found that both minority and mainstream children performed better in literature-based reading programs than in traditional classrooms on all measures of reading and writing development except on standardized tests, where there were no differences. Similarly, Karin Dahl and Penny Freppon (1995) found that minority children in literature-based classrooms do as well as children in skills-based classrooms, plus they develop a greater sense of the purposes of literacy and see themselves as readers and writers.

ANSWERING TEACHERS' QUESTIONS ABOUT . . .

Writing Strategies and Skills

I think skills are more important than strategies. Don't you think so?

It's true that both skills and strategies are important. Spelling errors, unsophisticated sentence structure, lack of paragraphing, and handwriting problems stand out on some children's papers, and we want to fix these problems. We know how to fix them; we know how to teach these skills. In contrast, other writing problems—disorganization, single-draft compositions, lack of audience awareness— are less obvious when we first look at a paper. These are strategy problems, and they are much harder to fix, but it is crucial that we teach children about organization, revising, editing, audience awareness, and other writing strategies. Good writers use both strategies and skills effectively.

I teach second grade, and my students are too young to learn strategies. I think I should focus on skills instead.

Your students already know and use some strategies. For example, they activate background knowledge when they draw pictures or make clusters before writing, and they make predictions when they read. Activating background knowledge and making predictions are strategies that readers and writers use. Teachers at every grade level are responsible for teaching both strategies and skills. You demonstrate strategies as well as skills when you do modeled and shared writing, and you support your second graders' use of strategies and skills during interactive and guided writing.

I have only one computer in my classroom. How can is use it to teach writing?

Although an ideal situation would be to have a computer available on each child's desk, it is, unfortu- nately, not yet a reality. When you have only one or two computers in the classroom, children will probably prewrite and write rough drafts with paper and pencil, and then type their compositions on the word processor before revising them. A schedule is needed so that all children can have access to the computer. Expect children to volunteer to collaborate on compositions so they can have more time on the computer. This collaboration will also benefit their writing.

I don't know enough about computers to teach my students how to use word processing and other computer tools. What can I do?

It isn't necessary for you or your students to know much about computers or word processing programs. These programs are user-friendly, and you and your students can learn to use them with several hours of practice and a few basic commands. The programs designed for children are even easier to use than programs for adults. Also, in almost every class, one or two children will be familiar with computers and word processing programs, and they will quickly become the resident computer experts.

How do I know when to teach formal minilessons and when to take advantage of "teachable moments"?

You're asking about instructional strategies, and as with other types of strategy use, there are several factors to consider. Is the skill or strategy a grade-level expectation? How many children need the instruction? Does it fit into your instructional plan? Would it be more effective to teach a formal lesson or to take a minute and explain the skill or strategy now? There is no hard-and-fast rule. You must consider various factors and decide what to do. If you decide to take advantage of a teachable moment and children need more practice, then teach a more formal minilesson later. Or, if you teach a lesson and several children need more support, teach another minilesson or use teachable moments. It's fortunate that teachers have more than one opportunity to teach strategies and skills.

Chapter 4
Assessing Children's Writing

Preview

- The goal of writing assessment is to help children become better writers.

- Teachers regularly use informal monitoring procedures to keep track of children's progress.

- Teachers examine the process children use as they write in process assessment, and they focus on the quality of children's finished compositions in product assessment.

- Children collect their best pieces of writing in portfolios to document their growth as writers.

- Teachers prepare children for district- and state-mandated writing assessments.

Third Graders Assess Their Writing

*I*n Mrs. Meyers's third-grade classroom, children keep writing workshop folders in their desks. They place all the materials they are working on, checklists, and other records in their folders as they work. (They have reading, math, and theme folders in their desks, too.) After they complete a thematic unit or at the end of a grading period, children organize the materials in these folders, self-evaluate their work, and choose materials from their works-in-progress folders to put into their portfolios.

Portfolios are more than collections of children's work; they are a tool for systematically documenting children's growth as learners. Mrs. Meyers's children assume an important role in keeping track of what they are learning. Each child's portfolio is an accordion file subdivided into three sections: language arts, math, and thematic units. In each section, children place samples of their completed and graded work, including writings that have been revised and edited, and informal writings, such as journal entries, quickwrites, clusters, charts, and diagrams.

A Third Grader's Reflection

During the last week of the fall semester, Tiffany reviews the work in her portfolio. She selects the following pieces for the second grading period:

- A photocopy of the final version of her autobiography along with her rough drafts, prewriting clusters, and life line
- A simulated journal about Eleanor Roosevelt, written after reading a biography about the famous First Lady
- A collection of Christmas poems
- Her reading log with entries written to classmates about books she read during reading workshop
- Story problems written in math as part of a money unit
- A math log for a unit on fractions, with quickwrites and drawings
- A report about games the Plains Indians played written as part of a theme on Native Americans, with rough drafts and other preliminary writings
- A learning log from the thematic unit, including maps, clusters, and quickwrites

Mrs. Meyers has already read and graded these writings. Some assignments, such as the math log, were scored using a point system for daily work, and other assignments, such as the autobiography and report, were graded using rubrics.

As she adds each item to her portfolio, Tiffany writes a reflection, or self-assessment, pointing out her accomplishments and explaining why she selected the item for her portfolio. She considers the grades received on each writing, but the grade is not her primary reason for choosing a piece. She clips a reflection to the top of each item. One of these reflections is shown on this page: it's about her autobiography, and her comments reflect her pride in this book. Her parents value it greatly, and Tiffany points out some of her accomplishments, including the table of contents, three chapters, and photo illustrations.

Mrs. Meyers keeps two crates holding children's portfolios on a counter in the classroom; it is accessible to the children at any time. She encourages them to review their own portfolios and look for ways their writing and their knowledge about written language have developed.

By the end of the year, children's portfolios will be thick with papers that document the activities in which they have been involved and each child's learning during third grade. During the last week of the school year, children will review their portfolios and remove three-quarters of the materials. The other quarter will be passed on to the fourth-grade teacher. Children make a take-home portfolio for the materials they remove to document their third-grade year. Mrs. Meyers adds a cover letter for these take-home portfolios, in which she comments on the portfolios, reflects on the class and their year together, and invites parents to celebrate their children's successes as learners as they review the portfolio.

---

*A*ssessment provides information about what writers know and what they can do. It's something that teachers do every day, in one form or another. Assessing writing involves more than just looking at pieces of writing; instead, teachers should focus on the writers themselves (Anderson, 2005). There are five purposes of writing assessment:

- Documenting children's growth as writers
- Informing students and parents about writing achievement
- Guiding writing instruction
- Substantiating that children meet grade-level standards
- Evaluating the effectiveness of the instructional program

Three approaches are used to assess writing today. Kuhs, Johnson, Agruso, and Monrad (2001) explain that "more frequent assessment and the use of different approaches will improve the reliability, validity, and fairness of classroom assessment" (p. 6). First, teachers informally monitor children's writing progress. They regularly observe children as they write and conference with them about their writing to monitor their progress and make informed decisions about instruction. Second, teachers use process and product measures, including checklists, rubrics, and portfolios, to assess students' compositions. In the vignette, for example, Mrs. Meyers used portfolios to document her third graders' writing. Third, teachers administer district- and state-mandated writing assessments where children respond to writing prompts under test conditions. Even though many teachers don't like these performance-based assessments, they're being used to judge students, teachers, and schools.

Informal Monitoring of Children's Writing

Keeping track of children's progress in writing is a demanding task because writing is multidimensional and not adequately measured simply by counting the number of compositions a child has written. Three procedures for daily monitoring of children's progress in writing are observing, conferencing, and collecting writing in folders. These informal procedures allow teachers to interact daily with children and to document the progress they make in writing.

Observing

Careful, focused observation of children as they write (and keeping detailed notes of these observations) is part of good teaching as well as part of assessment in writing classrooms (Graves, 1994; Kuhs, Johnson, Agruso, & Monrad, 2001). Teachers watch children as they write, participate in writing groups, revise and proofread their writing, and share their finished compositions with genuine audiences. They observe to learn about children's attitudes toward writing, the writing strategies that children use, how children interact with classmates during writing, and whether classmates seek out particular children for assistance or sharing writing.

While observing, teachers ask questions (e.g., "Are you having a problem?" "What are you planning to do next?") to clarify what they have observed. Observing is not necessarily time-consuming. Even though teachers watch and interact with children throughout writing projects, these observations take only a few minutes, and for experienced teachers who know their children well, a single glance may provide the needed information about a child's progress.

Conferencing

Teachers hold short, informal conferences to talk with children about their writing or to help them solve a problem related to their writing. These conferences can be held at children's desks as the teacher moves around the classroom, at the teacher's desk, or at a special writing conference table. Here are eight types of conferences:

1 *On-the-Spot Conferences.* Teachers visit briefly with children at their desks to monitor some aspect of the writing assignment or to see how they're progressing. These conferences are brief, with the teacher often spending less than a minute at a child's desk before moving on.

2 *Prewriting Conferences.* The teacher and child make plans for writing. They may discuss possible writing topics, how to narrow a broad topic, or how to gather and organize information before writing.

3 *Drafting Conferences.* Children bring their rough drafts and talk with the teacher about specific trouble spots in their writing. Together they discuss the problem and brainstorm ideas for solving it.

4 *Revising Conferences.* A small group of children and the teacher meet in a revising conference to get specific suggestions about how to revise their compositions. These conferences offer student writers an audience to provide feedback on how well they have communicated.

5 *Editing Conferences.* Teachers review children's proofread compositions and help them correct spelling, punctuation, capitalization, and other mechanical errors.

6 *Instructional Conferences.* Teachers meet with individual children or small groups to provide instruction on a strategy or skill (e.g., writing a lead, using commas in a series) that is confusing to these children.

7 *Assessment Conferences.* Teachers meet with children after they complete a composition to talk about their growth as writers and their plans for future writing. Teachers also ask children to set goals for their next writing assignment.

8 *Portfolio Conferences.* Teachers meet individually with children to review the writing samples and other materials they have placed in their portfolios. Children might explain why they chose to include particular writing samples in the portfolio, or the teacher might read and respond to the self-evaluations attached to each writing sample.

At these conferences, the teacher's role is to be a listener and a guide. Teachers learn a great deal about children and their writing when they listen as children talk.

Figure 4–1 Writing Conference Questions

Prewriting	What are you going to write about? How did you choose your topic? What prewriting activities are you doing? How are you organizing your writing? What do you plan to do next?
Drafting	How is your writing going? Are you having any problems? What do you plan to do next?
Revising	What did you learn about your draft from the rubric? What questions do you have for your writing group? What help do you want from your writing group? What compliments or suggestions did your writing group give you? What changes are you planning to make?
Editing	What kinds of mechanical errors have you found? How has your editor helped you proofread? How can I help you identify (or correct) errors? Have you completed the editing checklist? What do you plan to do next?
Publishing	Are you ready to make your final copy? How will you format your final copy? Are you ready to share your writing with the class? What do you like best about this piece of writing? What would you like to learn to do better?

Once children explain a problem they are having, teachers are often able to help them decide on a way to work through it. A list of questions that teachers can use in conferences to encourage children to talk about their writing is presented in Figure 4–1. Teachers try to balance the amount of their talk with the child's talk during the conference, and at the end reflect on what the child told them, what responsibilities the child can take, and whether the child understands what to do next (Calkins, Hartman, & White, 2005).

Collecting Writing Samples

Children keep their current writing in manila writing folders; these folders contain works-in-progress, including stories, poems, reports, and other pieces being developed and refined using the writing process. All prewriting activities and drafts are kept together to document the process that children use. They also keep their informal writing, including learning logs, quickwrites, diagrams, and clusters, in literature focus unit, literature circle, or theme folders.

Children's completed writing projects are often placed in portfolios. Children collect all pieces related to a project—prewriting notes and graphics, rough drafts, writing group notes, checklists and rubrics, the final copy, self-assessment, and teacher assessment—and clip them together to provide a complete picture of their writing process. These collections are important because they document children's growth as writers. For example, teachers can monitor children's use of strategies and skills by examining their writing samples.

In a writing process classroom, children rarely throw away a piece of writing or take it home to stay because part of the record of the child's writing development is lost. Also, these pieces of writing may be used in the classroom for minilessons on specific writing skills and strategies.

Keeping Records

Teachers need to document the data collected through observations and conferences. Simply recording a grade in a grade book does not provide an adequate record of a child's writing progress; instead, teachers should keep a variety of records, including copies of children's writing, rubrics, anecdotal notes from observations and conferences, checklists of strategies and skills taught in minilessons, strategies and skills applied in children's writing, and writing process activities that children participate in as they write.

Anecdotal Notes ■ Teachers make brief anecdotal notes as they observe children writing informally—making clusters or writing in journals—and doing writing projects using the writing process. Anecdotal notes provide teachers with rich details about children's writing and their knowledge of written language. These notes are a powerful tool for ongoing literacy assessment (Rhodes & Nathenson-Mejia, 1992). As teachers take notes, they describe the specific event and report what they have observed, without evaluating or interpreting the information. A yearlong collection of these notes provides a comprehensive picture of a child's development as a writer. Instead of recording random samples, teachers should choose events that are characteristic of each child's writing.

Several organizational schemes are possible, and teachers should use the format that is most comfortable for them. Some teachers make a card file with dividers for each child and write anecdotes on note cards. They feel comfortable jotting notes on these small note cards or even carrying around a set of cards in their pockets. Other teachers divide a spiral-bound notebook into sections for each child and write the anecdotes in the notebook, which they keep on their desks. A third scheme is to write anecdotes on sheets of paper and clip these sheets to the children's writing portfolios. Another possibility is to use self-stick notes that can be attached to note cards or in notebooks. Like note cards, little pads of these notes are small enough to fit into a pocket.

Teachers need a routine for making anecdotal notes. Teachers generally concentrate on one small group of children each day and use note cards, a notebook, or little pads of paper to take notes. Later they transfer the notes to a more permanent file. Periodically, teachers review and analyze the notes they have collected. Rhodes and Nathenson-Mejia (1992) recommend that teachers identify patterns that emerge over time (including similarities and differences), identify strengths and weaknesses, and make inferences about children's writing development. It is important that teachers make time to both record and analyze anecdotal notes.

An excerpt from an anecdotal record documenting a fifth grader's progress in writing is presented in Figure 4–2. In this excerpt, the teacher has dated each entry, used writing terminology such as "cluster" and "drafting," and offered compliments. Each entry provides information about the strategies and skills the child has demonstrated.

Figure 4–2 Anecdotal Notes

NAME: ___Matthew___   GRADE: ____5____

American Revolution Theme

March 5	Matthew selected Ben Franklin as the historical figure for his American Revolution project.
March 11	Matthew fascinated with information about B. F. Brought several sources from home. Is completing B. F.'s life line with many details.
March 18	Simulated journal. Four entries in four days! Interesting how he picked up language style of the period in his journal. Volunteers to share daily. I think he enjoys the oral sharing more than the writing.
March 25	Nine simulated journal entries, all illustrated. High level of enthusiasm.
March 29	Conferenced about cluster for B. F. biography. Well developed with five rays, many details. Matthew will work on "contributions" ray. He recognized it as the least-developed one.
April 2	Three chapters of biography drafted. Talked about "working titles" for chapters and choosing more interesting titles after writing that reflect the content of the chapters.
April 7	Drafting conference. Matthew has completed all five chapters. He and Dustin are competitive, both writing on B. F. They are reading each other's chapters and checking the accuracy of information.
April 12	Writing group. Matthew confused Declaration of Independence with the Constitution. Chapters longer and more complete since drafting conference. Compared with autobiography project, writing is more sophisticated. Longer, too. Reading is influencing writing style, e.g., "Luckily for Ben." He is still somewhat defensive about accepting suggestions except from me. He will make 3 revisions—agreed in writing group.
April 15	Revisions: (1) eliminated "he" (substitute), (2) resequenced Chapter 3 (move), and (3) added sentences in Chapter 5 (add).
April 19	Proofread with Dustin. Working hard.
April 23	Editing conference—no major problems. Discussed use of commas within sentences, capitalizing proper nouns. Matthew and Dustin more task-oriented on this project; I see more motivation and commitment.
April 29	Final copy of biography completed and shared with class.

Checklists ■ Teachers can develop a variety of checklists to use in assessing children's progress in writing. Possible checklists include inventories of the following:

Writing forms
Writing strategies
Punctuation marks and other mechanical skills
Writing topics or themes
Writing process activities
Misspelled words by category
Types of revisions
Writing competencies

These checklists help teachers focus their attention (Kuhs, Johnson, Agruso, & Monrad, 2001). A sample checklist is presented in Figure 4–3. Teachers add checkmarks, dates, comments, or other information to complete checklists. The forms can be clipped inside children's writing portfolios.

Figure 4–3 Checklist for Monitoring Children's Writing Skills

Punctuation Mark Skills Checklist	
PERIOD at the end of a sentence	COMMA to separate words in a series
after abbreviations	between day and year
after numbers in a list	between city and state
after an initial	after greeting in a friendly letter
QUESTION MARK at the end of a question	after closing of a letter
	after an initial <u>yes</u> or <u>no</u>
EXCLAMATION MARK after words or sentences showing excitement or strong feeling	after a noun of direct address
	to separate a quote from the speaker
QUOTATION MARKS before and after direct quotations	before the conjunction in a compound sentence
around title of a poem, short story, song, or TV program	after a dependent clause at the beginning of a sentence
APOSTROPHE in contractions	PARENTHESES to enclose nonessential information
to show possession	to enclose stage directions in a script
COLON before a list	HYPHEN between parts of a compound number
in writing time	to divide a word at the end of a line
after the greeting of a business letter	between parts of some compound words

Name: _____ Grading Period 1 2 3 4

Process and Product Measures

Traditionally, the formal assessment of writing focused on the quality of children's finished compositions; however, the writing process and its emphasis on what children actually do as they write have spawned a different approach to writing assessment. Process assessment is designed to probe how children write, the decisions they make as writers, and the strategies they use, rather than the quality of their finished products. Three measures for process assessment are writing process checklists, student-teacher assessment conferences, and children's self-assessment. Information from these three measures, together with the product assessment measures, provides a more complete assessment picture.

Writing Process Checklists

As teachers observe student writers, they note how children move through the writing process stages: gathering and organizing ideas during prewriting; pouring out and shaping ideas during drafting; meeting in writing groups to get feedback about their writing and then making substantive changes during revising; proofreading and correcting mechanical errors during editing; and publishing and sharing their writing. The checklist presented in Figure 4–4 lists characteristic activities for each stage of the writing process. Teachers observe children as they write, and they place checkmarks and sometimes add comments. Children also use the checklist for self-assessment to help them become aware of the activities involved in the writing process. Temple, Nathan, Burris, and Temple (1992) advocate periodic process assessments to determine whether children are using the writing process.

The writing process checklist can also be adapted for various types of writing projects. For example, if children are writing autobiographies, items can be added in the prewriting stage about developing a life line and clustering ideas for each chapter topic, and in the publishing stage, items focusing on adding a table of contents, providing an illustration for each chapter, and sharing the completed autobiography with classmates can be included. A checklist for an autobiography project is presented in Figure 4–5 to show how the basic writing process checklist can be adapted for a specific genre.

Figure 4–4 A Writing Process Checklist

Name _____ Date _____
Title _____

PREWRITING
_____ Considers purpose, audience, and form
_____ Gathers ideas for writing
_____ Organizes ideas using a graphic organizer
_____ Conferences with classmates or the teacher

DRAFTING
_____ Writes fluently
_____ Labels paper as a "draft" and double-spaces text
_____ Focuses on content rather than mechanics

REVISING
_____ Rereads writing
_____ Uses rubric to self-assess writing
_____ Participates in a writing group
_____ Conferences with the teacher
_____ Makes substantive changes

EDITING
_____ Proofreads writing to identify errors
_____ Proofreads with a partner
_____ Corrects most errors
_____ Conferences with the teacher

PUBLISHING
_____ Prepares a final copy
_____ Formats the composition
_____ Shares writing from the author's chair

Figure 4–5 Genre-Specific Checklist

Autobiography Checklist		

Writer: _____

_____

PREWRITING	_____	Created a life line
	_____	Brainstormed eight chapter topics
	_____	Chose four topics for chapters
	_____	Clustered each topic for a chapter
DRAFTING	_____	Wrote a draft of each chapter
	_____	Wrote on every other line and marked papers as a ROUGH DRAFT
REVISING	_____	Participated in a writing group
	_____	Made at least three changes in the draft
EDITING	_____	Completed an editing checklist with a partner
	_____	Conferenced with the teacher
PUBLISHING	_____	Added a title page and a table of contents
	_____	Recopied the autobiography
	_____	Added an illustration for each chapter
	_____	Shared the autobiography in the author's chair

Writing process checklists can also be used in conjunction with product assessment; teachers can base a percentage of children's grades on how well they used the writing process and the remaining percentage on the quality of the writing.

Assessment Conferences

Through assessment conferences, teachers meet with individual children, and together they discuss the child's writing and decide on a grade based on their goals for the writing project. These discussions may focus on any aspect of the writing process, including topic selection, prewriting activities, word choice, writing group activities, types of revisions, consistency in editing, and degree of effort and involvement in the writing project. These questions encourage children to reflect on their writing:

> What was easy (or difficult) about writing this paper?
> What did you do well on this writing assignment?
> What did you do to gather and organize ideas before writing?
> What kinds of help did you get from your writing group?
> What kinds of revisions did you make?
> How do you proofread your papers?
> What mechanical errors are easy (or difficult) to locate?
> What is your favorite part? Why?

Through the judicious use of these questions, teachers help children probe their understanding of the writing process and their own competencies. Atwell (1998) keeps these conferences brief, and at the end of the meeting, she and the student develop a set of goals for the following writing project or grading period. This list of goals can be added to the child's writing folder and used to begin the next assessment conference. A seventh grader's list of goals might include the following:

> I will have my rough drafts ready for my writing group on time.
> I will write five poems during the next grading period.
> I will locate 75% of my spelling errors when I proofread.
> I will explain the purpose in the first two paragraphs of the essays I write.

Self-Assessment

Temple and his colleagues (1992) recommend that we teach children to assess their own writing and writing processes. In self-assessment, children assume responsibility for assessing their own writing and for deciding which pieces of writing they will share with the teacher and classmates and place in their portfolios. This ability to reflect on one's own writing promotes organizational skills, self-reliance, independence, and creativity. Furthermore, self-evaluation is a natural part of writing (Fletcher & Portalupi, 2001).

Children assess their writing throughout the writing process; they assess their rough drafts as well as their finished compositions. Before sharing their writing with classmates in a writing group, for example, children examine their rough drafts and make some preliminary assessments. This self-assessment may deal with the quality of writing—that is, whether the writing communicates effectively and how adequately the writing incorporates the requirements for the composition as stipulated by the teacher. For example, fifth graders who are writing reports on states can verify that they have included geographic, historical, and economic information as well as other information that the teacher has specified. Teachers can guide children as they assess their writing by listing questions on the chalkboard or developing a checklist that children complete as they review their writing. A checklist for fifth graders who are writing state reports is presented in Figure 4–6.

After children meet in a writing group, they use self-assessment again as they decide which revisions to make. This assessment is often difficult for children because

Figure 4–6 Self-Assessment Checklist

State Report Checklist

Name: _____ State: _____

After you have written the rough draft of your state report, complete this checklist to make sure that you have included all the necessary information.

Yes	No	
☐	☐	Have you written information about the <u>geography</u> of the state?
☐	☐	Have you drawn a <u>map</u> of the state?
☐	☐	Have you written information about the <u>history</u> of the state?
☐	☐	Have you made a <u>time line</u> of the state?
☐	☐	Have you written information about the <u>economy</u> of the state?
☐	☐	Have you written information about <u>places to visit</u> in the state?
☐	☐	Have you written <u>something special</u> about the state?
☐	☐	Have you included maps and other information that the <u>state tourist department</u> sent to you?

Figure 4–7 A Self-Assessment Questionnaire

Name _____ Date _____
Title _____

As you finish your writing, reflect on your writing processes and this piece of writing.
Respond briefly to at least two questions in each section.

Part 1: Your Writing Processes
What stage of the writing process was most successful for you?
Which writing strategies did you use?
What stage of the writing process was least successful for you?
What do you need help with?

Part 2: This Piece of Writing
What do you like best about this piece of writing?
How comfortable are you with this topic and genre?
How did you organize your writing?
Does your lead grab your readers' attention? Why or why not?
Which mechanical errors caused you the most trouble?

Note. Adapted from Tompkins, 1992.

they struggle to deal with their own egocentricity as well as with the sometimes laborious suggestions made by others. They also consider the teacher's revision suggestions, but in the end, they often choose to make a revision suggested by a classmate instead.

Teachers can develop a self-assessment questionnaire for children to complete after they share their writing. Some questions should deal with the writing process and others with the composition itself. A self-assessment questionnaire for eighth graders is presented in Figure 4–7. As children gain experience with self-assessment, they write more sophisticated reflections.

Children often use self-assessment as they select pieces of writing to place in their portfolios. They choose favorite compositions as well as those that demonstrate new competencies or experimentation with new techniques. During evaluation conferences, teachers help children make selections and talk about how the writing demonstrates the child's growth as a writer. Children also write self-assessments or reflections to attach to compositions that are placed in portfolios, as Mrs. Meyers's student did in the vignette at the beginning of this chapter. In their reflections, children comment on their reasons for selecting a particular piece of writing.

Self-assessment can also be used for an assessment at the end of the school year. Coughlan (1988) asked his seventh graders to "show me what you have learned about writing this year" and to "explain how you have grown as a written language user, comparing what you knew in September to what you know now" (p. 375). These upper-grade children used a process approach to develop and refine their compositions, and they submitted all drafts with their final copies. Coughlan examined both the content of their compositions and the strategies they used in thinking through the assignment and writing their responses. He found this "test" to be a very worthwhile project because it "forced the children to look within themselves . . . to realize just how much they had learned" (p. 378). Moreover, the children's compositions verified what they had learned about writing and that they could articulate that learning.

Even though assessment of the process children use when writing may be of greater importance in assisting children to improve their writing, it is the finished composition, the product, that parents and administrators use to judge writing. Product assessment focuses on the quality of children's compositions and often is equated with assigning a grade.

Assessing the quality of children's writing is a laborious and time-consuming responsibility, so much so that some teachers assign few writing projects in order to avoid it. Teachers can decrease the time spent assessing children's writing in two ways. First, they teach children to use a process approach to writing. Assessment then is not as difficult because children write better compositions. Second, teachers identify the requirements of the writing project when it is assigned; if children understand the requirements of the project before they begin, the finished compositions are easier to grade because they more closely meet those requirements.

When teachers assess children's writing, they should have specific criteria in mind. These criteria vary according to the writing project and the purpose of the assessment, but they should get to the heart of writing and not focus solely on mechanical errors.

The most common way to assess student papers is for teachers to mark mechanical errors, make a few comments, assign a grade, and return the composition to the student. However, writing is a complex cognitive activity, which means that measuring only one or two dimensions of a student's work, as in this common procedure, is inadequate. Two ways to provide a broader assessment of children's writing are holistic scoring and primary trait scoring. These two measures, which consider the multiple dimensions of writing, are discussed in the next two sections.

Holistic Scoring

Teachers read children's writing for a holistic or general impression, and they use this general impression to sort compositions into three, four, five, or six piles ranging from strongest to weakest. Then the compositions in each pile can be awarded a numerical score or letter grade. Every aspect of the composition, both content and mechanical considerations, affects the score, but none of them are specifically identified or directly addressed using a checklist. Instead, the focus is on overall performance.

Holistic scoring is often used for large-scale school, district, state, or national writing assessments because it's rapid and efficient. Compositions are typically rated on 4- or 6-point numerical scales; even-number scales are favored so there is no middle number for average compositions. Before the scoring begins, trainers teach readers how to do the assessment. They begin by reviewing a small group of compositions to identify anchor papers representative of each point on the scale, and they share these with the readers. The readers practice scoring papers by matching them to the representative papers. Then all compositions are read by at least two readers, and numerical scores are averaged or added together for a cumulative score.

The holistic approach is used to judge overall writing performance without emphasis on any particular writing skill; however, it's not an appropriate measure when teachers want to assess how well children have used a particular writing form or applied specific writing skills in a composition. The major drawback of this approach is that teachers may unintentionally place too much emphasis on mechanical correctness—particularly spelling, grammar/usage, and handwriting—and therefore bias their assessment (Searle & Dillon, 1980).

Primary Trait Scoring

The focus in primary trait scoring is on whether children have incorporated specific traits or qualities in their compositions. These primary, or most important, traits vary depending on the assignment. For example, the primary traits that teachers want to assess in friendly letters differ from those in personal narratives or reports.

Primary trait assessment is based on two ideas: first, that compositions are written using specific genres for specific purposes and audiences; and second, that writing should be judged according to situation-specific criteria. Because the criteria are specific, primary traits differ from one writing project to another, depending on the nature of the assignment. Strong compositions exemplify the primary traits, and weak compositions do not, even though they might be interesting, well organized, or free of mechanical errors.

The first step in primary trait scoring is to determine which traits are essential to a specific writing project; these are the traits that will be scored. The next step is to develop a scoring guide with a list of the primary traits to use in assigning scores. Teachers distribute the scoring guide to children before they begin writing so that they know the criteria to be used to assess their finished compositions.

As with holistic scoring, this measure was first used for large-scale writing assessments, but teachers use it when they specify what children are to include in the writing project. For example, if children are writing a report and they are directed to include an introduction, three topics, a conclusion, and a bibliography, these are primary traits, and children's compositions can be assessed as to whether each component was included, In large writing assessments, if children include one item, they receive a score of 1, a 2 for two items, and so on. A 4-point system generally is used, but the number of points depends on the number of traits being assessed.

A primary trait scoring guide for reading logs written by fifth graders is presented in Figure 4–8. The criteria are divided into two parts. The reading log must meet the basic criteria presented in the first part before the quality of the entries can be assessed using the criteria in the second part. The criteria in the second part are listed in order of increasing difficulty. For children to receive the highest grade, the entries must exhibit almost all of the criteria.

Figure 4–8 A Primary Trait Scoring Guide

Reading Log Scoring Guide

Name: _____   Book: _____

Part 1: Required Criteria
_____ Bibliographic information about the book
_____ A list of 20 interesting or new words found in the book
_____ At least 8 entries
_____ A cover with title and illustration

Part 2: Grading Criteria (1 for C; 2 for B; 3 or 4 for A)
_____ Entries include opinions and feelings
_____ Entries include 2 interesting words from the book
_____ Entries make comparisons with other books
_____ Entries make comparisons between the book and the reader's life

Rubrics

Rubrics are scoring guides that teachers and children use to assess achievement on particular writing projects (Bratcher, 2004). Rubrics apply elements of primary trait scoring to simplify the assessment and grading of children's writing. Teachers use rubrics to assess children's writing, and rubrics are often used in districtwide and statewide writing assessment because they make the assessment process more reliable and consistent.

Rubrics can have 3, 4, 5, or 6 levels, with descriptors at each level. In most rubrics, the descriptors are related to ideas, organization, language, and mechanics, but they vary to fit the writing project. The levels range from weak to strong, and the level just above the midpoint usually specifies grade-level proficiency standards—that's 3 on a 4- or 5-point rubric and 4 on a 6-point rubric. On a 3-point rubric, however, 2 usually indicates expected progress. Primary-grade teachers sometimes use rubrics with 3 levels, but middle- and upper-grade teachers generally use rubrics with 4, 5, or 6 levels. Researchers recommend either 4 or 6 levels on a rubric so that there isn't a "middle" score, but teachers often prefer rubrics with 5 levels so that scores can be equated more easily to letter grades.

Some rubrics are general and appropriate for almost any writing assignment, and others are designed for specific types of writing assignments. Two general writing

Figure 4–9 Two General Writing Rubrics

Kindergarten Writing Rubric
4 EXCEPTIONAL WRITER
• Writes several complete sentences or one more-sophisticated sentence. • Spaces between words and sentences consistently. • Spells some high-frequency words correctly. • Spells some CVC words correctly. • Begins some sentences with capital letters. • Uses periods and other punctuation marks to end some sentences.
3 DEVELOPING WRITER
• Writes a complete sentence. • Spaces between some words. • Spells one or more high-frequency words correctly. • Spells beginning and ending sounds in most words. • Uses both upper- and lower case letters.
2 BEGINNING WRITER
• Writes from left to right and top to bottom. • Writes one or more words using one or more letters that represent beginning or other sounds in the word. • Can reread the writing with one-to-one matching of words.
1 EMERGENT WRITER
• Uses random letters that do not correspond to sounds. • Uses scribbles to represent writing. • Draws a picture instead of writing. • Dictates words or sentences.

Figure 4–9 *Continued*

Fifth-Grade Writing Rubric
5   EXCEPTIONAL ACHIEVEMENT
• Creative and original • Clear organization • Precise word choice and figurative language • Sophisticated sentences • Essentially free of mechanical errors
4   GOOD ACHIEVEMENT
• Some creativity, but more predictable than an exceptional paper • Definite organization • Good word choice, but no figurative language • Varied sentences • Only a few mechanical errors
3   NEARLY ADEQUATE ACHIEVEMENT
• Predictable paper • Some organization • Adequate word choice • Little variety of sentences, and some run-on sentences • Some mechanical errors
2   LIMITED ACHIEVEMENT
• Brief and superficial • Lacks organization • Imprecise language • Incomplete and run-on sentences • Many mechanical errors
1   MINIMAL ACHIEVEMENT
• No ideas communicated • No organization • Inadequate word choice • Sentence fragments • Overwhelming mechanical errors

rubrics are shown in Figure 4–9; one is a 4-level kindergarten writing rubric, and the other is a 5-level rubric for assessing fifth graders' writing. The same qualities of writing are described at each level on a rubric. For example, the first bulleted item on the fifth-grade writing rubric focuses on ideas, the second on organization, the third on vocabulary, the fourth on sentences, and the fifth on mechanics. Notice that the bulleted qualities are scaled from weak at the first level to strong at the fifth level. The fourth bulleted quality in each level on the fifth-grade rubric in Figure 4–9, for example, deals with sentences, and the qualities range from "sentence fragments" at level 1 to "sophisticated sentences" at level 5. Each level represents improvement in students' application of that quality of writing.

Many teachers use rubrics incorporating Spandel's (2004, 2005) six traits or qualities of effective writing; these traits are *ideas, organization, voice, word choice, sentence fluency,* and *conventions,* and they're explained in Figure 4–10. Teachers typically introduce the traits one by one through a series of minilessons in which they explain the characteristics of the trait and use stories and other trade books as models. Once children have some understanding of the trait, they examine how it was applied in sample compositions and then revise other sample compositions to incorporate the trait. Next, they apply what they've learned about the trait in their own writing and use rubrics based on the six traits to assess their writing. In a multiyear study, Culham (2003) found that teaching children about the six traits and using rubrics that incorporate them improve the quality of children's writing.

Other rubrics address specific genres or particular writing projects. For example, the second-grade rubric shown in Figure 4–11 is designed for assessing stories, and it specifies genre characteristics at each level. Both types of rubrics are useful; teachers choose which rubric they'll use depending on the writing project and children's familiarity with that genre.

Although commercially prepared rubrics are available, teachers and children often develop their own rubrics because it provides the opportunity to teach children valuable lessons about what makes a strong piece of writing. Teachers often find that developing rubrics with 6 levels is difficult because it's hard to clearly articulate writing qualities at so many levels; nonetheless, children are more likely to show growth during a school year when rubrics have more levels. It seems obvious, for example, that a child's writing could improve from a 3 to a 4 when a rubric has 6 levels instead of 4.

Figure 4–10 The Six Traits

Ideas
Ideas are the "heart of the message" (Culham, 2003, p. 11). When ideas are well developed, the writing is clear and focused. Effective details elaborate the big idea and create images in readers' minds.

Organization
The internal structure of a composition is the organization; its function is to enhance the central idea. Spandel (2001) explains that organization is putting "information together in an order that informs, persuades, or entertains" (p. 39). The logical pattern of ideas varies according to genre; stories are organized differently than nonfiction or poetry.

Voice
The writer's style is known as *voice*; it's what breathes life into writing. The writer's voice can be humorous or compelling, reflective or persuasive. What matters most is that the author connects with readers.

Word Choice
Carefully chosen words have the power to clarify meaning or to create a mood. It's important for writers to choose words to fit both their purpose and the audience to whom their writing is directed. Children increase their word knowledge through lots of reading.

Sentence Fluency
Sentence fluency is the "rhythm and flow of carefully structured language that makes it both easy and pleasurable to read aloud" (Spandel, 2001, p. 101). Effective sentences vary in structure and length, and children are now encouraged to include some sentence fragments to add rhythm and energy to their writing (Culham, 2003).

Conventions
Mechanics, paragraphing, and design elements are three types of conventions that guide readers through a composition. Writers use standard English mechanics—spelling, punctuation, capitalization, and grammar—as a courtesy to readers. They divide the text into paragraphs to enhance their presentation of ideas. They also create a design for their compositions to enhance readability.

Figure 4–11 A Specific Writing Rubric

Second-Grade Rubric for Stories	
5	Writing has an original title. Story shows originality, sense of humor, or cleverness. Writer uses paragraphs to organize ideas. Writing contains few spelling, capitalization, or punctuation errors. Writer varies sentence structure and word choice. Writer shows a sense of audience.
4	Writing has an appropriate title. Beginning, middle, and end of the story are well developed. A problem or goal is identified in the story. Writing includes details that support plot, characters, and setting. Writing is organized into paragraphs. Writing contains few capitalization and punctuation errors. Writer spells most high-frequency words correctly and spells unfamiliar words phonetically.
3	Writing may have a title. Writing has at least two of the three parts of a story (beginning, middle, and end). Writing shows a sequence of events. Writing is not organized into paragraphs. Spelling, grammar, capitalization, or punctuation errors may interfere with meaning.
2	Writing has at least one of the three parts of a story (beginning, middle, and end). Writing may show a partial sequence of events. Writing is brief and underdeveloped. Writing has spelling, grammar, capitalization, and punctuation errors that interfere with meaning.
1	Writing lacks a sense of story. An illustration may suggest a story. Writing is brief and may support the illustration. Some words may be recognizable, but the writing is difficult to read.

Teachers present the rubric when they're introducing the writing project so that children understand how they'll be assessed, and they distribute copies of the rubric so children can refer to it as they write. Sometimes children also use the rubric to self-assess their rough drafts during the revising stage. The step-by-step feature on page 92 lists the steps in using rubrics.

Portfolios

Portfolios contain a collection of writings that provide evidence of both the products children create and the process they use (De Fina, 1992; Farr & Tone, 1998). It is a more authentic form of assessment because entire writing projects—rough drafts that have been revised and edited, prewriting notes and diagrams, and checklists and rubrics that have been marked—are included to document learning.

Reflection is an important component of portfolio assessment (D'Aoust, 1992) because it requires children to pause and become aware of themselves as writers. Indeed, reflection is part of the writing process itself: Children write, pause, reflect, write some more, reflect, and so on. Many children initially lack the vocabulary to

Step by Step: Rubrics

1. **Choose a rubric.** Teachers choose a rubric that is appropriate to the writing project or create one that reflects the assignment.

2. **Introduce the rubric.** Teachers distribute copies to children and talk about the criteria listed at each level; they focus on the requirements at the proficiency level, which specifies grade-level expectations.

3. **Have children self-assess their writing.** Children use one color pen to mark the rubric as they self-assess their writing, often during the revising stage. They highlight phrases in the rubric or check off items that best describe their writing. Then they determine which level has the most highlighted words or checkmarks; that level is the overall score, and children circle it.

4. **Assess children's writing.** Teachers use another color pen to assess children's writing by highlighting phrases in the rubric or checking off items that best describe the composition. Then they assign the overall score by determining which level has the most highlighted words or checkmarks and circling it.

5. **Conference with children.** Teachers talk with children about the assessment, identifying strengths and weaknesses. Afterward, children set goals for the next writing project.

be reflective; they do not know what to say or how to apply writing concepts to themselves as writers, but as teachers conference with children about their writing, they become more reflective.

Three types of portfolios are showcase, collaborative, and benchmark portfolios (Jenkins, 1996); they differ according to who selects the compositions to be included. The portfolios that Mrs. Meyers's third graders developed in the vignette at the beginning of the chapter are showcase portfolios: The children self-assessed their writing and chose the pieces they wanted to include. In contrast, teachers select writing samples for benchmark portfolios: The pieces they select demonstrate "benchmarks" of children's writing development. Somewhere in between showcase and benchmark portfolios are collaborative portfolios, in which children and the teacher work together to collect compositions for their portfolios (Tierney, Carter, & Desai, 1991).

Large-Scale Writing Tests

Large-scale writing tests are a fact of life today. Most states require that children participate in large-scale writing tests at least three times during their school careers, often in 4th, 7th, and 11th grades. The prompts that are used typically reflect the state's language arts standards. Many school districts conduct writing assessments at least once each year: Children at each grade level, beginning in kindergarten, write in response to prompts that focus on particular genres, and teachers work in teams to score the writing samples. Writing tests are also part of high school exit exams in some states, and the College Board's SAT now includes a writing requirement.

Large-scale writing tests assess writing directly by having students write in response to prompts. These tests, however, measure students' ability to write rough drafts, not their ability to use the writing process to craft and refine a piece of writing.

The tests are usually administered in an hour or two, and real writing takes much longer (Hillocks, 2002).

Students respond to prompts in writing tests. A prompt includes two parts: the writing topic and the directions for writing. Prompts must be stated clearly and must accommodate students' varied backgrounds and experiences. For example, here's a prompt that's appropriate for fourth graders:

> Think of a time you helped a friend to do something. Then write a story about what you did, telling what happened and what you learned from it.

The first sentence introduces the topic, and the second sentence presents the directions for writing. Students should also recognize that they're supposed to write a personal narrative because they're asked to write a story about a personal experience. It's crucial that students understand what the prompt is asking them to do. They also need to be knowledgeable enough about the topic or have had the prerequisite experiences specified in the prompt to have something to say and be able to generate ideas and respond to the prompt quickly.

Most prompts require that students apply what they know about a genre. Here are the most common genres used in large-scale writing assessments in kindergarten through eighth grade:

- Personal narratives
- Responses to literature
- Stories
- Informative writing
- Summaries
- Persuasive writing

The prompts don't specify a particular writing genre, but they provide clue words that signal the genres to students who have been taught about them (Kiester, 2000). When students are asked to convince someone about something, for instance, they're usually doing persuasive writing. In upcoming chapters, you'll find Preparing for Writing Tests features that present information about each of these genres.

Students' papers in large-scale writing assessments are usually evaluated holistically or using a combination of holistic and primary trait scoring by trained readers, as explained earlier in the chapter. In state and national assessments, professional readers are used, and for district assessments, trained teachers do the scoring. The rubrics that the readers use are normally available before the testing, so students should be aware how their writing will be assessed.

National Assessment of Educational Progress

In addition to taking district- and state-mandated writing tests, many children from across the United States participate in the National Assessment of Educational Progress (NAEP) assessments. These tests are administered once every 4 years to determine what American 4th, 8th, and 12th graders know and can do in reading, writing, mathematics, and other subject areas.

In the writing assessment, students respond to prompts that ask them to write in these three genres:

- Narrative genre, where students write personal narratives or creative stories to capture readers' imagination
- Informative genre, where students share knowledge with readers
- Persuasive genre, where students seek to influence readers

The prompts also suggest an intended audience; for example, "encourage your teacher to . . ." or "write to your grandparent to explain . . ." Students are encouraged to use the writing process as they respond to the prompt. Space is provided in the test booklet for students to plan their writing before they begin to write. After they generate a draft, they're advised to revise and edit their writing. Trained raters score students' writing and rank it as "basic" (below grade-level expectations), "proficient" (meeting grade-level expectations), or "advanced" (beyond grade-level expectations).

In 2002, nearly 300,000 students participated in the writing assessment. The results indicated that fourth and eighth graders wrote better compositions than students at these grade levels had in the 1998 testing. Twelfth graders, however, didn't show significant improvement over past years.

Preparing for Writing Tests

Excellent writing instruction is the best way to prepare for large-scale writing tests (Angelillo, 2005). Regie Routman (2005) says that "research shows that high achievement and high test scores result when what is tested is woven into daily teaching and challenging curriculum in a relevant manner" (p. 245). Through writing workshop, children learn to

- use the writing process to develop and refine compositions;
- vary their writing according to particular genres;
- spell most words conventionally;
- use standard English grammar;
- demonstrate legible and fluent handwriting.

In addition, teachers should prepare children for writing tests because there's a huge difference between writing workshop and large-scale tests where children respond to a prompt and write a composition within time constraints.

Teachers prepare students for writing tests in several ways. They teach students how to read prompts and recognize the specialized vocabulary used in them through a series of minilessons. Teachers model how to interpret a prompt and how to write responses and score them using a rubric. They provide sample papers for students to examine and score to get a better understanding of what they're expected to do. Students write practice tests with prompts similar to those used in the writing tests to learn what to expect on test days and how to pace themselves. Students also self-assess their practice tests with the same rubrics used in the large-scale assessment to understand how they'll be assessed and to identify the areas for improvement. Information about how to prepare students for large-scale writing tests is summarized in the feature on the next page.

Most teachers spend too much time practicing for writing tests, not too little. Mark Overmeyer (2005) spends 10 days spread throughout the year on test practice in his fifth-grade classroom. He teaches his fifth graders how to write to a prompt, has

Preparing for Writing Tests

Large-Scale Writing Tests

Students write in response to a prompt, usually within a specific time period, in large-scale writing tests. In their writing, students are expected to demonstrate their ability to perform these tasks:

- Respond directly to a prompt.
- Control specific genres.
- Develop the main idea in an organized and thoughtful way.
- Add details to support the main idea.
- Choose specific vocabulary.
- Vary the sentence structure.
- Express an individual voice.
- Make few mechanical errors.

State-mandated writing tests are administered several times during students' school careers, and school districts often require quarterly or yearly writing assessments.

Parts of a Prompt   Prompts have two parts, the topic and the directions for writing. They can be formatted as a question, an issue, or a hypothetical situation. Students need to understand the writing process terms (e.g., *organize, revise, complete sentences*) and genre-specific words (e.g., *explain, describe, argue*) that are often used in the prompts.

How to Respond to a Prompt   Before beginning to write, students read the prompt several times and examine any accompanying visuals. They use an abbreviated writing process to respond to the prompt. Students gather and organize ideas before beginning to write. Sometimes they have scratch paper to use for making notes and drawing graphic organizers. Then they write a rough draft that they reread, revise, and edit within the allotted time. Students don't usually have the opportunity to get feedback from classmates or recopy their writing.

How Are Writing Tests Scored?   Writing tests are generally assessed holistically or using a combination of holistic and primary trait scoring, using a 4- or 6-point scale. On a 4-point scale, a score of 3 is considered "proficient" or "on-grade level," and on a 6-point scale, a score of 4 is considered "proficient" or "on-grade level." Tests are read and scored by two trained readers, and the two readers' scores are averaged.

them practice doing timed writings, examines their responses to identify areas of need, and plans instruction and additional practice test based on their needs.

Benefits

It's easy to argue against large-scale writing tests because they're artificial writing situations that use up valuable instructional time, but these tests highlight the importance of writing for teachers, students, and parents (Spandel & Stiggens, 1997).

When students participate in large-scale writing tests, teachers are more likely to emphasize writing instruction and to raise their expectations about students' performance. In addition, teachers who take part in scoring writing tests learn more about teaching writing. Even though there are problems with these assessments, there's no doubt that they're much better than multiple-choice tests for assessing children's writing performance.

ANSWERING TEACHERS' QUESTIONS ABOUT . . .

Assessing Children's Writing

Don't I have to grade every paper my students write?

No. In a writing process classroom, children write many more papers than teachers can read and critique. As often as possible, children should write for themselves, their classmates, and other genuine audiences rather than for the teacher. Teachers need to ask themselves whether assessing each piece of writing will make their students better writers, and most teachers will admit that such a rigorous critique won't. More likely, grading every composition will clear teachers' conscience about whether they are good teachers; it won't do much, however, to improve children's writing. Teachers should use the informal monitoring procedures and process assessment measures discussed in this chapter as well as grades. Donald Graves (2003) recommends that teachers grade only the compositions that children identify as their best ones.

There are so many ways to assess writing; I don't know which one to use.

How you assess a piece of writing depends on the writing project and on your reason for assessing it. Informal monitoring provides one measure that children are writing and completing assignments. Using process measures can help assess children's use of the writing process and various writing strategies. Process assessment should be used when teachers want to measure how well children are using the writing process. Most teachers are more familiar with product assessment and more inclined to use a product-oriented measure. If the goal of the assessment is to determine the relative merits of one composition over another, then a product measure is appropriate. Over the grading period, teachers should use a variety of assessment measures for a more complete picture of children as writers.

If I don't correct children's errors, how will they learn not to make the errors?

You do help children correct many, many errors during the editing stage of the writing process, but always

focusing on error correction doesn't ensure that children become capable writers. Writing researchers have documented that children with differing amounts of writing experience make different kinds of writing errors, and that the errors of inexperienced writers are less sophisticated than those made by more experienced writers. Teachers can make a far more important contribution to children's learning by structuring worthwhile writing experiences, providing instruction in writing as it relates to the writing projects that children are involved in, and providing opportunities for children to share their writing with classmates than by correcting children's errors after the writing has been completed.

I just don't agree with you. The mechanics are important—they are the mark of a good writer—and they should count the most in grading a child's writing.

It's true that using correct spelling, grammar, and other mechanics is one indication of a good writer, and when the conventions of written English are followed, the writing is easier to read. However, literary prizes are not awarded for technically correct writing; they are awarded for writing that exhibits unique content. Writing that is clever, creative, and well organized that makes the reader laugh or cry, even if it has some mechanical errors, is preferable to a bland, error-free composition. Think for a moment about book reviews: Are books ever recommended because they don't have mechanical errors, or are they recommended because of their memorable characters or vivid language? The mechanics of writing are important, but they are better dealt with in the editing stage, after children have drafted and revised their writing, than in the early stages of the writing process, when children are concerned with gathering and organizing ideas and finding the words to express those ideas.

We've tried keeping portfolios, but they're too much work. And what are we supposed to do with all the stuff we collect? Upper-grade teachers don't have space in their classrooms for collections of 5 years' worth of papers. What do you suggest?

Teachers can find many reasons for not using portfolios, and they are a great deal of work; nonetheless, portfolios are an essential component of a writing process classroom, whether or not they are passed on to the next teacher. Children's writing changes substantially when they reflect on their writing and collect it in portfolios. When teachers don't use portfolios, children often view their writing simply as work to be completed for a grade.

Teachers can begin by having children put all of their completed projects into their portfolios; at the end of each grading period, they sort what they have placed in their portfolios, select several pieces to keep, and take the rest home. Having children sort through their own writing helps them to set purposes for themselves as writers, and the end of a grading period is an appropriate time for self-reflection. If the other teachers at your school aren't interested in implementing a schoolwide portfolio program, then children can take their portfolios home at the end of the school year. However, portfolios can be manageable if only four writing projects are passed on each year. That way, portfolios moving to sixth grade would contain 24 compositions with attached information from the teacher assessments and the child self-assessments.

Chapter 5
Journal Writing

Preview

Purpose Children use journals to record personal experiences, explore reactions and interpretations to books they read and videos they view, and record and analyze information about literature, writing, and social studies and science topics.

Audience The audience is usually very limited. Sometimes the writer is the only audience, and when writers share journal entries with others, these readers are typically well known and trusted.

Forms Journal forms include personal journals, dialogue journals, reading logs, learning logs, double-entry journals, and simulated journals. Children often write personal and dialogue journal entries in spiral-bound notebooks, and use small stapled booklets for other types of journal entries.

Sixth Graders Keep Journals

To begin a literature focus unit on Natalie Babbitt's classic *Tuck Everlasting* (2000), the story of a family who unknowingly drinks from a magic spring that stops them from growing any older (a condition they find to have some surprising disadvantages), Mrs. Wheatley asks her sixth-grade class, "Would you like to live forever?" After a lively discussion of the advantages and disadvantages of immortality, she becomes more specific and asks children to write their answers to this question: "If I offered you a drink of water from a magic spring that would allow you to stay the same age you are right now forever, would you drink it?"

Children quickwrite their answers on the first page of their reading logs. Veronica answers:

> I think I would save the water until I finish college and started my career. Then I would drink it because I would like to know how the world would be in about 200 years, and if I lived forever I could become a very important person.

After Veronica and her classmates share their writings, Mrs. Wheatley introduces the book. They read the Prologue together and talk about the author's comparison of August to the top of a huge Ferris wheel. Mrs. Wheatley explains that *Tuck Everlasting* is a "think-about" story. Like their impromptu writing about immortality, their other writings in this log will be informal and personal, written for and about themselves rather than for the teacher. They will be thinking on paper, she explains, because by writing about the story, they will comprehend it better.

Each day, Mrs. Wheatley and her students read a chapter or two, and afterward they talk about the story in small groups or together as a class. Then children spend approximately 10 minutes writing entries in their reading logs. The discussions serve as prewriting, and in their entries, children often comment on topics they discussed. Rather than having them simply summarize the chapter, Mrs. Wheatley emphasizes that they should relate the story to their own lives and gives them this list of possible writing topics:

Who is your favorite or least favorite character?
Does one character remind you of a friend or family member?
Does one character remind you of yourself?
Do any of the events in this story remind you of your own life?
What event would you have handled differently if you were the character?
Does anything puzzle you about the story? If so, explain.
Does the setting remind you of somewhere you have been?
What do you like best or least about the story?
How does this story make you feel?
What other stories that you have read does this story remind you of?
What would you change about this story, if you could?

After writing, some children will eagerly share their entries with the class, whereas others will keep their entries private. Here are excerpts from Veronica's reading log:

> *Chapter 1:*   I found the book quite boring although the author did use a lot of imagination in making the animals seem like real people.
>
> *Chapter 4:*   At this point of the story I am beginning to like it a lot. My favorite character right now is Winnie. She seems like quite a little girl and the elf music I think is coming from Mae's music box. Winnie's grandmother seems pretty funny also.
>
> *Chapter 6:*   Winnie has been kidnapped by the Tucks and you can tell she has a big imagination when you think about how she imagined the kidnappers. In a way I think she kind of enjoys this but as they go farther she begins to become more scared. Mae started playing the music box and the music was the same music her grandmother had told her was elf music.
>
> *Chapter 8:*   Indomitable—unstoppable; eddies of dust—small whirlpools or swirls; mirage—illusion, trick of eyes. I did notice the food they ate is rarely eaten today. I never really thought about chewing but

<table>
<tr><td>Chapter 18:</td><td>now that I do think about it, it is kind of a personal thing. I don't really like people watching me chew.

Right now in the story I like Jesse the best because he has big dreams and seems intent on making them come true. He's always looking at the bright side of things.</td></tr>
</table>

Chapter 18:

now that I do think about it, it is kind of a personal thing. I don't really like people watching me chew.

Chapter 18:   Right now in the story I like Jesse the best because he has big dreams and seems intent on making them come true. He's always looking at the bright side of things.

Chapter 22:   Winnie is feeling really guilty about Mae so she is going to help them get her out of jail. If I was Winnie I think I might run away with them because they are really nice people and she has grown to love them. She would probably miss her family a lot but if she drank the water, they wouldn't have to worry about her getting hurt.

Chapter 24:   I wish I was more like Winnie in a way. She is a very brave person and would do anything to help someone. "Stone walls do not a prison make" means there are other kinds of prisons besides rock walls and you can put yourself in a prison by shutting out others and not helping other people.

Epilogue: I think Tuck is happy that Winnie died and didn't have to live forever. I think it was neat that they saw the toad that lived forever. I liked the way the story ended but I kind of wanted Winnie to find Jesse and the Tucks and to drink the water and live forever.

Veronica's use of the first-person pronoun "I" in this log demonstrates that she wrote about what she thought, what she liked, and what was meaningful to her. She didn't try to second-guess what author Natalie Babbitt intended or what Mrs. Wheatley thought. She wrote for herself. Also, Veronica used the log to note unfamiliar words and phrases (e.g., "eddies of dust" in Chapter 8) and sayings (e.g., "Stone walls do not a prison make" in Chapter 24).

After finishing the story, Mrs. Wheatley asks the children to respond again to the question, "If I offered you a drink of water from a magic spring that would allow you to stay the same age you are right now forever, would you drink it?" This time Veronica writes:

> If someone offered me some magic water that would let me live forever, I wouldn't take it because I believe if the Lord wanted us to live forever he would let us. And I wouldn't want to because forever is an awful long time.

The about-face in Veronica's second response demonstrates the power of a reading log to stimulate thinking and verifies Toby Fulwiler's statement that "when people write about something they learn it better" (1987, p. 9). Having thought about immortality, Veronica has become less egocentric and more perceptive in her response.

---

*A*ll sorts of people—artists, scientists, dancers, politicians, writers, assassins, and children—keep journals. In most of these journals, people record the everyday events of their lives and explore the issues that concern them. These journals are personal records, not intended for public display. In other journals, which might be termed "working journals," writers record observations and other information that they will use for another purpose. For example, farmers might record weather or crop data, or gardeners might note the blooming cycle of their plants.

The journals of some well-known public figures have survived for hundreds of years and provide a fascinating glimpse of their authors and the times in which they

Instructional Overview: Journal Writing	
Grades	**Goals and Activities**
Kindergarten–Grade 2	**Goal 1: Write personal journals** • Children use a combination of drawing and writing in entries. • Children use a dialogue format and write back and forth with the teacher. • Children brainstorm ideas for writing topics.
	Goal 2: Respond to stories in reading logs • Children write responses that summarize the beginning, middle, and end of stories. • Children write responses that make connections to self, world, and other texts. • Children write responses that evaluate the story.
Grades 3–5	**Goal 1: Keep learning logs during thematic units** • Children brainstorm lists of words or ideas. • Children make clusters and other diagrams in the logs. • Children write quickwrites in the logs. • Children create data charts to organize information.
	Goal 2: Continue to respond to books in reading logs • Children write entries using prompts. • Children write entries without prompts.
Grades 6–8	**Goal 1: Assume another point of view and create simulated journals** • Children choose a book character and write a journal from that character's viewpoint. • As part of a history unit or while reading a biography, children choose a historical figure and write a journal from that person's viewpoint. • Children use the writing process to draft, revise, and edit the simulated journal.
	Goal 2: Write double-entry journals • Children choose a quote while reading and respond to it. • Children use the double-entry format to compare characters or for other purposes.

lived. For example, the Renaissance genius Leonardo da Vinci recorded his daily activities, dreams, and plans for his painting and engineering projects in more than 40 notebooks. In the 1700s, Puritan theologian Jonathan Edwards documented his spiritual life in his journal. In the late 1700s, American explorers Meriwether Lewis and William Clark kept a journal of their travels across the North American continent, more for geographical than personal use. In the 19th century, the American writer Henry David Thoreau filled 39 notebooks with his essays. American author F. Scott Fitzgerald filled his notebooks with snippets of conversation that he overheard, many of which he later used in *The Great Gatsby* and other novels.

Anne Frank, who wrote while hiding from the Nazis during World War II, is the best-known child diarist.

Children use journals for a variety of purposes, much like adults do:

To record experiences
To explore ideas
To ask questions
To activate prior knowledge
To engage the imagination
To assume the role of another person
To solve problems

As they write, children shape their thinking and personalize their learning. Because writing is such a powerful tool for thinking and learning, teachers involve children in a variety of journal-writing activities (Armbruster, McCarthey, & Cummins, 2005; Emig, 1977). The Instructional Overview on page 101 lists many of the goals and activities for journal writing in kindergarten through eighth grade.

Types of Journals

Children use these six types of journals:

- Personal journals
- Dialogue journals
- Reading logs
- Learning logs
- Double-entry journals
- Simulated journals

These journals are used for different purposes, which are summarized in Figure 5–1. Reading logs, for example, are used to help children deepen their comprehension of the stories they're reading, as the entries that Veronica wrote in the vignette at the beginning of the chapter demonstrated. Children's journal writing is often spontaneous and loosely organized, and it contains more mechanical errors than other types of writing because children are focusing on thinking, not on spelling and other mechanical considerations. James Britton and his colleagues (1975) compare journal entries to a written conversation, and that conversation may be with oneself or with trusted readers who are interested in the writer.

Personal Journals

Children can keep personal journals in which they recount the events in their lives and write about topics that they choose themselves. These third graders' entries show the variety of topics children may choose. Kerry reviews the events of a school day:

I came to school and cleaned out my desk and got my work all done and put a layer on a pumpkin and went to lunch. On recess me, Rex, Ray and Tray got chased and then we came in and worked.

Figure 5–1 Six Types of Journals

Personal Journals
Children write in personal journals about events in their own lives and other topics of special interest. Teachers respond as interested readers, often asking questions and offering comments about their own lives.

Dialogue Journals
Dialogue journals are similar to personal journals except that they are written to be shared with the teacher or a classmate. The person who receives the journal reads and responds to the entry. These journals are like a written conversation.

Reading Logs
Children respond in reading logs to books they're reading. They write and draw entries after reading, record key vocabulary words, make charts, and write memorable quotes.

Learning Logs
Children write in learning logs as part of social studies and science thematic units and math units. They write quickwrites, draw diagrams, and take notes.

Double-Entry Journals
Children divide each page into two columns and write different types of information in each column. Sometimes they write quotes from a story in one column and add reactions to the quotes in the other, or they write predictions in one column and what actually happened in the story in the other.

Simulated Journals
Children assume the role of a book character or a historical personality and write entries from that person's viewpoint. They include details from the story or historical period in their entries to add authenticity.

Andrea tells about Thanksgiving vacation:

> Yesterday was the end of Thanksgiving break. I went to the church crafts fair and they served soup. I got a gingerbread cookie and it was about 6 inches long. We had for Thanksgiving dinner: mashed potatoes, turkey, stuffing, sweet potatoes, pumpkin pie, Dutch apple pie, oregano beans, and water. We put up our Christmas tree. So far it has almost drunk a gallon of water and we have some presents.

Micah describes a grandparent's death:

> My PaPa had a heart attack by sitting down and he could not get up. My Grandma called the ambulance and I saw the people in the ambulance help. And he died.

Michael shares a problem:

> Today I made a friend an enemy, and I am glad of it, too. It all started about the beginning of the year. My brother and somebody else and me started a club, so the person that I am mad at was jealous. He started hanging around us and we didn't like it so we didn't pay attention to him. So yesterday he started a club. Today I talked some of his people in his club into being in my club. That's why he is mad at me and I am mad at him.

Micah writes about his plans for the future:

> I am going to be a golfer when I grow up. Now I can hit a golf ball almost 80 yards. My dad can hit a golf ball almost 300 yards. I go golfing almost every 2 months. And I might be a baseball player or a basketball player.

And Jenna writes about a disappointment:

> My class all got pen pals. My pen pal's name is Eric. He is 8 1/2 years old and lives in Washington. See I wanted a girl but when I went up to Mrs. Carson she was fresh out of girls.

Many teachers develop a list of possible journal-writing topics with children. This list is then displayed in the classroom or duplicated for children to clip inside their journals so that they can refer to it when they have trouble thinking of something to write about. A first- and second-grade class brainstormed these possible topics: pets, jokes, holidays, my family, basketball, playing jumprope, things to do, Disneyland, and friends. Referring children to the list or asking them to brainstorm a list of topics encourages them to become more independent writers and discourages them from depending too much on teachers for writing topics.

Privacy is an important issue as children grow older. Most primary-grade students are very willing to share what they have written, but by third or fourth grade, some children become reluctant to share their writing with classmates. Usually they are willing to share their journal entries with a trusted teacher, so teachers must be scrupulous about protecting children's privacy. It is also important to require children to respect each other's privacy and not read each other's journals. To protect children's privacy, many teachers keep personal journals on a shelf out of the way when they are not being used.

When children share personal information with teachers through their journals, a second issue also arises: Sometimes teachers learn details about children's family life that they may not know how to deal with. Entries about child abuse, suicide, or drug use may be the child's way of asking for help. Although teachers are not counselors, they have a legal obligation to report possible problems to appropriate school personnel. Occasionally a child may invent a personal problem as an attention-getting tactic; however, asking the child about the entry or having a school counselor do so will help to ensure that the child's safety is being fully considered.

How to Address Struggling Writers' Problems

The Problem	Children complain, "I don't know what to write."
What Causes It	Children often have trouble getting started when they are assigned to write about an unfamiliar topic or when they don't know how to generate ideas for writing.
How to Solve It	*Quick fix:* During prewriting, have children brainstorm a list of ideas and pick the most promising one to write about. Sometimes it's effective for children to draw pictures to explore an idea, read a book to learn more about a topic, or talk with classmates to exchange ideas. Children can also brainstorm a list of vocabulary words related to the topic to use as they write. *Long-term solution:* Teach children how to choose topics for writing and develop ideas in a series of minilessons. Teachers should also think about the topics they assign and how they can help children prepare for writing. It's crucial that children have adequate background knowledge before beginning to write.
How to Prevent the Problem	Children who have strategies for choosing topics and generating ideas for writing are more successful in getting started and carrying their writing to completion.

Dialogue Journals

Children converse in writing with the teacher or a classmate through dialogue journals (Bode, 1989). Young and older children can also be paired to write back and forth (Harwayne, 2001). Children write informally on topics of their own choosing, and the teacher or child who is responding writes back. These journals are interactive and conversational in tone, and, most important, they provide an opportunity for authentic writing and genuine communication.

Teachers' responses do not need to be lengthy; a sentence or two is often enough. Even so, it is very time-consuming for teachers to respond to 20, 25, 30, or more journal entries every day. Often teachers read and respond to children's journal entries on a rotating basis; for example, they might respond to one group's writing one week and another group the next week.

In this fifth grader's dialogue journal, Daniel shares the events and problems in his life with his teacher, and she responds sympathetically. Daniel writes:

> Over spring break I went down to my grandma's house and played basketball in their backyard and while we were there we went to see some of my uncles who are all Indians. Out of my whole family down there they are all Indians except Grandpa Russell.

And Daniel's teacher responds:

> What a fun spring break! That is so interesting to have Indians in your family. I think I might have some Indian ancestors too. Do you still plan to go to Padre Island for the summer?

The next day Daniel writes:

> My family and I plan to go to Padre Island in June and I imagine we will stay there for quite a while. I think the funnest part will probably be swimming or camping or something like that. When we get there my mom says we will probably stay in a nice motel.

Daniel's teacher responds:

> That really sounds like a fun vacation. I think swimming is the most fun, too. Who will go with you?

Daniel continues to talk about his family, now focusing on the problems he and his family are facing:

> Well, my mom and dad are divorced so that is why I am going to court to testify on Tuesday but my mom, me, and my sister, and brother are all going and that kind of makes me sad because a couple of years ago when my mom and dad were together we used to go a lot of places like camping and hiking but now after what happened we hardly go anywhere.

His teacher responds:

> I am so sorry your family is having problems. It sounds as if your mom and dad are having problems with each other, but they both love you and want to be with you. Be sure to keep talking to them about how you feel.

Daniel replies:

> I wish my mom and dad did not have problems because I would have a lot more fun and get to go and do a lot more things together, but since my mom and dad are divorced I have to take turns spending time with both of them.

His teacher offers a suggestion:

> I'm sure that is hard. Trevor and Carla have parents who are divorced, too. Maybe you could talk to them. It might help.

This journal is not a series of teacher questions and student answers. Instead, Daniel and his teacher are having a dialogue or conversation, and their interchange is built on mutual trust and respect.

Dialogue journals are especially effective in promoting the writing development of English learners. Researchers have found that these children are more successful writers when they choose their own topics for writing and when their teachers contribute to the dialogue with requests for a reply, statements, and other comments (Reyes, 1991). Not surprisingly, children wrote more in response to teachers' requests for a reply than when teachers made comments that did not require a response. Peyton and Seyoum (1989) found that when a child was particularly interested in a topic, it was less important what the teacher did, and when the teacher and child were both interested in a topic, the topic seemed to take over as they shared and built on each other's writing.

Figure 5–2 presents an excerpt from a fourth grader's dialogue journal. This child is a native speaker of Lao and is learning English. In this entry, the fourth grader writes fluently about a trip to a county fair, recounting his activities there, and his teacher responds briefly to the account.

Reading Logs

Children write in reading logs about the stories and other books they are reading during literature focus units and reading workshop (Atwell, 1998; Hancock, 2004). As children read or listen to books read aloud, they respond to the book or relate it to events in their own lives, as Veronica did in the *Tuck Everlasting* reading log described in the vignette at the beginning of the chapter. Children can also list unfamiliar words, jot down quotable quotes, and take notes about characters, plot, or other elements of the story, but the primary purpose of these journals is for children to think about the book, connect literature to their lives, and extend their comprehension.

Researchers have examined children's responses and noticed patterns in their reading log entries. Hancock (1993) identified these eight categories:

- *Monitoring Understanding.* Children get to know the characters and explain how the story is making sense to them. These responses usually occur at the beginning of a book.
- *Making Inferences.* Children share their insights into the feelings and motives of a character. They often begin their comments with "I think."
- *Making, Validating, or Invalidating Predictions.* Children speculate about what will happen later in the story and also confirm or reject predictions they made previously.
- *Expressing Wonder or Confusion.* Children reflect on the way the story is developing. They ask "I wonder why" questions and write about confusions.
- *Character Interaction.* Children show that they are personally involved with a character, sometimes writing "If I were _____, I would . . ." They express empathy and share related experiences from their own lives. Also, they may give advice to the character.

- *Character Assessment.* Children judge a character's actions and often use evaluative terms such as "nice" and "dumb."
- *Story Involvement.* Children reveal their involvement in the story as they express satisfaction with how the story is developing. They may comment on their desire to continue reading or use words such as "disgusting," "weird," or "awesome" to react to sensory aspects of the story.
- *Literary Criticism.* Children offer "I liked/I didn't like" opinions and praise or condemn an author's style. Sometimes they compare the book with others they have read or compare the author with other authors with whom they are familiar.

The first four categories are personal meaning-making options in which children make inferences about characters, offer predictions, ask questions, or discuss confusions. The next three categories focus on character and plot development; children become involved with the story, and they offer reactions to the characters and events of the story. The last category is literary evaluation, in which children evaluate books and reflect on their own literary tastes.

Figure 5–2 Shared Writing: An Excerpt From a Fourth Grader's Dialogue Journal

> Yesterday I went to the Fair with my brother-in-law and my brother, sister my sister tell me to use the three doller to get that big miorrow so I use the three doller but I only got one dart to throw at the balloon then I hit the balloon and I got a big miorrow for my sister my brother-in-law tell me to get one for my brother-in-law so I got a biger one then I give to my sister and I got my self some tiket to ride I went on the super sidle and I got scard then I was sitting and I jump up hight when I was going down.
>
> You must have good aim to be able to throw a dart and hit a balloon. I'm glad you won some mirrors. Was this your first trip to the Fair?

These categories can extend the possibilities of response by introducing teachers and children to a wide variety of response options. Hancock (1993; 2004) recommends that teachers begin by assessing the kinds of responses children are currently making. They can read children's reading logs, categorize the types of responses, tally the categories, and make an assessment. Often children use only a few types of responses, not the wide range that is available. Teachers can teach minilessons and model types of responses that children aren't using, and they can ask questions when they read journals to prompt children to think in new ways about the story they are reading.

For example, a third grader wrote this reading log entry during an author study of Eve Bunting; the focus is literary criticism:

> I just read *Fly Away Home* [Bunting, 1991] and it is the best book that Eve Bunting ever wrote. The boy was like the bird and I know he made it out of the airport.

A sixth grader wrote this entry after reading the third chapter of *Summer of the Swans* (Byars, 1970); the focus is on character interaction:

> I think looks are not the most important thing because the way you act is. When some people look good and still act good—that's when people are really lucky, but I just think you should go ahead and appreciate the way you look.

The next two entries were written by seventh graders after finishing *The Giver* (Lowry, 1993). Even though they reach different conclusions about the book, their focus is story involvement:

> I can't believe it ended this way. They froze to death. I think they died but I wish they found freedom and happiness. It is very sad.
>
> The ending is cool. Jonas and Gabe come back to the community but now it is changed. There are colors and the people have feelings. They believe in God and it is Christmas.

Learning Logs

Children use learning logs to record or react to what they are learning in social studies, science, or math. They write in these journals to reflect on their learning, to discover gaps in their knowledge, and to explore relationships between what they are learning and their past experiences (Topping & McManus, 2002).

Children often keep learning logs as a part of thematic units in social studies. In their logs, children write in response to informational books, write vocabulary related to the theme, create time lines, and draw diagrams and maps. For example, as part of a study of the Pilgrims, middle-grade students might include the following in their learning logs:

- Informal quickwrites about Pilgrims
- A list of words related to the theme
- A chart comparing the Pilgrims of 1620 to modern-day pilgrims
- A time line showing when groups of Pilgrims came to America
- A brainstormed list of questions to ask parents about how each child's family came to America, and answers to these questions
- A picture of the Statue of Liberty with labels for the various parts
- Notes from interviewing a recent immigrant to America
- A response to *Molly's Pilgrim* (Cohen, 1983)

Through these learning log activities, children explore concepts they are learning and record information they want to remember about the Pilgrims.

Figure 5–3 Independent Writing: A First Grader's Seed Log

Translation: We planted a plant.

Translation: It cracked open.

Translation: We dug up the seed. It grew a root.

Translation: It got fatter. It grew roots.

Science-related learning logs can take several forms. One type of learning log is an observation log in which students make daily entries to track the growth of a plant or animal. Figure 5–3 presents a first grader's seed journal. In this journal, Tyler makes each entry on a new page. Drawing is as important as writing, and he uses invented spelling. Because several pages are difficult for adults to decipher, the text has been translated into standard orthography.

A second type of learning log is one in which children make daily entries during a unit of study. Children may take notes during a presentation by the teacher or a classmate, after viewing a video, or at the end of each class period. Sometimes children make entries in list form, sometimes in clusters or charts, and at other times in paragraphs. A lab report is a third type of learning log. In these logs, children list the materials and procedures used in the experiment, present data on an observation chart, and then discuss the results.

Children also use learning logs to write about what they are learning in math (Armbruster, McCarthey, & Cummins, 2005). They record explanations and examples of concepts presented in class and react to any problems they may be having. Some upper-grade teachers allow students the last 5 minutes of math class to summarize the day's lesson and react to it in their learning logs. They write about what they have learned during class, the steps involved in solving a problem, definitions of mathematical terms, or things that confuse them. Writing in learning logs has several advantages over class discussion: All children participate simultaneously in writing, and teachers can review written responses more carefully than oral ones. Also, children use mathematical vocabulary and become more precise and complete in their answers.

Double-Entry Journals

Children divide double-entry journal pages into two parts and write different types of information in each part (Barone, 1990; Berthoff, 1981). They can use double-entry journals for reading logs or for learning logs. When they make double-entry reading logs, children often write quotes from the book they are reading in the left column and then relate each quote to their own life, to the world around them, or to literature they have read in the right column. Through this type of journal, children become more engaged in what they are reading and become more sensitive to the author's language.

Fifth graders drew and wrote in double-entry journals as they read *Bunnicula: A Rabbit-Tale of Mystery,* a hilarious Halloween story by Deborah and James Howe (1996). Before reading each chapter, children wrote predictions about what would happen in the chapter in one column, and after reading, they drew and wrote about what actually did happen. An excerpt from a fifth grader's journal is presented in Figure 5–4. This child's responses indicate that she is engaged in the story and is connecting it to her own life as well as to another story she has read.

Double-entry journals can be used in several other ways. For example, instead of recording quotes from the book, children can write "Reading Notes" in the left column and "Reactions" in the right column. In the left column, children write about the events they read about in the chapter, then they make personal connections to the events in the right column. As an alternative, children can use the heading "Reading Notes" for one column and "Discussion Notes" for the second column; in this case, children write reading notes as they read or immediately after reading. Later, after they discuss the story or chapter of a longer book, children add discussion notes.

Younger children can use the double-entry format for a prediction journal, labeling the left column "Predictions" and the right column "What Really Happened" (Macon, Bewell, & Vogt, 1991). In the left column, they write or draw a picture of what they predict will happen in the chapter before reading it. Then, after reading, they draw or write what actually happened in the right column.

Children also use the double-entry format in learning logs: They write important facts in the left column and their reactions to the facts in the right column, or questions about the topic in the left column and answers in the right column. As with the other types of double-entry journals, it is in the second column that children make more interpretive comments. Figure 5–5 shows a sixth grader's double-entry

Figure 5–4 Independent Writing: An Excerpt From a Fifth Grader's Double-Entry Journal on *Bunnicula: A Rabbit-Tale of Mystery*

Chapter	Prediction	What Really Happened
3	I think that Chester will have night mares becose of the story.	They found a WHITE tomato.
4	I think that Chester will want to learn about vampires and he might even turn into one. ALL ABOUT VAMPIRES	He fond a Zuckini. It was white and it had 2 little holes in it.
5	I think they will find a white squash or some other vegatables.	Toby doent no that the rabbit is a VAMPIRE.

Figure 5–5 Independent Writing: A Sixth Grader's Double-Entry
Journal Page

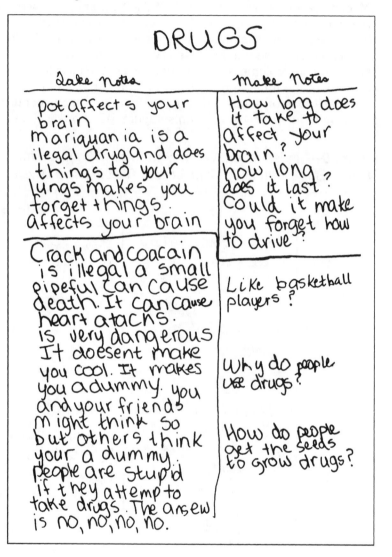

journal written during a unit on drug prevention. In the left column, the child wrote information she was learning, and in the right column, she made personal connections to the information.

Simulated Journals

In some children's books, such as *Catherine, Called Birdy* (Cushman, 1994) and *Amelia's Notebook* (Moss, 2006), the author assumes the role of a character and writes from the character's point of view. These books can be called *simulated journals*. They are rich with historical details and feature examples of both words and phrasing of the period. At the end of the book, authors often include information about how they researched the period and explanations about the liberties they took with the characters or events that are recorded. Scholastic Books has created four series of historical journals that are appropriate for fourth through eighth graders. The "Dear America" series features diaries written from girls' viewpoints, including *A Journey to the New World: The Diary of Remember Patience Whipple* (Lasky, 1996), *A Picture of Freedom: The Diary of Clotee, a Slave Girl* (McKissack, 1997), and *A Time for Courage: The Suffragette Diary of Kathleen Bowen* (Lasky, 2002b). The second series, "My Name Is America," features historical diaries written from boys' viewpoints, including *The Journal of Augustus Pelletier: The Lewis and Clark Expedition, 1804* (Lasky, 2000), *The Journal of Biddy Owens: The Negro Leagues, 1948* (Myers, 2001), and *The Journal of Patrick Seamus Flaherty: United States Marine Corps, Khe Sanh, Vietnam, 1968* (White, 2002). The third series, "My America," has shorter books with larger print that are written at the third-grade reading level. Most of the diaries in this series continue through two or three related books such as *Freedom's Wings: Corey's Underground Railroad Diary* (Book1) (Wyeth, 2001) and the continuation in *Flying Free: Corey's Underground Railroad Diary* (Book 2) (Wyeth, 2002). The fourth series, "The Royal Diaries," features the simulated diaries of Elizabeth I (Lasky, 2002a), Cleopatra (Gregory, 1999), and other famous queens from Europe, Africa, and Asia. Each of these books provides a glimpse into history from a child's perspective, and they are handsomely bound to look like an old journal. The paper is heavy and rough cut around the edges, and a ribbon page marker is bound into the book.

Children can write simulated journals, too: They assume the role of another person and write from that person's viewpoint. As children read biographies or study social studies units, they can assume the role of a historical figure. As they read stories, they can assume the role of a character in the story. In this way, children gain insight into the lives of other people and into historical events. A look at a series of diary entries written by a fifth grader who has assumed the role of Betsy Ross shows how she carefully chose the dates for each entry and wove in factual information:

May 15, 1773
Dear Diary,
This morning at 5 o'clock I had to wake up my husband John to get up for work but he wouldn't wake up. I immediately called the doc. He came over as fast as he could. He asked me to leave the room so I did. An hour later he came out and told me he had passed away. I am so sad. I don't know what to do.

June 16, 1776
Dear Diary,
Today General Washington visited me about making a flag. I was so surprised. Me making a flag! I have made flags for the navy, but this is too much. But I said yes. He showed me a pattern of the flag he wanted. He also wanted six-pointed stars but I talked him into having five-pointed stars.

July 8, 1776
Dear Diary,
Today in front of Carpenter Hall the Declaration of Independence was read by Tom Jefferson. Well, I will tell you the whole story. I heard some yelling and shouting about liberty and everyone was gathering around Carpenter Hall. So I went to my next door neighbors to ask what was happening but Mistress Peters didn't know either so we both went down to Carpenter Hall. We saw firecrackers and heard a bell and the Declaration of Independence being read aloud. When I heard this I knew a new country was born.

June 14, 1777
Dear Diary,
Today was a happy but scary day. Today the flag I made was adopted by
Congress. I thought for sure that if England found out that a new flag was taking
the old one's place something bad would happen. But I'm happy because I am
the maker of the first American flag and I'm only 25 years old!

Another type of simulated journal is a multivoiced journal, in which children write
entries from the viewpoints of different characters as they read a novel or examine
a historical event from a variety of perspectives. In a recent study, Styslinger and
Whisenant (2004) asked eighth graders to write in the role of various characters as
they read *Crossing Jordan* (Fogelin, 2000), the story of a friendship between two
girls, one African American and one white. The teachers stopped reading at pivotal
points in the story for children to write entries that reflected on the racism some
characters felt and the prejudice other characters exhibited. Through the experience,
grounded in tenets of critical literacy, the eighth graders not only deepened
their comprehension but also grew in their ability to "see" the world through other
people's eyes.

Children can use simulated journals in two ways: as a tool for learning or as a project. When children use simulated journals as a tool for learning, they write the entries as they are reading a book in order to get to know the character better, or during
a thematic unit as they are learning about the historical period. In these entries, children are exploring concepts and making connections between what they are learning and what they already know. These journal entries are less polished than when
children write a simulated journal as a project. Children might choose to write a simulated journal as a culminating project for a literature focus unit or a thematic unit.
For a project, children plan out their journals carefully, choose important dates, and
use the writing process to draft, revise, edit, and publish their journals. They often
add covers typical of the historical period. For example, a simulated journal written
as part of a unit on ancient Greece might be written on a long sheet of butcher paper and rolled like a scroll, or a pioneer journal might be backed with paper cut from
a brown grocery bag to resemble an animal hide.

Young Children's Journals

Young children can write in journals by drawing, or they can use a combination of
drawing and writing (McGee & Richgels, 2003). Children may write scribbles,
random letters and numbers, simple captions, or extended texts using invented
spelling. These invented spellings often seem bizarre by adult standards, but they are
reasonable in terms of children's knowledge of phoneme-grapheme correspondences and spelling patterns. Other children want parents and teachers to take their
dictation and write the text. After the text is written, children can usually read it
immediately, and they retain recognition of the words for several days.

Young children usually begin writing in personal or dialogue journals and then expand their repertoire of journal forms to include reading logs and learning logs. Four
journal entries made by kindergartners are presented in Figure 5–6. The top two entries are from personal journals, and the bottom two are from reading logs. In the top
left entry, this 5-year-old focuses on the illustration, drawing a detailed picture of a
football game (note that the player in the middle right position has the ball); he adds
five letters for the text so that his entry will have some writing. In the top right entry,

Figure 5–6 Independent Writing: Entries From Young Children's Journals

the kindergartner writes, "I spent the night at my dad's house." The child wrote the entry on the bottom left after listening to his teacher read *The Three Billy Goats Gruff* (Stevens, 1987). As he shared his entry with classmates, he read the text this way: "You are a mean bad troll." The kindergartner wrote the entry on the bottom right after listening to the teacher read *The Jolly Postman, or Other People's Letters* (Ahlberg & Ahlberg, 2001). This child drew a picture of the three bears receiving a letter from Goldilocks. She labeled the mom, dad, and baby bear in the picture and wrote, "I [am] sorry I ate your porridge."

Teaching Children to Write in Journals

Children usually write in journal notebooks. Spiral-bound notebooks are used for long-term personal and dialogue journals and writing notebooks, and small booklets of paper stapled together are more often used for learning logs and simulated journals. Children often decorate the covers of these short-term journals, as Mrs. Wheatley's students did with their reading logs for *Tuck Everlasting.* Most teachers prefer to keep the journals in the classroom so they will be available for children to write in each day.

Children usually write in journals at a particular time each day. Many teachers have children make personal or dialogue journal entries while they take attendance or immediately after recess. Learning logs and simulated journals can be written in as part of a daily assignment or as part of social studies or science class. For example, children may go over to an incubator of quail eggs, observe them, and then make an entry in their learning log during their daily language arts time. Children who are writing simulated journals as part of a social studies unit on medieval life might make their entries during language arts time or during social studies class.

Introducing Children to Journal Writing

Teachers introduce children to journal writing using minilessons in which they explain the purpose of the journal-writing activity and procedures for gathering ideas, writing in a journal, and sharing with classmates. Teachers often model the procedure by writing a sample entry on the chalkboard or on chart paper as children observe; this sample demonstrates that the writing is to be informal, with content being more important than mechanics. Then children make their own first entries, and several read their entries aloud. Through this sharing, children who are still unclear about the writing activity have additional models on which to base their own writing.

Similar procedural minilessons are used to introduce each type of journal. Although all journals are informal, the purpose of the journal, the information included in the entries, and the point of view of the writer vary according to the type of journal. The minilesson feature on page 119 shows how a third-grade teacher introduces a new type of journal.

Journal writing can also be introduced with examples from literature. Two well-loved characters in children's literature—Harriet in *Harriet the Spy* (Fitzhugh, 1964) and Leigh in *Dear Mr. Henshaw* (Cleary, 1983)—keep journals in which they record the events in their lives, their ideas, and their dreams. A list of books in which characters and historical personalities keep journals is presented in Figure 5–7. In these books, the characters demonstrate the process of journal writing and illustrate both the pleasures and the difficulties of keeping a journal.

Figure 5–7 Books in Which Characters and Historical Personalities Keep Journals

Altman, S. (1995). *My worst days diary.* New York: Bantam. (P)

Banks, L. R. (2000). *Alice-by-accident.* New York: HarperCollins. (M)

Bowen, G. (1994). *Stranded at Plimoth Plantation, 1626.* New York: HarperCollins. (M–U)

Creech, S. (1995). *Absolutely normal chaos.* New York: HarperCollins. (U)

Cronin, D. (2003). *Diary of a worm.* New York: HarperCollins. (P)

Cruise, R. (2000). *Fiona's private pages.* San Diego: Harcourt Brace. (U)

Cushman, K. (1994). *Catherine, called Birdy.* New York: Clarion Books. (U)

Denenberg, B. (1996). *When will this cruel war be over? The Civil War diary of Emma Simpson.* New York: Scholastic. (M–U)

Denenberg, B. (1999). *The journal of Ben Uchida: Citizen 13559, Mirror Lake Internment Camp.* New York: Scholastic. (M–U)

Denenberg, B. (2000). *One eye laughing, the other weeping: The diary of Julie Weiss, Vienna, Austria to New York, 1938.* New York: Scholastic. (U)

Fitzhugh, L. (1964). *Harriet the spy.* New York: Harper & Row. (M)

Frank, A. (1995). *Anne Frank: The diary of a young girl.* New York: Doubleday. (U)

Hermes, P. (2001). *Westward to home: Joshua's diary, the Oregon Trail, 1848.* New York: Scholastic. (M)

Hest, A. (1998). *The great green notebook of Katie Roberts: Who just turned 12 on Monday.* New York: Candlewick Press. (M–U)

Kalman, E. (1995). *Tchaikovsky discovers America.* New York: Orchard Books. (M–U)

Krupinski, L. (1995). *Bluewater journal: The voyage of the Sea Tiger.* New York: HarperCollins. (M–U)

Lasky, K. (2001). *A journey to the new world: The diary of Remember Patience Whipple.* New York: Scholastic. (M–U)

Lewis, C. C. (1998). *Dilly's big sister diary.* New York: Millbrook. (P)

McKissack, P. C. (1997). *A picture of freedom: The diary of Clotee, a slave girl.* New York: Scholastic. (M–U)

Meyer, C. (2000). *Isabel: Jewel of Castilla, Spain, 1466.* New York: Scholastic. (M–U)

Moss, M. (2005). *Amelia's 6th-grade notebook.* New York: Simon & Schuster. (M–U)

Murphy, J. (1998). *The journal of James Edmond Pease: A Civil War Union soldier.* New York: Scholastic. (M–U)

Murphy, J. (2001). *My face to the wind: The diary of Sarah Jane Price, a prairie teacher.* New York: Scholastic. (M–U)

Myers, W. D. (1999). *The journal of Scott Pendleton Collins: A World War II soldier.* New York: Scholastic. (M–U)

Osborne, M. P. (2000). *My secret war: The World War II diary of Madeline Beck.* New York: Scholastic. (M–U)

Parker, S. (1999). *It's a frog's life.* Pleasantville, NY: Reader's Digest. (P)

Philbrick, R. (2001). *The journal of Douglas Allen Deeds: The Donner party expedition.* New York: Scholastic. (M–U)

Platt, R. (1999). *Castle diary: The journal of Tobias Burgess, page.* Cambridge, MA: Candlewick Press. (U)

Pratt-Serafini, K. J. (2002). *Saguaro moon: A desert journal.* Nevada City, CA: Dawn. (M)

Rinaldi, A. (2000). *The journal of Jasper Jonathan Pierce: A Pilgrim boy.* New York: Scholastic. (U)

Roop, C., & Roop, P. (Eds.). (2000). *The diary of Mary Jemison, captured by the Indians.* New York: Benchmark. (M–U)

Ruby, L. (1994). *Steal away home.* New York: Macmillan. (U)

Weston, C. (2000). *The diary of Melanie Martin: Or how I survived Matt the brat, Michelangelo, and the leaning tower of pizza.* New York: Knopf. (M–U)

White, E. E. (1998). *Voyage on the great Titanic: The diary of Margaret Ann Brady.* New York: Scholastic. (M–U)

Yep, L. (2000). *The journal of Wong Ming-Chung: A Chinese miner.* New York: Scholastic. (M–U)

P = primary grades (K–2), M = middle grades (3–5), U = upper grades (6–8)

Instructional Procedures for Journal Writing

Children use brainstorming, quickwriting, clusters, and data charts as they write in journals. They also draw maps and diagrams, write key words, and draw pictures. None of the instructional procedures are better than the others; instead, children choose the procedure that is most appropriate for the writing activity and the most useful for supporting their thinking and learning.

Brainstorming ■ Children generate a list of words or ideas on a topic when they brainstorm; they think about the topic and then list as many examples, descriptors, or characteristics as possible. Afterward, they circle the most promising ideas to use in a writing activity. First graders generated these ideas about police officers before listening to their teacher read *Officer Buckle and Gloria* (Rathmann, 1995):

They have guns.
They put bad people in jail.
You have to do what they say.
Police officers will help you if you get lost.
They drive police cars with blue lights and sirens.
They fly in police helicopters.
They give tickets when your dad is speeding in the car.
They have handcuffs.
Don't be scared of them.

After reading the book, children added more information about police officers and then chose one idea to explore in a quickwrite.

EL *Scaffolding English Learners*

Taking time to brainstorm a list of words with struggling writers before they begin to write a journal entry or another writing assignment often pays big dividends. The brainstorming activity activates background knowledge, provides direction for the writing assignment, and generates words and ideas that can be used in the writing activity. In addition, having the correct spelling of key words available ensures that children's writing will be more readable.

Quickwriting ■ Children quickwrite when they write informally, rambling on paper, generating ideas, and making connections among the ideas. They often write on a topic for 5 to 10 minutes, letting their thoughts flow from their minds to their pens without focusing on mechanics or revisions. This strategy, originally called *freewriting* and popularized by Peter Elbow (1998), is a good way to help children focus on content rather than on mechanics. Young children can do "quickdraws" in which they use a combination of drawing and writing to explore concepts.

During a thematic unit on the solar system, third graders each chose a word from the word wall (a thematic list of words hanging in the classroom) to quickwrite about as an end-of-the-unit review. Here is one child's quickwrite on the sun:

The sun is an important star. It gives the planets light. The sun is a hot ball of gas. Even though it appears large, it really isn't. It's pretty small. The sun's light takes time to travel to the planets so when you see light it's really from a different time. The closer the planet is to the sun the quicker the light reaches it. The sun has spots where gas has cooled. These are called sun spots. Sun spots look like black dots. The sun is the center of the universe.

Clusters ■ Children make spider web–like diagrams called *clusters* to organize ideas and other information (Bromley, 1996; Rico, 2000). Clusters can be organized or unorganized. To make an organized cluster, children write the topic in the center circle on a sheet of paper and draw out branches for main ideas, then they add details to expand each main idea. A sixth grader's organized cluster on Poseidon is shown in Figure 5–8. In contrast, in unorganized clusters, ideas are not organized into main ideas and details; instead, branches are drawn out from the center circle and the

Reading Logs

Mrs. Ford has taught a series of minilessons to her third graders about comprehension strategies, most recently about making connections. The children understand that good readers think while they are reading or listening to a book being read aloud and that they make personal, world, and book connections. Today she teaches a minilesson on writing about connections in their reading log entries.

1. Introduce the topic

Mrs. Ford reminds the third graders that they have been learning to make connections, and they identify the three types of connections.

2. Share examples

The third graders reread a chart they created that lists the connections they made after Mrs. Ford read *The Runaway Tortilla* (Kimmel, 2000), a southwestern version of "The Gingerbread Man" story. They recall that Arlene made a personal connection to the Mexican food that her grandmother cooks, Lupe made a world connection by locating Texas on the map of the United States, and Martee compared this version to the original "The Gingerbread Man" story.

3. Provide information

Mrs. Ford explains that the children can write about the three types of connections in their reading logs by dividing a page into three columns and labeling them "Personal Connections," "World Connections," and "Book Connections." Mrs. Ford models the procedure: She divides a sheet of chart paper into three columns and labels each column. Then she asks Arlene, Lupe, and Martee to restate their connections as she writes them in the appropriate columns. Children read the chart and Mrs. Ford points out the qualities she expects to see in the childrens' reading log entries.

4. Guide practice

The next day, Mrs. Ford reads aloud *Chato's Kitchen* (Soto, 1995), a story about a cool cat named Chato who entices the barrio mice to come to his house by cooking lots of tasty Mexican food, and the third graders talk about the story and make all three types of connections. Then Mrs. Ford asks the children to open their reading logs, divide a page into three columns, and write at least one connection in each column.

5. Assess learning

For the next week, Mrs. Ford reads aloud a picture-book story each day and asks the third graders to write connections. She monitors their work and provides assistance as needed.

MINILESSON

ideas are added in any order. A third-grade class's unorganized cluster on Saturn is shown in Figure 5–9. The steps in making a cluster are listed in the step-by-step feature on page 123.

Children use clusters in two ways: as tools for organizing thinking during prewriting, and as a report to present information. Figures 5–8 and 5–9 are examples of clusters used as finished pieces of writing, and they report information. Children used neat handwriting, conventional spelling, and artistic touches as they created these clusters.

Figure 5–8 Independent Writing: A Sixth Grader's Organized Cluster on Poseidon

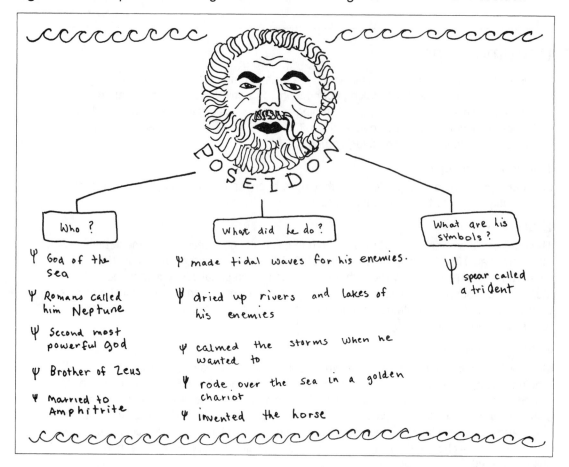

Figure 5–9 Shared Writing: A Third-Grade Class's Unorganized Cluster on Saturn

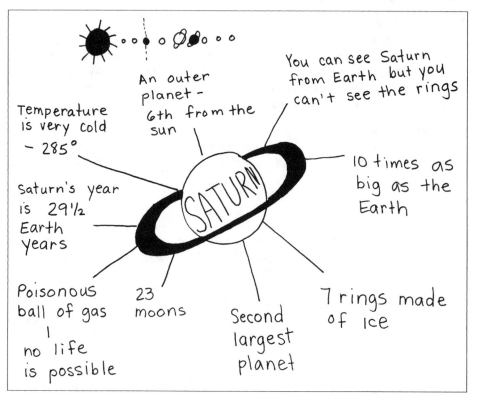

Data Charts ■ Children use data charts to categorize and record information about a topic. They make a data chart by drawing a grid and labeling the column headings with characteristics and the rows with examples. Then they fill in the boxes with information to complete the chart. Children can make data charts together as a class, in small groups, or individually. An excerpt from a fourth grader's data chart on the regions of California is shown in Figure 5–10. Children created the data charts at the beginning of a thematic unit on California, and then they added the information for each section after studying that region. Because the children followed the teacher's directions and demonstration as they created the chart and the teacher guided the children as they completed each section, the figure is an example of guided writing.

Sustaining Journal Writing

Children write in journals on a regular schedule, usually daily. Once they know how to write the type of entry, children write independently. Although some children prefer to write private journals, others will volunteer to read their journal entries aloud each day no matter what type of journal they are writing. Young children share their picture journal entries and talk about them. If the sharing becomes too time-consuming, several children can be selected each day on a rotating basis to share. Teachers and classmates may offer compliments about the topic, word choice, humor, and so on.

Children can select entries from their journals and develop them into polished compositions if they wish. However, the journal entries themselves are rarely revised and edited because the emphasis is on writing fluency and self-expression rather than on correct spelling and neat handwriting.

Children may continue to write in personal journals throughout the school year, but their writing in other types of journals begins and ends with particular literature focus units and thematic units. Sometimes children seem to lose interest in personal journals. If this happens, many teachers find it useful to put the journals away for several weeks and substitute another type of journal or free reading.

Assessing Children's Journals

Sometimes children write in journals independently with little or no sharing with the teacher, or at other times, they make daily entries that the teacher monitors or reads regularly. Typically, children are accustomed to having teachers read all or most of their writing, but the quantity of writing that children produce in their journals is often too great for teachers to keep up with. Some teachers try to read all entries, and others read selected entries and monitor remaining entries. Still others rarely check their children's journals. These three management approaches can be termed *private journals, monitored journals*, and *shared journals*. When children write private journals, they write primarily for themselves, and sharing with classmates or the teacher is voluntary. The teacher does not read the journals unless invited to do so by children. When children write monitored journals, they write primarily for themselves, but the teacher monitors the writing to ensure that entries are being made on a regular basis. The teacher may simply check that entries have been made and not read them unless they are specifically marked "Read me." When children write shared journals, they write primarily for the teacher; the teacher regularly reads all entries except for those personal journal entries marked "Private" and offers encouragement and suggestions.

Figure 5-10 Guided Writing: A Fourth Grader's Data Chart on California

REGION	VEGETATION	ANIMALS	PLACES	HISTORY	ECONOMY
North	Redwood tres	Grizzly Bears Salmon	Eureka Napa Valley	Sutter's Fort GOLD!	Logging Wine
North Coast	Redwood trees Giant Sequoia tres	Seals Sea Otters Monarch Butterflies	San Francisco	Chinatown Cable Cars Earthquake	Computers Ghirardelli chocolate Levis
South Coast	Palm tres orange tres	Gray whales Condors	Los Angeles Hollywood	El Camino Real missions O.J. Simpson Earthquake	Disneyland TV + movies airplanes
Central Valley	Poppies	Quail	Fresno Sacramento	capital Pony Express Railroad	grapes Peaches Cotton Almond
Sierra Nevada	Giant Sequoia Lupine	Mule Deer Golden eagles Black Baers	Yosmite	John Muir	skiing

Step by Step: Clusters

1. ***Choose a topic.*** Children choose a topic and write it in the center of a circle drawn on a chart or a sheet of paper. The center circle can be drawn in the middle or at the top of the sheet.

2. ***Brainstorm words.*** Children brainstorm as many words and phrases as they can that are related to the topic and write them on another sheet of paper. To complete an unorganized cluster, children write the words on rays drawn out from the center circle to make a diagram that looks like a sun.

3. ***Organize the words.*** For an organized cluster, children or the teacher identifies three to six categories and draws rays from the center circle for each category. Next, children write the name of the category in a box or smaller circle at the end of the ray. Then they choose words from the brainstormed word list related to each category and write them on rays drawn out from the category box or circle.

4. ***Complete the cluster.*** Children reread the words and phrases recorded and brainstorm more ideas to complete the cluster. The teacher may prompt children for additional words and phrases. In addition, children sometimes complete the cluster with small drawings.

The matter of how to grade journal entries is a concern. Because the writing is informal and usually not revised and edited, teachers generally don't grade the quality of the entries. One option is to give points for each entry made, especially with personal journals. For learning logs and simulated journals, though, some teachers grade the content because they can check to see if particular pieces of information are included in the entries. For example, when children write simulated journals about medieval life, they can be asked to include a specific number of pieces of historically accurate information in their entries. (It is often helpful to ask children to identify the pieces of information by underlining or highlighting them.) Rough draft journal entries should not be graded for mechanical correctness; children need to complete the writing process and revise and edit their entries if they are to be graded for mechanical correctness. A rubric for grading simulated journals that have been revised and edited is shown in Figure 5–11. When children develop simulated journals as a literature or theme project, it is appropriate to grade the entries.

ANSWERING TEACHERS' QUESTIONS ABOUT . . .

Journal Writing

My fourth graders get tired of writing in their personal journals. What can I do?

Many teachers report this problem. During the first month or two of the school year, children are eager to write in their journals, but then they get tired of it. There are several things you might try. First, you can alternate journal writing with independent reading activities so that children write in their journals only every other day, or give children a choice of reading a book or writing in their journals during this time. Second, change from personal journals to a different type of journal. Third, read aloud a book in which the main character keeps a journal, and ask children to reflect on their journal-writing activities by comparing them to the character's.

Figure 5–11 An Eighth-Grade Rubric for Simulated Journals

Historical Journal Rubric
A   Excellent
• Assumes the "voice" of the historical figure. • Incorporates many words and phrases from the period in each entry. • Contains few, if any, capitalization, punctuation, spelling, or grammar errors. • Adds explanatory and decorative illustrations in the margins.
B   Good
• Writes detailed entries with at least three paragraphs. • Uses at least two vocabulary words related to the historical period in each entry. • Uses an easily understood sequence of events from entry to entry. • Contains only minor capitalization, punctuation, spelling, or grammar errors that do not interfere with understanding.
C   Adequate
• Organizes entries into at least two paragraphs. • Develops a sustaining idea in each entry. • Includes at least one vocabulary word related to the historical period in each entry. • Contains some capitalization, punctuation, spelling, or grammar errors that do not interfere with understanding.
D   Poor
• Recounts an event or a day's activity in each entry. • Writes at least one paragraph for each entry. • Writes from the first-person point of view. • Contains many capitalization, punctuation, spelling, or grammar errors that may interfere with understanding.
F   Failing
• Does not accomplish what is expected for a D.

How does quickwriting differ from personal journals? They seem like the same thing to me.

You're right. These two types of writing are very similar, and the differences between them can be confusing. Quickwriting is a specific strategy that children use to write more fluently. They can use quickwriting to write a journal entry, but they can use it for other informal writing activities as well. In contrast, a personal journal is a place where children write informally for themselves about almost any topic. They may use quickwriting or any other approach to writing these entries.

Which type of journal should I use with my fifth-grade class?

Choosing a type of journal depends on your purpose for having your students keep journals. If you want your students to develop writing fluency, or if this is your students' first experience with journals, the personal journal is a good choice. If you want your students to gain writing practice and you also want to get to know them better, you might try dialogue journals. In connection with your literature focus units, try reading logs. If you want to use journals in content-area classes, learning logs or simulated journals are two options. Many teachers have students keep personal (or dialogue) journals and reading logs in separate notebooks throughout the school year and have them staple together booklets of paper for learning logs and simulated journals for thematic units.

My students don't like to write in reading logs when they're reading. They say they want to spend more time reading. What should I do?

Listen to what your students are telling you. The purpose of reading logs is to support them as they comprehend what they are reading; the logs shouldn't interfere with their reading. You might offer children more options in how often they write in their reading logs, or change the time when they write. They might prefer to write after they discuss the book, or write journal entries at home after reading in school (or the other way around).

I have to disagree with not correcting errors in children's journals. I'm a teacher, and it's my job to correct children's spelling, capitalization, punctuation, and other errors.

Many teachers agree with you; it's difficult to ignore many of the errors in children's journal entries. But what good would the corrections do? Would the effect of your corrections be to teach children how to spell or use punctuation marks correctly, or would your emphasis on correctness convince children that they're "no good at this writing thing," a conclusion that causes many children to stop writing? Many teachers have found that focusing on children's mechanical errors rather than on the content of their writing teaches children that correctness is more important than meaning, and that is just not true. Journal entries are a form of personal and private writing, in contrast to public writing, in which mechanical correctness counts. In more formal types of writing, mechanics do count, and through the writing process, children learn to identify and correct their mechanical errors. If you focus on errors in children's journals, you are defeating the purpose of informal writing.

Chapter 6
Letter Writing

Preview

Purpose Children write friendly letters to develop relationships and share information. They write business letters to conduct business and to offer opinions. In simulated letters, children use their imagination to assume the role of another person and to reflect on their learning.

Audience Children usually write friendly letters to known audiences and business letters to more distant known or unknown audiences, and these letters should be mailed. Simulated letters are often written for a more limited audience—the children themselves, teachers, and classmates.

Forms The two basic forms of letters are friendly letters and business letters. Children write friendly letters to pen pals, family members, teachers, classmates, favorite authors and illustrators, and other known audiences. They write business letters to companies, nonprofit organizations, and political leaders.

Third Graders Write Postcards

The students in Mrs. Donnelly's third-grade classroom spend 45 minutes after lunch in reading workshop. After reading two, three, or four books, children select and work on a project to extend their reading of one of the books. One of the most popular projects in Mrs. Donnelly's classroom is to make and mail a picture postcard to share information about a favorite book with a friend or relative. Children make the postcard from a piece of posterboard. On the front, they draw and color a picture of a scene from the book, and on the reverse, they write a message.

When Mrs. Donnelly introduced this project at the beginning of the school year, she taught three minilessons. One was about drawing pictures on postcards. The class examined Mrs. Donnelly's collection of picture postcards. Some were vacation postcards, and others were postcards advertising books of children's literature she had picked up at a convention. Together the class developed guidelines for the pictures they would draw on postcards: The picture should be about something special in the book, the picture should touch all four sides of the card, and the title and author should be listed. These guidelines were recorded on a chart about postcards that was hung in the classroom.

The second minilesson was about how to address a postcard. The information about writing an address was added to the poster so that children could refer to it when they addressed their postcards. The third minilesson was on writing the message on the postcard. The children decided to include both personal information and information about the book in the message. Mrs. Donnelly also reviewed how to begin and end the message. This information was added to the chart.

Children used the writing process to create postcards. They began by reviewing the book to choose a high point or favorite episode for the illustration. They also planned what they would write on the postcard. Next, children drafted the message for the postcard on scratch paper and drew the picture on the postcard. Mrs. Donnelly encouraged the children to begin the message with personal information but also to include information about the book. Many times, children's messages were persuasive, saying that they are sure this is a book the recipient of the postcard would enjoy reading.

The third graders met briefly with Mrs. Donnelly to revise and edit their messages, and they also shared the picture they drew on the postcard with Mrs. Donnelly. Then the children copied their message on the postcard and addressed the card.

Children shared their completed cards with the class during sharing time (the last 5 minutes of reading workshop), and then they were mailed.

One child's postcard about *Iktomi and the Berries* (Goble, 1989) is shown on page 128; both sides of the postcard, showing the picture and the message, are included in the figure. This postcard exemplifies many of the characteristics that Mrs. Donnelly taught through the series of minilessons on postcard projects: The picture is about the book, it covers the entire postcard, and the title and author are included. The child focuses on information about the book in the message and begins and ends the message appropriately for a letter to his parents. The address is also written correctly.

People write postcards and other types of letters for genuine communicative purposes. Mrs. Donnelly's students wrote to get someone's attention, to sustain friendships, to share information, to persuade, and to recount events. Other purposes

Guided Writing: A Third Grader's Postcard About *Iktomi and the Berries*

IKTOMI AND THE BERRIES By Paul Goble

Dear Mom and Dad,
This book is called
Iktomi and the Berries.
It's a terrific book. It is
about a man that goes
hunting and can't see
anything so he sees some
berries and makes a
lot of mistakes.
I think you would like
thise book.

love,
Brian

Connie and Steve Kyser

736 Valley Lane

Penn Valley, Ca

Zip 98946

for letter writing include asking questions, asking permission, apologizing, and requesting information (Karelitz, 1988).

Children's interest in letter writing often begins with writing notes. Young children often write "I love you" notes to their parents and messages to Santa Claus. Sometimes parents continue the practice by writing "Have a good day" notes to primary-grade children and then tucking them into lunch boxes for children to find and read at school. Reta Boyd (1985) is a firm believer in the value of note writing, and she encourages her students to write notes and post them on a special message board in the classroom. The children write notes for a variety of purposes, but Boyd

Instructional Overview: Letter Writing

Grades	Goals and Activities
Kindergarten–Grade 2	**Goal 1: Write friendly letters** • Children write short messages to classmates and the teacher. • Children use the mailbox mail system set up in the classroom to exchange messages with classmates and the teacher. • Children use interactive writing to write class-collaboration friendly letters. • Children write friendly letters to pen pals and authors.
	Goal 2: Write courtesy letters • Children write invitations to classroom and school events. • Children write thank-you notes. • Children make and send birthday, get well, and good-bye cards.
Grades 3–5	**Goal 1: Learn the forms and uses of business letters** • Children examine sample business letters to learn about their form and function. • Children write business letters to request information as part of thematic units.
	Goal 2: Correspond with pen pals • Children write friendly letters to students in another school. • Children send e-mail letters to pen pals. • Children become pen pals with college students training to be teachers. • Children write back and forth about a book they are reading or a thematic unit. • Children make postcards to send to relatives and friends.
	Goal 3: Correspond with authors and illustrators • Children write letters to favorite authors and illustrators as part of an author study. • Children write letters to favorite authors read during reading workshop.
Grades 6–8	**Goal 1: Assume another point of view and write simulated letters** • Children write simulated letters from one book character to another. • Children write simulated letters from one historical or scientific personality to another.
	Goal 2: Review friendly and business letters • Children compare the forms and purposes of the two types of letters. • Children write friendly and business letters as part of language arts and content-area classes.

emphasizes their educational value: Children practice reading and writing skills, and they recognize the functional and social nature of writing.

Letter writing is the logical extension of these informal notes. As with note writing, audience and function are important considerations, but in letter writing, form also is important. Although letters may be personal, they involve a genuine audience of one or more persons. Not only do children have the opportunity to sharpen their writing skills through letter writing, but they also increase their awareness of audience. Because letters are written to communicate with a specific and important audience, children think more carefully about what they want to say, write more legibly, and are more inclined to use spelling, capitalization, and punctuation conventions correctly. The Instructional Overview on page 129 outlines the goals and activities for letter writing in kindergarten through eighth grade.

Types of Letters

Letters that children write and mail are typically classified as friendly or business letters. The forms of these two types of letters, which are shown in Figure 6–1, reflect the purpose of the letter. When children write informal, chatty letters to pen pals or thank-you notes to a television newscaster who has come to the classroom, they use the friendly letter form. When they write letters to a cereal company requesting information about the nutritional content of breakfast cereals or letters to the mayor expressing an opinion about current events, they use the more formal, business letter form. Before children write either type of letter, they need to learn to use the forms.

Friendly and business letter formats are accepted writing conventions, and most teachers simply explain the formats and prepare a set of charts to illustrate them. This attention to format should not suggest that form is more important than content; rather, it highlights the fact that children are typically unfamiliar with the formatting aspects of this genre.

Friendly Letters

Children write friendly letters to friends who live out of town, relatives, and pen pals. In these casual letters, children share news about events in their lives and ask questions to learn more about the person to whom they are writing and to encourage that person to write back. Receiving mail is the real reward of letter writing!

After learning about the friendly letter form, children write to real people. Writing authentic letters that are delivered is a much more valuable experience than writing practice letters to be graded by the teacher. Children may draw names and write letters to classmates, to pen pals (by exchanging letters with children in another class in the same school or in a school in another town), or to friends and relatives. They also may want to list addresses of people to whom they can write friendly letters on a special page in their journals.

Children generally use the writing process to write letters. In prewriting, they decide what to say in their letters. Children brainstorm information to include and questions to ask in their letters. Next, they write rough drafts using the brainstormed ideas to make their letters interesting. Then they meet in writing groups to revise their rough drafts and edit them to correct mechanical errors. Children are especially interested in revising and editing when they're writing letters that will be mailed. Last, they

Figure 6–1 Forms for Friendly and Business Letters

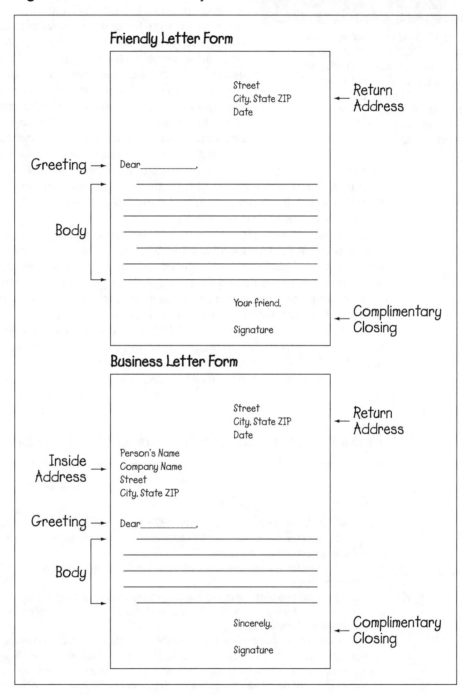

recopy the final draft, address envelopes, and mail their letters. One child's letter is presented in Figure 6–2.

Pen Pal Letters ■ Teachers can arrange for children to exchange pen pal letters with students in another class by contacting a teacher in a nearby school, through local educational associations, or by answering advertisements in educational magazines. Sometimes teachers arrange for children to write to pen pals who are the same age, and sometimes they set up cross-age groups; both arrangements have benefits. When children write to same-age pen pals, they have many things in common on which to build relationships. When they write to older or younger children, the relationship changes: Younger children work to impress the older children, and older children assume a parental regard for their pen pals.

Children usually write about school activities and their families and friends in pen pal letters, but they can also write to pen pals about the literature they are reading. In an innovative reading-writing program in Houston, third graders write to pen pals about their thoughts and reactions to books they are reading (Dorotik & Betzold, 1992).

Children can also arrange for pen pals through pen pal organizations. Two reputable pen pal organizations are the Student Letter Exchange (www.pen-pal.com) and World Pen Pals (www.world-pen-pals.com). These organizations match children with American pen pals and English-speaking pen pals from around the world.

Sometimes teachers arrange for their students to become pen pals with college students who are training to become teachers. Children and preservice teachers write back and forth to each other four, five, or six times and then get together at the end of the semester. This arrangement benefits both the children and the preservice teachers: Children correspond with caring adults, and the college students get to know children who are similar to those they will soon be teaching. Berrill and

Figure 6–2 Guided Writing: A Third Grader's Pen Pal Letter

December 10

Dear Annie,

I'm your pen pal now. My name is Allison and I'm 8 years old. My birthday is on April 1st.

I go to Jefferson Elementary School. Our mascot is a dragon. We are in construction because we're going to have a new gym in January.

My hobbies are soccer, sewing, and cooking. I play soccer, sewing I do in free time, and I cook dinner sometimes.

My pets are two cats and a dog. The dog's name is Casey and he's a boy. He is two years old. The cat is a girl and her name is Snuffles. She is four year old. The kitten is a girl and her name is Sprinkles. She is two months old.

My dad's name is Mark and my mom's name is Charlotte. Her birthday is the day after Mother's Day. My brother's name is Lenny. He is 13 years old. My sister's name is Nicole. She is 3 years old.

I have some questions for you. Do you have a sister or a brother? Are your mom and dad divorced? Mine aren't. What is your school's name? What is your mascot? What is your teacher's name? Do you have a pet? How many pets do you have? Will you send me a photograph of yourself?

Your friend,

Allison

Gall (2000) studied a class of second graders who became pen pals with a class of preservice teachers, and they compared the children's letters with letters written by a control group of children who wrote letters to imaginary audiences and received traditional teacher comments on their letters. The researchers found that the children who wrote pen pal letters wrote longer and more complex letters once they received responses to their letters. The results emphasized the importance of providing real audiences for children's writing.

In another study (Crowhurst, 1992), sixth graders corresponded with preservice teachers, and the children's letters showed similar growth. The sixth graders wrote increasingly longer letters, and their later letters were syntactically more complex with more adverbials and more embedded clauses. Only a few children wrote more than one paragraph in their first letters, but many used a series of paragraphs in later letters. Over the semester, the children also experimented with more mature ways of beginning and ending letters and became more skillful in introducing new topics. In addition, the children themselves changed as writers: As they developed a sense of purpose and audience, they became more eager to write and more concerned about expressing themselves clearly.

E-mail Messages ■ The Internet has created a completely new way for children to correspond with people around the world. It's a fast and simple way to send and reply to mail, and messages can be saved and stored on the computer, too. Because it's becoming a pervasive form of communication in our culture, children need to learn how to write e-mail messages. They learn the genre-specific conventions—brevity, conversational language, and innovative mechanics—and how these messages differ from other types of letters (Wollman-Bonilla, 2003).

Children learn to write in e-mail boxes. They type the correspondent's e-mail address in the top window, specify a topic in the subject window, and then write their message in the large window. They begin by greeting their correspondent and then write a message, often using shorthand spellings and innovative punctuation. Children keep their messages short—no longer than one or two screens in length—so that they can easily be read on the computer screen. They end their message with a closing, much as in other types of friendly letters.

E-mail can be used in a variety of ways. Children write e-mail messages to friends and family members, and they use e-mail to correspond with pen pals. Teachers also use e-mail to build relationships with their students. Niday and Campbell (2000) found that warm, humorous, and genuine dialogue on the Internet changed the way that they got to know their seventh- and eighth-grade students.

Courtesy Letters ■ Invitations and thank-you notes are two other types of friendly letters that children write. They may write to parents to invite them to an after-school program, to the class across the hall to ask to visit a classroom exhibit, or to a community person to be interviewed as part of a content-area unit. Similarly, children write letters to thank people who have been helpful.

A sixth-grade social studies class developed a multimedia presentation about the United States Constitution and shared their presentation with a fourth-grade class. The fourth graders each wrote a thank-you note to a sixth grader, and they included a question in their letters so that the sixth graders would write back. One of the thank-you notes is presented in Figure 6–3 together with the sixth grader's response.

Letters to Authors and Illustrators ■ Children write letters to favorite authors and illustrators to share their ideas and feelings about the books they read. They ask

Figure 6–3
Independent Writing:
A Fourth Grader's
Thank-You Note and
the Response by a
Sixth Grader

Dear Marci,

You did a good job in the play that we watched. Can you tell me what union means please? Also what does tranquility mean? Well I just wanted to write you to ask you questions and tell you that you did good. Well got to go now. Bye.

Your friend,
Amy

Dear Amy,

Thank you for telling me I was good. Union means when all states get together and tranquility means peace!

Your friend,
Marci

questions about how a particular character was developed or why the illustrator used a certain art medium. Children also write about the books they have written. Most authors and illustrators will reply to children's letters; however, they receive thousands of letters from children every year and cannot be pen pals with them.

When children write to authors and illustrators, they should write meaningful letters to share thoughts and feelings about the books they've read. They should write only to authors and illustrators with whose work they are familiar. It's important that

How to Address Struggling Writers' Problems

The Problem	The composition has weak sentence structure.
What Causes It	Children write the way they talk, and those who speak in short, choppy sentences, use run-on sentences, or lack sentence variety in their conversation will write the same way.
How to Solve It	*Quick fix:* During revising, have children read their rough drafts aloud to locate short, choppy sentences that they can combine, run-on sentences that they can correct, or places where they can vary the types of sentences they use. As children participate in writing groups, they can also ask their classmates for suggestions about how to improve the quality and variety of sentences in their compositions.
	Long-term solution: In a series of minilessons, teach children about the types of sentences, run-on sentences and how to eliminate them, and how to combine sentences to make their writing more interesting. Children can work in small groups to practice combining sentences and improving the sentence variety of sample compositions. In addition, children can examine the variety of sentences in books they're reading and collect favorite sentences from these books.
How to Prevent the Problem	Children who do a lot of reading learn more sophisticated sentence structures through their reading, and they apply these structures in their own writing.

children follow the friendly letter format and use the process approach to write, revise, and edit their letters. If they want to receive a reply, children need to include their return address in the letter and on the envelope. It's also courteous to include a self-addressed, stamped envelope for a reply.

Children send letters to the author or illustrator in care of the publisher. Publishers' names are listed on a book's title page, and addresses are usually located on the copyright page (the page following the title page). If the complete mailing address isn't listed, children can find the publisher's address on the Internet. There are also websites, including www.kidsreads.com, that provide addresses for hundreds of authors and illustrators.

Beverly Cleary's award-winning book *Dear Mr. Henshaw* (1983) provides a worthwhile lesson about what children can realistically expect from authors and illustrators. Children shouldn't ask personal questions, such as how much money the author earns, send writing samples for the author to critique, or ask for free books.

Young Children's Letters ■ Young children can write individual letters, too. They prewrite as older children do, by brainstorming possible ideas before writing. A quick review of how to begin and end letters is also helpful. In contrast to older children's letters, kindergartners' and first graders' letters may involve only a single draft in which invented spellings and the artwork carry much of the message.

Primary-grade students also compose class letters. The children brainstorm ideas that the teacher records on a large chart. After the letter is finished, children add their signatures. They might write these collaborative letters to thank people from the community who have visited the class, to invite another class to attend a puppet show, or to compliment a favorite author. Class collaboration letters can also be used as pen pal letters to another class.

Business Letters

Children write business letters to seek information, to complain and compliment, and to transact business. These more formal letters are used to communicate with businesses, local newspapers, and governmental agencies. Children write to businesses to order products, ask questions, and complain about or praise specific products. They write letters to the editors of local newspapers and magazines to comment on recent articles and to express their opinions on a particular issue. It's important that children support their comments and opinions with facts if they hope to have their letters published. Children can also write to local, state, and national government leaders to express their concerns, make suggestions, or seek information.

Addresses of local elected officials are listed in the telephone directory, and the addresses of state officials are available in the reference section of the public library. Here are the addresses of the president and United States senators and representatives:

President's name
The White House
Washington, DC 20500

Representative's name
House of Representatives Office Building
Washington, DC 20515

Senator's name
Senate Office Building
Washington, DC 20510

Children can also write other types of business letters to request information and free materials. For example, they can write to NASA, the National Wildlife Federation, publishers, state tourism bureaus, and businesses to request materials as part of social studies and science units.

As part of an author unit on Laura Ingalls Wilder and her series of Little House books, a fourth-grade class decided to write a letter to the Laura Ingalls Wilder–Rose Wilder Lane Memorial Museum and Home in Missouri to request some information about the author and the museum. The class discussed what information needed to be included in the letter, and one child was selected to write the letter. A copy of this business letter is presented in Figure 6–4.

Simulated Letters

Children write simulated letters, in which they assume the identity of a historical or literary figure and write letters from that point of view. As part of a social studies unit, they might write letters as though they were Davy Crockett defending the Alamo, or during a science unit as though they were Thomas Edison inventing the electric light. They also assume the role of a character in a book they are reading and write from one book character to another. For example, after reading Patricia MacLachlan's *Sarah, Plain and Tall* (1985), third grader Adam assumed the persona of Sarah and wrote this letter to her brother William:

> Dear William,
> I'm having fun here. There was a very big storm here. It was so big it looked like the sea. Sometimes I am very lonesome for home but sometimes it is very fun here in Ohio. We swam in the cow pond and I taught Caleb how to swim. They were afraid I would leave. Maggie and Matthew brought some chickens.
> Love, Sarah

Even though these letters are never mailed, they give children an opportunity to focus on a specific audience as they write. After they write simulated letters, children can exchange letters with classmates who assume the role of the respondent and reply to the letter.

Figure 6–4 Shared Writing: A Fourth-Grade Class Letter to a Nonprofit Organization

Horace Mann Elementary School
1201 Whisenant Street
Duncan, Oklahoma 73533
February 23, 2003

Ms. Irene V. Lichty, Director
Laura Ingalls Wilder–Rose Wilder Lane
   Memorial Museum and Home
Mansfield, Missouri 65704

Dear Ms. Lichty:

My fourth grade class has been studying about Laura Ingalls Wilder because February is the month of her birthday. We even have a learning center about her. Our teacher has put a few chapters on tape of <u>The Little House in the Big Woods</u>. It is a very good book.

We'd like to learn more about Laura. If you wouldn't mind, could you please send our class some brochures about the museum and any other information about her?

Thank you.

Sincerely,

Kyle Johnson and
Mrs. Wilkins's Class

Teaching Children to Write Letters

Teachers teach children to write friendly and business letters and involve them in a variety of letter-writing activities during language arts and content-area units. For example, children write letters to children's authors, pen pal letters about books they are reading to children in another school, letters to governmental agencies and businesses requesting information and free materials, and simulated letters from one book character to another or from one historical personality to another.

Teaching children to write letters, however, involves more than just assigning letter-writing activities; teachers need to model how to write letters, teach minilessons on letter-writing formats and other strategies and skills, write collaborative letters with children, and have children use the writing process to write and send letters to real audiences.

Introducing Letter Writing

Many kindergarten and first-grade classrooms have classroom mailboxes or message boards so that children can write notes and other messages to classmates. The teacher begins by modeling how to write, deliver, and respond to short notes, and soon the children are exchanging messages. Teachers in middle-grade classrooms often introduce letter-writing activities by writing collaborative letters.

A good book to use in introducing young children to letter writing is the Alhbergs' *The Jolly Postman, or Other People's Letters* (2001), a storylike introduction to the reasons why people write letters. This book has a collection of small letters that children can remove from envelopes and read. Another useful book is *Detective LaRue: Letters From the Investigation* (Teague, 2004); this story of a dog detective named Ike who locates two missing cats is told through a series of letters. A list of books about letter writing is shown in Figure 6–5. Some of the books demonstrate how to write letters or to be a pen pal; other share letters written to literary characters.

Writing Letters

For children to be successful in writing letters, teachers combine instruction about letter writing with authentic opportunities to write and send letters. Children use the process approach to write letters so that they can make their letters interesting, complete, and readable. The steps in teaching children to write a letter are listed in the step-by-step feature on this page.

Teachers regularly teach minilessons so that children will know how to write letters and how the format and style of letters differ from those of stories, informational books, and journals. Topics for minilessons include using the letter-writing forms, focusing on audience, organizing information in the letter, and asking questions to encourage a response. Teachers also teach minilessons on capitalizing proper nouns, addressing an envelope, using paragraphs, and using courteous phrases. Two minilessons are presented: The one on page 140 shows how Mr. Diaz teaches

Step by Step: Writing a Letter

1. ***Gather and organize information for the letter.*** Children participate in prewriting activities, such as brainstorming and clustering, to decide what information to include in their letters. If they are writing friendly letters, particularly to pen pals, they also identify several questions to ask.

2. ***Review the friendly or the business letter form.*** Before children write the rough drafts of their letters, the teacher reviews the friendly or the business letter form so that children will understand how to arrange the message on the paper.

3. ***Develop or share an assessment checklist or rubric.*** The teacher and children develop an assessment checklist or rubric based on the writing assignment that will be used to assess the letters, or the teacher shares an already developed assessment tool that will be used to grade the letters. In both cases, children know what is expected before they write the letters.

4. ***Draft the letter.*** Children write a rough draft, incorporating the information developed during prewriting and following the friendly or the business letter format.

5. ***Revise the letter.*** Children meet in a writing group to share their rough drafts, receive compliments, and get feedback. They make changes based on the feedback in order to communicate more effectively.

6. ***Edit the letter.*** Children work with a partner to edit their letters, proofreading to identify errors and correcting as many as possible. They also make sure they have used the appropriate letter format.

7. ***Make the final copy of the letter and mail it.*** Children recopy their letters, address envelopes, and mail them.

Figure 6–5 Books That Include Letters

Ada, A. F. (1998). *Yours truly, Goldilocks.* New York: Atheneum. (P)

Ada, A. F. (2001). *With love, Little Red Hen.* New York: Atheneum. (P)

Ahlberg, J., & Ahlberg, A. (2001). *The jolly postman, or other people's letters.* Boston: Little, Brown. (P)

Avi. (1991). *Nothing but the truth.* New York: Orchard Books. (U)

Ayres, K. (1998). *North by night: A story of the Underground Railroad.* New York: Delacorte. (M–U)

Beller, S. P. (2001). *The Revolutionary War.* New York: Benchmark. (M–U)

Bonners, S. (2000). *Edwina victorious.* New York: Farrar, Straus & Giroux. (M)

Boudalika, L. (1998). *If you could be my friend: Letters of Mervet Akaram Sha'ban and Galit Fink.* New York: Orchard Books. (M–U)

Bryant, J. (2006). *Pieces of Georgia.* New York: Knopf. (U)

Cherry, L. (1994). *The armadillo from Amarillo.* New York: Gulliver Green. (M)

Dahan, A. (2000). *Squiggle's tale.* San Francisco: Chronicle Books. (P)

Danziger, P., & Martin, A. M. (1998). *P.S. Longer letter later.* New York: Scholastic. (M)

Danziger, P., & Martin, A. M. (2000). *Snail mail no more.* New York: Scholastic. (M–U)

Fleming, C. (2003). *Boxes for Katje.* New York: Farrar, Straus & Giroux. (P–M)

George, J. C. (1993). *Dear Rebecca, winter is here.* New York: HarperCollins. (M)

Heisel, S. E. (1993). *Wrapped in a riddle.* Boston: Houghton Mifflin. (M–U)

Hesse, K. (1992). *Letters from Rifka.* New York: Holt. (U)

Hobbie, H. (1997). *Toot and Puddle.* Boston: Little, Brown. (P)

Holub, J. (1997). *Pen pals.* New York: Grosset & Dunlap. (P)

Ives, D. (2005). *Scrib.* New York: HarperCollins. (M–U)

James, J. (1996). *Dear Mr. Blueberry.* New York: Simon & Schuster. (P)

Klise, K. (1998). *Regarding the fountain: A tale, in letters, of liars and leaks.* New York: Avon. (U)

Klise, K. (1999). *Letters from camp.* New York: Avon. (U)

Lorbiecki, M. (1997). *My palace of leaves in Sarajevo.* New York: Dial Books. (M–U)

Lyons, M. E. (1992). *Letters from a slave girl: The story of Harriet Jacobs.* New York: Scribner. (U)

Lyons, M. E., & Branch, M. M. (2000). *Dear Ellen Bee: A Civil War scrapbook of two Union spies.* New York: Atheneum. (U)

Nichol, B. (1994). *Beethoven lives upstairs.* New York: Orchard Books. (M–U)

Orloff, K. K. (2004). *I wanna iguana.* New York: Putnam. (M)

Pak, S. (1999). *Dear Juno.* New York: Viking. (P)

Pattison, D. (2003). *The Journey of Oliver K. Woodman.* San Diego: Harcourt Brace. (M)

Pinkney, A. D. (1994). *Dear Benjamin Banneker.* San Diego: Gulliver/Harcourt Brace. (M)

Pinkney, A. D. (2001). *Abraham Lincoln: Letters from a slave girl.* New York: Winslow. (M–U)

Potter, B. (1995). *Dear Peter Rabbit.* New York: Warne. (P–M)

Stewart, S. (1997). *The gardener.* New York: Farrar, Straus & Giroux. (P)

Teague, M. (2004). *Detective LaRue: Letters from the investigation.* New York: Scholastic. (P–M)

Tryon, L. (1994). *Albert's Thanksgiving.* New York: Atheneum. (P)

Wheeler, S. (1999). *Greetings from Antarctica.* Chicago: Peter Bedrick Books. (M)

Winthrop, E. (2001). *Franklin D. Roosevelt: Letters from a mill town girl.* New York: Winslow Press. (U)

Woodruff, E. (1994). *Dear Levi: Letters from the Overland Trail.* New York: Knopf. (M–U)

Woodruff, E. (1998). *Dear Austin: Letters from the Underground Railroad.* New York: Yearling. (M–U)

P = primary grades (K–2), M = middle grades (3–5), U = upper grades (6–8)

E-mail Messages

At the beginning of the year, Mr. Diaz taught his second graders to write e-mail messages, and his students became pen pals with children at another school in the district. Because he has noticed that the children's messages are getting shorter and less interesting, Mr. Diaz teaches this minilesson on how to write a good e-mail message.

1. Introduce the topic

Mr. Diaz explains that he's noticed that some of the children's e-mail messages to their pen pals are getting shorter and less interesting. Also, he points out that some of them have complained to him that their pen pals don't write back regularly and speculates that the pen pals are not responding because they've lost interest in being pen pals.

2. Share examples

Mr. Diaz shares several very short and uninteresting e-mail messages, such as:

> Hi! How are you? I was sick but now I'm not.
>
> Bye.

He asks the children to tell him why the messages aren't interesting.

3. Provide information

Mr. Diaz uses modeled writing to compose an interesting e-mail message:

> Hi Joey,
>
> My Grandma and Grandpa are visiting at my house. They live in Houston and they come to visit in the winter because they like to see some snow. My Grandma says that she likes to see it but not to drive in it. Ha! Ha! I have to sleep with my brother when they are here, but it's OK because Grandpa always gives me some money. Do you have grandparents that come to visit? Bye for now.

After reading the message aloud, the teacher asks the children to pick out the characteristics of an interesting message. The children recognize that Mr. Diaz's e-mail message includes five sentences, detailed information, and a question.

4. Guide practice

Together the children and Mr. Diaz develop a rubric with the characteristics of interesting e-mail messages, and the children refer to it as they write e-mail messages to their pen pals.

5. Assess learning

Mr. Diaz asks the second graders to print out a copy of their e-mail messages and attach the rubric so that he can check that they wrote messages with at least four sentences and included detailed information and one or more questions.

his second graders about writing interesting e-mail messages, and the one on page 141 shows how Mrs. Ramirez teaches her fifth-grade class about punctuation marks.

Assessing Children's Letters

Traditionally, children wrote letters that were turned in to the teacher to be graded. After they were graded, the letters were returned to the children, but they were never mailed. Teachers now recognize the importance of having a real audience for children's writing, and research suggests that children write better when they know their writing will be read by people other than the teacher. Although it is often necessary to assess children's writing, it seems unimaginable for the teacher to place a grade at the top of the letter before mailing it. Instead of placing a grade on children's letters, teachers can develop a checklist to use in evaluating the letters without marking on them.

The third-grade teacher whose students wrote the pen pal letters described earlier developed the checklist presented in Figure 6–6; this checklist identifies specific behaviors and products that are measurable. Checklists are shared with children before they begin to write so they understand what is expected of them and how they will be graded. At an evaluating conference before the letters are mailed, the teacher reviews the checklist with each child. Then the letters are mailed without any evaluative comments or grades written on them, but the completed checklist

Punctuation Marks

Mrs. Ramirez's fifth graders are writing letters to their favorite authors, and as many of them move into the editing stage of the writing process, Mrs. Ramirez teaches this minilesson to review the punctuation marks used in letters and on envelopes.

1. Introduce the topic

Mrs. Ramirez asks her fifth-grade students to examine the chart with punctuation marks posted in the classroom and to name the punctuation marks that are commonly used in writing letters and addressing envelopes; they name *period, comma,* and *colon.* She writes one punctuation mark on each of three pieces of chart paper taped to the chalkboard.

2. Provide examples

Mrs. Ramirez passes out highlighters and a collection of letters and envelopes; some are copies of letters written by students, and others are letters and envelopes she has received at home. She asks the children to examine the letters and envelopes and to locate and highlight the punctuation marks.

3. Provide information

The children work in small groups to make lists of the ways periods, commas, and colons are used in letters and on envelopes. After the groups have completed their lists, Mrs. Ramirez brings the class back together and they list the uses of the punctuation marks on the pieces of chart paper. Periods, for example, are used after abbreviations (e.g., *Mr.* and *Jan.*) and initials and at the ends of sentences.

4. Guide practice

Mrs. Ramirez asks her students to get out their language arts notebooks and turn to the page with letter-writing and envelope forms. She asks them to highlight all punctuation marks shown on the letter and envelope forms. Then she asks them to get out their rough drafts and check that they have used the punctuation marks correctly. Some of the children also trade papers and have classmates check their use of punctuation marks.

5. Assess learning

Mrs. Ramirez reminds the children that one item on the rubric she will use to assess their letters is "uses punctuation correctly in letters and on envelopes," so she will check that they have used punctuation marks correctly when she grades their work.

MINILESSON

Figure 6–6 A Checklist for Assessing Children's Pen Pal Letters

Pen Pal Letter Checklist

Name _____

	Yes	No
1. Did you complete the cluster?	☐	☐
2. Did your include questions in your letter?	☐	☐
3. Did you put your letter in the friendly-letter form?	☐	☐
_____ return address		
_____ greeting		
_____ 3 or more paragraphs in the body		
_____ closing		
_____ salutation and name		
4. Did you write a rough draft of your letter?	☐	☐
5. Did you revise your letter with suggestions from people in your writing group?	☐	☐
6. Did you proofread your letter and correct as many errors as possible?	☐	☐

is placed in childrens' writing folders. A grading scale can be developed from the checklist; for example, points can be awarded for each checkmark in the *yes* column, or five checkmarks can be required for a grade of A, four checkmarks for a B, and so on.

ANSWERING TEACHERS' QUESTIONS ABOUT . . .

Letter Writing

Don't my children need to write practice letters before they write real pen pal letters that we mail?

Writing practice letters is a waste of time because the activity is artificial. When writing just for practice or for a grade, children feel little impetus to do their best work, but when they are writing to an authentic audience—their pen pals—they are careful about their writing because they want to communicate effectively. The instructional strategy for letter writing presented in this chapter provides the opportunity for teachers to introduce or review the friendly letter format during the prewriting stage and to help children revise the content of letters after meeting in writing groups, and for children to identify and correct mechanical or formatting errors during the editing stage. With these activities built into the instructional strategy, children can eliminate most errors before they mail their letters, making the writing of practice letters unnecessary.

How can I tie letter writing to my literature-based reading program?

Here are three ways you can tie letter writing to literature study. First, children can write letters to you or to classmates about the books they are reading, or they can write postcards to friends and relatives, as Mrs. Donnelly's students did. In these letters, they share their reactions to the book, compare the book to others they have read or to others by the same author, or offer a recommendation about whether the reader would like the book. A second suggestion is for children to write letters to favorite authors and illustrators. Let children choose whom they write to, and be sure to review the guidelines for writing letters to authors and illustrators before they begin writing. Third, children can assume the role of a character from a favorite book and write a simulated letter from one character to another. Then they can trade letters with classmates and write back and forth.

What do you think about having children correspond using e-mail?

It's a terrific idea! Here is a wonderful example: Children in a school on a naval base write and send e-mail messages to their parents who are away at sea. Computers are a center at that school, and each day, children check for messages from their parents and respond to the messages. Of course, children in other schools could use e-mail to write to pen pals.

I'd like to have my students write letters to an author, but I don't know how to do it. I mean, should all of my students write letters to the same author, or should they pick different authors?

Children should write to authors when they have something to say, not because it is an assignment. The letters shouldn't have a "My teacher is making me do this" tone. Instead, children should write when they have something that they really want to say to the author. Children who want to write letters to an author as a project after reading a book should do so. Other children should choose favorite authors to write to, perhaps as part of reading workshop activities. Children have a much better chance of getting a reply when they write an honest letter, with insightful comments and interesting questions.

I have a lot of things to teach in fifth grade. Are you saying that I need to do one unit on friendly letters, a second unit on business letters, and a third unit on simulated letters? That's a lot to do!

You don't need to do units on letter writing. Instead, incorporate letter writing as a tool for learning and communicating as part of other classroom activities. Children might write friendly letters because you have a pen pal program in your classroom, or they might write friendly letters to authors as part of your reading program. They could also write simulated letters as part of literature focus units or during social studies units. Your students might have opportunities to write business letters as part of social studies, science, or other community activities. Think of letters as tools for learning.

Chapter 7
Biographical Writing

Preview

➤ *Purpose* Children use biographical writing to chronicle events in their own and other people's lives, to reflect on experiences, and to draw generalizations about life.

➤ *Audience* The audience for personal narratives is often the writers themselves and their classmates and families. Autobiographies and biographies are more sophisticated forms of biographical writing, and these compositions are often shared with wider audiences.

➤ *Forms* Forms are personal narratives, autobiographies, and biographies.

First Graders Write a Class Biography

Mrs. Jordan's first-grade class is studying plants, and as part of the thematic unit, the children want to learn about people who work with plants. They take a field trip to a local plant nursery, interview an agricultural extension agent, and learn about George Washington Carver. Mrs. Jordan reads Aliki's *A Weed Is a Flower: The Life of George Washington Carver* (1988), and after listening to the book read aloud, the children get into a circle to talk about the book.

Mrs. Jordan starts by asking, "Who would like to begin our conversation about George Washington Carver?" and then the first graders take turns sharing ideas and asking questions. They talk about how Carver was born a slave and was taken away from his mother, how he struggled to learn about plants, and the many uses he found for common plants such as peanuts and sweet potatoes. One child asks why Carver has George Washington's name, another asks if the class can make a meal entirely from peanuts like the botanist did, and another child says that Carver reminds her of Martin Luther King, Jr., whom they had studied earlier in the school year.

Mrs. Jordan seizes this opportunity to review the concept of biography. She asks the first graders if they know what kind of book *A Weed Is a Flower* is, and when no one recalls the term *biography,* she writes the word on the chalkboard and pronounces it. Then one child remembers that a biography "is a story of someone's life," and another child says, "It's a book that tells about the important things that happened in somebody's life." A third child recalls that a biography "tells why a person is remembered today."

Mrs. Jordan suggests that the children brainstorm a list of reasons why George Washington Carver is special and remembered today. One child suggests, "He invented stuff like peanut butter," another says, "He was a scientist," and a third child comments, "People admired him a lot." Then Mrs. Jordan points out that people like Carver are also a lot like us. The children make a second list of the ways that Carver is "just like us." The list includes "he liked peanut butter," "he was black," "he was good," "he went to college and I'm going to college too," and "he wanted people to like him." Each child chooses something from the "special" list or the "just like us" list as the topic for a quickwrite or a quickdraw.

Mrs. Jordan has a set of eight paperback copies of Aliki's book, and children reread the book in small guided reading groups with her. Several children remember Carver's saying, "A weed is a flower growing in the wrong place," and after rereading the book, they decide to make a mural about it. Other children work together in a group to make a life line (a line marked into 10-year intervals on a long sheet of chart paper) of Carver's life, noting the most important events, from his birth in 1864 to his death at age 79 in 1943. Children take turns identifying important events in Carver's life and writing them on the chart. Mrs. Jordan shares other information about the famous botanist and adds some of the information to complete the life line. For the year 1890, for instance, one child wrote, "GWC finally earned enough money to go to college in Ames, Iowa." Another group of children marked the locations that Carver traveled to on the large laminated map of the United States that hangs in the classroom, and several others made mobiles about the uses of peanuts. After they finish work, children share their projects with the class.

The class then plans two special whole-class activities: They cook a meal made entirely of vegetables, including peanut butter, and they make a class collaboration book about the great botanist. Individually or with a classmate, children choose events from Carver's life to write about. On each page, they write a sentence or two about an event in the botanist's life and add an illustration. Children use the writing process to make their class book the best it can be. They begin by drawing their illustration on "good" paper and writing a rough draft of their text on "draft" paper.

Then the class gets into a circle, arranging themselves so the pages of the book are in sequential order, and the children take turns reading their pages. They read through the entire book; then each page is reread and children offer compliments and suggestions about how to communicate more effectively. As children find gaps in their biography, several volunteers do additional pages to complete the book. Then children make revisions and meet with the teacher to edit their compositions. Finally, children add the text to the illustrations they have already done, and the book is compiled. They line up to sequence the pages, one child makes a cover and a title page, and then the book is bound with a plastic spiral. One page from the collaborative biography is presented on page 146.

Mrs. Jordan inserts a blank page at the back of most books for children, parents, and other readers to make comments after reading. Children read the book during independent

Shared Writing: A Page From a First-Grade Class's Biography of George Washington Carver

George had a traveling School. He went across Alabama telling farmers how to plant cowpeas, Sweet potatoes, cotton, and peanuts.

reading, and they take turns taking the book home for parents to read. Here is a sampling of comments on the "Readers' Comments" page:

This book is so good I read it twice!!
The writers and illustrators of this book did a great job!
The children really learned a lot about George Washington Carver.
Cool, dude.
We have enjoyed each of the books this year.
This book was very interesting; we never get too old to learn.
Very, very good book!

Mrs. Jordan teaches thematically, and she ties reading and writing into science and social studies activities. She uses the themes to introduce genres, such as biography, and as jumping-off places for writing activities. Mrs. Jordan's first graders use informal writing as they brainstorm lists and quickwrite in learning logs, and they use the writing process as they write biographies. Her children used the writing process to write their class biography of George Washington Carver, and because each child or pair of children wrote one page, Mrs. Jordan could model the writing process and complete the book in four days.

Instructional Overview: Biographical Writing	
Grades	**Goals and Activities**
Kindergarten–Grade 2	**Goal 1: Write personal narratives** • Children write personal narratives during writing workshop. • Children apply the writing process as they write and refine their personal narratives. • Children bind writings into books and place them in the classroom library for classmates to read.
	Goal 2: Write autobiographies • Children write "All About Me" books. • Children collect materials for life boxes.
Grades 3–5	**Goal 1: Write biographies** • Children read biographies and examine the genre. • Children choose personalities to write about and make life lines. • Children write simulated journal entries from the person's viewpoint. • Children make biography clusters. • Children write multichapter biographies. • Children give oral presentations as their personalities.
	Goal 2: Write autobiographies • Children read autobiographies and examine the genre. • Children make "me" quilts. • Children write chapter-book autobiographies.
Grades 6–8	**Goal 1: Write biographies** • Children compare and contrast biographies and autobiographies. • Children choose personalities to study and read biographies and collect other information. • Children write simulated journal entries from the person's viewpoint. • Children create multigenre biographies with at least three genres (e.g., simulated journal, biographical sketch, life line, collection of objects, poems, and photos).

*B*iographical writing is writing about people. Children like to investigate the lives of well-known personalities as they read biographies and share information about themselves and their lives as they write personal narratives and autobiographies. Taylor (2002/2003) explains that biography study engages children's imaginations: When they read biographies, they step into other lives and different worlds as they read about people they know from television shows and movies or men and women who have changed the course of history.

Children' biographical writing goes beyond writing traditional autobiographies and biography reports: Children create bio boxes, for example, by collecting objects representing their lives or the life of another person and writing about each object. They also write personal narratives highlighting events in their own lives, and they create multigenre projects with collections of letters, poems, and other pieces of writing. The Instructional Overview on page 147 lists goals and activities for teaching biographical writing.

Types of Biographical Writing

Biographical writing can be organized into three categories: personal narratives, autobiographies, and biographies. *Personal narratives* are accounts of events from the writers' own lives, told much like a story. *Autobiographies* are more sophisticated, multiple-episode stories about the writer's life, and *biographies* are other people's life stories.

Personal Narratives

Personal narratives are often one of the first types of sustained writing that children do. In this form of biographical writing, children write about themselves and their experiences in the community in which they live. Young children as well as older students (and even adults!) become more active, engaged writers as they write about themselves in personal narratives (Steinberg, 1991). One reason that children are so successful in writing personal narratives is that they can draw on what they know best—themselves.

Teachers do not assign topics for personal narratives; instead, children draw from their own lives and experiences and write about things that interest them. A writing might begin as a journal entry about a field trip to the zoo or a birthday party and then be developed and polished through writing process activities. In the writing workshop approach, children keep a list of possible topics in their writing notebooks. They choose a topic from this list or an event in their life and work through the writing process stages to organize, draft, revise, edit, and publish their writing.

In contrast, very young writers often use an abbreviated writing process. They draw and write their personal narratives directly into a booklet of paper stapled together. Drawing the pictures is their prewriting activity, and writing the words is drafting. They usually omit the revising and editing stages, but they increasingly make changes while they are drafting. In fact, children's desire to go back and make some changes is the best indication that they are becoming aware of their audience and can handle all five stages of the writing process. Whether or not children revise and edit, they publish and share their books, usually with classmates and their families.

Young children's personal narratives are often written with an illustration and a line of text on each page. First grader Jessica, for example, writes a line of text on each page of her "We Went to the Zoo" book:

Page 1:	We went to the zoo.
Page 2:	We saw a turtle.
Page 3:	We saw a bunny and we saw a snake.
Page 4:	We saw a monkey.

Jessica wrote this book after a class trip to the zoo, and her experiences are evident in the text and accompanying illustrations.

Preparing for Writing Tests

Personal Narrative

Writers recount personal experiences using a story structure when they write personal narratives: They let readers live through the experience they're retelling. These first-person stories are often told in chronological order, but more experienced writers also use flashbacks. These writings have a clear, identifiable story line and include sensory details and dialogue to make them interesting. Prompts usually have two parts: First, they ask writers to tell about a personal experience, and then they ask writers to explain what they learned or gained through the experience—that's the "why" question. Personal narratives are similar to stories except that they focus on real-life experiences, whereas stories are imaginative.

What Do Writers Do?

- Tell the story of a personal experience from the first-person viewpoint
- Create a focus with a controlling idea based on the prompt
- Organize the writing like a story with a beginning, middle, and end
- Add description and details to make the story interesting
- Create dialogue that reveals the characters' personalities
- Build suspense as they tell the story
- Answer the "why" part of the question by explaining what they learned or gained through the experience

What Mistakes Do Writers Make?

- Don't tell about a single specific experience
- Provide insufficient details to develop the story
- Ignore the "why" part of the prompt

Sample Prompts

- Think of a time you helped a friend to do something. Then write a story about what you did, telling what happened and what you learned from it.
- All of us have had a special adventure in our lives. It could be a time you visited a relative, a party you went to, a time you went somewhere special, a game you played, or something else. Write a story about your special adventure, and give enough details in your story to make it interesting. Also, be sure to tell why it was special.

Young children also write books of lists. Sometimes they write lists of favorite toys, family members, or things they like to do. One example of a book of lists is first grader Jason's "I Like" book:

Page 1:	I like pizza.
Page 2:	I like ice cream.
Page 3:	I like cookies.
Page 4:	I like salad.
Page 5:	I like fish.
Page 6:	But I don't like spinach.

In both of these personal narratives, the first-grade writers repeated a pattern ("We saw," "I like"), which structures the text and simplifies the writing task.

Older children and more experienced writers are able to sustain their account without a sentence pattern, as third grader Sean's account demonstrates:

> When I was three and a half years old, my mother and I had a discussion about cleaning my room. She was a little on the upset side. She told me I couldn't play until I cleaned my room up. She went into the kitchen to cook and left me to clean my room up. About ten minutes later I walked in the kitchen and stood there. My mother asked, "That was fast. Did you already get your room cleaned?" I said, "God told me that I didn't have to clean my room." With a shocked look on my mom's face, she asked again, "What? God will forgive me this day, so get back in your room and get it cleaned up!"

Sean is a more experienced and more fluent writer than the first graders. He wrote several drafts to develop his account and shared the drafts with classmates, each time revising his writing to extend and elaborate his account in order to communicate more effectively. He also met with the teacher to edit his writing and add conventional spelling, capitalization, and punctuation.

Children can also write personal narratives using their family members' stories. Dworin (2006) tells about a class of immigrant children who wrote down their parents' stories using Lulu Delacre's *Salsa Stories* (2000) as a model. The children asked family members to share a story about something that really happened with them, and they wrote the stories down. They brought their rough drafts to school and used the writing process to refine them, and finally they published an anthology of the family stories, with both English and Spanish versions that they shared with their families.

Teachers typically call personal narratives "stories" even though they don't have the plot and character development of a story. However, it is a disservice to children to call all writing "stories" when the writing might be a report, a poem, or a personal narrative because the terminology is confusing and children are less likely to learn to distinguish the various genres or writing forms.

Some picture books written in the first person that tell about realistic life events might be classified as personal narratives; Jane Yolen's *Owl Moon* (1987), an account of a child's walk into the woods on a snowy night to see a great horned owl, is one example, and Cynthia Rylant's *The Relatives Came* (1985), about a time when relatives came from Virginia for a visit and everyone had a good time, is another. A list of children's books that are written like personal narratives is presented in Figure 7–1. These books might be shared with children as examples of published personal narratives that have the same characteristics as the personal narratives they write.

EL *Scaffolding English Learners*

Have you noticed that English learners tend to write the same personal narratives using the same familiar vocabulary words over and over? Teachers can break this cycle by helping children brainstorm other topics and the vocabulary words to describe them. Children need opportunities to talk about a new topic to develop it before they begin to write. With support and guidance, English learners can move on to new topics, vocabulary, and sentence structures.

Autobiographies

An *autobiography* is the story of a person's life narrated by that person. In writing an autobiography, children relive and document events in their lives, usually in chronological order. They describe memorable events, the ones that are necessary to understand their personalities. A limited number of autobiographies have been written for children, and these life stories of scientists, entertainers, sports figures,

Figure 7–1 Books That Are Written Like Personal Narratives

Ackerman, K. (1992). *Song and dance man.* New York: Dragonfly. (P–M)

Baylor, B. (1997). *The other way to listen.* New York: Aladdin Books. (M–U)

Brinckloe, J. (1986). *Fireflies!* New York: Aladdin Books. (P–M)

Brown, R. (1986). *Our cat Flossie.* New York: Dutton. (P)

Bunting, E. (1990). *The wall.* New York: Clarion Books. (M–U)

Bunting, E. (1998). *Going home.* New York: HarperCollins. (P–M)

Crews, D. (1996). *Shortcut.* New York: HarperCollins. (M)

Crews, D. (1998). *Bigmama's.* New York: HarperCollins. (P–M)

Gray, L. (1999). *My mama had a dancing heart.* New York: Scholastic. (M–U)

Johnson, A. (1993). *Do like Kyla.* New York: Orchard Books. (P)

Juster, N. (2005). *The hello, goodbye window.* New York: Hyperion Books. (P)

Kellogg, S. (1986). *Best friends.* New York: Dial Books. (P–M)

Martin, B., Jr., & Archambault, J. (1985). *The ghost-eye tree.* New York: Holt, Rinehart & Winston. (M–U)

Mayer, M. (1968). *There's a nightmare in my closet.* New York: Dial Books. (P)

Ringgold, F. (1991). *Tar beach.* New York: Crown. (P–M)

Rylant, C. (1985). *The relatives came.* New York: Bradbury Press. (M)

Rylant, C. (1991). *Night in the country.* New York: Aladdin Books. (M)

Waber, B. (1988). *Ira says goodbye.* Boston: Houghton Mifflin. (P–M)

Williams, V. B. (1982). *A chair for my mother.* New York: Mulberry. (P–M)

Yolen, J. (1987). *Owl moon.* New York: Philomel. (M–U)

P = primary grades (K–2), M = middle grades (3–5), U = upper grades (6–8)

and others provide useful models of the autobiography form. A list of recommended autobiographies for children is presented in Figure 7–2.

Autobiographical writing grows out of children's personal narratives and "All About Me" books that they write in kindergarten and first grade. Children's greatest source of information for writing is their own experiences, and when they write autobiographies, they draw from this wealth of experiences. Children can also share their life stories by collecting items that represent their lives in life boxes and "me" quilts.

"All About Me" Books ■ Kindergartners and first graders often compile "All About Me" books. These first autobiographies usually contain information such as the child's birthday, family members, friends, and favorite activities, with drawings as well as text used to present the information. Two pages from a first grader's "All About Me" book are presented in Figure 7–3. In these books, children and the teacher decide on the topic for each page, and after brainstorming possible ideas for the topic, children draw a picture and write about the topic. Children may also need to ask their parents for information about their birth and events during their preschool years. In Figure 7–3, for example, first grader Jana reports that it was her father who told her she was choosy about the clothes she wore when she was 5.

Life Boxes ■ Autobiographies don't have to be written in books: Children can collect four or five small items that represent themselves and events in their lives and place these things in a shoebox, cereal box, or other box (Fleming, 1985). Items

Figure 7–2 Recommended Autobiographies for Children

Aldrin, B. (2005). *Reaching for the moon.* New York: HarperCollins. (P–M)

Bunting, E. (1995). *Once upon a time.* Katonah, NY: Richard C. Owen. (M)

Cohen, S., & Maciel, A. (2005). *Fire on ice: Autobiography of a champion figure skater.* New York: HarperCollins. (M–U).

Cole, J., & Saul, W. (1996). *On the bus with Joanna Cole: A creative biography.* Portsmouth, NH: Heinemann. (M–U)

Dahl, R. (1999a). *Boy.* New York: Farrar, Straus & Giroux. (M–U)

Dahl, R. (1999b). *Going solo.* New York: Farrar, Straus & Giroux. (U)

de Paola, T. (1989). *The art lesson.* New York: Putnam. (P–M)

de Paola, T. (1999). *26 Fairmount Avenue.* New York: Putnam. (P)

de Paola, T. (2000). *Here we all are.* New York: Putnam. (P)

de Paola, T. (2001). *On my way.* New York: Putnam. (P)

Ehlert, L. (1996). *Under my nose.* Katonah, NY: Richard C. Owen. (P–M)

Fleischman, S. (1996). *The abracadabra kid: A writer's life.* New York: Greenwillow. (M–U)

Fritz, J. (1999). *Homesick: My own story.* New York: Putnam. (M–U)

Goodall, J. (1988). *My life with the chimpanzees.* New York: Simon & Schuster. (M)

Herrera, J. F. (2000). *The upside down boy/El nino de cabeza.* San Francisco: Children's Press. (P)

Howe, J. (1994). *Playing with words.* Katonah, NY: Richard C. Owen. (M)

Huynh, Q. N. (1982). *The land I lost: Adventures of a boy in Vietnam.* New York: Harper & Row. (M–U)

Jiménez, F. (2001). *Breaking through.* Boston: Houghton Mifflin. (M–U)

Lowry, L. (1998). *Looking back: A book of memories.* New York: Delacorte. (M–U)

Lu, C. F., & White, B. (2001). *Double luck: Memoirs of a Chinese orphan.* New York: Holiday House. (M–U)

Myers, W. D. (2001). *Bad boy: A memoir.* New York: HarperCollins. (U)

Paulsen, G. (2001). *Guts: The true stories behind Hatchet and the Brian Books.* New York: Delacorte. (M–U)

Polacco, P. (1994). *Firetalking.* Katonah, NY: Richard C. Owen. (M)

Russo, M. (2005). *Always remember me.* New York: Atheneum. (M–U)

Stine, R. L., & Arthur, J. (1997). *It came from Ohio! My life as a writer.* New York: Scholastic. (M–U)

Tallchief, M. (1999). *Tallchief: America's prima ballerina.* New York: Viking. (M–U)

Figure 7–3 Independent Writing: Two Pages From a First Grader's "All About Me" Book

such as a baby blanket, a stuffed animal, family photos, postcards from a vacation, pictures of favorite toys or other items cut from magazines, maps showing places the child has visited, a letter from grandma, a mask worn on Halloween, a favorite book, or an award the child has received might be included. Children write a label to explain each item and attach the labels to the things. They also decorate the box and add an appropriate title. They can use a favorite color of paper, drawings of life events, words and pictures cut from magazines, or wallpaper scraps to decorate the box. Children can share the items with classmates orally or use the items in writing an autobiography.

Children can also make a life box after reading a biography. As with autobiographical life boxes, children collect or make three, four, or five items that represent a person's life, add labels to explain the objects, and place them in a decorated box. Life boxes are effective as a first biographical project because children think more critically about the important events in a person's life as they read and plan the items they will use to symbolize the person's life.

Bio Bags ■ Another way to document a person's life is by the books he or she has read and loved. Children can collect some of their favorite books to create bio bags (Weih, 2006): They select three, four, or five books that are important to them, write brief comments explaining why they value each book, insert the writing inside the book, and put the books into a decorated bag. The best part of the project is the sharing. Children take turns displaying the books they've collected, explaining why each book is important to them.

"Me" Quilts ■ "Me" quilts are another autobiography project. Children draw a self-portrait and a series of eight pictures to symbolize special events in their lives. Then they attach the pictures to a large sheet of butcher paper to look like a quilt with the self-portrait in the middle, as shown in Figure 7–4. Children write paragraphs to describe each picture, add these to the quilt, and then share their quilts with classmates. They can display their quilts on the classroom wall or present them orally to the class, explaining the pictures and what they represent.

Children can also make biographical quilts with a picture of a well-known person in the center and eight pictures representing special events or objects related to that person's life. They add paragraphs describing each picture, following the same procedure as with "me" quilts.

✍ How to Address Struggling Writers' Problems

The Problem	The composition lacks focus.
What Causes It	Sometimes children begin writing too quickly. If they don't understand the writing assignment, or if they begin drafting without generating enough ideas to sustain the composition, their writing may lack focus.
How to Solve It	*Quick fix:* During revising, have children read their rough drafts and highlight those sentences that pertain to the focus; they cut the other parts and elaborate the highlighted ideas. Sometimes they'll have to generate more ideas and reorganize their writing. *Long-term solution:* Demonstrate how to sustain a focus through the writing process by doing collaborative compositions with children. In prewriting, show children how to generate and organize ideas, and in revising, have them check that all of their sentences pertain to the focus. Also, explain that children choose titles for their compositions after they finish writing so that their titles will reflect the focus of their writing.
How to Prevent the Problem	Children who use the writing process to generate ideas, draft, and refine their writing create compositions that sustain a clear focus from beginning to end.

Figure 7–4 Independent Writing: A Fifth Grader's "Me" Quilt

Figure 7–5 Independent Writing: An Excerpt From a Second Grader's Autobiography, "A Story About Me"

ME!

My name is Enrico Juan Zapata.
Most peple call me Rico but my
Mom calls me Ricky.
I am 7½ yaers old.
My birthday is on March 28.
Then I will be 8.
I have brown hair and brown eyes.
I have tan skin.
I am a funny boy.

FREDDY

I got a Furby from my Mom for
Christmas.
I named him Freddy.
He is so awsome.
He is a furry animale that can talk.
I can talk to him and he will learn.
Freddy is very valuble so I can't
bring him to school.

SWIMMING

I love to swim.
I can swim fast in our pool in the
backyard.
My brother named Carlos taught me how.
My Dad says I am a FISH!
That's very funny!
I want to be in the Olympics
so I can win a Gold Medle in
swimming.

FAVORITES

My favorite color is blue.
My favorite number is 100.
Summer is my favorite season.
Whales are my favorite animale
but I like dogs alot too.
My favorite president is
George Washington.
And Mrs. Kasner is my favorite
teacher.

Chapter Books ■ Children write chapter books about important events in their lives. They choose three, four, or five important events to write about and use the writing process to develop and refine their compositions. A second grader's autobiography is presented in Figure 7–5; in this autobiography, you learn about Rico through four chapters in which he describes himself and his toys, his hobbies, and his "favorites."

Biographies

A *biography* is an account of a person's life written by someone else. Writers strive to make this account as accurate and authentic as possible. In researching biographies, they consult a variety of sources of information. The best source of information, of course, is the person himself or herself, and through interviews, writers can learn many things about the person. Other primary sources include diaries and letters written by the person, photographs, mementos, historical records, and recollections of people who know that person. Secondary sources are books, newspapers, and films about the person written by someone else.

Biographies of well-known people such as explorers, kings, queens, scientists, sports figures, artists, and movie stars, as well as ordinary people who have endured hardship and shown exceptional courage, are available for children to read. A list of recommended biographies is presented in Figure 7–6. Jean Fritz has written many biographies for middle-grade students, one of which is included in the list.

Authors use several approaches in writing biographies (Fleming & McGinnis, 1985). The most common one is historical: In this approach, the writer focuses on the dates and events of the person's life and presents them in chronological order. Many biographies that span the person's entire life, such as *Michelangelo* (Stanley, 2000) and *A Picture Book of Helen Keller* (Adler, 1990), follow this pattern.

A second approach is the sociological approach, in which the writer describes what life was like during a historical period, providing information about family life,

Figure 7–6 Recommended Biographies for Children

Adler, D. A. (2000). *A picture book of Sacagawea.* New York: Holiday House. (P)

Adronik, C. M. (2001). *Hatshepsut, his majesty, herself.* New York: Atheneum. (M–U)

Appelt, K. (2005). *Miss Lady Bird's wildflowers: How a first lady changed America.* New York: HarperCollins. (P–M)

Brown, D. (2000). *Uncommon traveler: Mary Kingsley in Africa.* Boston: Houghton Mifflin. (P–M)

Christensen, B. (2001). *Woody Guthrie: Poet of the people.* New York: Knopf. (P–M)

Cooper, F. (1996). *Mandela: From the life of the South African statesman.* New York: Philomel. (M–U)

Dash, J. (2001). *The world at her fingertips: The story of Helen Keller.* New York: Scholastic. (U)

Delano, M. G. (2005). Genius: A photobiography of Albert Einstein. Washington, DC: National Geographic. (M–U)

Demi. (2005). *Mother Teresa.* New York: McElderry. (M–U)

Fisher, L. E. (1999). *Alexander Graham Bell.* New York: Atheneum. (M–U)

Fleming, C. (2005). *Our Eleanor: A scrapbook look at Eleanor Roosevelt's remarkable life.* New York: Atheneum. (M–U)

Freedman, R. (1996). *The life and death of Crazy Horse.* New York: Holiday House. (M–U)

Fritz, J. (1999). *Why not, Lafayette?* New York: Putnam. (M–U)

Giblin, J. C. (2000). *The amazing life of Benjamin Franklin.* New York: Scholastic. (M–U)

Hesse, K. (2005). *The young Hans Christian Andersen.* New York: Scholastic. (M–U)

Hodges, M. (1997). *The true story of Johnny Appleseed.* New York: Holiday House. (P)

Levinson, N. S. (2001). *Magellan and the first voyage around the world.* New York: Clarion Books. (M–U)

Marrin, A. (2000). *Sitting Bull and his world.* New York: Dutton. (U)

Pinkney, A. D. (2002). *Ella Fitzgerald: The tale of a vocal virtuosa.* New York: Hyperion Books. (P–M)

Poole, J. (2005). *Joan of Arc.* New York: Knopf. (M–U)

Rappaport, D. (2001). *Martin's big words: The life of Dr. Martin Luther King, Jr.* New York: Hyperion Books. (P–M)

Rockwell, A. (2000). *Only passing through: The story of Sojourner Truth.* New York: Knopf. (M–U)

Stanley, D., & Vennema, P. (2001). *Good Queen Bess: The story of Elizabeth I of England.* New York: HarperCollins. (M–U)

Szabo, C. (1997). *Sky pioneer: A photo biography of Amelia Earhart.* Washington, DC: National Geographic Society. (U)

Wallner, A. (2001). *Abigail Adams.* New York: Holiday House. (P)

Winter, J. (1999). *Sebastian: A book about Bach.* New York: Browndeer. (P)

food, clothing, education, economics, transportation, and so on. For instance, in *Molly Bannaky* (McGill, 1999), the author describes how difficult life was in Colonial America for an indentured servant named Molly Bannaky, who would become Benjamin Banneker's mother.

A third approach is psychological: The writer focuses on the conflicts that the person faces. These conflicts may be with oneself or with other people, nature, or society. (For more information about conflict, see Chapter 9, "Narrative Writing.") This approach has many elements in common with stories and is most often used in the shorter event or phase biographies. One example is Jean Fritz's single-event biography *And Then What Happened, Paul Revere?* (1973), in which Paul Revere faces conflict with the British army.

Biographies may be categorized as *contemporary* or *historical*. Contemporary biographies are written about a living person, especially a person whom the writer can interview. In contrast, historical biographies are written about people who are no longer alive.

When children study someone else's life to prepare for writing a biography, they need to become personally involved in the project (Zarnowski, 1988). There are several ways to engage children in biographical study—that is, to help them walk in the footsteps of the other person. For contemporary biographies, meeting and interviewing the person is the best way. For other biography projects, children read books about the person, view films and videos, dramatize events from the person's life, and write about the personalities they are studying. An especially valuable activity is simulated journals, in which children assume the persona of the person they are studying and write journal entries from that person's viewpoint. (See Chapter 5 for more information about simulated journals.)

Life Lines ■ Children sequence the information they gather for a biography on a life line or a time line about a person's life. This activity helps children identify the milestones and other events in the person's life. Children can use the information on the life line to identify topics for the biography, or the life line can be the entire biography project if children write a sentence or paragraph about each event and add illustrations.

Bio Boxes ■ Children make "bio" or biography boxes similar to "me" boxes. They begin by identifying items that represent the person, then collect them and put them in a box they have decorated. They also write cards to put with each object on which they explain the object's significance to the person. A fifth grader created a bio box for Paul Revere and decorated the box with aluminum foil, explaining that it looked like silver and that Paul Revere was a silversmith. Inside the box, he placed the following items:

    A spoon to represent Paul Revere's career as a silversmith
    A toy horse to represent his famous midnight ride
    A tea bag to represent his involvement in the Boston Tea Party
    A copy of Longfellow's poem "The Midnight Ride of Paul Revere"
    An advertisement for Revere pots and pans along with an explanation that
        Paul Revere is credited with inventing the process of layering metals
    A portrait of the patriot
    Photos of Boston, Lexington, and Concord that were downloaded from the
        Internet
    A life line the student had drawn marking important events in Paul Revere's life

The child wrote a card describing the relationship of each object to Paul Revere and attached it to the item.

Biography Posters ■ Children present the information they have learned about the subject of their biography project on a poster. Posters can include a portrait of the person and information about the person's life and accomplishments. Eighth graders made a biography quilt with paper squares, and each square was modeled after the illustrations in *My Fellow Americans: A Family Album,* by Alice Provensen (1995). One student's square about Martin Luther King Jr. is presented in Figure 7–7. This student drew a portrait of the civil rights leader set in Washington, DC, on August 28, 1963, the day he delivered his famous "I Have a Dream" speech. The student also added well-known sayings and other phrases related to Martin Luther King Jr. around the outside.

Collaborative Biographies ■ Children share the writing, as Mrs. Jordan's first graders did in the vignette at the beginning of the chapter, when they write collaborative biographies. They divide the biography into pages or chapters, and

Figure 7–7 Independent Writing: A Biography Poster About Martin Luther King Jr.

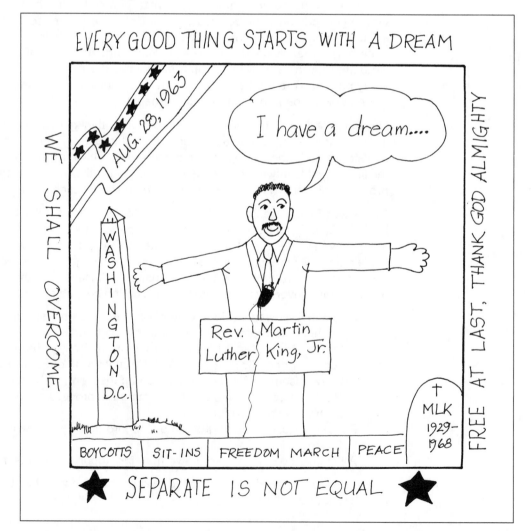

Figure 7–8 Shared Writing: A Page From a Second-Grade Class's Collaborative Biography of the School Principal

children each write one section, using the writing process to draft and refine their writing. A second-grade class interviewed their principal, Mrs. Reno, and compiled a picture-book biography that became the most popular book in the school. Before the interview, the second graders brainstormed questions, and each child selected a question to ask. Then Mrs. Reno came to the classroom and answered the children's questions. After the interview, the students wrote pages with their questions and Mrs. Reno's answers and compiled the pages into a book. A page from their collaborative biography is presented in Figure 7–8. You will also notice that the children practiced using quotation marks in their report.

Multigenre Biographies ■ Children write and draw a variety of pieces about a person to create a multigenre biography, which is like a multigenre report (Romano, 1995, 2000). Children collect and create some of the following items for a multigenre biography:

life line	found poem or other poem	story
quotations	open-mind portrait	poster
photographs	report	newspaper articles
collection of objects	maps	advertisements
simulated journal	letters	

Each item is a complete piece by itself and contributes to the overall impact of the biography. Children compile their biographies on posters or in notebooks. Figure 7–9 presents excerpts from a seventh grader's multigenre biography of Maya Angelou.

Figure 7–9 Independent Writing: Excerpts From a Seventh Grader's Multigenre Biography of Maya Angelou

---

Maya Angelou

In Maya's Heart

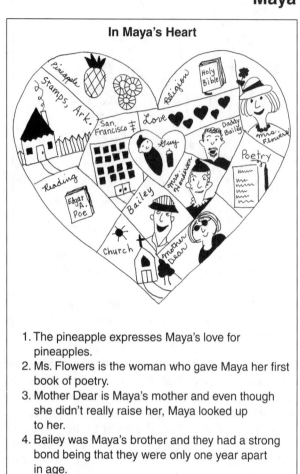

1. The pineapple expresses Maya's love for pineapples.
2. Ms. Flowers is the woman who gave Maya her first book of poetry.
3. Mother Dear is Maya's mother and even though she didn't really raise her, Maya looked up to her.
4. Bailey was Maya's brother and they had a strong bond being that they were only one year apart in age.
5. Guy is her son and her entire life.

Quotes

"Cleanliness is next to Godliness."

"God blessed everyone with an intelligent mind. Only we can decide how we use it."

Dear Diary,
One night I was scared and momma let me sleep in the bed with her and Mr. Freeman. Then when momma left early to run an errand, I felt a strange pressure on my left leg. I knew it wasn't a hand because it was much too soft. I was afraid to move and I didn't budge. Mr. Freeman's eyes were wide open with both hands above the covers. He then said, "Stay right here, Rite, I'm not gonna hurt you." I really wasn't afraid, a little curious, but not afraid. Then he left and came back with a glass of water and poured it on the bed. He said, "see how you done peed in the bed." Afterwards, I was confused and didn't understand why Mr. Freeman had held me so gently, then accused me of peeing in the bed.
Marguerite

Dear Diary,
While I was sitting talking to Miss Glory, Mrs. Cullinan called for someone. She said, "Mary P." We didn't know who she was calling, but my name is Marguerite. Now I settled for Margaret, but Mary was a whole nother name. Bailey told me bout Whites and how they felt like they had the power to shorten our names for their convenience. Miss Glory told me her name used to be Hallelujah and Mrs. Cullinan shortened it to Glory. Mrs. Cullinan sent me on an errand, which was a good idea because I was upset and anything was bound to come out of my mouth at the time.
Marguerite

Dear Diary,
Graduation day was a big event in Stamps. The high school seniors received most of the glory. I'm just a twelve year old 8th grader. I'm pretty high-ranked in my class along with Henry Reed. Henry is also our class valedictorian. The tenth grade teacher helped him with his speech. Momma was even going to close the store. Our graduation dresses are a lemon yellow, but momma added ruffles and cuffs with a crocheted collar. She added daisy embroideries around the trim before she considered herself finished. I just knew all eyes were going to be on me when graduation day came.
Marguerite

Teaching Children to Write Biographies

Teachers prepare children for writing biographies by teaching them about the organization of information in biographies and by sharing trade-book versions of biographies. With this experience, children can write personal narratives, autobiographies, and biographies using the writing process.

Introducing Biography With Personal Narratives

Children usually write personal narratives during writing workshop when they are free to choose their own topics for writing and write about topics that are important to them. It is important that children choose topics they care about and want to write about; otherwise, writing workshop can seem like an assembly line with children producing book after book without thoughtful work or careful bookmaking. Children get ideas for their writing as they listen to classmates sharing their books and from books of children's literature they are reading. The writing process itself also helps to nurture children's interest in writing because they learn how to develop and refine their compositions.

The procedure for writing personal narratives is described in the step-by-step feature on this page.

Writing Biographies and Autobiographies

Children write life stories as part of literature focus units and social studies and science thematic units. During an author unit, children might write a biography of a favorite author, or during a unit on the American Revolution, children read and write biographies of Paul Revere, George Washington, and other historical personalities. They also write biographies of scientists in connection with science themes. Children write autobiographies as part of literature focus units, writing workshop, and thematic units on self-awareness, families, and change.

The steps in the procedure are described in the step-by-step feature on page 162. Although it involves steps similar to those used for writing personal narratives, these two writing forms are different and should be taught separately.

Step by Step: Personal Narratives

1. ***Introduce personal narratives.*** Teachers use minilessons to teach children how to write personal narratives. In one minilesson, teachers explain that children write about events in their own lives. They share examples that students in a previous class have written or books written like personal narratives. In another minilesson, teachers help children brainstorm a list of possible writing topics such as a family trip, birth of a baby brother or sister, a pet, a hobby, an accident, a special holiday, a scary experience, or a grandparent's visit.

2. ***Use the writing process.*** Children begin by making a cluster or drawing a series of pictures to gather and organize their ideas. Then they write a rough draft, meet with classmates in a writing group, and revise their drafts based on feedback they receive from classmates. Next they proofread to identify and correct spelling, capitalization, and punctuation errors. Finally, children write the final draft of their composition, add a title page, and compile the pages to make a book.

3. ***Publish and share the writing.*** Children publish their personal narratives in books and share them with the class. Often they sit in an author's chair to read their books aloud to a group of classmates. They might also place their books in the classroom library for classmates to reread.

Step by Step: Autobiographies and Biographies

1. ***Examine the format and the unique conventions of the genre.*** Children read autobiographies and biographies to examine how authors organize and format life stories. In particular, they note which events the author focuses on, how the author presents information, and what the author's viewpoint is.

2. ***Gather information.*** Children gather information in several ways. For autobiographical writing, the children themselves are the best source of information, but they may need to ask parents and other family members for additional information. For biographical writing, they read books and view videotapes and movies to learn about the person and the time period in which he or she lived. If children are researching a living person, it might be possible to interview him or her in person or by e-mail. As they conduct research, children take notes about information they learn.

3. ***Organize the information.*** Children usually choose three, four, or five important events in their subject's life and develop clusters with these important events as the main ideas. Then they complete the cluster by adding details from the information they have gathered. Or, children can develop life lines or life boxes to organize their writing. They make life lines about events in their own lives or in the life of a historical personality. Or, they choose three, four, or five objects or photos from their life boxes and brainstorm ideas about each one.

4. ***Write the life story.*** Children use the clusters they developed to write their rough drafts: The main ideas become topic sentences, and the details are expanded into supporting sentences. After they write their rough drafts, children meet in writing groups to get feedback on their writing and then make revisions. Next, they edit their writing and recopy it or word process it. They add drawings, photographs, or other memorabilia. For biographies, children also add a bibliography, listing the sources of information they consulted.

Assessing Children's Biographies

Personal narratives are often the first type of sustained writing that young children do, and teachers watch for this accomplishment as a significant development in children's growth as writers. Teachers look for the following traits in children's first personal narratives:

- There is a common thread through the book.
- There is one line of text and an illustration on each page.
- The illustrations and the text are coordinated.
- The writer uses the first person.
- The child willingly shares the book with classmates.

As children gain more writing experience and begin working through all five stages of the writing process, their personal narratives become more developed and polished. Their writings should display many of these qualities:

- The account focuses on one event or experience.
- Specific people, locations, and objects are named.

- Sensory details about the people, locations, and events are included.
- Actions are described.
- Dialogue or monologue is included.
- The events are arranged in an appropriate sequence.
- There is suspense or a surprise at the end.

These qualities do not develop simultaneously, nor does any one personal narrative necessarily incorporate all of them. Think back to the three personal narratives presented earlier in the chapter; each of the accounts includes some of these qualities. Jessica's "We Went to the Zoo" piece, for instance, focuses on a single event, and Jason's "I Like" account has a surprise at the end. Sean's personal narrative is sequential, uses dialogue, and describes actions.

A second-grade checklist for assessing children's personal narratives is presented in Figure 7–10. Children use this checklist as they revise and edit their writing.

Before they begin work, children need to understand the requirements for their autobiography or biography project and how they will be graded. Teachers often create a rubric or assessment checklist with children so that they will understand what is expected of them. A seventh-grade teacher developed the rubric shown in

Figure 7–10 Second-Grade Personal Narrative Checklist

	Yes	No
Story Structure I used the "I" point of view. I wrote a beginning, middle, and end. I described the characters. I described the setting. I told why it was important to me.		
Ideas I wrote about one event. I wrote about the event in sequence. I added vivid details. I chose descriptive words to paint a picture.		
Mechanics I spelled most words correctly. I capitalized the beginning of sentences and names. I used punctuation marks correctly. I used complete sentences. I indented paragraphs.		

Figure 7–11 Assessment Rubric for a Multigenre Biography

A	**Genres:** The biography includes five genres. **Information:** The information is presented in the "voice" of the personality. **Vocabulary:** The compositions are rich with specific vocabulary terms. **Mechanics:** There are few, if any, mechanical errors. **Writing Process:** Rough drafts provide evidence of the writing process. **Design/Graphics:** The design is eye-catching, and four or more graphics extend the text. **Bibliography:** There are five or more references, and one is an Internet reference.
B	**Genres:** The biography includes four genres. **Information:** The information is accurate, detailed, and interesting. **Vocabulary:** The compositions include many specific vocabulary words used correctly. **Mechanics:** There are a few mechanical errors, but they do not interfere with understanding. **Writing Process:** Rough drafts provide evidence of the writing process. **Design/Graphics:** The design is attractive, and three or more graphics support the text. **Bibliography:** There are four or more references, and one is an Internet reference.
C	**Genres:** The biography contains three genres. **Information:** The information is accurate and interesting. **Vocabulary:** The compositions include a few specific vocabulary words. **Mechanics:** There are some mechanical errors, but they do not interfere with understanding. **Writing Process:** Rough drafts provide evidence of the writing process. **Design/Graphics:** The design is attractive, and two or more graphics support the text. **Bibliography:** There are three or more references.
D	**Genres:** The biography includes two genres. **Information:** A lot of information is confusing. **Vocabulary:** Very few specific vocabulary words are used. **Mechanics:** There are many mechanical errors. **Writing Process:** The rough drafts are not attached. **Design/Graphics:** The design is confusing, and there is one graphic. **Bibliography:** There are two references.
F	**Genres:** The biography includes one genre. **Information:** Very little information is provided, or it is not accurate. **Vocabulary:** No specific vocabulary words are used. **Mechanics:** There are many mechanical errors. **Writing Process:** The rough drafts are not attached. **Design/Graphics:** The biography has no design, and there are no graphics. **Bibliography:** There is one reference or none at all.

Figure 7–11 for a multigenre biography project. She began by listing these seven components on the chalkboard: genres, information, vocabulary, mechanics, writing process, design/graphics, and bibliography. She and her students discussed each component, and the teacher explained her expectations for their assignment. For example, for the genres component, the children knew that they had to include at least three genres—a report of information, a simulated journal with five entries, and a poem. Then they developed the genres component of the rubric. Three genres was the C expectation; if they wrote fewer genre pieces, their grade would be a

D or F. For a B, children needed to write four genre pieces, and for an A, they needed to write five. Together as a class, the children brainstormed the genres they might use. Then they repeated the process with each of the other six components. Through this activity, the children developed the rubric and the teacher reviewed the requirements for each grade.

Teachers usually give children copies of checklists and rubrics to keep in their writing folders so that they can check their work against the guidelines. At the end of the project, children self-assess their work and attach the checklists and rubrics to their work. Through this approach, children assume a greater responsibility for their own learning and better understand why they receive a particular grade.

ANSWERING TEACHERS' QUESTIONS ABOUT . . .

Biographical Writing

My second graders are writing personal narratives. In fact, that's all most of them write. How can I get them into writing stories, poems, letters, and other writing forms?

Choose one of the forms you mentioned and introduce it to your students, perhaps using a class collaboration. Then invite your students to use the form for a genuine writing purpose. For example, they might become pen pals with children in another school. The first letter might be a class letter, and you can demonstrate how to write a friendly letter as you compose the letter together with your students. Then they can write individual letters to their pen pals several times during the school year. Then continue to introduce other writing forms in connection with literature the children are reading or social studies and science units.

At which grade levels do you think children should write biographies and autobiographies?

Primary-grade students can do almost all types of writing, including biographical writing. First graders typically write personal narratives, and they can also begin writing collaborative biographies, as Mrs. Jordan's first graders did in the vignette at the beginning of the chapter. Second graders (see Figure 7–5) can write chapter autobiographies, and some experienced first-grade writers might also. Most children write personal narratives, but they shouldn't have to write an autobiography or a biography in every grade. Children can write a chapter autobiography once or twice and several biographies in connection with science and social studies themes.

Can I use stories such as *Sarah, Plain and Tall* (MacLachlan, 1985) for biographical writing?

The book you mentioned is a story, not a biography, so it shouldn't be used as an example of biographical writing. Like biographies, however, the story focuses on the main character, and the main character might even be based on a real person. The line between historical fiction and biography can sometimes be fuzzy, but biographies are written about people who actually lived, and the events described in them really happened and have been researched, not invented, by the author.

I don't have my students write autobiographies because they aren't middle class. Many of them are homeless. Others have parents who are in jail or deal in drugs. They don't have anything good to write about. What do you think?

It's important to be sensitive to your students and their family life; however, all children have some experiences they could share in an autobiography. However, if you don't think it's appropriate for your students, have them use other genres instead.

I like the idea of having my fourth graders write biographies or autobiographies, but do you have any ideas other than written books?

Sure! Writing an autobiography or biography is just one of many ways of presenting biographical information. After your students collect information, they can make life boxes, draw life lines, or make biography posters.

Chapter 8
Expository Writing

Preview

Purpose Children use expository writing to learn and to share information.

Audience Expository writing is often done for a wide, unknown audience. Reports in book format can be placed in the school library. Information presented on posters, in diagrams, and on other charts can be displayed in the hallways of the school or in the community.

Forms The forms include reports, "All About . . ." books, ABC books, riddles, posters, diagrams, charts, and multigenre projects. Children can also incorporate information into stories and poems that they write.

Fifth Graders Write Guide Books

As part of their unit on pioneers, Mr. Garcia's fifth-grade class is playing *The Oregon Trail* (1997), a CD-ROM simulation game, on the computers in the classroom. Children play in small-group teams, assuming the role of pioneers and traveling 2,000 miles from Independence, Missouri, to the Willamette Valley in Oregon in 1848. As they play the game, Mr. Garcia's students learn about the geography of the Oregon Trail, dangers that the pioneers faced along the way, and how the pioneers solved problems. They make decisions about their travel, and the computer generates a trail log with their decisions and important events.

Tyler, Luz, Marianne, Stacy, and George form one team; they call themselves the "Oregon or Bust" team. They choose to begin their simulated journey on April 1, 1848, and buy supplies, including 5 oxen, 500 bullets, and 250 pounds of food. Four days later, they reach the Kansas River and hire a ferry to take their wagon across. As they travel to Fort Laramie and then to Independence Rock, one member of their team dies from a snakebite and another breaks an arm. Periodically they run short of food and have to hunt deer, rabbits, and buffalo. They get lost twice and deal with not having grass for the oxen to eat. They travel past the Grande Ronde in the Blue Mountains, Fort Boise, The Dalles, and then reach the Columbia River. After resting for several days, the remaining members of the team decide to raft down the Columbia River. The river is treacherous, but at first the team navigates it well. Then disaster strikes: Their wagon falls off the raft and into the river, and all but one person is drowned. At the end of the game, that person reaches the Willamette Valley safely on August 5, 1848.

The teams take turns using the three computers in the classroom to play the simulation game, and the children who have completed the game are involved in a variety of related activities: They make maps of their journey, read books from a text set about pioneer life, write letters home from some point on the trail, work on a classroom display of trail life, and create a simulated journal using information from the game's trail log. Here are four entries from the "Oregon or Bust" team's collaborative journal:

April 1, 1848
Dear Diary,
Today we left Independence, Missouri, for the Oregon Trail. It was sad when we had to say good-bye to our families. We may never see them again, but we really want to go west because we are adventurers. We have lots of supplies. We have 5 oxen, 5 sets of clothing, 500 bullets (in case we get in a fight with the Indians), 2 wagon wheels, 2 wagon axles, 1 wagon tongue, 250 pounds of food, and more than $900. We are strong and healthy and young. We want to make it to Oregon by October before the snows begin.

May 17, 1848
Dear Diary,
Life on the trail is very hard now. Everyone is too tired to sing or dance. We have been out of water until we thought we would go crazy and die. There was no water for us or for the animals. Now we have reached Fort Bridger and we drank and drank lots of water. We rested for two days and drank lots more water. We used some of our money to buy more food at the store in the fort. Now we have decided to continue.

August 3, 1848
Dear Diary,
Today we are resting beside the Columbia River. It is a great and dangerous river. We want to be strong before we raft down it to the Willamette Valley. We think it will take us three days to reach Oregon. We have talked to lots of people here to get advice about how to travel on the river. It will be very dangerous because there are rocks and broken wagons and other stuff in the river. There are still four of us who are alive on this wagon. We are sure that we will make it to Oregon now.

August 5, 1848
Dear Diary,
It's just me, Stacy, now. I am alive and I made it to the Willamette Valley. It was terrible on the Columbia River. We were doing fine and then what happened is that the side of our raft hit a rock and it turned over. All the oxen drowned real fast. We tried to swim to shore but I was the only good swimmer. When I got to shore, I tried to look for them but I couldn't find them. I saw some pioneers on another raft and they came to the shore and picked me up. They let me go with them. I'm happy for me but I am sad for my friends.

After all teams complete their journey on the Oregon Trail, they have a class meeting to share their experiences. Each team recounts its trip and whether everyone on the team survived to reach Oregon. Children talk about the decisions they made, what they learned, and how they would play the game differently next time.

Mr. Garcia smiles as he listens to them talk knowledgeably about the Oregon Trail; they have learned so much. Now they are ready to write reports, which is one of the language arts standards for fifth-grade level in Mr. Garcia's district. He has planned an innovative expository writing project: guidebooks for pioneers who travel the Oregon Trail. "I know what we should do next," Mr. Garcia explains. "You've learned so much about the Oregon Trail, I think you'd really enjoy writing a guidebook for pioneers who travel on the Oregon Trail. You could write the most important information that you've learned about life on the trail."

Mr. Garcia's enthusiasm is contagious, and his students agree eagerly. "We could share these guides with the other fifth-grade classes before they play *The Oregon Trail*. And you could give the guides to your students to read before they play the game next year," the children suggest.

The children are eager to share what they have learned, and Mr. Garcia reviews the form, purpose, and audience for this project. They will fold two sheets of paper in half and staple them together to make a guidebook. He shows them several travel guidebooks from his trip to Europe a few years ago. After examining the guides, the class brainstorms these topics that they might include in their guides:

- Map of the Oregon Trail
- Lists of supplies to bring
- Information about the dangers
- Advice about how to pack a covered wagon, how to caulk a wagon to cross a river, how to find the trail when you get lost, and how to hunt for food
- Directions for medical emergencies
- A calendar showing the best months to travel the Oregon Trail
- Questions and answers
- Quotes from pioneers who made the trip

Mr. Garcia explains that each team will create one guidebook, and children can choose topics from this list or think of other important information to include in their guides. The children use the writing process to create their guidebooks. They create rough draft guides and share them with Mr. Garcia. Some teams write the guides by hand, and others use the computers in the classroom for some or all of their guidebooks. They revise and edit their guides, draw the illustrations, and make the final copies of the guidebooks. Then each team shares its guide with the class. Two pages from the "Oregon or Bust" team's guide are shown on the next page; one page shows the cover, and the other presents information about food.

Mr. Garcia also develops a rubric with the children soon after they begin creating their guides. As a class, they decide which qualities the guides should exemplify: useful and interesting information, attention-getting design, historically accurate and technical vocabulary, mechanical correctness, and illustrations that support and extend the text. Mr. Garcia divides a sheet of butcher paper into six rows and five columns. In the top row, he writes the scores 1 (Poor) to 4 (Great), and down the left column, he writes labels for the five qualities the class has identified, as shown in the box on page 170. Then Mr. Garcia and the class talk about the characteristics of each of the five qualities and choose descriptors to complete the rubric. With this information, the children are better able to create quality guides.

Shared Writing: Two Pages From a Collaborative Guide on the Oregon Trail

Guide for Pioneers On the Oregon Trail

DON'T LEAVE HOME WITHOUT THIS BOOK!

**Written by Pioneers Who Know First Hand
The Hardships of the Trail**

Food

You must take lots of food with you. Take food that does not spoil quickly because if the food is spoiled you have to throw it away. Never eat spoiled food or you will get sick or die! You can only do three things to get more food on the Oregon Trail:

1. **You can hunt for food. You will need bullets so that you can hunt for deer, birds, rabbits, and buffalo. Don't be greedy because you can only carry some food like one deer back to your wagon. Remember that the food you hunt is perishable. It will spoil fast.**

2. **You can buy food at the forts. You need money to buy food. The food at the fort is not perishable but you might get sick of eating it.**

3. **You can trade for food, but you must have something that Indians or pioneers want or no one will trade with you.**

Rubric for Assessing Fifth Graders' Oregon Trail Guides

	1 Poor	2 Satisfactory	3 Good	4 Great
Information	Little information or incorrect information	Some useful information and no incorrect information	More useful information	Lots of very detailed and useful information
Design of the guide	Confusing arrangement and no headings	Organized into sections with some headings	Attractive organization with headings for every section	Attention-getting organization and headings make it easy to read
Vocabulary and style	No special words and hard to read	A few special words	More special words and easy to read	Lots of special words and interesting to read
Mechanics • spelling • capitals • punctuation	Many errors	Some errors	A few errors	No errors
Illustrations	No pictures, or pictures aren't related to the Oregon Trail	A few pictures or charts	Useful pictures and charts	Very detailed pictures and charts

Instructional Overview: Expository Writing	
Grades	**Goals and Activities**
Kindergarten–Grade 2	**Goal 1: Recognize and use the description, sequence, and comparison structures** • Children notice examples of the structures when reading. • Children record information in graphic organizers. • Children use the structures to organize their writing. • Children use the cue words that signal the structure.
	• **Goal 2: Share information they have learned in reports** • Children write "All About . . ." books. • Children write class collaborative reports. • Children write riddles. • Children make posters, diagrams, and charts.
Grades 3–5	**Goal 1: Recognize and use all five expository text structures** • Children notice examples of the structures when reading. • Children record information in graphic organizers. • Children use the structures to organize their writing of paragraphs and longer compositions. • Children use the cue words that signal the structure.
	• **Goal 2: Research and write reports** • Children write small-group collaborative reports. • Children write class ABC books as part of thematic units. • Children write riddles using social studies or science information they have learned. • Children make posters, diagrams, and charts. • Children write individual reports. • Children participate in developing class multigenre projects.
Grades 6–8	**Goal 1: Research and write reports** • Children write small-group collaborative reports that are structured using the expository text structures. • Children write individual reports that are structured using the expository text structures. • Children write cubes to explore a topic from different perspectives. • Children report information in diagrams and charts.
	• **Goal 2: Create multigenre projects** • Children explore a topic by writing, using several genres. • Children use three or more genres and graphics to create a multigenre project on a poster or in a book.

xpository writing is factual; its purpose is to convey information about the world (Duke & Bennett-Armistead, 2003). The information might be an explanation of the importance of recycling, the steps of how a bill becomes a law, a comparison of Islam and Christianity, or a description of the struggles facing pioneers traveling on the Oregon Trail. James Britton (1970a) explains that this type of writing is intended "to interact with people and things and to make the wheels of the world, for good or ill, go round" (p. 8).

Too often, teachers assume that children are more comfortable writing stories instead of nonfiction, but researchers, including Tom Newkirk (1989), have provided compelling evidence that children, even those in kindergarten and first grade, can write expository text. Other researchers have reported that through instruction and reading and writing experiences, children grow in their ability to differentiate among genres (Donovan, 2001; Kamberelis, 1998). The Instructional Overview on page 171 lists the goals and activities for expository writing in kindergarten through eighth grade.

Expository Text Structures

Writers organize different kinds of writing in different ways. When they write to share information, writers use expository patterns or text structures. In each pattern, information is organized in a particular way, and words often signal the structure. Five of the most commonly used patterns are *description, sequence, comparison, cause and effect,* and *problem and solution* (Harvey, 1998; Robb, 2003).

Description

Writers describe a topic by listing characteristics, features, and examples. Phrases such as *for example* and *characteristics are* cue this structure. When children delineate any topic, such as cobras, the planet Jupiter, and Russia, they use description.

Sequence

Writers list items or events in numerical or chronological order. Words that signal the sequence structure include *first, second, third, next, then,* and *finally.* Children use this structure when they write directions for completing a math problem, steps in the life cycle of a plant or animal, or events in a biography.

Comparison

Writers explain how two or more things are alike or how they are different. *Different, in contrast, alike, same as,* and *on the other hand* are words and phrases that signal this structure. When children compare and contrast book and movie versions of a story, insects with spiders, or life in colonial America with life today, they use this organizational pattern.

Cause and Effect

Writers explain one or more causes and the resulting effects. *Reasons why, if . . . then, as a result, therefore,* and *because* are words and phrases that signal this structure. Children write explanations of why the dinosaurs became extinct, the effects of pollution on the environment, or the causes of the American Revolution using the cause-and-effect pattern.

Problem and Solution

Writers state a problem and provide one or more solutions. A variation is the question-and-answer format, in which the writer poses a question and then answers it. Cue words and phrases include *the problem is, the puzzle is, solve,* and *question . . . answer.* When children write about why money was invented, saving endangered animals, and building dams to stop flooding, they use this structure.

Reading researchers identified these five patterns by examining content-area reading materials to devise ways to help children comprehend those materials more easily. Most of the research on expository text structures has focused on older children's use of these patterns in reading; however, young children also use the patterns and cue words in their writing.

How Children Apply the Patterns

Just as children develop a concept of story and learn specific information about story structures, they learn about the organization of informational books and apply what they have learned as they write about information. A class of second graders examined the five expository text structures and learned that authors use cue words as a "secret code" to signal the structures. They read informational books exemplifying each of the expository text structures, and after reading, they wrote paragraphs to share what they had learned. Working in small groups, they developed graphic organizers and added main ideas and details from their reading. Then they wrote paragraphs modeling each of the five organizational patterns. These graphic organizers and paragraphs are presented in Figure 8–1. The cue words in each paragraph are underlined. The minilesson feature on page 177 shows how an eighth-grade teacher used the sequence structure in a minilesson about writing instructions.

Types of Expository Writing

Contrary to the popular assumption that young children's first writing is narrative, researchers have found that kindergartners and first graders write many nonnarrative compositions in which they provide information about familiar topics, such as "All About Swimming Lessons," or write directions for familiar activities, such as "How to Bake Cookies" (Duke & Bennett-Armistead, 2003; Harvey, 1998; Robb, 2004). Children in the middle grades continue to use expository writing to write summaries and to search for answers to questions that interest them. Through early, successful experiences with expository writing, children not only learn how to write reports but also gain knowledge in different subject areas.

"All About . . . " Books

Young children write entire booklets on a single topic; these small booklets are known as "All About . . . " books. Usually one piece of information is presented on each page. An example of an "All About . . . " book is presented in Figure 8–2. First grader David wrote an "All About . . . " book about sea animals as a part of a unit on the sea. Notice that he numbered each page of his book, 1 through 4, in the upper right corner of the page. Then he added a cover, and after a minute of confusion,

Figure 8–1 Second Graders' Graphic Organizers and Paragraphs Illustrating the Five Expository Text Structures

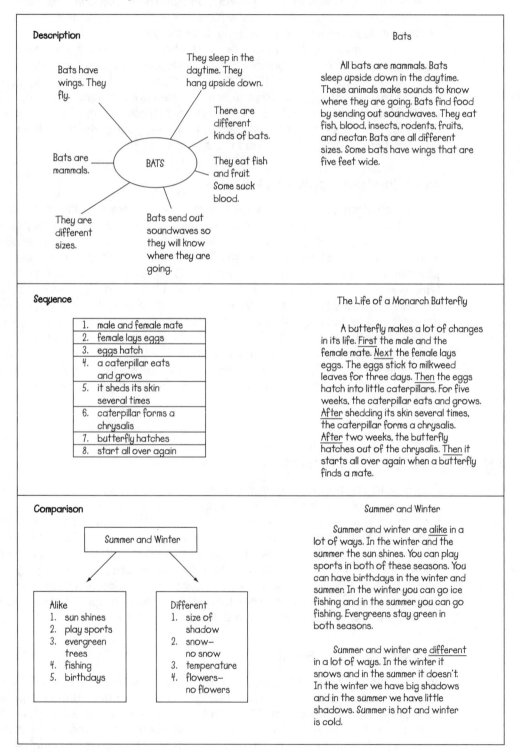

Figure 8–1 (*Continued*)

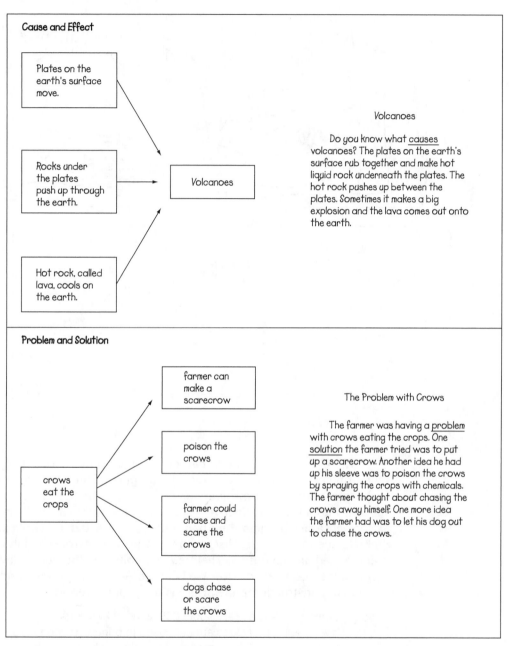

he added a zero to the cover so that each page would be numbered. David used invented spelling for many words, but the information can be deciphered easily. Also, on page 1, David was experimenting with word boundaries and chose to use a dot to mark the division between words that he recognized as separate; he considered "The dolphin" and "swim fast" as single units. When he wrote other pages, David's attention changed and he focused on other dimensions of writing.

Figure 8–2 Independent Writing: A First Grader's "All About . . ." Book

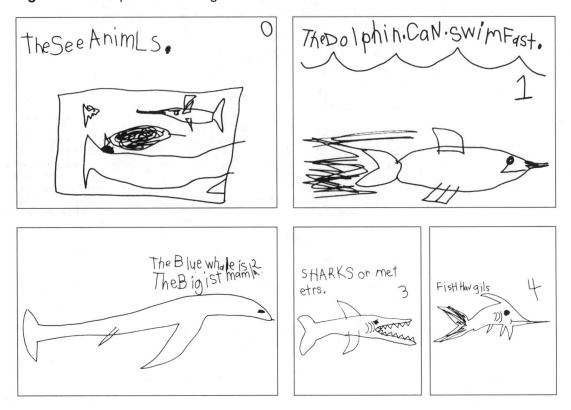

An "All About . . . " book can be a collaborative production in which each child contributes one page. For example, as part of the unit on insects, primary-grade children collected some ladybugs to observe in the classroom and read several books about these distinctive insects. Then, working in small groups, children brainstormed a list of facts they had learned about ladybugs. Next, the children each chose one fact from the list for their page. They wrote the information interactively and added an illustration. Their teacher collected the pages, included a sheet at the end of the book called "How We Learned About Ladybugs," and then added a cover made of construction paper. Here is the group's report:

Page 1: There are about 600 kinds of ladybugs.
Page 2: Ladybugs are supposed to bring you good luck.
Page 3: Ladybugs pretend to be dead when frightened.
Page 4: Ladybugs like the rain.
Page 5: Ladybugs spend the winter in pinecones, cracks, under leaves, and even in houses sleeping and waiting for spring.
Page 6: Ladybugs don't bite!
Page 7: How We Learned about Ladybugs:
   1. We watched three ladybugs that we kept in a jar in our classroom.
   2. We read these books: *Insects* by Illa Podendorf, 1981. *Ladybug, Ladybug, Fly Away Home* by Judy Hawes, 1967.

Writing Instructions

Mr. LeBeau's eighth graders are learning to write instructions in preparation for his district's quarterly writing assessment. The students began by examining instructions on food packages, games, and household appliances and identifying the characteristics of clear, well-sequenced instructions. Next, they wrote instructions for making a peanut butter and jelly sandwich, and their classmates tried to follow the instructions to actually make a sandwich. Afterward, they revised their instructions to make them clearer. The purpose of today's minilesson is for the students to use the district's rubric for technical writing to assess the sandwich-making instructions written by students in another of Mr. LeBeau's classes.

1. Introduce the topic

Mr. LeBeau explains that he has made copies of five students' sandwich-making instructions that he wants them to read and assess. (The students' names were covered before the copies were made.)

2. Share examples

Mr. LeBeau passes out copies of two students' papers and asks the students to read the papers and compare them. The students discuss the papers and agree that the second one is stronger because the instructions are more concise and easier to follow. Then he passes out a third paper for the students to read and compare to the other two. This paper, the students conclude, is even better than the other two because the student has used spatial detail words, such as *underneath* and *top*.

3. Provide information

The teacher passes out copies of the district's 4-point technical writing rubric, which the students use to score the three papers; one paper is ranked a 2, the second a 3, and the third a 4. The students provide reasons for ranking each paper as they did.

4. Guide practice

Students divide into groups of two to read and assess two more student papers; they score one paper as a 2 and the other as a 3 and give reasons to support their scores. Next, Mr. LeBeau asks students how they might revise these papers to improve the scores.

5. Assess learning

Students use the rubric to self-assess their compositions and then make revisions if they do not score at least a 3, because a score of 3 is considered "on grade level." Later, Mr. LeBeau conferences with students to discuss their rankings.

MINILESSON

Collaborative Reports

Small groups of children work together to write collaborative reports. Each child writes a section, and then they compile their sections to form the report. Children benefit from writing a group report, first, because the group provides a support system, and second, because group members share the laborious parts of the work.

A group of four fourth graders wrote a collaborative report on hermit crabs. These children sat together at a table and watched the hermit crabs that lived in a terrarium on their table. They cared for these crustaceans for 2 weeks and recorded their observations in learning logs. After this period, the children were bursting with questions about the hermit crabs and were eager for answers: They wanted to know what the crabs' real habitat was, what the best habitat was for them in the classroom, how they breathed air, why they lived in borrowed shells, why one pincer was bigger than the other, and so on. Their teacher gave some answers and directed them to books that would provide additional information. As they collected information, the children created a cluster that they taped to their table next to the terrarium. Soon the cluster wasn't an adequate way to report information, so they decided to share their knowledge by writing a book they called "The Encyclopedia About Hermit Crabs." This book is presented in Figure 8–3.

The children decided to share the work of writing the book, and they chose four main ideas, one for each child to write: what hermit crabs look like, how they act, where they live, and what they eat. One child wrote each section and then returned to the group to share the rough draft. The children gave each other suggestions for revisions. Next, they edited their report with the teacher and added an introduction, a conclusion, and a bibliography. Finally, they recopied their report and added

Figure 8–3 Shared Writing: Fourth Graders' Collaborative Report on Hermit Crabs

---

The Encyclopedia About Hermit Crabs

How They Look
Hermit crabs are very much like regular crabs but hermit crabs transfer shells. They have gills. Why? Because they are born in water and when they mature they come to land and kill snails so they can have a shell. They have two beady eyes that look like they are on stilts. Their body is a sight! Their shell looks like a rock. Really it is an exoskeleton which means the skeleton is on the outside. They have two pincers. The left one is bigger so it is used for defense. The right one is for feeding. They also have ten legs.

Where They Live
Hermit crabs live mostly on beaches in Florida where the weather is 65°–90°. They live in fresh water. They like humid weather and places that have sand, wood, and rocks (for climbing on). The best time to catch hermit crabs is a low tide.

What They Eat
Hermit crabs are omnivorous scavengers which means they eat just about anything. They even eat leftovers.

How They Act
Hermit crabs are very unusual. They go back into their shell if they think there is danger. They are funny because they walk sideways, forwards, and backwards. They can go in circles. They can also get up when they get upside down. And that's how they act.

Preparing for Writing Tests

Summary

Summaries are shorter, condensed versions of a text that maintain the integrity of the original. They present a clear and accurate overview of a text. Writing a summary requires a thorough understanding of the text's message and the ability to paraphrase—that is, to rewrite something using different words without changing the original meaning. Summaries vary in length, depending on the length of the original text and its purpose, but as a rule of thumb, they're approximately one fourth of the length of the original source. In some state writing assessments, however, students are asked to paraphrase rather than summarize a text. Paraphrased texts are almost as long as the original text.

What Do Writers Do?

- Read the text several times, making notes on the text, if possible
- Cite the title, author, and source, if it's known
- Clearly articulate the main ideas
- Include the most important details that support the main ideas
- Show relationships among the ideas
- Arrange the information in the same order as in the original text
- Use their own words in writing the summary
- Stay true to the tone of the original text
- Remain objective without inserting personal ideas and opinions

What Mistakes Do Writers Make?

- Don't follow order of information in the original text
- Include nonessential information
- Incorporate quotes from the original text
- Share personal knowledge or opinions

Sample Prompts

- Read the informational article on the moon. After reading it, write a summary of what you have read. Make sure that you state the main ideas of the article and identify important details that support the main ideas.
- Read the selection "Why Do Kids Smoke?" Read it several times, and be sure to think about the main ideas as you read. You may take notes to help you remember the main ideas and important details. Then write a summary of the selection.

illustrations in a clothbound book that they read to each class in the school before placing it in the school library.

Individual Reports

Laura Robb (2004) and Tony Stead (2002) recommend that children do authentic research in which they explore topics that interest them or hunt for answers to

How to Address Struggling Writers' Problems

The Problem	The composition is plagiarized.
What Causes It	When children don't know how to write a report or other composition or if they run out of time, they may resort to copying directly from reference books or Internet sites.
How to Solve It	*Quick fix:* Work with children to create a graphic organizer with information for the composition and next write a rough draft together using information from the organizer. Then have children continue through the revising, editing, and publishing stages of the writing process. Also, have children turn in graphic organizers and rough drafts with revisions and editing corrections marked on them along with their final compositions to provide evidence that they developed their compositions themselves.
	Long-term solution: Teach children in a series of minilessons how to make graphic organizers, take notes, and develop original compositions using the notes. In addition, teachers write a class collaboration composition to demonstrate how to use graphic organizers and note cards before children write individual compositions.
How to Prevent the Problem	Children who write at school are less likely to plagiarize than children who complete assigned writing projects at home because teachers provide support and assistance, and children are less likely to run out of time.

questions that puzzle them. As children become immersed in thematic units, questions arise that they want to explore. For example, students in a fourth-grade class were studying dinosaurs, and they quickly asked more questions than the teacher could answer. She encouraged them to search for answers in the books they had checked out of the school library. As they located answers to their questions, the children were eager to share their new knowledge and decided to write reports and publish them as books.

ABC Books

Children can use the letters of the alphabet to organize the information they want to share in an ABC (or alphabet) book. These report books incorporate the sequence structure because the pages are arranged in alphabetical order. ABC books such as *A Is for America* (Scillian, 2001), *The Living Rain Forest: An Animal Alphabet* (Kratter, 2004), and *Alpha Bravo Charlie: The Military Alphabet* (Demarest, 2005) can be used as models. Children begin by brainstorming information related to the topic being studied and identify a word or fact for each letter of the alphabet. Then they work individually, in pairs, or in small groups to compose pages for the book. The format for the pages is similar to the one used in ABC books by professional authors: Children write the letter in one corner of the page, draw an illustration, and write a sentence or paragraph to describe the word or fact. The text usually begins "_____ is for _____," and then a sentence or paragraph description follows. The *H* page from a sixth-grade class's ABC book is presented in Figure 8–4.

Riddles

Children can compose riddles to share information they have discovered. Riddles use a question-and-answer format and incorporate two or three facts, or clues, in the question part. Sometimes the answer is written upside down on the page, on the back of the page with the question, or on the next page of a book. The writing process is important for creating riddles, and during the revising stage, children make sure they have provided essential descriptive information and that the information is correct.

Small groups of children or the whole class can compose books of riddles related to social studies or science themes. During a study of life in the desert, first graders wrote these riddles as part of a class book:

I live in underground cities of tunnels.
I get my name from my barking cry.
I eat grass and other plants.
What am I? (a prairie dog)

I fly in wide circles above the earth.
I sometimes am called a buzzard.
What am I? (a vulture)

Figure 8–4 Guided Writing: A Page From a Sixth-Grade ABC Book on Ancient Egypt

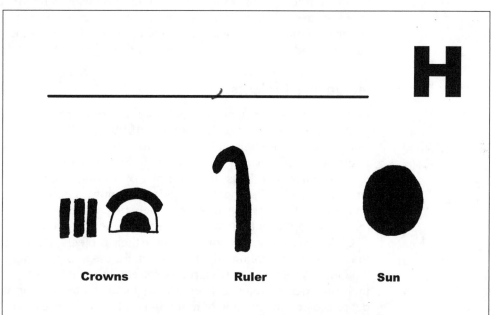

Crowns   **Ruler**   **Sun**

H is for hieroglyphics which is how the Ancient Egyptians wrote. Hieroglyphics aren't real letters, but they are more like picture symbols. All together there are more than 700 hieroglyphics. Scribes in Ancient Egypt used hieroglyphics to write religious books and royal documents. They wrote on papyrus. They used pens made of sharpened reeds and made ink using soot and water for their writing. Modern people couldn't read hieroglyphics until Jean Champollion discovered the Rosetta Stone in 1822.

Cubes

A cube has six sides, and in this expository writing activity, children explore a topic from six dimensions or sides by doing the following:

Describe it. Describe its colors, shapes, and sizes.
Compare it. What is it similar to or different from?
Associate it. What does it make you think of?
Analyze it. Tell how it is made or what it's composed of.
Apply it. What can you do with it? How is it used?
Argue for or against it. Take a stand and list reasons supporting it.

Almost any topic can be examined from these six dimensions, from earthquakes to the California gold rush, from eagles to the Internet, from the Great Wall of China to ancient Egypt. Figure 8–5 presents a sixth-grade class's cube on junk food that was written as part of a thematic unit on nutrition.

Children often work together in small groups to do a cube. They divide into six groups, and each group examines the topic from one dimension. Together, they develop a paragraph or two to explore their dimension. Children brainstorm ideas, use the ideas to develop a paragraph or two, revise, and edit. Then one child in the group writes the final copy. All six groups share their writing with the class. The final copies can be taped to a large square box and displayed in the classroom.

Multigenre Projects

Children explore a science or social studies topic through several genres in a multigenre project (Allen, 2001; Romano, 1995, 2000), combining content-area study with writing in meaningful ways. Tom Romano (2000) explains that each genre offers ways of learning and understanding that the others do not. Children gain different understandings, for example, by writing a simulated journal entry and by writing a riddle. Teachers or children identify a repetend, a common thread or unifying feature for the project, which helps children move beyond the level of remembering facts to a deeper, more analytical or critical comprehension level.

Children use a variety of genres for their projects, depending on the information they want to present and their repetend. Figure 8–6 presents a list of genres, including clusters, reports, poems, maps, letters, and data charts, that children can use in their multigenre projects. They usually incorporate three or more genres in a multigenre project and include both textual and visual genres. What matters most is that the genres amplify and extend the repetend.

The design of a third-grade class's multigenre project on honeybees is presented in Figure 8–7. The class studied bees as part of an agriculture unit, and they learned how the insects help farmers pollinate crops. The multigenre project included these textual and visual genres:

Collage. Children created a collage of honeybee words and pictures cut from magazines, and the title was printed over the collage.

Figure 8–5 Guided Writing: A Sixth-Grade Collaborative Cubing on Junk Food

Junk Food

1. Describe it

Junk food is delicious! Some junk food is made of chocolate, like chocolate ice cream and brownies. Some junk food is salty, like potato chips and pretzels. Other junk food is usually sweet or sugary, like sugar cookies, sweet rolls, or soft drinks. Junk food packages are colorful and often show you what's inside to get your attention. Most of the packages are made of paper or plastic, and they make crinkly sounds.

2. Compare it

Junk food tastes better than nutritious food, but nutritious food is better for you. Nutritious food is less sweet and salty. Parents would rather you eat nutritious food than junk food because nutritious food keeps you healthy, but kids would rather eat junk food because it tastes better and is more fun to eat.

3. Associate it

Most often you eat junk food at get-togethers with friends. At parties, junk food such as chips and dip and soft drinks are served. At movies, you can buy popcorn, candy, nachos, and many other kinds of junk food. Other places where people get together and eat junk food are skating rinks, sporting events, and concerts.

4. Analyze it

Junk food is not good to eat because of all the oils, sugar, salt, and calories. Most of them have artificial colorings and flavorings. Many junk foods are low in vitamins and protein, but they have a high percentage of fats.

5. Apply it

The most important thing you can do with junk food is to eat it. Some other uses are popcorn decorations at Christmas time, Halloween treats, and Easter candy. You can sell it to raise money for charities, clubs, and schools. Last year we sold junk food to raise money for the Statue of Liberty.

6. Argue for or against it

We're for junk food because it tastes good. Even though it's not good for you, people like it and buy it. If there were no more junk food, a lot of people would be unemployed, such as dentists. Bakeries, convenience stores, fast food restaurants, grocery stores, and ice cream parlors would lose a lot of business if people didn't buy junk food. The Declaration of Independence guarantees our rights and freedoms, and Thomas Jefferson might have said, "Life, Liberty, and the Pursuit of Junk Food." We believe that he who wants something pleasing shall have it!

From "Rx for Writer's Block," by G. E. Tompkins and D. J. Camp, 1988, *Childhood Education, 64*, p. 213. Copyright © 1988 by the Association for Childhood Education International. Reprinted with permission.

Figure 8–6 Genres for Multigenre Projects

Genre	Description
Acrostics	Children spell a key word vertically and then write a phrase or sentence beginning with each letter to create a poem or other composition.
Biographical sketches	Children write a biographical sketch of a person related to the topic being studied.
Cartoons	Children draw a cartoon or copy a published cartoon from a book or Internet article.
Charts	Children organize and display textual and visual information on a chart.
Clusters	Children draw clusters or other diagrams to display information concisely.
Cubes	Children examine a topic from six perspectives.
Data charts	Children create a data chart to list and compare information.
Found poems	Children collect words and phrases from a book or article and arrange the words and phrases to make a poem.
"I am" poems	Children create an "I am" poem about a person or a topic.
Letters	Children write simulated letters or make copies of real letters related to the topic.
Life lines	Children draw life lines and mark important dates related to a person's life.
Maps	Children make copies of actual maps or draw maps related to the topic.
Newspaper articles	Children make copies of actual newspaper articles or write simulated articles related to the topic.
Open-mind portraits	Children draw open-mind portraits of people related to the topic.
Photos	Children download photos from the Internet.
Postcards	Children create picture postcards about the topic.
Questions-answers	Children write a series of questions and answers related to the topic.
Quotes	Children collect quotes about the topic from materials they are reading.
Riddles	Children write riddles with information related to the topic.
Simulated journals	Children write simulated-journal entries from the viewpoint of a person related to the topic.
Songs	Children write lyrics about the topic that are sung to familiar tunes.
Stories	Children write stories related to the topic.
Summaries	Children paraphrase main ideas from books they've read.
Time lines	Children draw time lines to sequence events related to the topic.
Venn diagrams	Children draw Venn diagrams to compare the topic with something else.
Word wall	Children make an alphabetized word wall or word cards of key words related to the topic.

True or False Flip Books. Children used facts on the K-W-L chart to write flip books with true or false statements about honeybees. The statement is written on the first page and the answer on the second page. For example:

> First page: Bees do not communicate.
> Second page: False. Bees communicate by dancing.

Figure 8–7 The Design of a Third-Grade Class's Multigenre Project

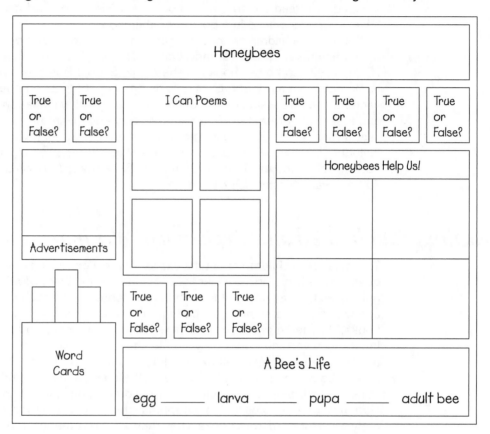

Advertisements. Third graders wrote advertisements from the viewpoint of a farmer who needs bees to pollinate the crops or from the viewpoint of a bee who offers the colony's services to farmers.

"I Can" Poems. Children assumed the role of a queen, drone, or worker bee and wrote a poem from that bee's viewpoint. For example:

> I am a busy worker bee.
> I gather food for the colony.
> I build combs with wax from my body.
> I defend the hive from our enemies.
> I am a brave worker bee.

Honeybees Help Us! Chart. Children drew pictures of four ways honeybees help people and wrote paragraph-long explanations to accompany the pictures.

Word Cards. Third graders wrote key vocabulary words on word cards, including *pollinate, drone, migrate, hive, communicate, comb, metamorphosis,* and *swarm,* and then drew and wrote definitions.

Life Line. Children drew a bee's life cycle, showing the stages that bees move through during the first 21 days of their lives from egg to adult.

The teacher displayed the multigenre project in the classroom, and the children often stopped to reread the true-false booklets, review the word cards, and look at the advertisements placed in a pocket on the chart.

Not only do children create multigenre projects; some authors/illustrators also use the technique in children's trade books. *The Magic School Bus on the Ocean Floor* (Cole, 1992) and other books in the Magic School Bus series are examples. Each book features a story about Ms. Frizzle and her students on a fantastic science adventure, and on the side panels of pages, a variety of explanations, charts, diagrams, and essays are presented. Together, the story and the informational side panels present a more complete, multigenre presentation or project. Other multigenre books include *Chocolate: A Sweet History* (Markle, 2005), *Nothing But the Truth* (Avi, 1991), *Regarding the Trees: A Splintered Saga Rooted in Secrets* (Klise, 2005), and *To Be a Slave* (Lester, 1998).

Teaching Children About Expository Writing

Teachers teach children about the expository text genre and how to write reports and other expository forms. Duke and Bennett-Armistead (2003) offer these three guidelines for teaching children about the genre. First, teachers should link reading and writing. Children need to read informational books because as they read these books, they learn about the characteristics of the genre and use the format of the books they've read when they create their own books. Second, teachers should teach children how expository text differs from other genres. As they read informational books, children identify some of the characteristics, and teachers point out others. Third, teachers should teach children about plagiarism. Children need to learn how to take notes and to paraphrase the information they've read so they won't copy word for word from books when they write summaries, reports, and other types of expository writing.

Introducing the Expository Text Structures

Teachers teach children about the expository text genre and the five structures that writers use through a series of minilessons involving both reading and writing (Robb, 2004). Children read informational books illustrating each of the five structures and identify characteristics of the genre. Figure 8–8 lists examples of books representing each structure as well as a combination of patterns. The steps in the instructional procedure are listed in the step-by-step feature on page 189.

Writing Collaborative Reports

Children learn how to write reports through a combination of minilessons and experiences writing class collaboration reports. Through the minilessons, teachers explain how to choose a topic, design research questions, use the writing process to develop and refine the report, and write a bibliography. Then children practice what they have learned as they work with partners or in small groups to write collaborative reports. Through these experiences, children gain both the expertise and the confidence to write individual reports.

Children use the writing process as they search for answers to questions about a topic and then compose a report to share what they have learned. Reports are usually

Preparing for Writing Tests

Informative Writing

Informative writing communicates facts and data to readers; writers report on events, explain ideas, analyze concepts, and develop generalizations. They use their background knowledge and experiences for informative writing, and sometimes they are asked to read a text or analyze the information presented visually and use that information to supplement their own knowledge as they write. Prompts often ask writers to write reports, instructions, reviews, and letters. The most effective informative writing is lively and engaging, showing the writer's commitment to the topic. Sometimes informative writing is confused with persuasive writing: Informative writing disseminates information; writers present facts but they don't try to persuade readers to agree with them as they do in persuasive writing.

What Do Writers Do?

- Present a thesis statement (older students only) and main ideas clearly
- Include facts, examples, illustrations, incidents, and explanations to elaborate main ideas
- Convey a feeling of knowledge and authority
- Craft an effective introduction and conclusion
- Use technical vocabulary related to the topic
- Adopt a more formal, academic writing style

What Mistakes Do Writers Make?

- Don't organize their presentation of ideas
- Include few details
- Ignore the "why" or "how" part of the prompt

Sample Prompts

- Everyone has a favorite movie. What's yours? Write a review about this movie that could be published in your school's newspaper. Be sure to explain why you like this movie.
- Think about a time of year that you really like. It could be a season, a special day, or a holiday. Write a letter to your teacher about this time of year and explain why it is special to you.
- Hunger is a problem in the world today that needs to be solved. Read the information about hunger on the next page. Then write a report explaining the problem and how people could work to solve it.

written in connection with thematic units, but some children enjoy expository writing or have special interests that they research and write about during writing workshop.

Children work with the partners or in small groups to write collaborative reports in connection with thematic units. Class collaboration reports are a good way for students to learn the steps involved in writing a report and to gain experience working through the writing process without the complexities of writing individual reports. The procedure is explained in the step-by-step feature on page 190.

Figure 8–8 Informational Books Representing the Expository Text Structures

Description

Cole, J. (2005). *Ms. Frizzle's adventures: Imperial China*. New York: Scholastic. (M)

Myers, W. D. (2004). *USS Constellation: Pride of the American Navy*. New York: Holiday House. (M–U)

Robbins, K. (2005). *Seeds*. New York: Atheneum. (P–M)

Simon, S. (2004). *Earth: Our planet in space*. New York: Simon & Schuster. (M–U)

Sequence

Goodman, S. E. (2004). *Skyscraper: From the ground up*. New York: Knopf. (P–M)

Keller, K. T. (2004). *From milk to ice cream*. Mankato, MN: Capstone. (P)

Lalicki, T. (2004). *Grierson's raid: A daring strike through the heart of the confederacy*. New York: Farrar, Straus & Giroux. (U)

Leedy, L. (2004). *Look at my book: How kids can write and illustrate terrific books*. New York: Holiday House. (M–U)

Comparison

Hollyer, B. (2004). *Let's eat! What children eat around the world*. New York: Holt. (P–M)

Markle, S. (2005). *Outside and inside mummies*. New York: Walker. (M)

Royston, A. (2003). *Magnetic and nonmagnetic*. Portsmouth, NH: Heinemann. (P–M)

Scott, E. (2004). *Poles apart*. New York: Viking. (M–U)

Cause and Effect

Branley, F. M. (2005). *Sunshine makes the seasons*. New York: HarperCollins. (P–M)

Karas, G. B. (2005). *On earth*. New York: Putnam. (M)

Meltzer, M. (2004). *Hear that train whistle blow! How the railroad changed the world*. New York: Random House. (M–U)

Pfeffer, W. (2004). *Wiggling worms at work*. New York: HarperCollins. (P–M)

Problem and Solution

Allen, T. B. (2004). *George Washington, spymaster: How the Americans outspied the British and won the Revolutionary War*. Washington, DC: National Geographic Society. (M–U)

Blumenthal, K. (2005). *Let me play: The story of Title IX, the law that changed the future of girls in America*. New York: Atheneum. (U)

Holub, J. (2004). *Why do snakes hiss: And other questions about snakes, lizards, and turtles*. New York: Dial Books. (P–M)

Skurzynski, G. (2004). *Are we alone? Scientists search for life in space*. Washington, DC: National Geographic Society. (U)

Combination

Dussling, J. (2004). *Earthquakes*. New York: Grosset & Dunlap. (M)

Giblin, J. C. (2004). *Secrets of the sphinx*. New York: Scholastic. (M–U)

Jenkins, A. (2004). *Next stop Neptune: Experiencing the solar system*. Boston: Houghton Mifflin. (M–U)

Simon, S. (2005). *Guts: Our digestive system*. New York: HarperCollins. (P–M)

P = primary grades (K–2), M = middle grades (3–5), U = upper grades (6–8)

Writing Individual Reports

Writing an individual report is similar to writing a collaborative report. Children identify questions, gather information to answer the questions, and then report what they have learned. However, writing individually makes two significant changes necessary: Children must narrow their topics and then assume the entire responsibility for writing the report. The procedure for writing individual research reports is presented in the step-by-step feature on page 192.

Step by Step: Expository Text Structures

1. ***Introduce an organizational pattern.*** Teachers explain the pattern and when writers use it, note cue words that signal the pattern, share an example of the pattern, and then describe the graphic organizer for that pattern.

2. ***Analyze examples of the pattern.*** Children locate examples of the expository text structure in informational books they are reading. Sometimes the pattern is signaled clearly using titles, topic sentences, and cue words, but sometimes it isn't. Children identify cue words when they are used, and they talk about why writers may or may not explicitly signal the structure. They also diagram the structure using a graphic organizer.

3. ***Write paragraphs using the pattern.*** Children write paragraphs using the pattern they're studying. The first writing activity may be a whole-class activity; later, children write paragraphs in small groups and individually.

4. ***Repeat for each pattern.*** Teachers repeat the first three steps as they teach children about each of the five expository text structures.

5. ***Choose the most appropriate pattern.*** Children experiment with the patterns by using different ones to write about a particular topic. Sometimes children divide into five groups, and each group uses a different expository text structure to write about the topic. As they use different patterns, children learn how to choose the appropriate one for the information they want to share.

Assessing Children's Expository Writing

Children need to know what the requirements are for the writing project and how they will be assessed. Many teachers develop a checklist or rubric with the requirements for the project and distribute this to children before they begin working. In this way, children know what is expected of them and assume responsibility for completing each step of the assignment. For an individual report, the checklist might include these observable behaviors and products:

- Choose a narrow topic.
- Identify four or five questions.
- Gather and organize information to answer the questions.
- Write a rough draft with a section (or chapter) to answer each question.
- Meet in writing groups to share your report.
- Make at least three changes in your rough draft.
- Complete an editing checklist with a partner.
- Add a bibliography.
- Write the final copy of the report.

This checklist can be made simpler or more complex depending on children's age and experiences. Figure 8–9 shows two assessment checklists for expository writing projects. The first is a checklist for a second grader's report poster on an insect, and the second is for the sixth-grade ABC book project. For both checklists, children

Step by Step: Collaborative Reports

1. ***Choose a topic.*** The teacher chooses a broad topic related to what children are studying for the collaborative research project. Almost any topic in social studies or science that can be subdivided into 4 to 10 parts works well for class reports.

2. ***Identify questions.*** As children study the topic, questions emerge. Partway through the unit, children brainstorm a list of possible questions that is posted on a chart in the classroom, and new questions are added as they're suggested. Children choose questions from this list to research.

3. ***Write one section together as a class.*** The teacher chooses a question that no one has chosen and models how to write a section of the report, demonstrating the procedures that children are to use.

4. ***Gather and organize information.*** Children work in pairs or small groups to read and find answers to their questions; these questions provide the structure for data collection. Before beginning to write, children take notes and use clusters or other graphics to organize the data they collect.

5. ***Write sections of the report.*** Children use the writing process to draft, revise, and edit their sections of the report using information they have gathered and organized. One child in the group serves as the scribe, and the other children dictate the sentences and paragraphs. Then each group shares its rough draft in a whole-class revising group and uses the feedback it receives to revise its writing. Then the children proofread their draft and correct as many mechanical errors as possible. Last, they meet with the teacher to correct any remaining errors.

6. ***Complete the report.*** The children meet as a class and write the introduction and the conclusion to the report. Next, they decide on the order for the sections of the report and make a table of contents and a cover. After all the parts are compiled, the entire report is read aloud so children can catch any inconsistencies or redundant passages. Older children also compile the bibliography at this time.

7. ***Publish the report.*** Children prepare the final copy of their sections and compile them. The introduction and conclusion are also added. Next, they add page numbers. If the report has been word processed, it is easy to print out the final copy, and the report looks very professional. Copies of the report are made for each child.

---

were involved in developing the checklists, and they received copies of the checklists at the beginning of the writing projects. They checked off the items as they worked, and then turned in the checklists with their completed projects.

Children staple the checklist to the inside cover of the folder in which they keep all the work for the project; as each requirement is completed, they check it off. In this way, children monitor their own work and learn that writing is a process, not just a final product.

When the project is completed, children submit their entire folder to the teacher to be assessed. All of the requirements on the checklist are considered in determining the grade. If the checklist has 10 requirements, each requirement might be worth

Figure 8–9 Two Assessment Checklists

Insect Poster Checklist

Name _____ Insect _____

❏ 1. Draw and color an insect.

❏ 2. Label the drawing.

❏ 3. Write 3 facts in sentences.

❏ 4. Add a title and your name.

❏ 5. Make the poster attractive.

The ABC Book Project

Name _____ Your Letter _____

As you create your page for our class ABC book on ancient Egypt, check off each item on this assessment checklist. Keep the checklist in your project folder and turn it in with your project.

____ 1. Brainstorm a list of at least three things beginning with your letter, and then choose the word for your page.

____ 2. Research your word and gather information in a cluster.

____ 3. Write a rough draft paragraph explaining the word for your page at the computer station. Begin with _____ is for _____.

____ 4. Design your page and sketch an illustration.

____ 5. Share your paragraph in writing group and revise based on feedback that you receive.

____ 6. Edit your paragraph and proofread for spelling errors.

____ 7. Print out your paragraph at the computer station.

____ 8. Add illustrations.

---

10 points, and the grading can be done objectively on a 100-point scale. Thus, if the child's project is complete with all required materials, the child scores 100 or a grade of A. Points can be subtracted for work that is sloppy or incomplete. If additional grades are necessary, each item on the checklist can be graded separately. If a quality assessment of the final copy of the research report is needed, then a second grade can be awarded.

Teachers also develop rubrics to assess the quality of children's reports, as Mr. Garcia did in the vignette at the beginning of the chapter. Sometimes teachers use general criteria about good writing to create the rubric, and at other times, they create a rubric for the specific writing project, such as the rubric for guidebooks shown on page 170.

Step by Step: Individual Reports

1. ***Choose and narrow a topic.*** Children choose topics for reports from content-area units, hobbies, or other interests. After choosing a general topic, they narrow their topic so that it is manageable. The broad topic of cats might be reduced to pet cats or tigers, for example.

2. ***Identify questions.*** Children brainstorm a list of questions for which they want to find answers. Then they review their list, combine some questions, delete others, and finally arrive at four to six questions that are worthy of answering. As they conduct their research, new questions may be added and others deleted if they reach a dead end.

3. ***Gather and organize information.*** Children read, take notes, and use clusters, data charts, or other graphics to gather and organize information.

4. ***Draft the report.*** Children write a rough draft incorporating the information they have gathered. Each research question can become a paragraph, a section, or a chapter in the report. As they draft each section of the report, children organize their writing using an appropriate text structure.

5. ***Revise and edit the report.*** Children meet in writing groups to share their rough drafts, and they make revisions based on the feedback they receive from their classmates. After they make the needed revisions, children use an editing checklist to proofread their reports and identify and correct mechanical errors.

6. ***Publish the report.*** Children recopy their reports in books and add bibliographic information.

ANSWERING TEACHERS' QUESTIONS ABOUT . . .

Expository Writing

You must be kidding! My second graders can't write reports. They still need to learn basic reading and writing skills.

The writing samples in this chapter show that second graders can write research reports. The question you seem to be asking is *why* second graders should write reports. Writing collaborative and individual reports is not frivolous! Children learn basic reading and writing skills as they develop research questions, read to find answers, and then write a report to share what they have learned. What is more basic than having children read to find answers to research questions? They apply decoding and comprehension skills as they read, searching for answers to their questions. What is more basic than having children share their findings through writing? They use the writing process to write their reports. Report writing is authentic

and meaningful, the kind of activity that promotes basic reading and writing skills.

When do I teach outlining?

Outlining is a sticking point for many writers. Because the format of an outline seems so formidable, children often write it *after* completing the report. Generally speaking, outlining isn't taught to elementary students. Instead, children should use graphic organizers to organize their writing; these forms are more effective and flexible than outlining. If you do teach outlining, have children make a cluster first and then transfer the information from the cluster to the outline. Each main idea from the cluster becomes a main idea in the outline and is marked with a roman numeral. The details are listed under the main ideas and are marked with uppercase letters. If additional details have been added, they are marked with numerals and written under the particular detail. For example, the "How they act" section of the cluster on hermit crabs presented in Figure 8–4 can be rewritten this way as an outline:

A. How they act
   1. Move sideways, backwards, and forwards
   2. Turn in circles, dig, climb, push objects
   3. Go back in shells if in danger
   4. Don't like water

Why do you insist that children, even first graders, should add a bibliography to their reports?

Children should give credit to the sources they used in their reports. Adding a bibliography lends credibility to the report and helps assure the reader that the information is accurate. Adding a bibliography to a report is not a complicated matter, even though some junior and senior high school students who have never written a report before seem overwhelmed when asked to write a bibliography—a word they often confuse with biography. In contrast, children accept the responsibility easily when it has been a natural part of report writing since kindergarten. Young children simply add a page at the end of their reports to tell everyone who reads it how they became experts about the subject and found answers to their research questions. It is sufficient if primary-grade students list only the name and author of the book. Students at each grade level gradually add more information; upper-grade students include author, title, city of publication, publisher, and copyright date for the books they reference.

Another benefit is that middle graders begin to note that the informational books they read have references, too, and they become more critical readers when they look for evidence of the accuracy of information they're reading.

I teach fifth grade, and I want my students to write reports as part of our unit on colonial life. Which type of report should I use?

You could use any of the types described in this chapter. Teachers choose the type of report depending on their students' prior experiences with expository writing, the amount of time available for the project, and their goals for the writing activity. When children haven't had many report-writing experiences, a collaborative report or ABC book might be a good choice. When time is limited, you might choose riddles or ABC books. If you want to help children think more critically about a topic or make connections to other curricular areas, cubes or charts might be a good choice. When you want children to learn to write a conventional report, individual reports are a good choice.

I think multigenre projects are a good idea for older students, but I have a kindergarten–first grade combination class. My students couldn't do them.

Many kindergarten and first-grade teachers develop multigenre projects with their classes. The children participate in a variety of writing activities, and then the teacher puts the display board or display book together using samples of the children's work. Working together as a class, young children can write reports and poems interactively, make clusters and other diagrams, and create new song lyrics. They can also work independently to draw pictures and write words and sentences.

Chapter 9
Narrative Writing

Preview

Purpose   Children use narrative writing to create both fictitious and true stories that entertain readers. A fully developed story involves a problem, which is introduced in the beginning, becomes more complicated in the middle, and is resolved at the end. Children retell familiar stories, write sequels and new episodes for favorite characters, and compose original stories.

Audience   Children write stories for classmates, their families, and other well-known and trusted audiences. They also publish their stories as books that are placed in the class library or school library.

Forms   Stories are often bound into books and may be written as class collaborations or individual stories, or as scripts for puppet shows and readers theatre.

First Graders Write Stories

"Clever trick number 4!" cries LaWanda. "That mean ol' crocodile is pretending to be a picnic bench."

"Don't worry, Trunky is going to warn the kids," replies Ashton.

The children in Ms. Dillen's first-grade classroom are listening to their teacher reread a favorite story, Roald Dahl's *The Enormous Crocodile* (1978), as part of a focus unit on the book. They eagerly listen to the crocodile's four clever (but unsuccessful) attempts to catch a fat and juicy child to eat for supper, and they join in as Ms. Dillen reads, predicting the failure of the crocodile's tricks again and again. Although many adults find Dahl's story repulsive, these first graders love it.

Shared Writing: Story Cluster for *The Enormous Crocodile*

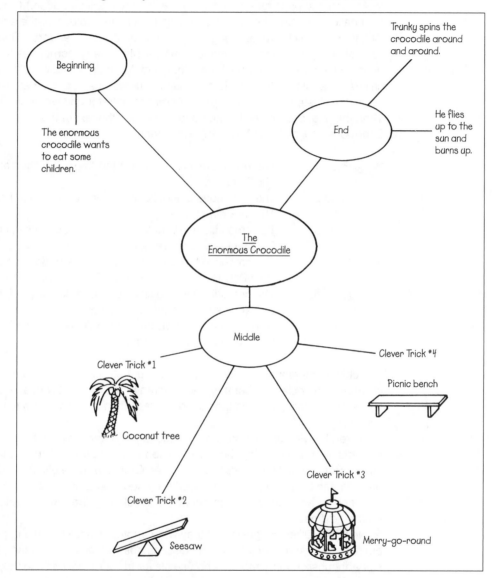

Recognizing the children's interest in this story, Ms. Dillen decides to use it to introduce her first graders to the most basic components of plot. She explains that stories have three parts: a beginning, a middle, and an end. She and the children retell the beginning, middle, and end of *The Enormous Crocodile*. Next, she draws a cluster on the chalkboard with the title of the story in a circle and three rays marked "Beginning," "Middle," and "End." The children identify the events that belong in each story part and complete the story cluster as shown on this page.

The following day, Ms. Dillen asks the children if they want to write their own version of the story in a big book (a large book made out of sheets of posterboard that the class can read together); they shout and clap their enthusiasm. Ms. Dillen begins by reviewing the story with the children, using the story cluster to organize the retelling. The children decide to write a six-page book, with one page for the beginning, one page for each of the four tricks, and one page for the end. (Later, a title page will be added.) Next, Ms. Dillen divides the chalkboard into six columns and asks the children to dictate the story; she records their dictation on the chalkboard, page by page. Then the children reread their story and suggest several changes. Using proofreaders' marks, Ms. Dillen incorporates the changes agreed upon by the class. After a final reading, the children draw and write the big book. Some children draw illustrations on large sheets of posterboard, and others write the text above or below the illustrations on each page. Another illustrator and writer create the title page. Then the pages are compiled and bound. Here is the text of their completed story, "The Enormous Crocodile in Ms. Dillen's Classroom":

Page 1:	The enormous crocodile wanted to eat the children in Ms. Dillen's class.
Page 2:	The enormous crocodile made himself look like a coconut tree. The trick didn't work.
Page 3:	The crocodile tried another trick. He made himself into a seesaw. But Muggle-Wump warned the children.
Page 4:	The crocodile turned himself into a merry-go-round. The Roly-Poly Bird warned the kids. Clever trick three didn't work!
Page 5:	The crocodile was a picnic bench. Trunky warned the children. Clever trick four did not work either.
Page 6:	Trunky spun the enormous crocodile around and around. He threw him up into the sun.

The children personalized the story by having the enormous crocodile want to eat the children in their class rather than the children in the nearby town, as Roald Dahl wrote in his version of the story, and they used the repetition of clever tricks to recall the story events.

Several days later, the children participate in other projects. Some make finger puppets to use in retelling the story. As soon as the puppets are made, they break into small groups to tell the story to each other. Others write retellings of the story, with one page for the beginning, four pages for the middle, and one page for the end. Then they add a cover and staple their completed booklets together. Barry's retelling is presented on the next page.

Next, Ms. Dillen suggests that they write another class story using clever tricks. They brainstorm a list of clever tricks and discuss possible plots. The class decides to write a story about six hungry rabbits who use clever tricks to fool a fox so they can eat the vegetables in the garden. The children decide on three clever tricks and develop a story cluster with a beginning, middle, and end. With this preparation, they dictate the story to Ms. Dillen, who records it on the chalkboard. They refine their story, and then Ms. Dillen makes copies for each child. Here is their story, "The Hungry Rabbits":

Page 1:	Once there were six rabbits. They wanted carrots and lettuce. But the fox chased the rabbits out of the garden.
Page 2:	The rabbits think of clever tricks. They tell the fox there's a deer in the forest so the fox will chase the deer instead of them. But the trick didn't work.

Independent Writing: A First Grader's Retelling of *The Enormous Crocodile*

There in The jugul. is a

Bad alugadr.

①

he can be ril Bad. he Can be a Cocunt tree.

②

and he can be. a See Suo. and wrs.

③

iI iS not a goob. ibi to be a

more go rod.

④

woj awt for The Bin. it is a alugatr.

⑤

The alugabr is ril Bad.

Help

⑥

Page 3:   The rabbits dig a hole trying to get to the garden but they didn't dig far enough. They were only by the fence.

Page 4:   Then the rabbits ran to the briar patch and jumped over it. The fox tried to jump over it but landed in it. "Ouch, ouch," cried the fox. He couldn't get out.

Page 5:   So the rabbits jumped real high over the briars and got the carrots and lettuce. And they lived happily ever after.

As the children are finishing their class story, many are already talking about clever trick stories they want to write. Ms. Dillen provides the guidelines: Like their class story, children's individual stories should have a beginning, three (or more) clever tricks in the middle, and an ending. Children stack five, six, or more pages of paper on their desks and begin to work. Some begin illustrating their stories, some begin writing, and others mark their papers with the words "beginning," "middle–1," "middle–2," "middle–3," and "end" before writing or drawing.

Eddie has his story already in mind. He quickly sets to work drawing a picture in the top half of each page. Then he writes his story, using the pictures he has drawn much as an adult uses an outline. As he writes, using a combination of invented and standard spelling, Eddie becomes more and more animated. As soon as he finishes writing, he gets construction paper for a cover and staples his storybook together. He goes over to Barry's desk to share his story with his best friend. "Hey, Bar', listen to this. You're gonna love it," he says. And Barry does. Other children crowd around to read Eddie's story, and soon Ms. Dillen moves this group of children over to the author's chair to share their stories. They clap as each story is read and offer compliments about their classmates' use of clever clues and surprise endings.

This is Eddie's story, "The Dog," written in standard spelling:

Page 1: The little dog is very, very hungry and he sees a little rabbit. He chases the rabbit but he ran too fast.

Page 2: Clever trick no. 1. The dog jumped on the rabbit's tail but the trick didn't work.

Page 3: Clever trick no. 2. He hid under the bushes and jumped out of the bush but he missed the rabbits and they ran away.

Page 4: Clever trick no. 3. The dog dressed up into a carrot and the rabbit walked by the dog and the dog ate him.

Page 5: That's the end.

Eddie's story is well developed: He established a conflict between the hungry dog and the rabbit in the beginning; in the middle, he presented three attempts to catch the rabbit; and with the third attempt, the dog is successful. Although the ending is not as elaborate as it might be, it follows the style often used in folktales (e.g., "Snip, snap, snout, this tale's told out!") and in television cartoon shows (e.g., "That's all, folks!").

The first graders in Ms. Dillen's class are learning about stories by listening to stories read aloud, examining how authors organize their stories, and writing stories themselves. Distinguished British educator Harold Rosen (1986) pleads for teachers to provide more opportunities, or "generous space," for storytelling—both oral and written—to teach children about narrative discourse, its meaning, voice, and seduction.

Children's concept of story begins in the preschool years; children as young as 2½ years of age have a rudimentary sense of story (Applebee, 1978; Pitcher & Prelinger, 1963). They acquire this concept of story gradually, first through listening

Instructional Overview: Narrative Writing	
Grades	**Goals and Activities**
Kindergarten–Grade 2	**Goal 1: Recognize the beginning-middle-end of stories and use this structure to organize stories** • Children make storybooks by drawing pictures of the beginning, middle, and end of stories. • Children write retellings of familiar stories in beginning, middle, and end parts. • Children write stories with beginning, middle, and end parts.
	Goal 2: Identify characters and settings in stories and include characters and settings in the stories children write • Children draw portraits of characters. • Children make character clusters. • Children draw setting maps and make tabletop displays of settings.
Grades 3–5	**Goal 1: Analyze the four ways authors develop characters in stories and how children use these methods in their stories** • Children examine the four ways authors develop characters. • Children make open-mind portraits. • Children create well-developed characters in the stories they write.
	Goal 2: Analyze the ways authors develop setting in stories and how children use setting in their stories • Children consider how the story would be different if the setting were different. • Children make setting maps.
	Goal 3: Analyze how authors develop plot in stories and how children use plot in their stories • Children make a plot profile as they read a novel. • Children draw story mountains.
Grades 6–8	**Goal 1: Identify explicit and implicit themes in stories** • Children make a theme cluster to explore a one-word theme (e.g., friendship). • Children write an essay to explain how the author developed a theme in a story.
	Goal 2: Identify the four points of view in stories and analyze the effect of viewpoint on the story • Children analyze the four viewpoints in stories they are reading. • Children consider how the story would differ if told from a different viewpoint.
	Goal 3: Analyze story structure • Children analyze the author's use of story structure in a familiar story. • Children analyze their use of story structure in stories they have written.

to stories read to them, later by reading stories themselves, and then by telling and writing stories. Not surprisingly, older children have a better understanding of story structure and conventions than younger children do. Similarly, the stories that older children write are increasingly more complex; plot structures are more tightly organized, and characters are more fully developed. Yet Applebee (1980) found that by the time children begin kindergarten, they have already developed a concept of what a story is, and these expectations guide them as they respond to stories and tell their own stories. For example, he found that kindergartners could use three story markers: the convention "Once upon a time . . . " to begin a story, the past tense for telling a story, and formal endings such as "The End" and "they lived happily ever after."

Most of the research examining children's understanding of story structure and conventions has been applied to reading. Children's concept of story plays an important role in their ability to comprehend the stories they read (Stein & Glenn, 1979). However, children's concept of story is equally important in writing (Golden, 1984): Just as they draw on their concept of story in reading stories, children use this knowledge in writing stories. Dressel (1990) found that children who read and discussed higher-quality stories wrote stories of greater literary quality than did children who read lesser-quality stories. A list of the goals and activities for teaching narrative writing is shown in the Instructional Overview on page 199.

Elements of Story Structure

Stories have unique structural elements that distinguish them from other genres. In fact, the structure of stories is quite complex because authors manipulate character, plot, setting, and other elements to produce interesting stories. Five elements of story structure—plot, setting, characters, theme, and point of view—are discussed in this section, with familiar and award-winning trade books used to illustrate each one.

Plot

Plot is the sequence of events involving characters in conflict situations in the beginning, middle, and end of a story. The plot is based on the goals of one or more characters (Lukens, 2006): The main character (or characters) wants to achieve a certain goal or solve a problem, and other characters try to prevent the main character from being successful. The story is put into motion as the main character attempts to overcome obstacles to reach the goal or solve the problem.

Beginning-Middle-End ■ The most basic aspect of plot is the division of the main events of a story into three parts: the beginning, the middle, and the end. (With upper-grade students, the terms often used are *introduction, development* or *complication,* and *resolution.*) In *Where the Wild Things Are* (Sendak, 1988), for instance, the three story parts can be picked out easily. As the story begins, Max plays a mischievous wolf and is sent to his room for misbehaving. In the middle, Max magically travels to the land of the wild things to become their king. Then Max feels lonely and returns home to find his supper waiting and still hot—the end of the story.

Authors include specific types of information in each part. In the beginning, they introduce the characters, describe the setting, and present a problem. The author uses the characters, setting, and events to develop the plot and sustain the theme through the story. In the middle, authors introduce conflict; they create roadblocks that keep the characters from solving their problems. How the characters deal with these obstacles adds suspense, which keeps readers interested. In the end, readers learn whether the characters' struggles are successful.

Conflict ■ *Conflict* is the tension or opposition between forces in the plot, and it is usually the element that entices readers to continue reading the story. Conflict usually takes one of four forms (Lukens, 2006):

- Conflict between a character and nature
- Conflict between a character and society
- Conflict between characters
- Conflict within a character

Conflict between a character and nature is represented in stories in which severe weather plays an important role, as in Jean Craighead George's *Julie of the Wolves* (2003), and in stories set in isolated geographic locations, such as Scott O'Dell's *Island of the Blue Dolphins* (1990), in which the Indian girl Karana struggles to survive alone on a Pacific island. In some stories, a character's activities and beliefs are different from those held by other members of the society, and these differences cause conflict. One example of this type of conflict is Elizabeth Speare's *The Witch of Blackbird Pond* (2001), in which Kit Tyler is accused of being a witch because she continues, in a New England Puritan community, activities that were acceptable in the Caribbean community where she grew up. Conflict between characters is commonly used in children's literature. In Judy Blume's *Tales of a Fourth Grade Nothing* (2003), for instance, the never-ending conflict between Peter and his little brother, Fudge, is what makes the story interesting. The fourth type of conflict is conflict within a character. In *The Puppeteer's Apprentice* (Love, 2003), for instance, a story set in medieval England, a timid orphan named Mouse escapes a miserable life and finds happiness when she learns to be a puppeteer. A list of stories representing the four types of conflict is presented in Figure 9–1.

Plot Development ■ Authors develop plot through the introduction, development, and resolution of the conflict. Plot development involves four steps:

- A problem that introduces conflict is presented in the beginning of a story.

📓 How to Address Struggling Writers' Problems

The Problem	The composition lacks an exciting lead.
What Causes It	Children often assume that a composition should be written from beginning to end, and that the lead has to be written first. However, it's often more effective if children postpone creating an exciting lead paragraph until after they've written the rest of the rough draft.
How to Solve It	*Quick fix:* During revision, have children generate several leads using a personal experience, a question, a quotation, humor, or a comparison, and then choose the best one for the composition. Children can get feedback about which lead is most effective from classmates in their writing group. *Long-term solution:* In a series of minilessons, teach children about the different types of leads and have them examine the leads in familiar stories and informational books. In addition, children can keep a list of interesting leads in their writers' notebooks or on a classroom chart.
How to Prevent the Problem	In classrooms where children do a lot of reading, they are better able to write different types of effective leads.

Figure 9–1 Stories That Illustrate the Four Types of Conflict

Conflict Between a Character and Nature

George, J. C. (2003). *Julie of the wolves*. Boston: HarperTrophy. (M–U)
Paulsen, G. (1987). *Hatchet*. New York: Bradbury Press. (M–U)
Polacco, P. (1990). *Thundercake*. New York: Philomel. (P–M)
Steig. W. (1986). *Brave Irene*. New York: Farrar, Straus & Giroux. (P–M)

Conflict Between a Character and Society

Bunting, E. (1994). *Smoky night*. San Diego: Harcourt Brace. (P–M)
Hesse, K. (2001). *Witness*. New York: Scholastic. (U)
Lowry, L. (1989). *Number the stars*. New York: Atheneum. (M–U)
Speare, E. G. (2001). *The witch of Blackbird Pond*. Boston: Houghton Mifflin. (M–U)

Conflict Between Characters

Avi. (2002). *Crispin: The cross of lead*. New York: Hyperion Books. (U)
Blume, J. (2003). *Tales of a fourth grade nothing*. New York: Puffin Books. (M)
Henkes, K. (1991). *Chrysanthemum*. New York: Greenwillow. (P)
Ives, D. (2005). *Scrib*. New York: HarperCollins. (M)

Conflict Within a Character

Naylor, P. R. (1991). *Shiloh*. New York: Atheneum. (M–U)
Ryan, P. M. (2000). *Esperanza rising*. New York: Scholastic. (M)
Taylor, T. (2002). *The cay*. New York: Yearling. (U)
Waber, B. (1972). *Ira sleeps over*. Boston: Houghton Mifflin. (P)

P = primary grades (K–2), M = middle grades (3–5), U = upper grades (6–8)

- Characters face roadblocks as they attempt to solve the problem in the middle of the story.
- The high point in the action occurs when the problem is about to be solved. This high point separates the middle and the end of the story.
- The problem is solved and the roadblocks are overcome at the end of the story.

The problem is introduced at the beginning of the story, and the main character (or characters) is faced with trying to solve it. This problem determines the conflict. Once the problem has been introduced, the author throws roadblocks in the way of an easy solution. As one roadblock is removed, another emerges to thwart the main character. Postponing the solution by introducing roadblocks is the core of plot development. Stories may contain any number of roadblocks, but children's stories typically contain three, four, or five.

The high point of the action comes when the solution of the problem hangs in the balance. Tension is high, and readers continue reading to learn whether the main characters will solve the problem. At the end of the story, the problem is solved.

Second-grade Riley wrote this animal story, "Charge!", for a district writing competition. Notice how clearly he identifies a problem in the beginning of the story and uses it to drive the plot through the middle and end:

It was a beautifully sunny day with the sun up bright 'n early. And so was the president! He was getting married! So as you probably already know, everybody else was up, too.

But the president was a worrywart, so as I'm sure you know, he was worried about what was on the front page of the newspaper. It said:

Rhino Escaped from Zoo!
1,000,000 Dollar Reward

"What if it blows down our wedding?" the president asked his future wife.

"Oh, but it won't, honey," she replied.

But she found out how wrong those very words could be. Right when he slipped the ring on her finger, the door blew down and the missing rhino (now not missing) came charging through the church. Pews were flyin', the church got shattered, and the rhino had its horn engraved in the organ, which it was shattering as well.

"Run for your lives!" someone shouted.

"Break for it!" shouted someone else.

"It's the rhino that escaped from the zoo!" shouted another.

All of the people but twelve got out. Those twelve, all mighty and strong if you hope to know, were trying to pick up the rambunctious rhino. After an hour and a half, they hauled off the mighty being. So they returned the rhino, got the million, split it up, and went home to tell the tale.

The president did the marriage again (without the rhino), and Washington had other marriages (without the rhino), and it lived happily ever after (without the rhino).

The rhino presents the conflict in this story, and it is classified as conflict between characters and nature. This story shows how even young children can create effective stories using the elements of plot structure, including conflict. This story is even more charming because of Riley's sophisticated vocabulary, expressions, and asides to the reader.

Setting

In some stories, the setting is barely sketched; this is a *backdrop setting*. In many folktales, for example, the setting is relatively unimportant, and the convention "Once upon a time . . . " is used to set the stage. In other stories, however, the setting is elaborate and is integral to the story's effectiveness; these settings are *integral settings* (Lukens, 2006). Whether the setting is important to plot and character development determines how much attention writers give to describing the setting. Some stories could take place anywhere, and the setting requires little description; others, however, require a specific setting, and authors take care to ensure the authenticity of the historical period or geographic location in which the story is set.

Of the elements of story structure, setting is the one many people feel comfortable with. Often they think that setting is simply where the story takes place. Certainly location is an important dimension of setting, but there are three other dimensions as well: weather, time, and time period.

Location ■ Location is a very important dimension of setting in many stories. The Boston Commons in *Make Way for Ducklings* (McCloskey, 1999), postwar Holland in *Boxes for Katje* (Fleming, 2003), and isolated Mount Eskel in *Princess Academy* (Hale, 2005) are integral to these stories' plots. The settings are artfully described and add something unique to the story. In contrast, many stories take place in everyday settings that do not contribute to the story's effectiveness.

Weather ■ Weather is a second dimension of setting and, like location, is crucial in some stories. At other times, the author may not even mention the weather because it doesn't have an impact on the story. Many stories take place on warm, sunny days. Think about the impact weather could have on a story; for example, what might have happened if a snowstorm had prevented Little Red Riding Hood from reaching her grandmother's house?

Time ■ The third dimension, time, involves both time of day and the passage of time within a story. The time of day is not significant in many children's stories, except for ghost stories, which typically take place after dark. Many stories span a brief period of time, often less than a day. Kevin Henkes's Caldecott Medal picture book, *Kitten's First Full Moon* (2004), for instance, takes place in an hour or two. Other stories, such as *Little Red Hen* (Pinkney, 2006) and *Sally Jean, the Bicycle Queen* (Best, 2006), span months or years.

Time Period ■ The fourth dimension of setting is the time period in which a story is set. The time period is important in stories that are set in the past or in the future. For example, Karen Hesse sets her lyrical novel *Witness* (2001) in 1924, and she uses the voices of 11 townspeople to bear witness to what happens when the Ku Klux Klan moves into a small Vermont town. Other stories, such as *Eager* (Fox, 2004), are set in the future and raise important questions about what it means to be human. A list of stories with integral settings is presented in Figure 9–2. These stories illustrate the four dimensions of setting—location, weather, time, and time period.

Even though settings are often taken for granted, an integral setting exerts a great deal of influence on a story. Watson (1991) recommends that teachers help children to recognize the importance of setting as a literary element and to see the connections between setting and plot, character, and other elements. For example, in *Number the Stars* (Lowry, 1989), a story of two friends—a Christian child and a Jewish child—set in Denmark during World War II, the setting is integral to the development of the story. The time period influences the plot development because readers

Figure 9–2 Stories With Integral Settings

Babbitt, N. (2000). *Tuck everlasting.* New York: Farrar, Straus & Giroux. (M–U)
Bunting, E. (1998). *So far from the sea.* New York: Clarion Books. (P–M)
Curtis, C. P. (1995). *The Watsons go to Birmingham—1963.* New York: Delacorte. (M–U)
Fleischman, P. (1997). *Seedfolks.* New York: HarperCollins. (M–U)
Fleming, C. (2003). *Boxes for Katje.* New York: Farrar, Straus & Giroux. (P–M)
George, J. C. (2003). *Julie of the wolves.* New York: HarperTrophy. (M–U)
Hale, S. (2005). *Princess Academy.* New York: Bloomsbury. (M–U)
Park, L. S. (2004). *The firekeeper's son.* New York: Clarion Books. (P–M)
Peterson, J. W. (2004). *Don't forget Winona.* New York: HarperCollins. (P)
Polacco, P. (1988). *The keeping quilt.* New York: Simon & Schuster. (M)
Ringgold, F. (1991). *Tar beach.* New York: Crown. (P–M)
Sachar, L. (1998). *Holes.* New York: Farrar, Straus & Giroux. (U)
Spinelli, J. (2003). *Milkweed.* New York: Knopf. (U)
Uchida, Y. (1993). *The bracelet.* New York: Philomel. (P–M).

Creating a Historically Accurate Setting

As part of a semester-long unit on ancient civilizations, Mrs. Clay's sixth-graders are working in small groups to make multigenre projects that focus on each of the civilizations, and each project will include a story set in that civilization. Mrs. Clay has emphasized that their stories must be historically accurate. She is meeting with the small groups during revising to help them examine the settings they have created. Today she is meeting with the "Greek Civilization" group.

1. Introduce the topic

Mrs. Clay explains that an important characteristic of historical fiction is that the setting is detailed and historically accurate. Today, she'd like the students to examine the historical information included in their story.

2. Share examples

Mrs. Clay distributes copies of the rough draft of the story to each student. She also passes out highlighter pens. While one student reads aloud, the others highlight words and phrases about life in Athens in the story. Then they take turns sharing what they have highlighted.

3. Provide information

The teacher commends the students for their use of many historical words, particularly at the beginning of the story, but she calls their attention to the fact that most of their highlighted words and phrases are on the first page of the story. She suggests the students draw a series of pictures to illustrate the story and add as many historical details to their drawings as possible. Then they can go back and add historically accurate words and phrases to the story.

4. Guide practice

The sixth graders each take a section of the story to illustrate and decide to add phrases using words from the word wall to mark the historical details in their drawings, for example, *citizens wearing linen tunics at the Temple of Nike on the Acropolis, vendors at the crowded agora selling goats and sheep, women in the looming room making clothes for their family, altars to Zeus in the courtyard of the home,* and *slaves who are craftsmen making pottery and shields.* Then they add many of these historical details to their story.

5. Assess learning

Mrs. Clay will assess students' use of historically accurate information and vocabulary when she reads the final draft of their story.

expect that the Nazis will try to relocate the Jewish girl and her family and that the Christian girl and her family will try to protect or rescue the Jewish family. The minilesson feature on this page shows how a sixth-grade teacher helped her students create historically accurate settings.

Characters

Characters are the people or personified animals who are involved in a story. Often character is the most important element of story structure because the experience the author creates for readers is centered on a character or group of characters. Usually, one fully rounded character and two or three supporting characters are introduced and developed in a story. Fully developed main characters have all the characteristics of real people. A list of fully developed main characters in children's stories is presented in Figure 9–3.

In *Olive's Ocean* (Henkes, 2005), for instance, 12-year-old Martha is the main character. On her family's summer visit to her grandmother's beach cottage, Martha gains perspective on the death of a classmate named Olive. We get to know her as a real person as she shares secrets with her aging grandmother, exchanges a kiss with an older boy who then betrays her trust, and decides to become a writer. Readers also get to know a little about the supporting characters in the story: the people in Martha's family; her boyfriend, Jimmy, and his brother, Tate; and even Olive and her mother.

Characters are developed in four ways. The first way is through appearance: Authors generally provide some physical description—facial features, body shapes, habits of dress, mannerisms, or gestures—when characters are introduced. Second is action: What a character does is the best way of knowing about him or her, and it drives the plot. Dialogue is a third way that authors develop characters: What characters say is important, but so is the way they speak. Fourth, authors develop characters through monologue: They provide insight into their characters by telling what they are thinking.

Authors use these four ways to bring their characters to life. Shannon Hale uses all four ways in her Newbery Honor book, *Princess Academy* (2005). In the story, 14-year-old Miri and all the teenage girls from her mountain village are sent to an academy for potential princesses, but the story's not about becoming a princess. Instead, it's about Miri, who feels she is a burden to her family. While she's at the academy, she discovers a way to improve the quality of life for the people in her village, and in the process, she learns to value herself. Her appearance is unremarkable: She's a slight girl, named for a tiny mountain flower. She's too delicate for strenuous quarry work, but Miri does her part by cleaning the house, caring for the goats, and bartering with the traders. Her actions are important: She learns to read easily, teaches the village elders how to improve the village's economy, and summons help

Figure 9–3 Stories With Fully Developed Main Characters

Character	Story
Crispin	Avi. (2002). *Crispin: The cross of lead.* New York: Hyperion Books. (U)
Amber	Danziger, P. (1994). *Amber Brown is not a crayon.* New York: Putnam. (M)
Edward	Dicamillo, K. (2006). *The miraculous journey of Edward Tulane.* Cambridge, MA: Candlewick Press. (M)
Olivia	Falconer, I. (2000). *Olivia.* New York: Atheneum. (P)
Miri	Hale, S. (2005). *Princess Academy.* New York: Bloomsbury. (U)
Lilly	Henkes, K. (1996). *Lilly's purple plastic purse.* New York: Greenwillow. (P)
Marty	Naylor, P. R. (1991). *Shiloh.* New York: Atheneum. (M–U)
Debbie	Perkins, L. R. (2001). *All alone in the universe.* New York: HarperCollins. (U)
Officer Buckle	Rathmann, P. (1995). *Officer Buckle and Gloria.* New York: Putnam. (P)
Armpit	Sachar, L. (2006). *Small steps.* New York: Delacorte. (U)
Maria	Soto, G. (1993). *Too many tamales.* New York: Putnam. (P)
Comfort	Wiles, D. (2005). *Each little bird that sings.* San Diego: Gulliver. (M)

when the girls at the academy are kidnapped. Miri's personality is unveiled through dialogue: She's cheeky, for example, when the soldiers come to take her to the academy. Through monologue, we understand that Miri fears she's a burden to her village, and we learn about her growing affection for her friend Peder.

Theme

Theme is the underlying meaning of a story and embodies general truths about society or human nature. According to Lehr (1991), the theme "steps back from the literal interpretation" to state more general truths (p. 2). The theme usually deals with the characters' emotions and values.

Themes can be stated explicitly or implicitly (Lukens, 2006). Explicit themes are stated openly and clearly in the story, whereas implicit themes are suggested through the characters' actions, dialogue, and monologue as they strive to resolve their problems. Friendship, responsibility, courage, and kindness to others are common topics around which authors build themes in children's literature.

In *Charlotte's Web* (1999), E. B. White builds a theme around the topic of friendship. Wilbur, who is grateful for Charlotte's encouragement and protection, remarks that "friendship is one of the most satisfying things in the world" (p. 115). Wilbur's statement is an example of an explicitly stated theme. Friendship is also central to *Bridge to Terabithia* (Paterson, 2005), but it is implied through Jess and Leslie's enduring friendship rather than explicitly stated in the text.

During the elementary grades, children develop and refine their understanding of theme. Kindergartners have a very rudimentary sense of theme, and through a wide exposure to literature and many opportunities to discuss books, children grow in their ability to construct and talk about themes (Au, 1992). Even so, students in the middle and upper grades often think about theme differently than adults do (Lehr, 1991). Older children become more sensitive to the structure of stories, develop a greater ability to generalize story events, increasingly understand the characters' motivations and the subtleties of the plot, and expand their own worldviews and ability to interpret literature.

Many stories have more than one theme, and as children talk about stories, they may head toward a different theme than the one the teacher had in mind. In this way, teachers can gain new insights about themes from their students (Au, 1992).

Point of View

People see the world from different points of view; listening to several people recount an event they have all witnessed proves the impact of viewpoint. The focus of the narrator determines to a great extent readers' understanding of the story—the characters, the events—and whether readers will believe what they are being told.

Authors use these four viewpoints to tell a story:

- *First-Person Viewpoint.* Authors tell the story through the eyes of one character using the first-person pronoun *I*. This viewpoint enables readers to live the story as the narrator tells it.

- *Omniscient Viewpoint.* Authors are godlike, seeing and knowing all. They tell readers about the thought processes of each character without worrying about how the information is obtained.

- *Limited Omniscient Viewpoint.* Authors use this point of view to overhear the thought of one of the characters without being all-knowing. The story is told in the third person, and authors concentrate on the thoughts and feelings of the main character.

Figure 9–4 Stories Illustrating the Four Points of View

First-Person Viewpoint
Bunting, E. (1994). *Smoky night.* San Diego: Harcourt Brace. (P–M)
Cushman, K. (1994). *Catherine, called Birdy.* New York: HarperCollins. (U)
MacLachlan, P. (1985). *Sarah, plain and tall.* New York: Harper & Row. (M)
Young, E. (2004). *I, Doko: The tale of a basket.* New York: Philomel. (P–M)

Omniscient Viewpoint
Babbitt, N. (2000). *Tuck everlasting.* New York: Farrar, Straus & Giroux. (M–U)
Lewis, C. S. (2005). *The lion, the witch and the wardrobe.* New York: Macmillan. (M–U).
Steig, W. (1982). *Doctor De Soto.* New York: Farrar, Straus & Giroux. (P)
White, E. B. (1999). *Charlotte's web.* New York: HarperCollins. (P–M–U)

Limited Omniscient Viewpoint
Cleary, B. (1981). *Ramona Quimby, age 8.* New York: Morrow. (M)
Hale, S. (2005). *Princess Academy.* New York: Bloomsbury. (U)
Lowry, L. (1993). *The giver.* Boston: Houghton Mifflin. (U)
Sachar, L. (1998). *Holes.* New York: Farrar, Straus & Giroux. (U)

Objective Viewpoint
Allard, H. (1997). *Miss Nelson is missing!* Boston: Houghton Mifflin. (P–M)
Lester, H. (1988). *Tacky the penguin.* Boston: Houghton Mifflin. (P–M)
Meddaugh, S. (1992). *Martha speaks.* Boston: Houghton Mifflin. (P)
Pinkney, B. (2006). *Little Red Hen.* New York: Dial Books. (P–M)

Multiple Viewpoints
Fleischman, P. (1991). *Bull Run.* New York: HarperCollins. (U)
Fleischman, P. (1997). *Seedfolks.* New York: HarperCollins. (M–U)
Hesse, K. (2001). *Witness.* New York: Scholastic. (U)
Konigsburg, E. L. (1998). *The view from Saturday.* New York: Aladdin Books. (U)

- *Objective Viewpoint.* Authors write as though they were making a film of the story and can learn only from what can be seen or heard. Readers are confined to the immediate scene. A limitation is that authors cannot probe very deeply into characters. (Lukens, 2006)

A list of stories written from each viewpoint is presented in Figure 9–4.

Sometimes authors tell stories from two or more viewpoints. Paul Fleischman, for example, has written two stories from multiple viewpoints: In *Bull Run* (1993), he paints a vivid portrait of the first battle of the Civil War using 16 voices, and using 13 voices in *Seedfolks* (1997), he tells how an inner-city vacant lot is transformed into a community garden.

These five elements are the building blocks of stories. With this structure, authors—both children and adults—can let their creativity flow and combine ideas with structure to craft a good story.

Literary Devices

In addition to the five elements of story structure, authors use literary devices to make their writing more vivid and memorable. Without these literary devices, writing can be dull (Lukens, 2006). A list of literary devices is presented in Figure 9–5. Imagery is probably the most commonly used literary device; many authors use imagery as they paint rich word pictures that bring their characters and settings to life. Authors use metaphors and similes to compare one thing to another, personification to endow animals and objects with human qualities, and hyperbole to exaggerate or stretch the truth. They also create symbols as they use one thing to represent something else. In Chris Van Allsburg's *The Wretched Stone* (1991), for example, the glowing stone that distracts the crew from reading, from spending time with their friends, and from doing their jobs symbolizes television or, perhaps, computers. For children to understand

---

Preparing for Writing Tests

Response to Literature

A response to literature essay demonstrates a writer's understanding of a story. Younger writers typically write a two-paragraph response: In the first paragraph, they summarize the story, and in the second paragraph, they offer an interpretation with evidence from the story and their own experiences. Older writers develop their multiple-paragraph essay around a thesis statement and several key ideas. Then they justify their interpretations using examples and evidence from the story. Sometimes writers confuse response to literature with summary writing, but they earn low scores if they summarize a story without offering a thoughtful interpretation.

What Do Younger Writers Do?

- Present a concise summary of the story, stating major events and suggesting the theme
- Offer an interpretation using their understanding of the author's message and their knowledge of literature
- Support their interpretation with appropriate details from the story and their own experiences

What Do Older Writers Do?

- Write a thesis statement and develop this central idea with relevant facts, details, and explanations
- Make inferences about the characters, events in the story, and the theme
- Justify their interpretation using quotations, paraphrases, examples, and details

What Mistakes Do Writers Make?

- Write only a summary
- Show incomplete understanding of the story
- Offer judgments without providing support for them
- Limit their responses to making text-to-self connections

Sample Prompts

- Read the following story. As you read, you may make marks or take notes. Then write an essay to show your understanding of the author's message and the ideas presented in the story.
- Read the story on the next page, and then write an essay in which you present your understanding of the overall meaning of the story. Support your ideas with examples and evidence from the text.

Figure 9–5 Literary Devices

Comparison	Authors compare one thing to another or view something in terms of something else. When the comparison uses the word *like* or *as,* it is a simile; when the comparison is stated directly, it is a metaphor. For example, "the ocean is like a playground for whales" is a simile; "the ocean is a playground for whales" is a metaphor. Metaphors are stronger because they make more direct comparisons.
Hyperbole	Authors use hyperbole when they overstate or stretch the truth to make obvious and intentional exaggerations for a special effect. "It's raining cats and dogs" and "my feet are killing me" are two examples of hyperbole. American tall tales also have rich examples of hyperbole.
Imagery	Authors use descriptive or sensory words and phrases to create imagery or a picture in the reader's mind. Sensory language stirs the reader's imagination. Instead of saying "the kitchen smelled good as grandmother cooked Thanksgiving dinner," authors create imagery when they write "the aroma of a turkey roasting in the oven filled grandmother's kitchen on Thanksgiving."
Personification	Authors use personification when they attribute human characteristics to animals or objects. For example, "the moss crept across the sidewalk" is personification.
Symbolism	Authors often use a person, place, or thing as a symbol to represent something else. For example, a dove symbolizes peace, the Statue of Liberty symbolizes freedom, and books symbolize knowledge.
Tone	Authors create an overall feeling or effect in a story through their choice of words and use of other literary devices. For example, some stories are humorous, and others are uplifting, feel-good stories.

the theme of the story, they need to recognize symbols. The author's style conveys the tone or overall feeling in a story; some stories are humorous, some are uplifting celebrations of life, and others are sobering commentaries on society.

Young children focus on the events and characters as they read and write stories, but children gradually become more sophisticated readers and writers. They learn to notice both what the author says and how he or she says it. Teachers facilitate children's growth by directing their attention to literary devices and to the author's style as they discuss stories they are reading and by encouraging children to use these devices in their own writing.

Teaching Children to Write Stories

Children develop their concept of story through listening to stories read aloud and telling stories during the preschool years. With this introduction to narratives, children are ready to learn more about how stories are organized and how authors use the elements of story structure to create stories. Children apply this knowledge to compose the stories they write as well as to comprehend stories they read.

The teaching strategy presented in this section builds on children's concept of story by examining the elements of story structure—plot, setting, character, theme, and point of view—and then having children apply these elements in writing stories. Rather than a collection of cookbook-like activities, this strategy is an integrated approach in which children read, listen to, discuss, view, visually represent, and write stories. The reading-writing connection is particularly crucial. As readers, children consider how the author used a particular structure and consider its impact; then, as writers, they experiment with the structure in the stories they write and consider the impact on their classmates who read them.

Teaching an Element of Story Structure

Teachers introduce children to an element of story structure using the stories that illustrate the element. Children read stories and analyze how authors use the element in them. Next, they participate in exploration activities, such as retelling stories and drawing diagrams, in which they investigate how authors used the element in particular stories. With this background, children write collaborative and individual stories applying what they have learned about the element. The teaching procedure is presented in the step-by-step feature on page 212.

Exploration Activities

Through exploration activities, children investigate how authors use plot, character, setting, theme, and point of view. As they retell and dramatize stories, compare versions of stories, and write new versions, children are refining their understanding of story and gaining the experience necessary to write well-developed stories. Here are 10 activities:

Class Collaboration Retelling of Stories. Teachers choose a favorite story that children have read or listened to several times, and they have each child draw or write a retelling of a page or short part of the story. Then they collect the pages and compile them to make a class book. Younger children can draw pictures and dictate their retellings, which the teacher prints in large type. Then these pictures and text can be attached to sheets of posterboard to make a big book that children can read together.

Retelling and Telling Stories. Children retell familiar stories to small groups of classmates using simple hand or finger puppets or with pictures on a flannel board. Similarly, children can create their own stories to tell.

Retelling Stories With Pictures. Children retell a favorite story by drawing a series of pictures and compiling them to make a wordless picture book. Young children can make a booklet by folding one sheet of drawing paper in quarters like a greeting card. Then they write the title of the book on the front; on the three remaining pages, they draw illustrations to represent the beginning, middle, and end of the story. A sample four-sided booklet is presented in Figure 9–6 on page 213.

Retelling Stories in Writing. Children write retellings of favorite stories in their own words. Predictable books—stories that use repetition—are often the easiest to retell. Children don't copy the text out of a book; rather, they retell a story that they know well. A sixth grader wrote the following retelling of "Little Red Riding Hood." Notice that her sentences are written in alphabetical order: The first sentence begins with *A*, the second with *B*, the third with *C*, and so on.

"Another plain day," said Little Red Riding Hood. "Boy, oh boy, oh boy," she wondered. "Could I do something fun today?"

"Dear," called her mother to Little Red Riding Hood. "Eat your breakfast and then take these goodies to grandma's house."

"Fine, I'll do it. Great," said Little Red Riding Hood, "my first time I get to go through the forest."

"Hold it," said a wolf in the forest. "I want to look in that basket of yours."

"Just stay out of there, you wolf. Keep your hands off me! Let go of me, you wolf." Mighty and brave, she slapped the wolf. Not knowing what to do, she ran down the path to grandma's house.

Open minded, the wolf ran to grandma's house. Putting his hands through the window, he climbed in and swallowed grandma. Quietly he jumped in her bed.

Running to grandma's house, still scared from the wolf, Little Red Riding Hood knocked on grandma's door. Silently the wolf came to meet her. Too late for Red Riding Hood to run, she panicked and yelled. Unaware she was. Very loudly her yell traveled through the forest.

Wondering what it was, a woodsman heard it and came to grandma's house and killed the wolf. X-raying the body of the wolf, he saw grandma.

"Your help sure has paid off," said Little Red Riding Hood after the woodsman saved her. Zooming from grandma's house came Little Red Riding Hood, to tell her mom what had just happened.

Step by Step: Elements of Story Structure

1. **Introduce an element.** Teachers introduce an element of story structure and develop a chart to define the element and/or list its characteristics. Next, teachers read aloud several stories illustrating the element or have children read the stories themselves. After reading, teachers and children discuss the story, focusing on how the author used the element.

2. **Analyze the element in stories.** Children read or listen to one or more stories that illustrate the element, and then they analyze how the author used the element in each story. Children also investigate how authors use the element in particular stories by retelling stories orally, with drawings, and in writing; dramatizing stories with puppets; and drawing diagrams to graphically display the structure.

3. **Review the element.** Teachers review the characteristics of the element using the chart developed earlier, and they ask children to restate the definition and characteristics of the element in their own words, using one book they have read to illustrate the characteristics.

4. **Write a class collaboration story.** Children apply what they have learned about the element of story structure by writing a class (or group) collaboration story. They follow the writing process stages by writing a rough draft on the chalkboard, on chart paper, or on an overhead transparency. Then they revise and edit the story and make a final copy to be shared with all class members.

5. **Write individual stories.** Using the process approach, children write individual stories incorporating the element being studied and other elements of story structure that they have already learned.

Figure 9–6 Independent Writing: A Four-Sided Booklet Retelling *The Tale of Peter Rabbit*

After writing, children can explain how they used the element of story structure being studied in their retelling. They can point out the conflict situation; the point of view; repeated words; or the beginning, middle, and end parts. This activity is a good confidence builder for children who can't seem to continue a story to its conclusion: By using a story they are familiar with, children are more successful.

Dramatizing Stories. Children dramatize favorite stories or use puppets to retell a story. These dramatizations should be informal; fancy props are unnecessary, and students should not memorize or read dialogue.

Drawing Story Diagrams. Children draw beginning-middle-end story clusters, repetition clusters, and plot diagrams for stories they have read.

Comparing Versions of Stories. Children compare different versions of folktales and fairy tales such as "The Hare and the Tortoise" and "Cinderella." They can compare the beginning, middle, and end of each version. For example, in one version of "The Hare and the Tortoise," the beginning is much longer as the author describes the elaborate plans for the race, whereas in other versions, the beginning is brief. Children can also compare the events in each story. In one version of "Cinderella," for instance, the heroine attends two balls.

Creating Open-Mind Portraits. Children choose a character and create an open-mind portrait showing both what the character looks like and what he or she is thinking. They begin by drawing and cutting out a portrait of the character. They trace an outline of the character's head on another piece of paper and draw pictures and then write words inside the outline to show what the character is thinking. Then children staple the portrait at the top of the mind drawing so that it opens from the bottom like a flip book.

Writing Dialogue. children choose an excerpt from a favorite story and create a script with dialogue, then they read the script to classmates as a readers theatre presentation. Also, children can draw comic strips for an excerpt from a story and add dialogue. They might also try varying the register of the language, from informal to very formal, from standard to nonstandard English, to appreciate the power of language.

Retelling Stories From Different Points of View. Children experiment with point of view to understand how the author's viewpoint can slant a story. Children can retell or rewrite a familiar story, such as *Red Riding Hood* (Marshall, 1993), from different points of view—through the eyes of Red Riding Hood, her sick, old grandmother, the hungry wolf, or the woodsman. As they shift the point of view, children learn that they can change some aspects of a story but not others.

EL

Scaffolding English Learners

Looking for ways to get your English learners involved in story-writing activities? These 10 activities are as appropriate for second-language learners as they are for other young children because they offer opportunities for children to become actively involved with stories and use talk, drama, and drawing to learn about the structure of stories. In addition, children who need more support can work with classmates on their activities.

Assessing Stories That Children Write

Assessing the stories that children write involves far more than simply judging the quality of the finished stories: Any assessment should also take into account both children's activities and learning as they study the element of story structure and the activities they engage in as they write and refine their stories. Three components should be considered in assessing children's stories:

- Children's knowledge about and application of the element in writing
- Children's use of the writing process
- The quality of children's finished stories

The first component is children's knowledge of the element of story structure and their application of the element in the stories they write. Determining whether children applied what they have learned in their stories is crucial in assessing their stories. Consider the following points:

- Can the child define or identify the characteristics of the element?
- Can the child explain how the element being studied was used in a particular story?
- Did the child apply the element in the story he or she has written?

Children's use of the process approach to write their stories is the second component. Learning about the element is a prewriting activity, and afterward, children draft, revise, edit, and share their stories, as they do with other types of writing. Teachers assess children's use of the writing process by observing them as they write and by asking these questions:

- Did the child participate in a writing group?
- Did the child revise the story according to feedback received from the writing group?
- Did the child proofread the story and correct as many mechanical errors as possible?
- Did the child share the story?

Preparing for Writing Tests

Stories

Stories are accounts of a series of events, told in chronological order, and they include characters, a setting, and a plot in which a problem is identified and later solved. They're organized into a beginning, middle, and end. The characters, setting, and problem are introduced in the beginning. In the middle, the problem gets worse and roadblocks are thrown in the way of the character trying to solve the problem; then the problem is finally resolved in the end. Stories are invented; they're based on the writer's imagination and creativity. Students write stories in either first or third person, and they use narrative strategies, including description, dialogue, and suspense, to make their writing more interesting. Stories also have a central idea or theme that provides insight into human nature. Stories are similar to personal narratives, but they're usually fictional whereas personal narratives are based on things that really happened.

What Do Writers Do?

- Develop the plot with dramatic action
- Organize the story into the beginning middle, and end
- Stay focused on story events
- Develop the characters and their goals
- Create a setting using descriptive details
- Tell the story from a clear, consistent viewpoint
- Use dialogue or another narrative strategy effectively
- Suggest a central idea or theme
- Use an interesting style to hold the readers' interest

What Mistakes Do Writers Make?

- List a series of events without tying them together
- Omit the middle of the story
- Describe a character without creating a story

Sample Prompts

- Imagine that you started to shrink: You got smaller and smaller. Create an interesting story about what happens to you.
- Imagine that you're a player on your favorite sports team. Write a story about your experience. Be sure to organize it with a beginning, middle, and end, and include details to help readers imagine the experience.

The third component is the quality of the story. Quality is difficult to measure, but it is often described as creativeness or inventiveness. In addition, a second aspect of quality is organization: Children who write high-quality, interesting stories use the elements of story structure to their advantage. Ask these questions to assess the quality of children's stories:

- Is the story interesting?
- Is the story well organized?

Figure 9–7 Third Graders' Self-Assessment Character Checklist

Name _____ Story _____	
Who is the main character?	**Who are the other characters?**
How did you develop the main character? _____ How the character looks _____ What the character does _____ What the character says _____ What the character thinks	**What is the most important thing about your main character?**

These three components and the questions that accompany each can be used to develop rubrics and checklists to assess children's stories. Assessing or grading children's stories is more than simply evaluating the quality of the finished product, and any assessment should reflect all components of children's involvement with stories.

Figure 9–7 shows a character checklist that a third-grade teacher developed for children to self-assess how well they had developed the characters in the stories they are writing. Children typically use the checklist during the revising stage of the writing process and make revisions based on their self-assessment.

ANSWERING TEACHERS' QUESTIONS ABOUT . . .

Narrative Writing

It sounds as if this approach is very time-consuming, and I don't have any time to spend on teaching writing. What can I do?

Your concern is a common one. Many teachers feel frustrated as they try to squeeze writing instruction into an already full school day. One way to make time to teach children about the elements of story structure and have them write stories is to incorporate the activities discussed in this chapter into the reading program. Stories in basal readers illustrate many of the elements of story structure, and they can be supplemented with class sets of some of the stories suggested in this chapter, stories that you read aloud to the entire class, and library books that children read independently. As children read the stories in the basal readers or in trade books, focus the discussion on the elements of story structure rather than on questions provided in teacher manuals. If you teach creatively, you can use a combination of basal readers and trade books to teach children about stories.

I told my sixth graders about plot and then they wrote stories. I was very disappointed with their stories. They weren't very good.

It sounds as if you explained plot to the children rather than helping them analyze stories to see how authors use plot. It is important to follow the instructional procedure laid out in this chapter and allow time for children to examine and experiment with plot before they write stories. It isn't enough to explain an element of story structure to children. Did they write a class collaboration story before they wrote individual stories? Writing a collaborative story is an important step because it gives you an opportunity to see if the children understand the element and how to apply it in their stories.

Is there a sequence I should follow in teaching the elements of story structure, or can I teach them all together?

Each element of story structure should be taught separately, and it is best to teach the elements in the order presented in this chapter. Plot (and the concept of beginning-middle-end in particular) is the most basic element of story structure. Even older children need to understand this basic organizational pattern before examining the other elements. If children haven't been taught about plot, setting, characters, theme, and point of view, they need to study each element and write stories incorporating each.

What should I do when Wilson can't write a story?

You should work with Wilson to find out why he can't write a story. First, check his understanding of the elements of story structure. Can he explain an element and give examples? If not, he isn't prepared to write a story incorporating that element and should be involved in additional activities to examine it. Second, check Wilson's ability to retell a story he has read that incorporates the element. Can he retell a story orally? If not, read a short story to him or have him read one himself and retell it to you. If he can retell a story successfully, you might want to have him retell a story in writing instead of writing an original story. Third, check to see if he has an idea for his story. If he doesn't, talk to him about possible story ideas, encourage him to write a sequel to a story he has read, or, if all else fails, suggest that he retell a favorite story. It's important for Wilson to write something so he can overcome his writer's block.

My third graders spend an hour each day in writing workshop and they write personal narratives. I don't have time to teach them about story elements.

Teaching your third graders about the elements of story structure would fit well within your writing workshop structure. You can teach minilessons about the elements of story structure as part of writing workshop and then have them apply what they are learning in their writing. You'll find that your students' personal narratives will become more sophisticated when they apply information about plot, characters, setting, and the other elements of story structure. There are benefits for reading, too, because knowing about story structure also improves their reading comprehension.

Chapter 10
Descriptive Writing

Preview

➤ *Purpose* Children use descriptive writing techniques to paint word pictures and to make their writing more concrete and vivid by noting specific information, choosing words carefully, creating sensory images, crafting comparisons, and adding dialogue.

➤ *Audience* No matter who the audience is, description makes writing more interesting to read. Children should always endeavor to add descriptive words and phrases to their writing.

➤ *Forms* Descriptive writing techniques are used in all genres, especially poetry and stories.

Sixth Graders Write Vivid Descriptions

The sixth graders in Mrs. Ochs's class are studying life in ancient Egypt. Their study occupies much of the school day because language arts and social studies are integrated into a thematic unit. The children in Mrs. Ochs's class read books about life in ancient Egypt, and they write in response to their reading. The type of response varies—it may be a simulated journal or a learning log, an essay or report, a biography, or a simulated letter. Children work cooperatively in small groups on projects that may involve reading, writing, talking, art, music, and drama in addition to social studies. They learn language arts and writing strategies and skills as they need them to respond to their reading or work on their projects. These are some of the specific activities:

- Children read informational books and keep a reading log.
- Each child researches an Egyptian god or goddess and makes a poster to share the information.
- Mrs. Ochs reads *The Egypt Game* (Snyder, 1967) aloud, a chapter or two a day.

- Children work in small groups on various projects. One group creates a salt map of ancient Egypt; one dresses dolls in clothes like those worn by ancient Egyptians; one makes a time line, chronicling the major events in the period; another designs a chart of hieroglyphic symbols.

One day, several children share with the class what they have learned about Howard Carter's discovery of King Tut's tomb in 1922 from *In Search of Tutankhamun,* by Piero Ventura and Gian Paolo Ceserani (1985). Mrs. Ochs capitalizes on the class's interest and shows a videotaped film of Carter's discovery that she rented from a local video store. Several children express the wish that they could have been with Carter when the tomb was discovered; they discuss what this would have been like. The children's interest gives Mrs. Ochs an idea: She asks if they would like to write a first-person "I was with Howard Carter" narrative of the discovery. Are the children interested? You bet they are!

Mrs. Ochs suggests that their writing, like the film, evoke a strong mood and focus on the description of the tomb. To gather words and ideas for writing, she and the children create a five-senses cluster on the chalkboard in which they brainstorm words for the sights, sounds, smells, tastes, and feelings they might have experienced as they entered the tomb. A copy of this collaborative cluster is presented in the box on page 220. Taste was the most difficult sense for the children because the explorers did not eat in the tomb, but children recognized that the explorers might have tasted dryness, sandy grit, and even fear. The sense of touch evoked perhaps the most powerful images as children suggested that the explorers might have felt guilt about their trespassing.

With the background of knowledge gained from the unit on ancient Egypt and the clustering experience, the children write the rough draft of their first-person narratives. After children finish their rough drafts, they meet in groups to share their writing. Mrs. Ochs asks them to focus on the mood created in the writing and the use of description as writing-group members comment about each other's writings.

In his writing group, Josh reads first:

> It was November 1922 and I was in Egypt with Howard Carter. We had uncovered one step in the Sahara Desert and then 15 more leading downward. As Howard and I walked down we heard the echo of our footsteps. When we got to the bottom we could not see our hands nor each other. I called, "Are you there, Howard?" And he called, "Yes." Both our voices echoed.
>
> As we waited for our eyes to adjust to the darkness we listened. It was quiet, so quiet. I could hear my heartbeat, and I think Howard could hear his too.
>
> My eyes had adjusted and I was amazed at what I saw. There was gold and jewels everywhere. There was a boat and a chariot. There were canopic jars, statues, tools, some kind of gameboards that looked like chess, and a child-size throne chair.
>
> Suddenly it hit me. I turned around and there it was—Tut's tomb!

There is a silence, and then his writing group members beg, "Read it again." Josh willingly reads his piece a second time, this time more dramatically. When he finishes, Matt says, "I've got chill bumps like I was with Howard Carter. That's my compliment." Then Amber tells Josh she liked the part about hearing his heartbeat, and Becky Lee says she liked the dialogue.

Shared Writing: A Cluster Describing King Tut's Tomb

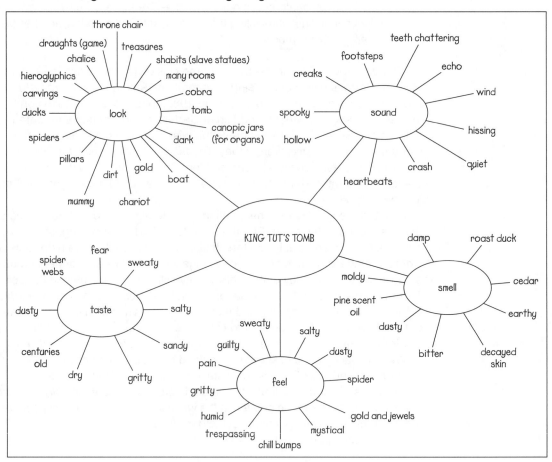

Next it's Josh's turn, as the writer, to ask a question: He asks if his classmates think he included enough details as Mrs. Ochs suggested. They count the details from the cluster that he included and after they reach 10, they quit counting and conclude that he did.

Finally, Josh asks the writing group members for suggestions to improve his writing. "I think you should keep writing and get to the part about the cobra," suggests Matt. "That's the best part and you could give it a lot of mood!" Becky Lee suggests that Josh call the game by its real name *draughts* instead of describing it and saying it was like chess. Josh agrees to continue writing but explains to Becky Lee that he didn't name the game on purpose because if he was just exploring with Howard Carter, not studying Egypt in sixth grade, he might not know the name!

The other children take turns sharing their rough drafts, listening to compliments and suggestions from the writing-group members, and asking questions themselves. After everyone in the group has shared, they move back to their desks to make revisions. Later, they will edit and recopy their "I was with Howard Carter" writings and add them to a bulletin board display about King Tut.

Instructional Overview: Descriptive Writing

Grades	Goals and Activities
Kindergarten–Grade 2	**Goal 1: Create sensory images** • Children brainstorm and cluster sensory words. • Children write five-senses poems. • Children write descriptive sentences.
	Goal 2: Add specific information • Children brainstorm lists of descriptive words for photos, paintings, and other illustrations and then choose the most appropriate words to use in sentences and poems. • Children build sentences and add specific information. • Children write sentences and paragraphs for wordless picture books.
Grades 3–5	**Goal 1: Write dialogue** • Children write dialogue to accompany photos and pictures. • Children add dialogue to stories they're writing. • Children write dialogue between characters in a story they're reading. • Children write dialogue for wordless picture books.
	Goal 2: Choose words carefully • Children brainstorm lists of synonyms using thesauri. • Children make character clusters with carefully chosen descriptive words.
	Goal 3: Make comparisons • Children make charts about metaphors and similes. • Children identify examples of metaphors and similes in stories and poems they're reading. • Children write comparisons in sentences and paragraphs.
Grades 6–8	**Goal 1: Use descriptive techniques** • Children identify examples of descriptive techniques in books they're reading. • Children use descriptive techniques (e.g., word choice, comparisons) as they draft and revise their compositions.

*D*escriptive writing is painting pictures with words. Children need to be keen observers, attentive to word choices and sensory images, as Mrs. Ochs's students were when they wrote about King Tut's tomb. They added specific details, such as the number of steps at the entrance to King Tut's tomb, and used the sensations of sound, touch, smell, and taste to paint a vivid picture for readers. Sometimes descriptive writing is a phrase, sentence, or paragraph embedded within a composition, and sometimes it is an entire composition.

Ken Macrorie (1985) advises writers to show, not tell, as they write. When writers show, they paint word pictures with details, dialogue, and sensory images. Telling, in contrast, keeps readers at a distance, not as involved as they might be because they are observers on the sideline rather than actively experiencing what the writing is describing. Readers have to supply the missing details and create their own sensory images. However, it does little good to simply admonish children to "show, don't tell." Macrorie's advice must be translated into practice by teaching children how to write descriptively and by encouraging them to revise their compositions to paint more vivid word pictures. The Instructional Overview on page 221 lists the goals and activities for descriptive writing.

Descriptive Techniques

Writers use specific techniques in descriptive writing to create vivid, multisensory word pictures. Here are five techniques that children can learn to use:

- Adding specific information
- Choosing words carefully
- Creating sensory images
- Making comparisons (metaphors and similes)
- Writing dialogue

These techniques help writers make their writing come alive for readers because they allow writers to shift from telling to showing.

Technique 1: Specific Information

Writers make their writing more descriptive when they add specific information and details. Rather than saying something is noisy, for example, the writer identifies the specific noise: a thunderstorm, a baby crying, a car engine roaring, or six dogs barking. Each of these noisy examples conjures up a distinct mental picture. Young writers can incorporate specific information in several ways:

EL
Scaffolding English Learners

Descriptive writing is especially difficult for English learners because they often lack a rich vocabulary; without these words, they can't provide specific information to make their writing interesting. You can help your English learners by brainstorming a word bank of words and phrases with them at least twice during the writing process—during prewriting and again during revising.

- *Identify specific activities and behaviors.* Instead of writing that "The bear was busy in the woods," the writer identifies the bear's activities: It climbed a tree, hunted for food, slept in its cave. Writers provide a wealth of information for readers when they identify specific activities rather than generalize with a word such as *busy*.

- *Name the characters.* Instead of writing about "a little girl," the writer gives the character a name and provides details about the character's appearance and personality.

- *Identify the setting.* Instead of writing "In a little town . . . ," the writer names the town or describes where it is located. The writer also identifies other aspects of setting, including weather, season, time of day, date, and day of the week.

- *List attributes.* Rather than writing that "The boy walked on the beach," the writer continues with details about the beach: noisy seagulls flying overhead, seashells spread across the sand like stars in the night sky, cold waves splashing against the boy's ankles. These attributes help the reader visualize the boy's walk on the beach.

Figure 10–1 Children's Books That Use Good Descriptions

Avi. (2004). *Crispin: The cross of lead.* New York: Hyperion Books. (M–U)
Babbitt, N. (2000). *Tuck everlasting.* New York: Farrar, Straus & Giroux. (U)
Barrett, J. (1987). *Cloudy with a chance of meatballs.* New York: Atheneum. (P–M)
Bouchard, D. (1995). *If you're not from the prairie . . .* New York: Simon & Schuster. (M)
Brown, R. (1996). *Toad.* New York: Puffin Books. (M–U)
Cooney, B. (1982). *Miss Rumphius.* New York: Viking. (M)
Creech, S. (1995). *Walk two moons.* New York: HarperCollins. (U)
Frame, J. A. (2003). *Yesterday I had the blues.* Berkeley, CA: Tricycle Press. (P–M)
Henkes, K. (2003). *Olive's ocean.* New York: Greenwillow. (U)
Johnson, A. (2003). *I dream of trains.* New York: Simon & Schuster. (M)
Juster, N. (2005). *The hello, goodbye window.* New York: Hyperion Books. (P)
King, E. (1990). *The pumpkin patch.* New York: Dutton. (P–M)
Martin, B., Jr., & Archambault, J. (1985). *The ghost-eye tree.* New York: Holt, Rinehart & Winston. (M)
Polacco, P. (1988). *The keeping quilt.* New York: Simon & Schuster. (M–U)
Ringgold, F. (1991). *Tar beach.* New York: Crown. (M–U)
Rylant, C. (1985). *The relatives came.* New York: Bradbury Press. (P–M)
Say, A. (1989). *The lost lake.* Boston: Houghton Mifflin. (M–U)
Scillian, D. (2001). *A is for America: An American alphabet.* Chelsea, MI: Sleeping Bear Press. (M–U)
Shannon, D. (1998). *A bad case of stripes!* New York: Blue Sky Press/Scholastic. (P–M)
Showers, P. (1991). *The listening walk.* New York: HarperCollins. (P)
Siebert, D. (1989). *Heartland.* New York: Crowell. (M–U)
Soto, G. (1992). *Neighborhood odes.* San Diego: Harcourt Brace. (U)
Sweet, M. (2005). *Carmine: A little more red.* Boston: Houghton Mifflin. (P–M)
Van Allsburg, C. (1984). *The mysteries of Harris Burdick.* Boston: Houghton Mifflin. (M–U)
Wood, A. (1984). *The napping house.* San Diego: Harcourt Brace. (P)
Yolen, J. (1987). *Owl moon.* New York: Philomel. (M–U)

P = primary grades (K–2), M = middle grades (3–5), U = upper grades (6–8)

As children write, they need to incorporate specific information into their writing. Many books of children's literature can be used as examples of descriptive writing; a list of useful books is presented in Figure 10–1. For example, in *The Best Town in the World* (1986), Byrd Baylor describes the town where her father grew up. Even though she does not name the town other than to say that it is in the Texas hills and that people called it "The Canyon," she shows, not tells, how the people lived and what the land was like. She writes about celebrations on the Fourth of July, going swimming in the creek, the toys the children played with, and the foods the people ate.

Technique 2: Word Choice

Children learn to choose words carefully in order to describe experiences and ideas effectively in their writing. Words that are specific and vivid give writing its energy, whereas more general nouns and weaker verbs force writers to use more modifiers; using too many modifiers robs writing of its power and makes it sound unnatural. Here are guidelines for choosing the best words:

- *Choose specific nouns.* Nouns can be general or specific. General nouns paint a fuzzy picture, but specific nouns give readers a much more colorful and detailed picture. *Car,* for example, is a general noun; nouns that are more specific include *minivan, sports car, station wagon, convertible,* and *SUV.*

- *Use vivid verbs.* Vivid verbs are more descriptive than ordinary verbs. *Walked,* for example, is an ordinary verb, but *trudged, hiked, marched, shuffled,* and *strutted* are more descriptive and give writing more energy. Children should avoid the "to be" verbs—*is, are, was, were.* For example, instead of using *is* in the sentence *The snake is on the rock,* the verbs *sunbathes, sleeps,* and *lurks* are more vivid alternatives.

- *Choose colorful adjectives and adverbs.* Adjectives modify and describe nouns, and adverbs describe the action of the verb. Children should incorporate adjectives and adverbs, but use them judiciously because they often use too many. For example, a sixth grader used too many modifiers in this sentence: *The tired and calm two-year-old child sat quietly in his lovely mother's lap to listen to a story at his 8 o'clock bedtime.* The sentence can be improved by shortening it and by substituting more specific nouns and verbs: *The tired toddler rested in his mother's lap listening to a bedtime story.*

- *Use synonyms to avoid repetition.* A thesaurus lists synonyms, words with similar meanings, that writers can use to avoid repetition; however, writers must take care to choose a synonym to fit the meaning of the sentence. For example, synonyms for *famous* include *noted, prominent, eminent,* and *notorious,* but not all of these words would be appropriate substitutes for *famous* in this sentence: *Charles Lindbergh was a famous aviator.*

- *Avoid "tired" words.* Children often overuse common words, such as *said, nice, bad, good,* and *pretty,* but they can choose fresher alternatives to make their writing more effective. For example, alternatives for *good* include *fine, excellent, outstanding, admirable, respectable,* and *splendid.* Children can use a thesaurus to locate alternatives for tired words during revising.

- *Differentiate among similar words.* Many similar word pairs and trios often confuse children, so they need to learn to choose the correct alternative. Some confusing words are homophones, words that sound alike but are spelled differently, such as *there–their–they're, capital–capitol, ant–aunt, through–threw,* and *it's–its.* Children confuse other word pairs, including *good–well, learn–teach, bring–take, lay–lie, who–whom,* and *leave–let* because of grammar and usage rules. In addition, they confuse word pairs that have similar spellings but do not sound alike, such as *desert–dessert* and *quiet–quite.*

Teachers help children learn to choose words carefully in a variety of ways. Whenever teachers read aloud a book and focus on vocabulary through word wall activities or through minilessons in which they examine the author's word choice in excerpts from the book, they are emphasizing the importance of word choice. Books such as Julie Mammano's series of "Rhinos" books, including *Rhinos Who Surf* (1996) and *Rhinos Who Skateboard* (1999), and Ruth Brown's *Toad* (1996) show children how energized writing can be when authors use specific words. Teachers also teach about word choice when they have children make charts of specific nouns, vivid verbs, and alternatives for overused words; study homophones and other confusing words; and learn how to use a thesaurus.

Technique 3: Sensory Images

Writers incorporate the senses into their writing to create stronger images and to make their word pictures more vivid. When Jane Yolen wrote about a father and child

How to Address Struggling Writers' Problems

The Problem	The writing lacks interesting vocabulary.
What Causes It	English learners and other children who have limited vocabularies often use conversational language rather than more sophisticated academic language in their writing.
How to Solve It	*Quick fix:* During revising, have children add some descriptive words to their writing or help them to identify several words they can replace with terms from a literature or thematic unit word wall in the classroom. They can also use a thesaurus to locate more sophisticated terms for several words in their compositions. Sometimes, however, children don't choose appropriate words when they consult a thesaurus.

Long-term solution: Teachers help children to become "word wizards" when they teach descriptive writing techniques, and they teach children to use a thesaurus so they can pick interesting words when they revise their writing. Teachers also post on word walls academic vocabulary related to books children are reading and thematic units. In addition, they encourage children to point out interesting words in the books they read. |
| **How to Prevent the Problem** | Children who are "word wizards" notice interesting words in books they read, use descriptive writing techniques, and include more sophisticated, academic vocabulary in their compositions. |

going owling on a cold winter night in the award-winning story *Owl Moon* (1987), she described how cold it was (touch), how the snow looked in the moonlight (sight), how the snow sounded as it crunched under their boots (hearing), how the wool scarf tied around the child's neck smelled (smell), and even how the fuzz from the scarf tasted (taste). Writers do not always use all five senses as Jane Yolen did; sometimes they include information about only one or two senses. Even so, the added sensory information makes the writing more memorable.

Too often, children's writing is limited to one sense—sight. Children often write a narrative of what they have seen, as though their writing were a home movie without any sound. To combat this tendency, teachers teach minilessons about writing sensory images and encourage children to incorporate more than one sense to enrich their writing. If a child is writing about a camping experience, for example, information about how things looked and sounded at night, how the food tasted, or how it felt sleeping in a sleeping bag on the ground might be included. The minilesson feature on page 226 shows how Mr. Uchida teaches his second-grade English learners to add sound words to their writing.

Technique 4: Comparisons

One of the most powerful techniques that writers use to describe something is to compare it to something else. Metaphors and similes are two types of comparisons. Strong comparisons go beyond the conventional uses of words. In Alfred Noyes's poem "The Highwayman," the moon is called a *ghostly galleon* and the road *a ribbon of moonlight* (Noyes, 1999), and in Lois Lowry's *Anastasia Krupnik* (1979), Anastasia's nervousness when she begins to read a poem to the class is compared to having ginger ale in her knees. These are fresh and unexpected comparisons.

Children grow in their understanding of figurative language and their ability to say, read, and write comparisons (Geller, 1985). Books, such as *Quick as a Cricket* (Wood, 1997), are a good way to introduce young children to traditional comparisons. In this book, a child is described using 22 comparisons, including "loud as a lion" and "wild as a chimp." After this introduction to traditional comparisons, children begin to notice traditional comparisons and then fresh comparisons in

EL
Scaffolding English Learners

You have probably noticed that your English learners rarely use comparisons in their writing, so encourage them to add comparisons during the revision stage of the writing process. Because they're often not familiar with our trite "butterflies in your stomach"-type comparisons, the ones they come up with are often unique and powerful. You may want to prompt them, by asking, "What is _____ like?" or "What does _____ make you think of?"

MINILESSON

Onomatopoeia

The English learners in Mr. Uchida's second-grade classroom are interested in words. For the past week, they have been collecting sound words from cartoons and books they're reading and adding them to a word wall in the classroom. They like collecting words, but so far they haven't begun to use the words in their speech or writing. Mr. Uchida's goal for today's minilesson is for his students to begin using sound words in sentences that they say and write.

1. Introduce the topic

Mr. Uchida reads aloud *Slop Goes the Soup: A Noisy Warthog Word Book* (Edwards, 2001), and the second graders repeat the sound words, giggling and savoring them.

2. Share examples

As Mr. Uchida rereads the book, the students add the sound words to their sound words word wall, and they take turns dramatizing each word and using it in a sentence.

3. Provide information

The teacher has copied sentences from the book and created others following the pattern used in the book (e.g., *Splash goes the water*) on sentence strips, omitting the sound words. He reads each sentence aloud and passes the sentence strip to a child. Then he asks the children to add a sound word to complete the sentence. Mr. Uchida encourages them to choose several sound words that are appropriate for each sentence (e.g., *swoosh, splish-splash, drip,* or *squirt goes the water*), but he corrects them when they choose an inappropriate word (e.g., *clatter goes the water*).

4. Guide practice

Mr. Uchida suggests that children make up a new noisy warthog story, beginning with this sentence: "Clip-clop, a warthog walks down the street . . ." Graciela begins the oral story, "Chatter, chatter go the people on the sidewalk. They see a bad warthog." The children invent a silly story full of sound words about the warthog's visit to Los Angeles.

5. Assess learning

After the minilesson, the second graders begin writing workshop, and Mr. Uchida encourages them to write sound stories about the warthog or to add sound words to stories they are writing. He explains that he will ask them about their use of sound words at their next writing conference.

the books and poems they are reading. Figure 10–2 presents a list of poems with fresh comparisons that are appropriate for middle- and upper-grade students. At the same time, children begin writing their own comparisons, as these third graders did about their classmates:

Eleanor's bangs are as curly as the ocean waves.
Joey is as smart as a computer.
Sanjay is as quiet as a burning candle.
Tim is as big as King Kong.
Sandra's hair shines like a black Corvette.

Technique 5: Dialogue

Another way writers show, not tell, is by adding dialogue to their writing instead of summarizing what the characters talked about. For example, instead of writing "The boy

Figure 10–2 Poems That Use Interesting Comparisons

From *Eric Carle's Animals Animals.*
  "Bat," by D. H. Lawrence. (The bat is compared to a glove.)
  "Tiger," by V. Worth. (The tiger's black stripes are compared to flames from a black sun.)

From Beatrice Shenk de Regniers's *Sing a Song of Popcorn: Every Child's Book of Poems*
  "The steam shovel," by R. Bennett. (A steam shovel is compared to a dinosaur.)
  "Dragon smoke," by L. Moore. (A person's cold breath is described as "dragon's smoke.")
  "Clouds," by C. G. Rossetti. (Clouds are called white sheep and the sky a blue hill.)

From X.J. and Dorothy Kennedy's *Knock at a Star: A Child's Introduction to Poetry* (rev. ed.)
  "Dreams," by L. Hughes. (Broken dreams are compared to an injured bird and to a barren field.)
  "The sidewalk racer or, on the sidewalk," by L. Morrison. (A sidewalk is compared to an asphalt sea and a skateboarder to an automobile.)
  "My fingers," by M. O'Neill. (Fingers are compared to antennae.)
  "The eagle," by A. Tennyson. (An eagle is compared to a thunderbolt.)
  "Dad," by J. S. Wong. (A father is compared to a turtle.)

From Jack Prelutsky's *The Random House Book of Poetry for Children: A Treasury of 752 Poems for Today's Child*
  "Dandelion," by H. Conkling. (A dandelion is compared to a soldier.)
  "The base stealer," by R. Francis. (A base stealer is compared to a tightrope walker.)
  "Air traveler," by L. Morrison. (An airplane is called "a silver cigar.")
  "What is orange?" by M. O'Neill. (The color orange is described as many things, including a parrot's feather. zip, and a marigold.)
  "What is red?" by M. O'Neill. (The color red is described as many things, including blood, embarrassment, and a valentine heart.)
  "Fog," by C. Sandburg. (Fog is compared to a cat.)
  "The toaster," by W. J. Smith. (A toaster is called a dragon.)
  "Zebra," by J. Thurman. (A fire escape on a city building is compared to a zebra.)

hesitantly asked Veronica for a date," the child writes, "The boy asked, 'Veronica, I, um, will you go to the dance with me?'" In this way, the child shows the boy's hesitation through the dialogue. Macrorie (1985) notes that dialogue gives force to writing and introduces a tension between characters.

Many examples of dialogue can be found in children's literature. In *The Ghost-Eye Tree* (Martin & Archambault, 1988), for example, a recounting of two children's spooky trip to get a pail of milk, the dialogue of the children is realistic: They use childlike language, with the big sister calling her little brother "a fraidy cat" and the boy's hat "dumb." The lines of talk are short, highlighting the children's fear. The anxious feeling created by the book would not be as strong without the dialogue.

Teaching Children to Write Descriptively

Children learn about descriptive techniques through minilessons. Teachers explain the techniques, share examples of descriptive writing in stories and poems, and then encourage children to practice the techniques in their own writing. After lessons on the descriptive techniques, children focus on making their writing more descriptive, whether they are writing in connection with thematic units or in writers' workshop.

Teaching Minilessons

In the lessons on the five descriptive techniques, teachers provide basic information about the techniques, share examples from literature, and involve children in writing activities. Teachers may want to refer to the list of books in Figure 10–1 and the poems in Figure 10–2 for these minilessons. Six descriptive writing activities are shown here:

> Creating five-senses clusters
> Listing attributes
> Building sentences
> Crafting comparisons
> Creating dialogue
> Adding words to wordless picture books

These activities can be incorporated into minilessons on the descriptive writing techniques.

Creating Five-Senses Clusters ■ To help children focus on the senses, they can create five-senses clusters. In this activity, children focus on each of the five senses as they explore an object or a concept and brainstorm words related to each sense. A step-by-step feature explaining how to create a five-senses cluster is presented on the next page. A class of first graders examined apples as part of a study of Johnny Appleseed and created the five-senses cluster shown in Figure 10–3. The teacher drew the cluster on a large piece of chart paper and then added the attributes that the children suggested. Later, children used words and phrases from the cluster in writing about apples.

Food is a very effective stimulus for a five-senses cluster because it evokes a response for each sense. Children can write about apples, pumpkins, popcorn, and other foods. For example, a fourth grader wrote this paragraph after doing a five-senses cluster about popcorn:

> ✐ I love to see popcorn pop. It looks like little white firecrackers. Sometimes it looks like a little white bunny. And it feels like bumpy little clouds shooting toward the sky. And they all get together and make one big smooth soft cloud. I like to hear it popping. It sounds like little stars falling from the sky and when they land it makes a whole bunch of popcorn for you to share with your friends. I love to eat it, too.

In this paragraph, the child incorporated three senses—sight, touch, and hearing—and made several comparisons. A seventh grader wrote the following poem, "Life Span of Popcorn," after making a five-senses cluster:

> ✐ In the beginning, I was a golden teardrop.
> An ancient, petrified, golden teardrop.
> I was tossed into a fountain of youth.
> where I became a sizzling teenager.
> Suddenly, the ground beneath me
> became hot—unbearably hot.
> I jumped into the air and P O P

(poem continues on p. 230)

Figure 10–3 Shared Writing: A First-Grade Class's Five-Senses Cluster for Apples

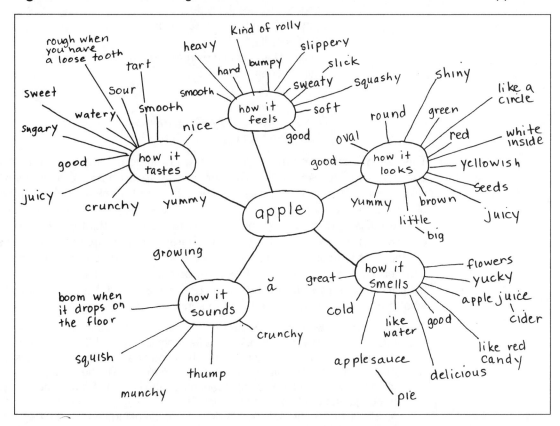

Step by Step: Five-Senses Cluster

1. **Draw a cluster diagram.** On the chalkboard, on a poster, or on an overhead transparency, the teacher draws a cluster consisting of a larger topic circle in the middle of the page and five smaller, main idea circles around the central circle.

2. **Label the diagram.** The teacher labels the circle in the center of the cluster with the topic to be examined and lists the five senses, one in each of the main idea circles. The teacher can use the five-senses labels (i.e., *see, touch, smell, hear,* and *taste*) or write questions or phrases in each main idea circle (e.g., *What we hear* or *What do you hear?*). Teachers may also ask children to write the labels.

3. **Brainstorm ideas.** Children discuss the topic using as many descriptive words as possible as they recall background knowledge, and the teacher draws their attention to other characteristics or features.

4. **Complete the cluster.** The teacher directs children to think about each of the five senses and to brainstorm words related to each sense. The teacher or a child writes the words on lines drawn out from the main idea circles. It is usually easier to begin with the most concrete sense, sight, and move to smell, hear, and touch before taste. Even if the topic is not something that children can eat or hear, for example, they can still think of sensory words.

my dull, indifferent shape
became unique—individual.
I was fluffy and almost weightless.
Filled with life,
I jumped into the air again and again
until I suddenly felt tired.
I could jump no more,
exhausted and old.
Now I lay in a bowl awaiting my inevitable fate—
the human being.

This sophisticated poem contains a comparison: The popping of popcorn is compared to a person's life. The sensory images come from the words this child wrote on her five-senses cluster as she examined a few kernels of unpopped corn, observed the popcorn being popped, and ate some of the popped popcorn.

The class can gradually move on to more sophisticated sensory writings. For example, after reading a story about courage, children can cluster sensory details related to this abstract concept. Or, for a social studies thematic unit on freedom, children can ask, What does freedom look like? sound like? feel like? smell like? taste like? A class of fifth graders wrote this class collaboration about freedom and what it means to them, incorporating sensory details:

> The men and women who fought in the American Revolution made America a free country, but many people today take freedom for granted. They shouldn't, but they do. Freedom is hard to explain, but when you see people pledging allegiance to the flag, going to the church they want to go to, and writing letters to the editor of the newspaper, you are seeing freedom. On the Fourth of July, freedom tastes like hot dogs and apple pie and it sounds like bands and fireworks. But every day, it smells like fresh air and sounds like people speaking their minds. George Washington and Abraham Lincoln and Martin Luther King Jr. symbolize freedom for many people, but we think we do, too. The pride and love we feel for the United States of America is our expression of freedom.

Listing Attributes ■ Writers are careful observers of life. They incorporate the attributes of people, places, and events in their writing so that readers feel as though they are eyewitnesses. Children need opportunities to develop observational skills to give an eyewitness quality to their writing. They can observe classroom pets and list attributes from their observations, cut pictures from magazines and list attributes from the picture, or watch a film or video about a historical event and write a description of it.

Another way to help children develop observational skills and the words they need to express these observations is through examining art prints. A sixth-grade class brainstormed these attribute words and phrases as they looked at a large print of Vincent van Gogh's famous painting *Starry Night:*

whirlwinds of light	lonely town
bursting out	darkness
cypress trees dancing	stars sparkle
frustration	glittering moon
anger	swirling
dark	round and round
few lights	scary
empty	frightening

Then children wrote quickwrites describing the painting, trying to incorporate many of the attributes from the brainstormed list. They shared their quickwrites with classmates and highlighted favorite descriptive sentences using highlighter pens. Then in a class read-around, children took turns reading their highlighted descriptive sentences, including the following:

> In the sky above, stars are bursting with light.
> The stars are whirlwinds of light.
> Clouds are swirling round and round.
> Sparkles of brightness shoot out of the moon as it gleams in the sky.
> The wind swiftly swings through the darkness.
> Cypress trees on a hillside are dancing in the wind.
> The coldness of the air puts ice into my bones.
> All I can see is the frustration of the sky on a gusty night.
> The sky above a small lonely town shatters the darkness.
> The sky waves good night.

These sentences are powerful because the children had learned descriptive techniques.

Building Sentences ■ Children can practice building sentences to see the power of specific information, sensory images, and comparisons. Teachers present an outline for a sentence, such as A _____ horse _____ _____. Children brainstorm a list of words and phrases for each blank and then choose words and phrases from the lists to create descriptive sentences. Here are some sentences that a fifth-grade class created:

> A startled horse reared up into the air when he heard the crash of thunder.
> The white stallion ran like the wind.
> The ancient chestnut horse snoozed contentedly in his stall in the barn.
> The hungry colt gobbled the oats in his feed bucket.
> The black and white horse pranced jauntily as he pulled the carriage down the drive.
> The mare gently licked her foal dry.

These sentences demonstrate some of the possible images that children can create about a horse in a single sentence. Children are often amazed by the variety of sentences their classmates create. Other topics for sentences might include an actor, a tree, a car, a space capsule, and other nouns that inspire a range of images.

Crafting Comparisons ■ Teachers should be alert to figurative language and provide opportunities for children to craft comparisons. After reading the folktale *Jack and the Beanstalk,* for instance, the teacher can encourage children to identify other things that grow as quickly as a beanstalk or things that are as big as a giant. Building on a shared experience and providing the attribute for the comparison (e.g., *fast* or *big*) are good ways to help children practice inventing comparisons. Even young children can create comparisons (Geller, 1981, 1985). For example, after petting a bunny and remarking on how soft the tail was, a kindergartner said, "My blue sweater is as soft as a bunny's tail." Then classmates began to name other things that were as soft as a bunny's tail.

To help children say and write comparisons once they have a subject, ask: What does _____ make you think of? What is it like? Children brainstorm several comparisons and then select the one that seems most powerful to them. Children exploring a Hershey's Kiss have compared it to a teepee, a mountain, a pyramid, an upside-down raindrop or tornado, a bell, the nose cone of a rocket, a volcano, and a castle. As they write, children add a phrase to complete the comparison or build a piece of writing around the comparison, as this second grader did:

> I like to eat Hershey's kisses.
> It is a chocolate mountain.
> My teeth climb up the mountain
> and my tongue sits on the pointy tip.
> Then I eat it.
> I like to eat Hershey's kisses.

Another second grader wrote:

> A little brown raindrop
> Good, chocolate, and sweet.
> A yummy chocolate kiss
> Dressed in silver.
> The little brown raindrop
> Melting in my mouth.
> Yummy, yummy in my tummy!

In the first poem, the Hershey's Kiss is called a mountain, and in the second, it is called a raindrop. These second graders are using comparison (metaphor) effectively in crafting their poems.

Poet Kenneth Koch (2000) has taught children to write poems using comparisons. To begin, Koch asked children to pretend something was like something else and to compare the two things using *like* or *as*. One child wrote "An octopus looks like a table and chair" (p. 104). Some children wrote a different and unrelated comparison in each line of their poems, and others expanded on one comparison in each line of the poem. After experience with similes, children tried metaphors. Koch asked them to think of a comparison and instead of saying one thing was like the other, to say that one thing *was* the other. Examples of childrens' poems are collected in *Wishes, Lies and Dreams: Teaching Children to Write Poetry* (Koch, 2000).

Creating Dialogue ■ Children gain experience in creating dialogue by drawing a picture of a scene from a favorite story and adding talk balloons for the characters they show. A fifth grader's drawing inspired by Chris Van Allsburg's fantasy *Jumanji* (1981), featuring a dialogue between two children (and a warning from a friendly sun), is shown is Figure 10–4.

Children can also practice writing dialogue on story boards. Story boards can be made by cutting pages from two copies of a picture book, backing the pictures with posterboard, and then laminating them. Children examine the story boards and write dialogue for the characters on self-stick notes, which they then attach to the story boards. The next step is to write about the story by referring to the pictures and adding the dialogue they have written on the notes, as well as other descriptions, to the composition. Children can collect all the writings, arrange them in sequence, and compile them to make a class retelling of the book.

Adding Words to Wordless Picture Books ■ In wordless books, authors tell the entire story using only pictures. A variety of wordless books are available today, and children enjoy "reading" these books and making up a text to accompany the pictures. A favorite book is *Frog Goes to Dinner* (Mayer, 2003), a hilarious story of a frog who goes to a fancy restaurant hidden in a small boy's jacket pocket. At the restaurant, the frog jumps out of the boy's pocket and causes all sorts of mayhem. A list of wordless picture books is presented in Figure 10–5.

Children can practice the descriptive writing techniques they are learning with wordless books. They brainstorm descriptive words and phrases on small self-stick notes and attach a note to each page in the book, or they can write dialogue on the notes. Then they incorporate the notes they have written into their retelling of the book. Here is an excerpt from a third grader's retelling of *Frog Goes to Dinner*:

Page 3: The boy is dressed in his Sunday best clothes. He bends over to pat his dog's head. "Good-bye and I will be home from the restaurant very soon," he says. He does not see the silly frog jump into his pocket.

Page 15: The lady wearing a flower hat puts a fork full of lettuce into her mouth. Then she looks down to the plate, and she sees the silly frog sitting in her salad. He has a smile on his face, but the woman screams anyway.

This is a very effective retelling because the child clearly conveys the plot and has incorporated descriptive words and dialogue.

Figure 10–4 Independent Writing: A Fifth Grader's Dialogue Picture Based on Van Allsburg's *Jumanji*

Figure 10–5 Wordless Picture Books

Anno, M. (1981). *Anno's journey*. New York: Philomel. (M–U)
Anno, M. (1983). *Anno's USA*. New York: Philomel. (M–U)
Bang, M. (1996). *The grey lady and the strawberry snatcher*. New York: Four Winds. (M–U)
Banyai, I. (1995). *Zoom*. New York: Viking. (M–U)
Blake, Q. (1996). *Clown*. New York: Holt (P–M)
Briggs, R. (1980). *The snowman*. New York: Random House. (P)
Day, A. (1991). *Good dog, Carl*. New York: Simon & Schuster.
Day, A. (1998). *Carl goes shopping*. New York: Farrar, Straus & Giroux. (P–M)
de Paola, T. (1978). *Pancakes for breakfast*. New York: Harcourt Brace. (P)
de Paola, T. (1981). *The hunter and the animals: A wordless picture book*. New York:
    Holiday House. (P–M)
Fleischman, P. (2004). *Sidewalk circus*. Cambridge, MA; Candlewick Press. (M)
Goodall, J. S. (1998). *Creepy castle*. New York: McElderry. (M)
Lehman, B. (2004). *The red book*. Boston: Houghton Mifflin. (P–M)
Mayer, M. (2003). *Frog goes to dinner*. New York: Dial Books. (P–M)
Mayer, M. (2004). *A boy, a dog, and a frog*. New York: Dial Books. (P–M)
McCully, E. A. (2005). *School*. New York: HarperCollins. (P)
Ormerod, J. (2004). *Moonlight*. London: Frances Lincoln. (P)
Ormerod, J. (2004). *Sunshine*. London: Frances Lincoln. (P)
Peddle, D. (2000). *Snow day*. New York: Doubleday. (P)
Popov, N. (1998). *Why?* New York: North South Books. (M–U)
Rogers, G. (2004). *The boy, the bear, the baron, the bard*. New York: Roaring Brook
    Press. (M–U)
Rohmann, E. (1994). *Time flies*. New York: Crown. (M)
Schories, P. (2004). *Jack and the missing piece*. Asheville, NC: Front Street. (P)
Spier, P. (1977). *Noah's ark*. New York: Doubleday. (P–M–U)
Spier, P. (1982). *Rain*. New York: Doubleday. (P–M–U)
Spier, P. (1995). *Circus*. New York: Dragonfly. (P–M–U)
Turkle, B. (1976). *Deep in the forest*. New York: Dutton. (P–M)
Weitzman, J. P. (2002). *You can't take a balloon into the Museum of Fine Arts*. New York: Dial Books. (M–U)
Wiesner, D. (1988). *Free fall*. New York: Lothrop; Lee & Shepard. (M–U)
Wiesner, D. (1991). *Tuesday*. New York: Clarion Books. (M)
Winters, P. (1988). *The bear and the fly*. New York: Knopf. (P–M–U)

Using Descriptive Writing Techniques

As children work in writers' workshop or on writing projects connected with thematic units, they apply the descriptive writing techniques they are learning. Children gather descriptive words and phrases during prewriting and incorporate them during drafting, but the revising stage is probably the most important for descriptive writing. During the revising stage, children compliment classmates on their use of description— vivid sensory images, specific details, dialogue, and comparisons—and they suggest where writers can add more description to their writing. Children then have the opportunity to return to their rough drafts to make changes.

In literature focus units and thematic units, children often use descriptive writing. A fourth-grade class, for example, was reading *Bunnicula: A Rabbit-Tale of Mystery* (Howe & Howe, 1996). In a minilesson, children learned about the roles of characters in a story and then chose their favorite character from *Bunnicula* to examine. They began by making a character map, or cluster: The character's name was written in a circle in the middle of a piece of paper, and then rays or lines were drawn out from the center circle. At the end of each ray, children wrote specific bits of information about the character. One child's character map for Harold, the literary dog in *Bunnicula,* is shown in Figure 10–6. The activity can end with the character map, or the child can use the information to write a paragraph-length description of Harold.

Another example is from a sixth-grade class that was involved in an author study of Chris Van Allsburg. Children each chose one of the illustrations from *The Mysteries of Harris Burdick* (1984), a collection of fantastic, surrealistic illustrations, and wrote a description of it. The teacher had taught several minilessons on descriptive writing before children wrote their descriptions, and they were encouraged to experiment with descriptive techniques. One child wrote about the illustration titled "Under the Rug":

> It was Tuesday evening and Harold Grimsley had had his dinner. He'd put on an old, comfortable sweater and his favorite leather slippers. He was in the family room reading the People magazine when he thought he heard a squeaky noise in the living room. So he went in to investigate. There was a round lump under the gray wall-to-wall carpet. It was the same thing that happened two weeks ago. Now it was back? Harold grabbed a chair from the dining room and hit the lump over and over. The lump squeaked louder and louder and grew larger and larger. Finally it broke through the carpet and a kind of fog spread throughout the room. Harold threw the chair down and ran out of the room and kept on running. He slammed the front door closed as he ran out of the house.

As children write on self-selected topics and work on projects during writing workshop, they often use description, whether they are describing a trip to New York City, the pizza they had for dinner last night, or the hermit crab living in a terrarium in the classroom. During a fourth-grade thematic unit on Antarctica, for instance, two

Figure 10–6 Independent Writing: A Fourth Grader's Character Map

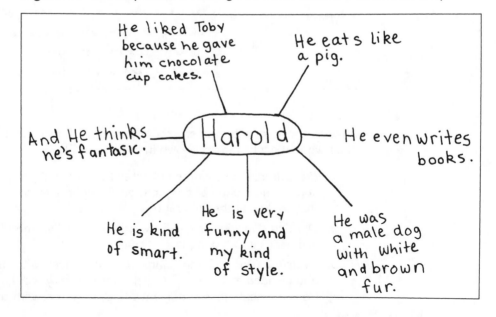

Figure 10–7 Shared Writing: The Process Used by Two Fourth Graders in Writing a Poem About Penguins

Prewriting	Feathers, feet, wing, beak, rock, yellow, black, white, orange, gray, penguin, red, chubby belly, black black, funny, likens
Drafting	① The penguins belly is white its back is black. ② The penguin has yellow and orange head feathers sticking out of its head. ③ The rock is covered with likens. ④ The penguin is up on a rock ledge in the sunshine.
Revising	The Penguins White belly and black back yellow and orange head feather sticking out of the side of its head. Up on a liken rock in the sunshine.
Final Copy	The Penguins White chubby belly. yellow and orange head feathers sticking out of the side of its head Up on a lichen-covered rock Standing in the sunshine.

children chose to write a poem about penguins. This is the procedure they followed (their work at each stage is shown in Figure 10–7):

1. *Prewriting.* The children collected books about penguins from the class library and looked at the pictures. They brainstormed a list of words as they looked at the illustrations.

2. *Drafting.* Drawing from the words in their list, the children wrote four sentences about penguins.

3. *Revising.* The children shared the sentences with their writing group and decided to "unwrite" (delete unnecessary words) to make a poem from the sentences. After unwriting, they met with their writing group

again to share their poem. Classmates complimented them on the word picture they had created and commented that the first line was the weakest one, offering commonly known information. Afterward, the children revised their poem by strengthening the first line and making several other changes.

4. *Editing.* The children proofread their poem and noticed that they had misspelled *lichen.* They made the correction and met with the teacher for a final editing. Then they wrote their final copy, which is shown at the bottom of Figure 10–7.

5. *Publishing.* The children pasted the final copy of their poem on a picture of a penguin they had drawn, colored, and cut out. At the class sharing time, they showed their final product and read their poem aloud to the class.

Assessing Children's Writing

Teachers assess children's descriptive writing in several ways. As they observe and conference with children, teachers use informal assessment procedures and note whether children use descriptive techniques. They examine children's use of specific information, careful choice of vocabulary words, sensory images, comparisons, and dialogue to show, not tell, in their writings.

Teachers also develop checklists and rubrics to assess children's use of descriptive techniques in their writing. Figure 10–8 shows a fifth-grade teacher's descriptive writing checklist. As part of a series of lessons about descriptive writing, the fifth graders used the checklist to assess descriptive paragraphs they wrote about photos of lions, tigers, and other big cats cut from calendars. Children assessed whether they had overused the descriptive techniques in their writing. In addition, teachers often incorporate one or more items about word choice and description in the rubrics they create for different writing genres because descriptive techniques play an important role in all types of writing.

Figure 10–8 Descriptive Writing Checklist

Too few	Just right	Too many	
			1. Choose vivid describing words.
			2. Include five senses words.
			3. Make comparisons.
			4. Describe emotions.
			5. Choose strong verbs.
			6. Use dialogue.

ANSWERING TEACHERS' QUESTIONS ABOUT . . .

Descriptive Writing

When should I teach descriptive writing?

Descriptive writing should be taught at all grade levels, beginning in kindergarten. Five- and six-year-olds can dictate lists of attributes, learn about the five senses, and use informal drama and puppets to create dialogue. Older children continue to write lists of attributes, develop five-senses clusters, and write dialogue, and they learn about other techniques as well. With these experiences, children become increasingly capable of incorporating description into their writing.

When children are writing dialogue, how important is it that they use quotation marks correctly?

When children begin to include dialogue in their writing, teachers should focus on the achievement, rather than criticizing them for not marking the dialogue with punctuation marks. However, teachers should build on children's interest in dialogue and give a series of minilessons on how to use quotation marks. Also, teachers can introduce quotation marks during the editing stage of the writing process and demonstrate their use by marking them on the child's rough draft.

What about children's trite expressions—*pretty* and *nice*? They use those words over and over!

Teaching children about descriptive writing will help them find alternatives for *pretty* and *nice.* As children brainstorm lists of words and draw five-senses clusters, they will realize that there are many better alternatives for these overworked words. Another way to combat the problem is to suggest to children in their writing groups that they revise their writing to include more descriptive words.

Is descriptive writing a separate genre, or is it part of every type of writing?

That's a good question. Some people consider it a genre, but others don't. Teaching children how to write more descriptively is more important than deciding whether it is a genre, and teachers usually find that it's more effective to focus children's attention on descriptive writing separately from other genres. Children can learn how to improve their word choice, write comparisons and dialogue, and create sensory images, and then they practice writing descriptive sentences and paragraphs. After this practice, children are more likely to add description to other genres.

I've seen children who start using a thesaurus and then their writing gets worse because they substitute inappropriate words—words they don't even know the meaning of—for the words they've written. What can a teacher do?

This is a common occurrence, but a thesaurus is an important writing tool, so children should learn to use it. Children need to learn how and when to use a thesaurus and why they should never change a word in their compositions to an unfamiliar word. When they consult a thesaurus, children learn new vocabulary words and shades of meaning for familiar words. This new knowledge will make children better readers and writers.

Chapter 11
Poetry Writing

Preview

➣ **Purpose** Children write poetry to create images, explore feelings, and entertain.

➣ **Audience** Poems are usually shared orally so that the audience can appreciate the alliteration, rhyme, and other poetic devices. Often children share their poems with classmates by reading them aloud or preparing an anthology.

➣ **Forms** Forms include formula poems, free-form poems, syllable- and word-count poems, rhymed verse forms, and poems modeled on other poems. Most children like to write poetry, but when they equate poetry with rhymed verse, the poems they compose are stilted and artificial. As they experiment with poetic forms and devices, children write interesting poems because of their spontaneity and playfulness with language.

Sixth Graders Read and Write Poems

Miss Clark's sixth-grade class is reading and writing poetry during a 4-week genre unit. During the first week, children focus on Jack Prelutsky and his poems. They read poems during reading workshop and write responses to them. Through minilessons, they learn about the poet and his poems. Then they apply what they have learned as they write poems during writing workshop. The daily schedule is as follows:

Text Set of Poetry Books Written by Jack Prelutsky

The baby uggs are hatching. (1982). New York: Mulberry.
The beauty of the beast: Poems from the animal kingdom. (1997). New York: Knopf.
For laughing out loud: Poems to tickle your funnybone. (1991). New York: Knopf.
The headless horseman rides tonight. (1992). New York: HarperCollins.
It's Christmas. (1995). New York: Greenwillow.
It's raining pigs and noodles. (2000). New York: Greenwillow.
My parents think I'm sleeping. (1985). New York: Greenwillow.
The new kid on the block. (1984). New York: Greenwillow.
Nightmares: Poems to trouble your sleep. (1992). New York: Greenwillow.
A pizza the size of the sun. (1996). New York: Greenwillow.
Ride a purple pelican. (1986). New York: Greenwillow.
Something big has been here. (1990). New York: Greenwillow.
Tyrannosaurus was a beast. (1988). New York: Greenwillow.
Zoo doings. (1983). New York: Greenwillow.

8:45–9:30	***Reading Workshop*** Children read poems independently and write responses in poetry logs.
9:30–9:45	***Sharing*** Children share poems they've read, and the class uses choral reading to reread favorite Prelutsky poems copied onto chart paper.
9:45–10:10	***Minilesson*** Miss Clark teaches reading and writing minilessons about Prelutsky and his poems, poetic forms, and poetic devices.
10:10–10:45	***Writing Workshop*** Using the writing process, children write poems, some of which are modeled on Prelutsky's poems.
10:45–11:00	***Sharing*** Children read poems they've written to the class.

During reading workshop, children read self-selected books from a text set (or collection) of poetry books written by Jack Prelutsky that are displayed in a special poetry crate in the classroom library. The box above lists the books in Miss Clark's text set. She has several copies of each book available for children to read. After independent reading time, children gather together to share some of the poems they've read. Three favorite poems are "The New Kid on the Block," "Mean Maxine," and "Louder Than a Clap of Thunder!"—all from Prelutsky's *The New Kid on the Block* (1984). Children have copied these poems on large chart paper, and the class rereads them as a choral reading or sings them to familiar tunes such as "Yankee Doodle" almost every day.

Each day, children write in a poetry log about the poems they're reading during reading workshop. In these entries, they write about poems they like, record observations about Prelutsky as a poet, list poetic devices that Prelutsky uses, and comment on relationships between the poems and their own lives. Here is one child's response to "Louder Than a Clap of Thunder!" from *The New Kid on the Block*:

I love this poem. It's cool to read because you can sort of yell and it's the truth for my dad. He snores real loud, real, real loud. And I think Jack Prelutsky was smart to use comparisons. He keeps you guessing until the last line that it is all about snoring. I think that's why the title is just the first line of the poem because if he called it "My Father's Snoring" it would give away the surprise. It's not a very good title. Sort of boring. I would call it "Can You Beat This?" I'm going to write a poem like this but change it to softer than and write about how soft my cat is when she tiptoes across my bed. Or when she curls up in my lap.

Miss Clark teaches a minilesson each day, and she uses Prelutsky's poems as examples for the concepts she's teaching. On Monday, her minilesson focuses on the poet and his life. Because rhyme is an important device in Prelutsky's poems, she makes this her topic for the minilesson on Tuesday. Miss Clark shares several poems with different rhyme schemes, and the children examine the arrangements. They also talk about repetition and imagery as alternatives to rhyme.

On Wednesday, Miss Clark reads "The Baby Uggs Are Hatching" (Prelutsky, 1982) and teaches a minilesson on inventing words. She suggests that during writing workshop, the children might want to create creatures like the uggs, invent names for them, and write their own verses following the format of the poem. On Thursday, she teaches a minilesson on alliteration after sharing several poems from Prelutsky's *The Headless Horseman Rides Tonight* (1992). The children especially enjoy these spooky poems, and Prelutsky uses alliteration effectively in them to evoke a frightening mood.

In the fifth minilesson, on Friday, Miss Clark explains how to write color poems after reading "What Happens to the Colors?" in *My Parents Think I'm Sleeping* (1985) and sharing other color poems from *Hailstones and Halibut Bones* (O'Neill, 1989). Later, during writing workshop, the children write color poems in which they begin each line or stanza with the name of the color. Here is one child's poem about gray:

> Gray is smoke,
> billowing from a burning house,
> Or clouds in a stormy sky,
> Gray is my Grandma's hair
> permed at the beauty salon,
> Or rocks on a mountainside.
> Gray is an elephant's hide
> wrinkled and covered with dust,
> Or me when I'm feeling down.

During writing workshop, children write their own poems. They experiment with the poetic forms that Miss Clark teaches and with other forms that they've learned previously. They draft their poems, meet in writing groups to revise them, edit them with Miss Clark, and then write the final copy in the second half of their poetry logs.

One day during writing workshop, the children work together as a class to write a new version of Prelutsky's poem "I'm Thankful," from *The New Kid on the Block*. They follow Prelutsky's format, even the "except" arrangement of the last line. Here is an excerpt from the class poem "I'm Thankful":

> I'm thankful for my telephone.
>   It hardly ever rings.
> I'm thankful for my cat.
>   He scratched me in the face.
> I'm thankful for my basketball.
>   It broke my mother's vase.
> I'm thankful for my bicycle.
>   I ran into a car.
> I'm thankful for my skateboard.

I fell and scraped my knees.
I'm thankful for so many things
Except, of course, for peas!

The children also prepare a reading-writing project at the end of the week. Miss Clark and the class brainstorm a list of more than 20 possible projects, and the children work individually or in small groups on self-selected projects. Some children write letters to Jack Prelutsky, and others make a collection of favorite Prelutsky poems. One group videotapes a choral reading of several Prelutsky poems to share with the class. Others write their own poems and compile them in an anthology or turn a Prelutsky poem into a picture book with one stanza illustrated on each page.

C hildren are natural poets. They have a natural affinity for songs, verses, and rhymes. Babies and preschoolers respond positively when their parents repeat Mother Goose rhymes, read A. A. Milne's Winnie-the-Pooh stories, and sing songs to them. Older children continue this interest in poetry as they create jumprope rhymes and other ditties on the playground. Miss Clark's students affirm this interest in poetry: They are enthusiastically involved in reading and writing poetry and think of themselves as poets. Jack Prelutsky and other poets have created many collections of poems that spark children's interest in poetry. These poets write about topics that appeal to children, such as poltergeists, parents, and dinosaurs. When children know how to write poems and use poetic devices, they can create vivid word pictures, powerful images, and emotional expressions. The Instructional Overview on page 244 outlines the goals and activities for teaching children to write poetry.

Poetic Forms

Children write poetry successfully using poetic formulas. They write formula poems by beginning each line with particular words, and they count syllables for haiku and create word pictures in concrete poems. Because these poems are brief and written quickly, children use the writing process to revise, edit, and share their writing more easily than with other types of writing. Poetry also allows children more freedom in how they use punctuation, capitalization, and page arrangement.

Many types of poetry that children write don't use rhyme. Rhyme is the sticking point for many would-be poets (Linaberger, 2004). In searching for a rhyming word, children often create inane verse:

> I see a funny little goat
> Wearing a blue sailor's coat
> Sitting in an old motorboat.

This is not to suggest that children shouldn't be allowed to write rhyming poetry, but rhyme should never be imposed as a criterion for acceptable poetry. Children should be encouraged to incorporate rhyme when it fits naturally into their writing. As children write poetry, they are searching for their own voices, and they need

	Instructional Overview: Poetry Writing
Grades	**Goals and Activities**
Kindergarten–Grade 2	**Goal 1: Write collaborative and individual formula poems** • Children write "I wish . . ." poems. • Children write color poems. • Children write five-senses poems. • Children write "If were . . ." poems.
Grades 3–5	**Goal 1: Identify syllables in words and write syllable-count poems** • Children break multisyllabic words into syllables. • Children write collaborative and individual haiku and cinquains.
	Goal 2: Develop a repertoire of poetic forms • Children write formula poems. • Children write free-form poems. • Children write found poems from books they are reading. • Children write poems for two voices related to stories and thematic units.
Grades 6–8	**Goal 1: Write model poems** • Children examine a poem written by an adult poet and create poems following its form.
	Goal 2: Analyze how poets use poetic devices • Children identify poetic devices in favorite poems. • Children write alliterative sentences and tongue twisters. • Children examine poems they have written to look for poetic devices or revise these poems to add one or more poetic devices.
	Goal 3: Review poetic forms • Children add information about each form to a poetry notebook. • Children write poems as part of writing workshop or as projects in literature focus units and thematic units.

freedom to do that. Using poetic forms, children create sensitive word pictures, vivid images, and unique comparisons in their poems.

Five types of poetry are presented in this section: formula poems, free-form poems, syllable- and word-count poems, rhymed poems, and model poems. Children's poems illustrate each poetic form. The poems written by kindergartners and first graders may seem little more than lists of sentences compared to the more sophisticated poems written by older children. The range of poems, however, shows effectively how children grow in their ability to write poetry through these writing activities.

Formula Poems

Poetic formulas may seem like recipes to be followed rigidly, but that is not how they are intended. Rather, they provide a skeleton for children's poems. After collecting words, images, and comparisons through brainstorming, clustering, or another prewriting strategy, children craft their poems, choosing words and arranging them to create a message. Meaning is always most important; form follows the search for meaning.

Poet Kenneth Koch (2000) worked with children and developed some simple formulas that make it easy for nearly every child to become a successful poet. Some of these forms seem more like sentences than poems, but the line between poetry and prose is blurry, and these poetry experiences help direct children toward poetic expression. Koch's forms involve repetition, a stylistic device that can be much more effective than rhyme for young poets.

"I Wish . . ." Poems ■ Children begin each line of their poems with the words "I wish" and then complete the line with a wish (Koch, 2000). In this second-grade class collaboration, children simply listed their wishes:

> I wish I had all the money in the world.
> I wish I was a star fallen down from Mars.
> I wish I were a butterfly.
> I wish I were a teddy bear.
> I wish I wouldn't rain today.
> I wish I didn't have to wash a dish.
> I wish I had a flying carpet.
> I wish I could go to Disney World.
> I wish I could go outside and play.

Then children choose one of their wishes and expand on the idea in several more lines. Seven-year-old Brandi chose her wish, "I wish I were a teddy bear," and wrote:

> I wish I were a teddy bear
> Who sat on a beautiful bed
> Who got a hug every night
> By a little girl or boy.
> Maybe tonight I'll get my wish
> And wake up on a little girl's bed
> And then I'll be as happy as can be.

Color Poems ■ Children begin each line of their poems with a color. The same color may be repeated in each line, or a different color may be used (Koch, 2000). For example, second-grade Cheyenne describes yellow in this color poem:

> Yellow is bright,
> Yellow is light.
> Yellow glows in the dark,
> Yellow likes to lark.
> Yellow is an autumn tree,
> Yellow is giving to you and me.

Cheyenne uses rhyming words effectively, and in searching for a rhyming word for *dark,* she creates a particularly powerful line, "Yellow likes to lark." Older children, like seventh-grade Nancy in the following poem, "Black," expand each of their ideas into a stanza:

> Black is a deep hole
> sitting in the ground

waiting for animals
that live inside.

Black is a beautiful horse
standing on a high hill
with the wind
swirling its mane.

Black is a winter night sky
without stars
to keep it company.

Black is a panther
creeping around a jungle
searching for its prey.

Mary O'Neill's book of color poems, *Hailstones and Halibut Bones: Adventures in Color* (1989), can also be shared with children; however, O'Neill uses rhyme, and it is important to emphasize that children's poems need not rhyme.

Five-Senses Poems ■ Children write about a topic by describing it with each of the five senses. These poems are usually five lines long, with one line for each sense, as the following poem, "Winter," written by a seventh grader, demonstrates:

Winter smells like chimney smoke.
Winter tastes like ice.
Winter looks like heaven.
Winter feels like a deep freeze.
Winter sounds like a howling wolf.

Sometimes children add a line at the beginning or end of a poem, as sixth-grade Amy did in this poem, entitled "Valentine's Day":

Smells like chocolate candy
Looks like a flower garden
Tastes like sugar
Feels like silk
Sounds like a symphony orchestra
Too bad it comes only once a year!

It is often helpful to have children develop a five-senses cluster to collect ideas for each sense. From the cluster, they select the strongest or most vivid idea for each sense to use in a line of the poem.

"If I Were . . ." Poems ■ Children write about how they would feel and what they would do if they were something else—a tyrannosaurus rex, a hamburger, or sunshine (Koch, 2000). They begin each poem with "If I were" and tell what it would be like to be that thing. For example, 8-year-old Jeff writes about what he would do if he were a giant:

If I were a giant
I would drink up the seas
And I would touch the sun.
I would eat the world
And stick my head in space.

In composing "If I were . . ." poems, children use personification, explore ideas and feelings, and consider the world from a different vantage point.

"I Used to . . ./But Now . . ." Poems ■ In these contrast poems, children begin the first line (and every odd-numbered line) with "I used to" and the second line (and every even-numbered line) with "But now" (Koch, 2000). Using this formula, children explore ways in which they have changed as well as how things in the world change. Eighth-grade Sondra writes from the point of view of a piece of gold ore:

> I used to be a hunk of gold sitting in
> A mine having no worries
> Or responsibilities.
> Now I'm a wedding band bonding
> Two people together, with all
> The worries in the world.

A third-grade teacher adapted this formula for her social studies class, and her students wrote a class collaboration poem using the pattern "I used to think . . . / But now I know . . ." and information they had learned during a unit on the Plains Indians. Here is their poem:

> I used to think that Indians always wore beads,
> but now I know they didn't until the white men came.
> I used to think that Indians used pouches to carry their babies,
> but now I know that they used cradle boards, too.
> I used to think that Indians didn't paint their teepees,
> but now I know that they did.
> I used to think that one chief ruled all the tribes,
> but now I know that there are different chiefs for each tribe.
> I used to think that Indians had guns,
> but now I know that Indians didn't before the white men came.
> I used to think that Indians burned wood,
> but now I know they burned buffalo chips.
> I used to think that Indians caught their horses,
> but now I know they got them from the Spaniards.

"_____ Is . . ." Poems ■ Children describe what something is or what something or someone means to them. To begin, the teacher or children identify a topic, filling in the blank with a word such as *anger, a friend, liberty,* or *fear.* Then children start each line in the same way and describe or define the thing they have chosen. Ryan, a sixth grader, wrote the following poem in which he described fear:

> Fear is not knowing what's around the next corner.
> Fear is strange noises scratching on my window at night.
> Fear is a cold hand touching you in an old, dusty hallway.
> Fear is being in a jet that's losing altitude at 50,000 feet.
> Fear is the earth blowing up.

Ryan evoked strong, concrete images of fear in his poem. Children often write very powerful poems using this formula when they move beyond "Happiness is . . ." and "Love is . . ."

Preposition Poems ■ Children begin each line of preposition poems with a preposition, and a delightful poetic rewording of lines often results. A fourth grader wrote this preposition poem, "We Ran Forever," about a race with a friend:

> About noon one day
> Along came my friend

To say, "Want to go for a run?"
Below the stairs my mom said, "Go!"
Without waiting, I flew out the door,
Down the steps,
Across the lawn, and
Past the world we ran, forever.

It is helpful for children to brainstorm a list of prepositions to refer to when they write preposition poems. As they write, children may find that they need to drop the formula for a line or two to give the content of their poems top priority, or they may mistakenly begin a line with an infinitive (e.g., "to say") rather than a preposition, as in the third line of "We Ran Forever." The forms presented in this section provide a structure or skeleton for children's writing that should be adapted as needed.

How to Address Struggling Writers' Problems

The Problem	Children do the bare minimum.
What Causes It	Children are often uninterested in a writing project when the topic doesn't appeal to them or when they lack confidence in themselves as writers.
How to Solve It	*Quick fix:* Have children write collaborative compositions. Children often become more interested in a topic when they work with classmates, and they gain confidence through the experience.
	Long-term solution: Teachers need to find ways to nurture children's interest in writing projects during the prewriting stage. One way to get children off to a successful start is to have them choose their own topics for writing. Another way is to connect the writing assignment to books children are reading or to thematic units. It's important that teachers think about the writing assignments they make and consider ways to offer children more opportunities to choose their own topics and work together with classmates.
How to Prevent the Problem	Children who choose their own topics for writing are usually more engaged in the writing experience, and they write longer, more interesting compositions.

Free-Form Poems

Children put words and phrases together in free-form poems to express a thought or tell a story without concern for rhyme, repetition, or other patterns. The number of words in a line and use of punctuation vary. In the following poem, eighth-grade Bobby poignantly describes loneliness using only 15 well-chosen words:

A lifetime
Of broken dreams
And promises
Lost love hurt
My heart
Cries
In silence

In contrast, Don, a sixth grader, writes a humorous free-form poem about misplaced homework:

Oh no, my English homework
Cannot be found—
Nor my science book.
Did my dog eat it?
Or maybe I dropped my mitt on it.
Possibly, Martians took it away,
Or it fell deep down in the hay.
Maybe it's lost or shut in the door.
Oh no, I broke my rule—
I forgot and left it at school!

Children use several methods for writing free-form poems. First, they can select words and phrases from brainstormed lists and clusters they have written and compile them to create a free-form poem. As an alternative, they write a paragraph and then "unwrite" to create the poem by deleting unnecessary words. The remaining words are arranged to look like a poem. Eighth-grade Craig wrote his poem, "A Step Back in Time," this way:

> It is late evening
> On a river bank.
> The sky has clouds
> That seem to be moving
> Towards the moon.
> The only light is my lantern,
> Which gives enough glare to see
> A few feet in front of me.
> Several sounds are heard
> In the distance: an owl
> Hooting in the trees,
> A deer crossing the river.
> Life overflows around me
> Like many different colored bugs.
> The wind is chilly,
> Making the large pines dance.
> The sand is damp.
> It's like the beginning of time,
> Before man existed,
> Just animals and plants.

Concrete Poems ■ Children create concrete poems by arranging words pictorially on a page or by combining art and writing. Words, phrases, and sentences can be written in the shape of an object, or word pictures can be inserted within poems that are written left to right and top to bottom on a sheet of paper. A seventh grader's "Lightbulb" poem is shown in Figure 11–1.

Found Poems ■ Children create poems by culling words from other sources, such as newspaper articles, songs, and stories. Seventh-grade Eric found this poem in an article about racecar driver Richard Petty:

> Moving down the track,
> faster than fast, is Richard Petty
> seven-time winner of the crowned jewel
> Daytona 500.
> At 210 mph—dangerous—
> pushing his engine to the limit.
> Other NASCARs running fast
> but Richard Petty takes the lead
> at last.
> Running across the line
> with good time.

Eric developed his poem by circling powerful words and phrases in the 33-line newspaper article and then writing the words in a poetic arrangement. After reading over the draft, he deleted two words and added three other words not included in the newspaper article that were needed for transitions in the poem. By writing found

Figure 11–1 Independent
Writing: A Child's Concrete
Poem

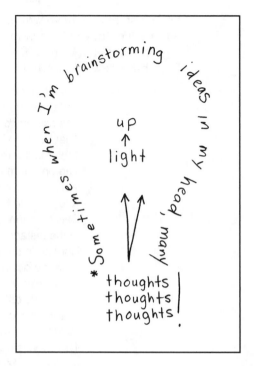

poems, children have the opportunity to manipulate words and experiment with sentence structures they don't write themselves.

Poems for Two Voices ■ Poems for two voices are a unique type of free verse. These poems are written in two columns, side by side, and the columns are read together by two readers or two groups of readers. One reader reads the left column, and the other reader reads the right column. When both readers have words—either the same words or different words—written on the same line, they read them simultaneously so that the poem sounds like a musical duet.

The two best-known books of poems for two readers are Paul Fleischman's *I Am Phoenix: Poems for Two Voices* (1985), which is about birds, and his Newbery Award–winning *Joyful Noise: Poems for Two Voices* (1988), which is about insects. Children, too, can write poems for two voices; Loraine Wilson (1994) suggests that topics with contrasting viewpoints are the most effective.

A class of second graders wrote this poem for two voices about Halloween:

Halloween is coming!	Halloween is coming!
Let's have some fun.	
	Fun! Fun! Fun!
Where are the black cats?	
	Hiss-ss.
	Me-ow.
You're here.	We're here.
	We're ready for some fun.
Where are the spooky ghosts?	
	Boo-oo.
	Boo-oo.

You're here.

Where are the bony skeletons?

You're here.

Where are the scary witches?

You're here.

Where are the children?

You're here.

Happy Halloween!
Fun! Fun! Fun!

We're here.
We're ready for some fun.

Rat-tle.
Rat-tle.
We're here.
We're ready for some fun.

Hocus pocus.
Hocus pocus.
We're here.
We're ready for some fun.

Trick or treat.
Trick or treat.
We're here.
We're ready for some fun.
Fun! Fun! Fun!
Happy Halloween!

Syllable- and Word-Count Poems

Haiku and other syllable- and word-count poems provide a structure that helps children succeed in writing; however, the need to adhere to the formula in these poems may restrict children's freedom of expression. In other words, the structure of these poems may both help and hinder children. The exact syllable counts force children to search for just the right words to express their ideas and feelings and provide a valuable opportunity for children to use a thesaurus.

Haiku ■ The best-known syllable-count poem is *haiku* (high-KOO), a Japanese poetic form consisting of 17 syllables arranged in three lines of 5-7-5. Haiku deals with nature and presents a single clear image. It is a concise form, much like a telegram. Ten-year-old Shawn wrote this haiku about the feeling of mud swishing between his toes:

> The mud feels slimy
> As it splashes through my toes
> Making them vanish.

Books of haiku poems to share with children include *Cool Melons—Turn to Frogs!* (Gollub, 1998), *Grass Sandals: The Travels of Basho* (Spivak, 1997), and *Don't Step on the Sky: A Handful of Haiku* (Chaikin, 2002). The artwork used in these books provides children with ideas for illustrating their haiku poems.

Cinquains ■ A *cinquain* (SIN-cane) is a five-line poem containing 22 syllables in a 2-4-6-8-2 syllable pattern. Cinquains usually describe something, but they may also tell a story. Teachers encourage children to search for words and phrases that are precise, vivid, and sensual, and they have children ask themselves what their subject looks like, smells like, sounds like, and tastes like and record their ideas using a five-senses cluster. Here is the formula:

Line 1:   A one-word subject with two syllables
Line 2:   Four syllables describing the subject

Line 3:   Six syllables showing action
Line 4:   Eight syllables expressing a feeling or observation about the subject
Line 5:   Two syllables describing and renaming the subject

This cinquain poem was written by sixth-grade Kevin:

> Wrestling
> skinny, fat
> coaching, arguing, pinning
> trying hard to win
> tournament

If you compare Kevin's poem to the cinquain formula, you'll notice that some lines are short a syllable or two; Kevin bent some of the guidelines in choosing words to create a powerful image of wrestling. The message of the poem is always more important than adhering to the formula.

An alternative cinquain form contains five lines but does not follow the syllable count. Instead, each line contains a specified number of words rather than syllables: The first line contains a one-word title, the second line has two words that describe the title, the third line has three words that express action, the fourth line has four words that express feelings, and the fifth line contains a two-word synonym for the title.

Diamantes ■ Iris Tiedt (1970) invented the *diamante* (dee-ah-MAHN-tay), a seven-line contrast poem written in the shape of a diamond. In this poetic form, children apply their knowledge of opposites and parts of speech. This is the formula:

Line 1:   One noun as the subject
Line 2:   Two adjectives describing the subject
Line 3:   Three participles (ending in *-ing*) telling about the subject
Line 4:   Four nouns, the first two related to the subject and the second two related to the opposite
Line 5:   Three participles telling about the opposite
Line 6:   Two adjectives describing the opposite
Line 7:   One noun that is the opposite of the subject

When the poem is written, it is arranged in a diamond shape. Sixth-grade Shelley wrote the following diamante about heaven and hell:

> HEAVEN
> happy, love
> laughing, hunting, everlasting
> pearly gates, Zion, Satan, netherworld
> burning, blazing, yelling
> pain, fire
> HELL

Shelley created a contrast between heaven, the subject represented by the noun in the first line, and hell, the opposite in the last line; creating the contrast gives children the opportunity to play with words and extend their understanding of opposites. The third noun, *Satan,* in the fourth line marks the transition from heaven to hell.

Rhymed Verse Poems

Several rhymed verse forms, such as limericks and clerihews, can be used effectively with older children. In using these forms, it is important that teachers try to ensure that the rhyme schemes don't restrict children's creative and imaginative expressions.

Limericks ■ The limerick is a form of light verse that uses both rhyme and rhythm. The poem consists of five lines. The first, second, and fifth lines rhyme, and the third and fourth lines rhyme with each other and are shorter than the other three lines. The rhyme scheme is a-a-b-b-a. Often the last line contains a funny or surprise ending, as shown in the following limerick written by eighth-grade Angela:

> There once was a frog named Pete
> Who did nothing but sit and eat.
> He examined each fly
> With so careful an eye
> And then said, "You're dead meat."

Writing limericks can be a challenging assignment for many upper-grade students, but middle graders can also be successful with this poetic form, especially when they work together and write a class collaboration. This class collaboration limerick, "Leprechaun," was written by fourth graders:

> There once was a lucky leprechaun
> That rode on a big, fat fawn.
> He ate a cat,
> And got so fat,
> To lose some weight he had to mow the lawn.

Limericks were popularized in the 19th century by Edward Lear (1812–1888). Teachers often introduce limericks by reading aloud some of Lear's verses so that children can appreciate the rhythm (stressed and unstressed syllables) of the verse. Three other collections of humorous limericks to share with children are *The Hopeful Trout and Other Limericks* (Ciardi, 1992), *There Once Was a Very Odd School* (Krensky, 2004), and *Pocketful of Nonsense* (Marshall, 2003).

Clerihews ■ A *clerihew* (KLER-i-hyoo) is a four-line rhymed verse that describes a person. The form is named for Edmund Clerihew Bentley (1875–1956), a British detective writer who invented it. Here is the formula:

Line 1:	The person's name
Line 2:	Rhymes with the first line
Lines 3 and 4:	Rhyme with each other

Clerihews can be written about anyone—historical figures, characters in stories, and even the students themselves. The following clerihew was written by an eighth grader named Johnny about another John:

> John Wayne
> Is in the Cowboy Hall of Fame.
> In movies he shot his gun the best,
> And that's how he won the west.

Model Poems

Children can write poems that are modeled on poems composed by adult poets, an approach Kenneth Koch suggests in *Rose, Where Did You Get That Red?* (1990). According to this approach, children read a poem and then write their own poems using the same theme expressed in the model poem. For other examples of model poems, see Paul Janeczko's *Poetry From A to Z: A Guide for Young Writers* (1994) and Nancy Cecil's *For the Love of Poetry: Poetry for Every Learner* (1994).

Apologies ■ Using William Carlos Williams's poem "This Is Just to Say" as the model, children write a poem in which they apologize for something they are secretly glad they did (Koch, 1990). Middle- and upper-grade students are very familiar with offering apologies, and they enjoy writing humorous apologies to inanimate things. For example, fifth-grade Clay wrote an apology to his eraser:

> Dear Eraser,
> This is just to say
> I'm so sorry
> for biting you off
> my pencil
> and eating you
> and putting you
> in my digestive system.
> Forgive me!
> Forgive me p-l-e-e-e-a-s-e-e-e.

Apology poems don't have to be humorous; they may be sensitive, genuine apologies, as in this poem, "Open Up," written by seventh-grade Angela:

> I didn't open
> my immature eyes
> to see the pain
> within you
> a death had caused.
> Forgive me,
> I misunderstood
> your anguished
> broken heart.

Invitations ■ Children write poems in which they invite someone to a magical, beautiful place full of sounds and colors and where all kinds of marvelous things happen; the model poem is William Shakespeare's "Come Unto These Yellow Sands" (Koch, 1990). The guidelines for writing an invitation poem are that it must be an invitation to a magical place and include sound or color words. The following invitation poem, "The Golden Shore," written by seventh-grade Nikki, follows these two guidelines:

> Come unto the golden shore
> Where days are filled with laughter,
> And nights filled with whispering winds.
> Where sunflowers and sun
> Are filled with love.
> Come take my hand
> As we walk into the sun.

Prayers From the Ark ■ Children write a poem from the viewpoint of an animal following the model poems *Prayers From the Ark* (1992) by Carmen Bernos de Gasztold, who wrote poems in the persona of animals on Noah's ark. Children can write similar poems in which they assume the persona of an animal. Second-grade Candice assumes the persona of the Easter Bunny for her poem:

> Dear Lord,
> I am the bunny.
> Why did you make me so fluffy?
> I thank you for keeping the carrots
> sweet and orange so I can be strong.
> Thank you for making me the Easter Bunny.
> Oh, I almost forgot, bless you
> for last month's big crop of carrots.

"If I Were in Charge of the World" ■ Children write poems in which they describe what they would do if they were in charge of the world; Judith Viorst's poem "If I Were in Charge of the World" (1981) is the model for this form. Children are eager to share ideas about how they would change the world, as this fourth-grade collaborative poem illustrates:

> If I were in charge of the world
> School would be for one month,
> Movies and video games would be free, and
> Foods would be McCalorieless at McDonalds.
> Poor people would have a home,
> Bubble gum would cost a penny, and
> Kids would have cars to drive.
> Parents wouldn't argue,
> Christmas would be in July and December, and
> We would never have bedtimes.
> A kid would be president,
> I'd meet my long lost cousin, and
> Candybars would be vegetables.
> I would own the mall,
> People would have as much money as they wanted, and
> There would be no drugs.

Poetic Devices

Good poets choose words carefully. They create strong images when they use unexpected comparisons, repeat sounds within a line or stanza, imitate sounds, repeat words and phrases, and choose rhyming words. These techniques are called *poetic devices*. Many children notice these devices when they read poems, and they need to be aware of them before they can use them in their writing. Knowledge of the appropriate terminology—*comparison, alliteration, onomatopoeia, repetition,* and *rhyme*—is also helpful in writing groups, when children compliment classmates on their use of a device or suggest that they try a particular device. The minilesson on page 256 shows how Ms. Cook, a fifth-grade teacher, teaches her students about poetic devices.

MINILESSON

Poetic Devices

The fifth graders in Ms. Cook's class are reading and writing poems during their workshop period. Ms. Cook has taught a series of minilessons on repetition, rhyme, alliteration, comparison, and onomatopoeia; as part of each minilesson, the children made a chart about the poetic device and posted it in the classroom. In today's minilesson, Ms. Cook asks her fifth graders to apply what they've learned about poetic devices to analyze some familiar poems and some new ones, too.

1. Introduce the topic

Ms. Cook says, "I'm wondering what poets do to craft a good poem. . . . " The children offer a variety of responses, including this one from Heather: "Poets choose the best words and sometimes make you laugh."

2. Share examples

The teacher shares three familiar poems on the overhead projector, reads each aloud, and asks if the poem is good. First, she rereads "Snow Rhyme," by Christine Crow (Yolen, 1993), and a child points out that it rhymes. Next, she rereads "Dad," by Janet Wong (Kennedy & Kennedy, 1999), and a child says that he likes the way the poet compared a dad to a turtle. Then, she rereads "A Pizza the Size of the Sun," by Jack Prelutsky (1996), and several children volunteer that the exaggeration is funny and the poet uses both rhyme and repetition. Finally, Darren blurts out: "I get it. You want us to think about the five kinds of poetic devices."

3. Provide information

"I agree that poets do many things to make their poems good," Ms. Cook says, "but you are right, Darren. I want to review poetic devices." Ms. Cook reviews the five posters. Then she reads aloud several new poems and asks the children to identify the poetic devices used in them.

4. Guide practice

Ms. Cook divides the class into small groups and gives each group copies of five poems to read and examine. She asks them to identify one or two poetic devices that the poet used effectively. Afterward, the children share their ideas with the class.

5. Assess learning

Ms. Cook asks children to examine one of the poems they read this week to see which poetic devices have been used and to write their reflections in their writers' notebooks.

Comparison ■ Children use comparisons—metaphors and similes—to describe images, feelings, and actions in the poems they write. As discussed in Chapter 10, "Descriptive Writing," a *metaphor* compares two things by implying that one thing is something else, and a *simile* is an explicit comparison of one thing to another, signaled by the use of *like* or *as*. Children learn traditional comparisons, such as "high as a kite" and "soft as a feather," during the primary grades, and then they experiment with creating new comparisons, such as this metaphor:

> Anger is a volcano
> Erupting with poisonous words.

Figure 11–2 Shared Writing: Two Pages From a Fourth-Grade Class Book, *The Z Was Zipped*

Sixth-grade Amanda uses a combination of traditional and unexpected similes in this poem, "People":

People are like birds
who are constantly getting their feathers ruffled.
People are like alligators
who find pleasure in evil cleverness.
People are like bees
who are always busy.
People are like penguins
who want to have fun.
People are like platypuses—
unexplainable!

Alliteration ■ *Alliteration* is the repetition of the same initial consonant sound in consecutive words or in words in close proximity. Repeating the same initial sound makes poetry fun to read, and children enjoy reading and reciting alliterative books such as Jane Bayer's *A My Name Is Alice* (1992), *Agent A to Agent Z* (Rash, 2004), and Chris Van Allsburg's *The Z Was Zapped* (1987). After reading one of these books, children can create their own versions. For example, a fourth-grade class created their own version of Van Allsburg's book, which they called "The Z Was Zipped." Children divided into pairs, and each pair composed a page for the class book. On the front of the sheet of paper, they illustrated their letter, and on the back, they wrote a sentence to describe their illustration, following Van Allsburg's pattern. Two pages from the book are presented in Figure 11–2. For the *D* page, the alliterative sentence is "The D got dunked by the duck," and for the *T* page, it is "The T was terrified."

Onomatopoeia ■ *Onomatopoeia* is a device in which poets use sound words to make their writing more sensory and more vivid; these sound words, such as *crash, slurp, varoom,* and *me-e-e-ow,* sound like their meanings. Children can compile a list of sound words found in stories and poems they read. The list can be displayed on a classroom chart or entered in their writing notebooks for children to refer to when they write.

In *Wishes, Lies, and Dreams* (2000), Kenneth Koch recommends having children write noise poems in which they include a noise or sound word in each line. These first poems may sound contrived (e.g., "A dog barks bow-wow"), but through these experiences, children learn to use onomatopoeia effectively. This poem, "Grey-hound," written by seventh-grade Brian, illustrates onomatopoeia:

> Fast and slick
> Out of the dogbox—
> ZOOM, ZOOM, ZOOM
> Burst into the air
> Then they smoothly touch the ground.

Repetition ■ Repetition of words and phrases is another device that writers of stories and poems can use effectively to structure their writing and add interest. Edgar Allan Poe's effective use of the fearful word *nevermore* in "The Raven" is one poetic example, as is the gingerbread boy's boastful refrain in *The Gingerbread Boy*. An easy way to introduce repetition of words in poetry is through a class collaboration poem. In this collaborative poem, "Wishing Time," a first grader's comment "Gee, it's fun wishing!" is repeated after every three wishes:

> I wish I could go to the moon.
> I wish I had a pony.
> I wish I was a professional baseball player.
> Gee, it's fun wishing!
>
> I wish I had a million dollars.
> I wish I could go to Disneyland.
> I wish I could be a movie star.
> Gee, it's fun wishing!
>
> I wish I owned a toy store.
> I wish I was the smartest kid in the world.
> I wish I could never stop wishing.
> Gee, it's fun wishing!

This repetition adds structure and enjoyment. As the class reads the poem aloud, the teacher reads each stanza and the children chant the refrain. In the following poem, "Chocolate," a fifth grader writes about a piece of chocolate, using the refrain "Here it comes" to heighten anticipation and to structure the poem:

> I drool.
>   Here it comes.
> The golden brown covering never looked
> so scrumptious, so tempting, so addicting.
>   Here it comes.
> I don't know anything that's going on around me.
> All I can concentrate on is chocolate.
>   Here it comes.
> I can feel the sweet, rich, thick chocolate
> on the roof of my mouth. A-a-a-ah!
>   And the chocolate is gone.

One way to encourage improvement in a child's poem is to suggest that he or she repeat a particularly effective phrase throughout the poem.

Rhyme ■ It is unfortunate that rhyme has been considered synonymous with poetry. Although rhyme is an important part of many types of poetry, it can dominate children's poems. When rhyme comes naturally, it adds a delightful quality, but it can interfere with vivid images. In the following Halloween poem, a fifth grader describes a witch's brew using rhyming words and an invented magical word, *allakaboo:*

> Bats, spiders, and lizards, too
> Rats, snakes—Allakaboo!
> Eggs and spiderwebs, a-choo
> Wings of a bug—Allakaboo—
> > a witch's brew!

Teaching Children to Write Poems

Children learn to write poems through minilessons about poetic forms and poetic devices, through reading poems, and through writing poems. It's not enough to simply invite children to read or write poetry; they need instruction and structured writing experiences in order to develop a concept of poetry. In the vignette at the beginning of the chapter, Miss Clark incorporated all three components in her poetry workshop, and her sixth graders were very successful.

Children learn poetic forms and write poems in connection with a unit on poetry, in response to literature they have read, and in writing workshop. They also write poetry in connection with social studies and science units. For example, they might write an "If I Were in Charge of the World" poem from Paul Revere's point of view or from the viewpoint of a favorite book character. Children might also write five-senses poems in connection with a thematic unit on the four seasons, or "If I were . . ." poems or concrete poems about animals as part of a unit on animals.

Introducing Children to Poetry

Many children have misconceptions about what poetry is and how to write it. Too often, they think poetry must rhyme or they are unsure about what it should look like on a page. Children need to have a concept of poetry before beginning to write poems. One way to expand children's knowledge of poetry is to share a variety of poems written by children and adults. Choose from poems included in this chapter as well as poems written by well-known poets who write for children, such as Karla Kuskin (2003), David McCord (1999), and Jack Prelutsky (1984, 1996, 2000). Include poems that don't rhyme, as well as concrete poems with creative arrangements on the page.

Another way to introduce poetry is to read excerpts from the first chapter of Lois Lowry's *Anastasia Krupnik* (1979). In this book, 10-year-old Anastasia, the main character of the story, is excited when her teacher, Mrs. Westvessel, announces that the class will write poems. Anastasia works at home for eight nights to write a poem. Lowry does an excellent job of describing how writers search long and hard for words to express their meaning and the delight that comes when writers realize their poems are finished. On the appointed day, Anastasia and her classmates bring their poems to class to read aloud. One child reads his four-line rhymed verse aloud:

> I have a dog whose name is Spot.
> He likes to eat and drink a lot.

Figure 11–3 Guidelines for Writing Poems

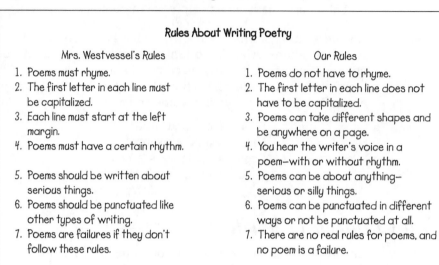

In this free-form poem without rhyme or capital letters, Anastasia has created a marvelous word picture with invented words such as *whisperwarm* and *wrinklesquirm*. Regrettably, Mrs. Westvessel has an antiquated view that poems should focus on serious subjects, use rhyme, and incorporate conventional capitalization and punctuation. She doesn't understand Anastasia's poem and gives Anastasia an F because she didn't follow directions.

Although this episode from the book presents a depressing picture of teachers and their lack of knowledge about poetry, it is a dramatic introduction to what poetry is and what it is not. After reading excerpts from this first chapter of *Anastasia Krupnik,* teachers develop a chart with their students comparing what poetry is in Mrs. Westvessel's class and what poetry is in their class. A class of upper-grade students developed the chart in Figure 11–3. Expanding children's understanding of poetry is a crucial first step because although most children have some knowledge about poetry, many of their notions are more like Mrs. Westvessel's than like Anastasia's.

Teaching Children to Write Poems Using a Poetic Form

After learning about poetry, children are ready to begin writing. Beginning with formula poems (e.g., "I wish . . ." poems and color poems) will probably make the writing easier for young children or for older students who have had little or no experience with poetry. The steps for writing any type of poetry are presented in the step-by-step feature below.

Children in a fourth- and fifth-grade remedial reading class composed the class collaboration poem "If I Were a Tornado" presented in Figure 11–4. The class began by clustering ideas about tornadoes, and then children used the words in the cluster in dictating a rough draft of the poem. After reading the draft aloud, one child commented that the poem looked "too full of words" and counted 52 words in the poem. The children decided to "unwrite" some of the unnecessary words (e.g., the repetitious "I'd" at the beginning of four lines) and reduced the number of words in the poem to 41. After making the changes and reading the revised poem aloud, the children declared the poem finished. It was then copied on a sheet of paper, and copies were made for each child.

Too often, teachers will simply explain several poetic forms and then allow children to choose any form they like and write poems. This approach ignores the teaching component; it's back to the "assign and do" syndrome. Instead, children need to learn and experiment with each poetic form. After these preliminary experiences, they can apply what they have learned and write poems adhering to any of the poetic forms they have studied. Class collaborations are a crucial component because they provide a practice run for children who aren't sure what to do. The 5 minutes it takes to write a class collaboration poem may make the difference between success and failure for many children.

Step by Step: Writing Poems

1. ***Explain the poetic form.*** Teachers describe the poetic form and explain what is incorporated in each line or stanza. Displaying a chart that describes the form or having children write a brief description of the poetic form in their writing notebooks will help them remember the information.

2. ***Share examples.*** Teachers read poems adhering to the poetic form. Poems included in this chapter can be shared, as well as poems published in books of poetry and poems written by children. They also point out how the writer of each poem used the form.

3. ***Review the poetic form.*** Teachers review the pattern or formula and share another poem that follows the form. Next, they ask children to explain how the poem fits the form.

4. ***Write class collaboration poems.*** Teachers have children compose a class collaboration poem before writing individual poems. The activity is guided writing when children each contribute a line for a class collaboration "I wish . . ." poem or a couplet for an "I used to . . . / But now . . ." poem; it is shared writing when children work together to suggest ideas and words for other types of poems, such as apology or concrete poems. They dictate the poem to the teacher, who records it on the chalkboard or on chart paper. Older children often work in small groups to create their poems.

5. ***Write individual poems.*** Children use the writing process to write poems. They prewrite to gather and organize ideas, write rough drafts, meet in writing groups to receive feedback, make revisions based on this feedback, and then edit their poems with a classmate and with the teacher. Then children share their poems in a variety of ways. Often they keep their poems in a poetry notebook.

Figure 11–4 Steps in Writing a Class Collaboration Poem

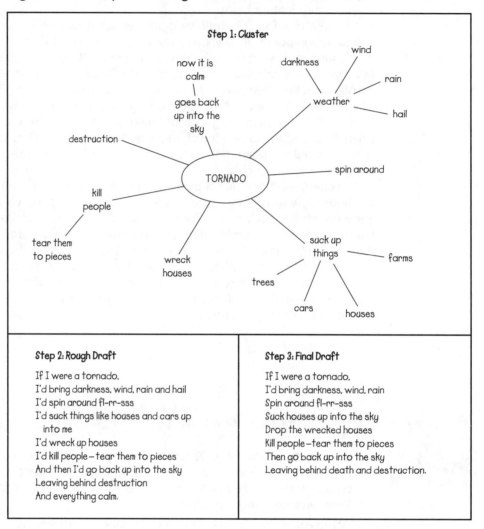

Step 1: Cluster

TORNADO

weather — wind, rain, hail, darkness

now it is calm — goes back up into the sky

destruction

kill people — tear them to pieces

wreck houses

spin around

suck up things — farms, trees, cars, houses

Step 2: Rough Draft

If I were a tornado,
I'd bring darkness, wind, rain and hail
I'd spin around fl-rr-sss
I'd suck things like houses and cars up
  into me
I'd wreck up houses
I'd kill people – tear them to pieces
And then I'd go back up into the sky
Leaving behind destruction
And everything calm.

Step 3: Final Draft

If I were a tornado,
I'd bring darkness, wind, rain
Spin around fl-rr-sss
Suck houses up into the sky
Drop the wrecked houses
Kill people – tear them to pieces
Then go back up into the sky
Leaving behind death and destruction.

Assessing Children's Poems

A variety of poetic formulas have been presented in this chapter. These formulas allow children to experiment with different ways to express their thoughts. Although children should experiment with a variety of forms, they should not be tested on their knowledge of particular forms. Knowing, for example, that a haiku is a Japanese form composed of 17 syllables arranged in three lines will not make a child a poet. Instead, information about the forms should be available in the classroom.

Assessing the quality of children's poems is especially difficult; instead of trying to give a grade for quality, teachers can assess children's writing on these three criteria:

- Has the child written the poem following the formula presented in class?
- Has the child used the process approach in writing, revising, and editing the poem?
- Has the child used a poetic device in the poem?

Teachers might also ask children to assess their own progress in writing poems. Children should keep copies of the poems they write in their writing folders or in poetry booklets so they can review and assess their work. If a grade for quality is absolutely necessary, children should be permitted to choose several of the poems in their writing folders to be evaluated.

ANSWERING TEACHERS' QUESTIONS ABOUT . . .

Poetry Writing

Isn't it true that children either have poetic ability or they don't?

Perhaps it is true that great poets are born, not made, but every child can write poems and enjoy the experience. Children benefit from experiences with poems; they develop a sensitivity to language and learn to play with words and evoke fresh images. The poetic forms presented in this chapter have been field-tested with children, and both teachers and children find these poetry-writing activities to be valuable learning experiences.

My students think that poems must rhyme. How can I convince them that poems don't have to rhyme?

Many children think that poems must rhyme. Reading the excerpt from Lowry's *Anastasia Krupnik* (1979) and developing a list of poetry rules for your class like the one described in Figure 11–3 will introduce the concept that poems are more than strings of rhyming words. Teaching children about concrete poems, haiku, and other forms that don't use rhyme will help them understand that they have options other than rhyming in poetry. Also, read aloud some poetry that doesn't rhyme.

My students' poems look more like paragraphs than poems. What can I do?

Have children examine the poems written in books to see how they are arranged on the page. Also, write class poems and discuss with children the various options that poets have for arranging their poems on the page. To demonstrate some of the options, have small groups of children each design a different arrangement for a class collaboration poem. Also, have children type their poems on the computer and arrange them in various ways. For example:

> Words
> written
> up and down
> and
> centered
> SMACK
> in the middle
> of the page—
> That's a poem to me!

If the poems also sound like a paragraph, some "unwriting," in which children delete unnecessary and repetitive function words, might be necessary. For example, the following paragraph was unwritten to create the poem just mentioned:

> In a poem you can write words up and down on a page. They are centered right in the middle of the page. They are fun to write. That's what a poem is to me.

How can I teach poetry when I've never liked it or been any good at writing poetry myself?

Teachers often ask this question. Note that this book offers a new way of writing poetry, in which the emphasis has changed from rhyming verse to expressing feelings and creating word pictures. Children's enthusiasm for this type of poetry is contagious; even the most skeptical teacher quickly becomes a convert.

Chapter 12
Persuasive Writing

Preview

Purpose Children use persuasive writing to argue logically with reasons, to present other viewpoints, to sway opinions, and to persuade someone to do something.

Audience The audience may be known or unknown: When children write to family members, friends, or a state legislator, the audience is known, but when they write to the editor of a newspaper, the audience is unknown. It is crucial that writers have a clear sense of audience and that they adapt their writing and the reasoning they use to their audience.

Forms Forms include posters, letters, letters to the editor, and essays.

Second Graders Write Persuasive Cards

It's a week before Mother's Day, and a group of second graders in Mrs. Carson's classroom meets to talk about the Mother's Day cards they want to make. Earlier that morning at the whole-class meeting that she uses to begin each writing workshop session, Mrs. Carson mentioned Mother's Day and encouraged the children to think about making Mother's Day cards or some other piece of writing for their mothers.

Five children are in the writing group: Maria, Bobby, Elizabeth, Teri, and John. John is a leader in the group, and as soon as Mrs. Carson asks the children what ideas they have for Mother's Day projects, he explains, "I want to make a card to tell my mom that she's the best mom in the world. I know she is and I want to tell her." Mrs. Carson follows his lead. "John, what does she do that makes you think she's the best mom?" John thinks for a minute and then begins to list her attributes: "My mom cooks me the best meals . . . she taught me to read when I was a little kid . . . you know, she takes care of me." Teri, Bobby, and the other children in the writing group join in the discussion, talking about their moms and what makes them special.

Four of the five children in the group decide to write letters to their moms telling why they are the best moms in the world. The fifth child chooses to write a poem instead, and she gets to work on her project. Mrs. Carson continues to meet with the other four children to talk about persuasive writing. Mrs. Carson says, "I think you are telling me that you want to convince your mom and everyone else who reads your Mother's Day card that your mom is the best. You will want to have lots of reasons or examples to make your point. John told us several reasons why his mom is the best. Can you think of some reasons why your mom is the best, too?"

The children share ideas, and then Mrs. Carson reviews the writing process and the steps they will follow in writing their cards. She asks them to draw a cluster and to include at least three reasons why their moms are the best, and she remains with the group while they get started. Then she moves off to another writing group.

Over the next 2 days, these four children write rough drafts of their cards. They all begin their cards by saying that their moms are the best and then incorporate the reasons and examples from their clusters into their writing. This group of four second graders is a very supportive group. As they write, they share their drafts with each other and get compliments and feedback on their writing. They also get ideas from each other. One child writes "I love you 100 times" on her rough draft, and soon others are writing "I love you 10,000 times" and another "I love you 1,000,000 times." The children aren't sure how to write such large numbers, so when Mrs. Carson checks on the group, she takes a moment to explain how to write large numbers.

On Wednesday, Mrs. Carson meets with the writing group about revising their cards. As each child reads his or her card aloud, Mrs. Carson and group members offer compliments and make suggestions for improvement. Mrs. Carson notices that John is the only child to have an ending for his card. Taking a moment to talk about writing, she reminds the group that many kinds of writing have a beginning, middle, and end. She uses a sandwich model made of two pieces of light-brown sponge cut into the shape of slices of bread, slices of meat and cheese cut from felt, rubber pickles, and mesh lettuce. She reminds them, "The beginning is the statement that your moms are the best," and she points to the top slice of bread. "The middle is where your reasons and examples go," and she points to the meat, cheese, and other ingredients. Then she points to the bottom slice of bread and asks, "Do your cards have an end?" John announces that his does, and he reads it aloud: "See I told you that you are the best mom on the Earth." No one else had an ending, so Mrs. Carson and John help the children write endings, such as "And that's why you are the bestest" and "Thank you for loving me so much."

After the children make their revisions, Mrs. Carson meets with the writing group again to help them edit their writing. The three editing skills that she focuses on are spelling, capitalization, and punctuation. For some writing assignments, Mrs. Carson focuses on punctuation marks or capital letters and ignores many of their invented spellings other than high-frequency words; however, this is an important writing project, and the children want their cards to be as adultlike as possible. Mrs. Carson reads over each paper and points out corrections. She explains some of the changes, and for others she simply says, "We usually put a comma here, so is it OK if I add it?"

After editing, the children copy their letters on "good" paper and glue the paper to the construction-paper cards they have decorated. On Thursday and Friday afternoons, the class meets to share their cards before they take them home. Mrs. Carson always makes time for the children to share their writing to help them develop a sense of authorship and feel that they are members of a community of writers.

Guided Writing:
A Second Grader's
Mother's Day
Message

> Dear Mom,
>
> You are the best mom on the entire Earth. I love you 1,000,000 times. You cook the best meals. You get me ready for school. You taught me to read when I was 5. See I told you that you are the best mom on the Earth.
>
> Love,
>
> John
>
> Happy Mother's Day!

John's Mother's Day message is presented here. This message, written by a second grader, includes the same three parts that older children who write more complex persuasive essays and letters use: a beginning, in which the position is stated; the middle, which provides at least three supporting reasons; and the end, in which the position is restated.

---

*P*arents have little doubt that children are effective persuaders as they argue to stay up beyond their bedtimes or plead to keep as a pet the stray puppy they've found. John's letter to his mother shows that young children can write persuasively, even though researchers have found that children's persuasive writing abilities develop more slowly than their abilities in any other genre (Applebee, Langer, & Mullis, 1986).

A sense of audience and the ability to tailor writing to fit that audience are perhaps most important in persuasive writing because the writer can judge how effective the persuasion is by readers' reactions. Although an audience's enjoyment of a story or poem or the information learned from a report can be hard to gauge, the effect of persuasion on others is not. Barry Kroll (1984) found that sixth graders could adapt to their audience in writing persuasive letters. He concluded that when students have a clear purpose and a plausible reason for writing, they can adapt their writing to meet the needs of their readers.

Persuasive arguments can be drawn on posters or written as essays or letters. Children write essays arguing against the use of drugs or make posters to recommend a book they've read. They present a point of view and then defend the position by citing several supporting reasons or examples. Children also write letters to legislators or to the editor of the local newspaper to express their opinions about community, state, or national issues and to try to persuade others to support their viewpoint. The Instructional Overview on the next page presents the goals and activities for teaching persuasive writing in kindergarten through eighth grade.

Instructional Overview: Persuasive Writing	
Grades	**Goals and Activities**
Kindergarten–Grade 2	**Goal 1: Create persuasive posters that offer an opinion** • Children make posters about favorite books. • Children make posters about nutrition, patriotism, ecology, and other issues.
	Goal 2: Write persuasive letters and books that present a position and provide some reasons or examples • Children write letters to persuade family members about a particular concern or issue. • Children use *The Important Book* (M. Brown, 1997) format to write persuasive cards and books.
Grades 3–5	**Goal 1: Write persuasive letters that express opinions, arguments, and feelings** • Children write letters to persuade friends or family members about a particular issue.
	Goal 2: Write persuasive essays that state an argument logically and with conviction • Children write book and movie reviews. • Children write essays comparing book and film versions of a story and explain why they prefer one version. • Children write persuasive essays about a health or contemporary issue.
	Goal 3: Create other persuasive materials • Children make persuasive posters. • Children design brochures and pamphlets that persuade the reader to a course of action or to a particular position.
Grades 6–8	**Goal 1: Present counterarguments** • Children create graphic organizers to consider counterarguments that could be used to refute their arguments. • Children add counterarguments to strengthen their arguments in letters and essays.
	Goal 2: Write convincing persuasive arguments • Children write persuasive letters to the editor of the school or city newspaper. • Children write persuasive essays in response to an article. • Children write persuasive essays as part of social studies and science units.

Persuasion

To persuade is to win someone over to your viewpoint or cause (Simon, 2005). In contrast to propaganda, which has a more sinister connotation, persuasion involves a reasoned or logical appeal. Propaganda can be deceptive, hyped, emotion-laden, or one-sided. Although the purpose of both is to influence, there are ethical differences.

Three Ways to Persuade

People can be persuaded in three ways. The first appeal a writer can make is based on reason. People seek to make logical generalizations and draw cause-and-effect conclusions, whether from facts or from strong possibilities. For example, people can be persuaded to practice more healthful living if told about the results of medical research. It is necessary, of course, to distinguish between reasonable and unreasonable appeals. For example, urging people to stand on their head every day for 30 minutes based on the claim that it will increase their intelligence is an unreasonable appeal.

A second way to persuade is through an appeal to character. Other people are important to us, and we can be persuaded by what another person recommends if we trust that person. Trust comes from personal knowledge of the person or the reputation of the person who is trying to persuade. Does the persuader have the expertise or personal experience necessary to endorse a product or a cause? For example, can we believe what scientists say about the dangers of global warming? Can we believe what a sports personality says about the effectiveness of a particular sports shoe?

The third way people can be persuaded is by an emotional appeal. Emotional appeals can be as strong as intellectual appeals because people have a deep concern for their well-being and for the rights of others. We support or reject arguments according to our feelings about what is ethical and socially responsible. At the same time, fear and the need for peer acceptance also influence our opinions and beliefs.

Any of the three appeals can be used to persuade another person. For example, when a child tries to persuade her parents that her bedtime should be delayed by 30 minutes, she might argue that neighbors allow their children to stay up later; this is an appeal to character. If the argument focuses on the amount of sleep that a 10-year-old needs, it is an appeal to reason. When the child finally announces that she has the earliest bedtime of anyone in her fourth-grade class and it makes her feel like a baby, the appeal is to the emotions.

These same three types of appeals are used for in-school persuasion. When trying to persuade classmates to read a particular book in a "book-selling" poster project, for example, children might argue that the book should be read because it is short and interesting (reason), because it is hilarious and you'll laugh (emotion), or because it is the most popular book in the second grade and everyone else is reading it (character).

Propaganda

The word *propaganda* suggests something shady or underhanded. Although propaganda, like persuasion, is designed to influence people's beliefs and actions, propagandists may use underhanded techniques to distort, conceal, and exaggerate the facts. People seeking to influence us often use words that evoke a variety of responses. For example, they claim something is "improved," "more natural," or "50% better." Such loaded words are deceptive because they have positive connotations but may have no basis in fact. For example, when a product is advertised as 50% better, consumers need to ask, "50% better than what?" That question is rarely answered in advertisements.

Doublespeak is another type of deceptive language; it is language that is evasive, euphemistic, confusing, and self-contradictory. For example, janitors may be called "maintenance engineers," and reruns of television shows may be termed "encore telecasts." William Lutz (1999) cites a number of kinds of doublespeak, including euphemisms and inflated language, that children can easily understand. Euphemisms are words or phrases, such as "passed away," used to avoid a harsh reality. They are often used out of concern for people's feelings rather than to deceive. Inflated language includes words designed to make the ordinary seem extraordinary. For example, car mechanics become "automotive internists," and used cars become "pre-owned." Children need to learn that people sometimes use words that only pretend to communicate; at other times, they use words to intentionally misrepresent. For instance, a wallet advertised as genuine imitation leather is a vinyl wallet, and a faux diamond ring is made of glass (the word *faux* is French for "false"). Children need to be able to interpret this deceptive language and to avoid using it themselves.

Organization of an Argument

Much like a story, an argument has a beginning, middle, and end. In the beginning, writers state their position, argument, or opinion clearly. In the middle, the opinion is developed as writers select and present three or more reasons or pieces of evidence to support their position; these reasons may appeal to logic, character, or emotions. Writers sequence the evidence in a logical order and use concrete examples whenever possible. They often use cue words such as *first, second,* and *third* to alert readers to the organization. Older students also refute counterarguments in the middle. In the end, writers lead their readers to draw the conclusion that they intend through giving a personal statement, making a prediction, or summarizing the major points. The organization of an argument is illustrated in Figure 12–1.

Marion Crowhurst (1991) identified several problems in children's persuasive writing that this organizational scheme can help to ameliorate. First, children's persuasive compositions are typically shorter than the stories and reports that they write. In these shorter compositions, children neither develop their arguments nor provide reasons to support their claims. Second, their persuasive essays show poor organization because children are unfamiliar with how an argument should be structured. Third, children's writing style is often inappropriate; their language is informal, and they use words such as *also* to tie arguments together rather than the more sophisticated stylistic devices, such as *if . . . then* statements, typically used in persuasive writing. When children talk their way through the graphic organizer as a prewriting activity and listen to classmates discuss their plans, they develop more sophisticated writing styles and tighter arguments.

How to Address Struggling Writers' Problems

The Problem	Ideas in the composition aren't sequenced.
What Causes It	When children begin to write before they've gathered and organized ideas, they tend to add ideas as they think of them, and the result is a disorganized composition.
How to Solve It	*Quick fix:* Write the sentences in a child's composition on sentence strips for the child to sequence or organize into related groups. Next, the child rereads the sentences and writes additional sentences on sentence strips, if necessary, to more fully develop the ideas. Once the ideas are developed and well organized, the child creates a new draft by copying the sentences on a piece of paper.
	Long-term solution: In a series of minilessons, teach children how to use graphic organizers to gather and organize ideas before beginning to write. They can also learn to meet with classmates to talk about their plans before beginning to write.
How to Prevent the Problem	Children who gather and organize ideas before beginning to write are more likely to write well-organized compositions that have a clear focus.

Figure 12–1 Graphic Organizer for an Argument

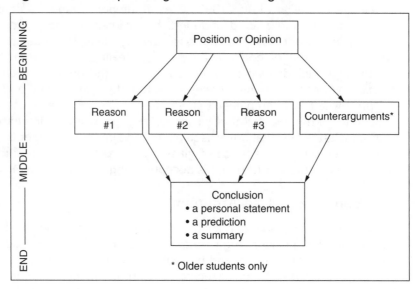

Although the organization of an argument typically involves a statement, the development of three (or more) reasons, and a conclusion, this organization isn't equivalent to a traditional five-paragraph theme. Persuasive writing requires a more elaborate organization than the simplistic, formulaic five-paragraph theme. In persuasive writing, children devise ways to introduce an argument, present supporting reasons, draw conclusions, and persuade the reader to accept the writer's viewpoint.

Types of Persuasive Writing

Persuasion is a part of everyday life. Children and adults frequently try to persuade others to do or believe a certain thing. Andrew Wilkinson and his colleagues (1980) investigated the ability of children (ages 7–13) to write persuasively: They found that children at all ages could state an opinion, and, not surprisingly, that as children grew older, they were better able to provide a logical justification for their opinions. Younger children were very egocentric in their reasoning and often failed to consider others' viewpoints. Furthermore, they found that children age 10 and older often wrote self-contradictory essays. In these essays, children started with a definite position, but through writing a justification for that position, they concluded with a position that was opposite of the one made in the beginning. However, it should be noted that these children wrote single-draft compositions and did not participate in writing groups to critique and revise their writing.

Topics for persuasive writing come from at-home and in-school activities as well as from literature focus units and thematic units. At home, children might try to persuade their parents to let them go to bed later, play on a football team, go to a slumber party, buy new clothes or shoes, join the Boy or Girl Scouts, have a larger allowance, buy a new toy, or have a pet. At school, children might try to persuade their teachers to let them have less homework, go outside for recess in cold weather, change lunchroom rules, or sponsor a student council election. Children also write to persuade others to stop smoking, avoid drugs, ban nuclear weapons,

Figure 12–2
Independent
Writing: A Fourth
Grader's Lost-
and-Found Poster

stop polluting the environment, endorse particular political candidates, read a certain book, see a certain movie, or support community, state, or national issues.

Persuasive Posters

A combination of drawing and writing is used to state a position on persuasive posters. Children are surrounded by persuasive posters, ranging from "Keep America Beautiful" billboard signs and "Don't drink and drive" bumper stickers to the motivational posters typically displayed in school hallways and cafeterias. As projects during literature focus units and thematic units, children make similar posters.

After reading Mercer Mayer's *Liverwurst Is Missing* (1981), fourth-grade Kyle designed the poster illustrated in Figure 12–2 to help locate Liverwurst, the baby rhinosterwurst that is missing from the circus. In the story, Liverwurst is finally found and saved from a terrible fate: becoming the world's first

EL
Scaffolding English Learners

Even though persuasive writing is often considered the most difficult genre, don't assume that English learners don't know how to use persuasion and can't be successful in persuasive writing. As a first step, try having them work with partners or small groups to make persuasive posters that use a combination of drawing and writing to express a viewpoint.

Figure 12–3 Independent Writing: A Sixth Grader's Poster About Drugs

rhino-burger. Kyle's poster provides the important logical-appeal information and picture typically found on lost-and-found posters. In addition, a reward is promised. Liverwurst's tears add a tug-at-your-heart emotional appeal, too.

As part of a unit on drugs, a class of sixth graders designed posters to display in their community to warn people about the dangers of drugs. In the poster presented in Figure 12–3, the child used a logical cause-and-effect appeal to warn of the dangers of driving under the influence of alcohol or drugs. The poster is particularly powerful because he used *gamble,* a loaded word, in his caption.

Persuasive Letters

Children write letters to persuade family members and friends. As with other types of letters, these letters are written to real audiences and are mailed. During a unit on drugs, children in a fifth-grade class each chose a family member or a friend to write a persuasive letter to. Some children wrote to parents or grandparents, arguing that they should stop smoking; others wrote to siblings or friends, urging them not to take drugs or not to mix drinking and driving. Fifth-grade Tom wrote this letter to his friend Mike:

Dear Mike,

I think drugs are very bad. They hurt people a lot and they can cost money. Mike, I know you're 15 and you don't think drugs can hurt you, but you can get addicted to drugs just the same as everybody else.

You can get hurt taking drugs, Mike. Some of the possible consequences are that you may get hurt dealing drugs, you may get AIDS by sharing infected needles or the pressure may become so great you just commit suicide. You might hurt others, too. You could rob a bank, hurt people in an auto accident, or just get violent and hurt someone. Michael, you might lose a friend and get into fights, be unpopular, or just be sad.

Drugs are out and it's the truth. More people are saying no to drugs. It isn't worth it, so be smart, not stupid, and don't get into trouble. Don't waste your time, and it costs lots of money to do drugs and you will be depressed a lot.

Many people say drugs are only as bad as cigarettes. That is not so. See Mike, you could go from $1 a day on cigarettes to $100 a day on heroin. Money and health problems arise from drugs. Each year, 200,000 are hurt by drugs and 25,000 people die from drug-related accidents. Half a million people are arrested for drugs each year.

So, doing drugs is wrong. This evidence is that you should not take any kind of drugs, Mike. I hope you make the right decision.

Your friend, Tom

In his letter, Tom uses appeals to reason, character, and emotion. He cites statistics and uses cause-and-effect arguments in his rational appeal to Mike not to use drugs. He says in his appeal to character that people who take drugs are stupid, and he evokes the universal fear of contracting AIDS in his appeal to emotion. Tom tells Mike that he might die or hurt other people if he takes drugs.

Persuasive letters can also be sent to newspapers. A letter sent to the editor of a local newspaper is presented in Figure 12–4. In this letter, seventh-grade Becky argues that the adult admission prices that teens pay at movies are unfair considering that they are not allowed to see adult movies.

Children also write persuasive letters as part of literature focus units, assuming the role of a character and writing simulated letters to another character. Even though these letters are not mailed, children can exchange letters and write back from the viewpoint of another character. As part of a literature focus unit on *The Giver* (Lowry, 1993), seventh graders wrote persuasive letters from one character to another in which they offered advice about how to make the community better. Josh writes from Jonas's viewpoint:

Dear Giver,

Gabe and I are here in Elsewhere. It is a loving community. We are safe and happy. Now it is up to you to help the community. I think you should let them deal with the memories themselves and let them make choices.

You have to teach them how to make choices and try to make them use them wisely.

Figure 12–4
Independent Writing: A Seventh Grader's Letter to the Editor

Source: The Norman (Okla.) Transcript. Reprinted with permission.

Editor, The Transcript:

I am a student at Longfellow Middle School. I am writing to express my feelings on the price teenagers pay to get into the movie theater. In most movie theaters at the age of 13, they consider you an adult, so you have to pay full price. But you pay the adult price to see a children's movie. They say we aren't old enough to see these movies, yet they consider us adult enough to pay the adult price. Why is this? I strongly urge the movie theaters to think this through and change the price, so if you are an adult you pay the adult price to see an adult movie and if you are a child you pay to see a children's movie. I am not saying that at the age of 13 you should be able to see "R" rated movies, but I'm saying don't make us pay for them. Let us pay for what we see.

REBECCA PIERCE
Norman

Let them use the memories for good. The memories of war would teach them that war is bad. The memories of color would let them enjoy life more, if they could see color. The feelings of love would make them very happy. They could learn from these memories. They could learn of the past, good or bad, sad or happy. If they have memories, they could have feelings. They could have wisdom. They could have happiness. They could be free.

I know what you think. You think there would be chaos if the community had the memories. Bad and evil things could happen, but Giver, life is like that. You have the memories and you know what could happen. That's why you are there to help them.

Your son,
Jonas

Josh's letter is persuasive. He argues that when people have memories, they can become wise, happy, and free. In the final paragraph, Josh refutes a counterargument, that giving the people memories will lead to chaos, by suggesting that the Giver can help the community through the difficult adjustment.

Persuasive Essays

Children write persuasive essays in which they argue on topics they have strong beliefs and opinions about. For example, sixth-grade Michael wrote the following essay about drinking soft drinks during class:

> I think we, the students of Deer Creek School, should be allowed to drink refreshments during class. One reason is that it seems to speed the passing of the day. Second, I feel it is unfair and rude for teachers to drink coffee and soft drinks in front of the students. Finally, I think if the students were not worried about making trips to the water fountain, they would concentrate more on school work. Being allowed to drink refreshments would be a wonderful addition to the school day.

Michael's essay is well organized with a well-articulated beginning, middle, and end. He clearly states his position in the first sentence. Next, he lists three reasons and cues readers to the reasons using the words *one reason, second,* and *finally.* In the last sentence, Michael concludes by making a prediction.

On the topic of girls' right to play any sport, sixth-grade Amy writes:

> I think there should be more sports for girls. Girls are capable of playing sports such as soccer and football. Some girls dislike basketball, but they want to participate in other sports. If girls could participate in other sports, they could learn to coordinate as a team. Everyone needs exercise and alternative activities would keep all females physically fit. Girls should have the chance to participate and excel in other sports.

Amy's essay also follows the three-part organizational structure, but she does not direct attention to her reasons using cue words as Michael did. She begins with a clear statement of her position, and at the end, she uses a summary to conclude her appeal.

As part of a thematic unit on the American Revolution, a class of fifth graders wrote persuasive essays. The teacher asked the children to think about whether the American Revolution was a necessary thing. Did they favor the patriot or the loyalist position? Children brainstormed a list of reasons in support of the Revolution and a list of reasons in opposition. Then they picked one side and

Preparing for Writing Tests

Persuasive Writing

Persuasive writing is winning people to a particular viewpoint or persuading them to take a specific action. Writers present a position and then try to persuade readers to agree with it. They provide meaningful facts, examples, evidence, and anecdotes in support of their position. Sometimes writers confuse persuasive writing with expository writing, but it does more than present information: Writers must take a stand and argue in support of it. The topics chosen for persuasive prompts are debatable, offering writers more than one point of view; older writers also refute contrasting positions.

What Do Writers Do?

- Clearly state a position
- Make at least three points in support of their position
- Provide examples, evidence, information, or anecdotes to explain each point
- Present an opposing point of view and argue against it
- Organize their writing with an introduction that presents a position, several reasons in support of that position (often set off in separate paragraphs), refutation of other viewpoints, and a conclusion
- Use standard English conventions effectively
- Adopt a style to appeal to the audience specified in the prompt
- Usually format the writing as an essay or a letter

What Mistakes Do Writers Often Make?

- Present information instead of articulating an argument
- Don't present convincing evidence for their arguments
- Present only one viewpoint (older writers only)

Sample Prompts

- Your principal is thinking about serving healthier food in the school cafeteria. Do you think that's a good idea? Write a persuasive letter to your principal to express your viewpoint and convince him to agree.
- Some people believe that laws requiring bicyclists to wear helmets are good, but others disagree. What is your viewpoint? Write a persuasive essay presenting the issues on both sides and convincing people to agree with your viewpoint.

wrote an essay articulating their position. They began by stating their position, provided at least three reasons to support their view, and then concluded the essay. Marshall wrote:

> I am in favor of the American Revolution and here are three of my reasons. First, after the colonists won the war, they could believe in God how they wanted. Next, if we didn't win the war, we would probably be British and not American. Third, after the war, the colonists could speak their mind without being tortured or killed. That is why I am for the American Revolution.

Tim took the opposing point of view and wrote:

> I'm against the American Revolution. I think it was a bad war and unnecessary for several reasons. The first reason is that the colonists were already pretty much free, and they didn't need to have a war. The second reason is that there was way too much suffering, fighting, and loss of life. The last reason was that it was a tremendous loss of lots of money. These are three reasons why I'm against the Revolutionary War.

Teaching Children to Write Persuasively

Teachers teach children about persuasive writing much like they teach the other writing genres. They introduce children to persuasive writing and explain what persuasion and propaganda are, share examples of persuasive writing in books children are reading, and provide opportunities for them to write persuasively.

Introducing Persuasive Writing

Teachers introduce persuasive writing by showing children how persuasion is used in everyday life. They talk with children about the points of view and positions that people take on various issues. Children might brainstorm a list of examples of persuasion they notice in their family, school, and community. They collect advertisements from magazines and newspapers or make a display of photos of billboards and posters with persuasive arguments that they notice in the community. Through a series of minilessons, teachers explain what persuasion is and compare it with propaganda.

Kindergarten and first-grade teachers often introduce persuasive writing using Margaret Brown's classic book, *The Important Book* (1997). On each page, something is described, and the most important attribute is identified. The same format is used on each page, and young children can use the format as a pattern for their persuasive writing. A first-grade class used this pattern to write about firefighters:

> The important thing about firefighters is that they are brave. They fight fires with hoses and axes. They save people and pets from getting burned. They wear hats, coats, gloves, and boots to stay safe. But, the important thing about firefighters is that they are brave.

Through this patterned writing activity, children learn about brainstorming ideas, identifying the most important idea, and trying to convince others of their viewpoint.

Other teachers also share examples of trade books in which persuasion is used. They might share *Molly's Pilgrim* (Cohen, 1983), *Encounter* (Yolen, 1992), or another book in which the authors try to persuade readers to adopt their viewpoint. A list of books with persuasive appeals is presented in Figure 12–5. In *Molly's Pilgrim,* for example, Barbara Cohen argues that there are modern-day Pilgrims like Molly's mother who emigrated from Russia and came to America for religious freedom.

Teachers introduce children to persuasive writing through a series of minilessons in which children investigate persuasive techniques, after which children apply what they have learned to write persuasive letters and essays as part of literature focus units and thematic units. The minilessons are important because research has shown that children benefit from direct instruction on persuasive writing (Crowhurst, 1991). Suggested topics for minilessons include the following: three ways to persuade people, how to organize an argument, how to develop a graphic organizer, and

Figure 12–5 Books With Persuasive Appeals

Baylor, B. (1982). *The best town in the world*. New York: Aladdin Books. (M)
Brown, M. W. (1997). *The important book*. New York: HarperCollins. (P)
Cohen, B. (1983). *Molly's pilgrim*. New York: Morrow. (M)
Cowcher, H. (1990). *Antarctica*. New York: Farrar, Straus & Giroux. (M)
Hesse, K. (2001). *Witness*. New York: Scholastic. (U)
Kelley, T. (2005). *School lunch*. New York: Holiday House. (P)
Scieszka, J. (1989). *The true story of the 3 little pigs!* New York: Viking. (P–M)
Siebert, D. (1991). *Sierra*. New York: HarperCollins. (M–U)
Turner, A. (1987). *Nettie's trip south*. New York: Macmillan. (M–U)
Van Allsburg, C. (1981). *Jumanji*. Boston: Honghton Mifflin. (M)
Van Allsburg, C. (1985). *The polar express*. Boston: Houghton Mifflin. (M)
Van Allsburg, C. (1990). *Just a dream*. Boston: Houghton Mifflin. (M)
Van Allsburg, C. (1991). *The wretched stone*. Boston: Houghton Mifflin. (M–U)
Weir, B., & Weir, W. (1991). *Panther dream: A story of the African rainforest*. New York: Hyperion Books. (M)
Yolen, J. (1992). *Encounter*. Orlando: Harcourt Brace. (M)
Zolotow, C. (1972). *William's doll*. New York: HarperCollins. (P)

P = primary grades (K–2), M = middle grades (3–5), U = upper grades (6–8)

how to refute counterarguments. Through these lessons, children increase their awareness of the power of persuasion and its pervasiveness today. Children also learn how arguments are organized so that they will be prepared to design persuasive posters and write persuasive letters and essays. Ms. Ohashi's minilesson on writing persuasive essays is presented in the minilesson feature on page 278.

Writing Persuasive Letters and Essays

Children use a process approach to develop and refine their persuasive letters and essays. Teachers often write a class collaboration composition with children to model the process before they begin writing their own letters or essays. Figure 12–6 shows the graphic organizer and final draft of a fourth-grade class's essay about pilgrims written after reading *Molly's Pilgrim* (Cohen, 1983), and Figure 12–7 shows the letter that fifth-grade Lance wrote to his Uncle Bobby to try to persuade him to stop smoking. Lance's graphic organizer is also shown in the figure. Then children use the writing process to write persuasive letters and essays. The steps are listed in the step-by-step feature on pages 281 and 282.

Assessing Children's Persuasive Writing

Teachers assess both the process that children use and the quality of their persuasive letters and essays. The assessment instrument should include the steps that children move through as they develop their compositions, such as the following:

- Children create a plan using a graphic organizer.
- Children write a rough draft.
- Children complete a "Writer's Revision Checklist."

- Children meet in writing groups to share their rough drafts.
- Children have classmates complete a "Reader's Revision Checklist."
- Children compare the revision checklists.
- Children make revisions based on the revision checklists and suggestions made in writing groups.
- Children proofread their compositions and correct as many mechanical errors as possible.

Persuasive Essays

Ms. Ohashi's fourth graders have studied persuasion, collected examples of persuasion in their community, and examined television commercials to determine the advertisers' purpose. Today the teacher is going to reread *The True Story of the 3 Little Pigs!* (Scieszka, 1989) and ask children to decide if they believe the wolf's version.

1. Introduce the topic

Ms. Ohashi quickly retells "The Three Little Pigs" to familiarize the children with the traditional folktale and then introduces Scieszka's version of the story, told from the wolf's viewpoint.

2. Share examples

Ms. Ohashi reads *The True Story of the 3 Little Pigs!* aloud to the children and asks them to think about the wolf's use of persuasion in the story.

3. Provide information

The children talk about the wolf's version, noting the wolf's persuasive techniques, including his friendly attitude and the repeated use of the word *true*. Next, they make a chart with three columns. In the left column, children list the wolf's bad deeds as described in the folktale; in the middle column, they list the wolf's arguments and excuses; and in the right column, they indicate whether they believe the wolf. For example, the pigs said that the wolf huffed and puffed and blew two houses down, and the wolf argued that he went to the pigs' houses to borrow a cup of sugar and sneezed. The children decide that they don't believe the wolf. After they finish the chart, it becomes clear that although they enjoyed the wolf's story, they believe the traditional version of the story.

4. Guide practice

"You don't believe the wolf's story, and you can explain your thinking in a persuasive essay," Ms. Ohashi explains. She quickly reviews how to complete a graphic organizer and write a persuasive essay. The children begin by identifying lines of reasoning for their arguments from the chart they developed in the previous step. They complete graphic organizers by listing three reasons for their decisions and their conclusions. Ms. Ohashi circulates around the classroom, providing assistance as needed and checking their completed graphic organizers. Then children write their essays independently.

5. Assess learning

Ms. Ohashi checks the children's graphic organizers as they complete them, and she will read their completed essays to assess their learning.

Figure 12–6 Shared Writing: Fourth Graders' Graphic Organizer and Essay About *Molly's Pilgrim*

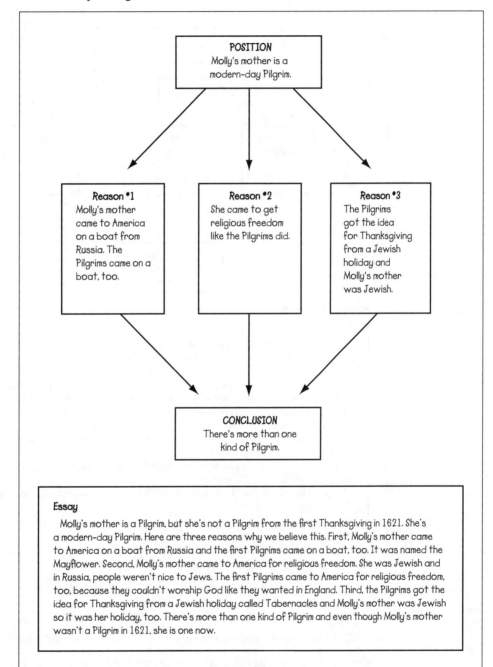

POSITION
Molly's mother is a
modern-day Pilgrim.

Reason #1
Molly's mother
came to America
on a boat from
Russia. The
Pilgrims came on a
boat, too.

Reason #2
She came to get
religious freedom
like the Pilgrims did.

Reason #3
The Pilgrims
got the idea
for Thanksgiving
from a Jewish
holiday and
Molly's mother
was Jewish.

CONCLUSION
There's more than one
kind of Pilgrim.

Essay

Molly's mother is a Pilgrim, but she's not a Pilgrim from the first Thanksgiving in 1621. She's a modern-day Pilgrim. Here are three reasons why we believe this. First, Molly's mother came to America on a boat from Russia and the first Pilgrims came on a boat, too. It was named the Mayflower. Second, Molly's mother came to America for religious freedom. She was Jewish and in Russia, people weren't nice to Jews. The first Pilgrims came to America for religious freedom, too, because they couldn't worship God like they wanted in England. Third, the Pilgrims got the idea for Thanksgiving from a Jewish holiday called Tabernacles and Molly's mother was Jewish so it was her holiday, too. There's more than one kind of Pilgrim and even though Molly's mother wasn't a Pilgrim in 1621, she is one now.

Figure 12–7 Independent Writing: A Fifth Grader's Graphic Organizer and Persuasive Letter

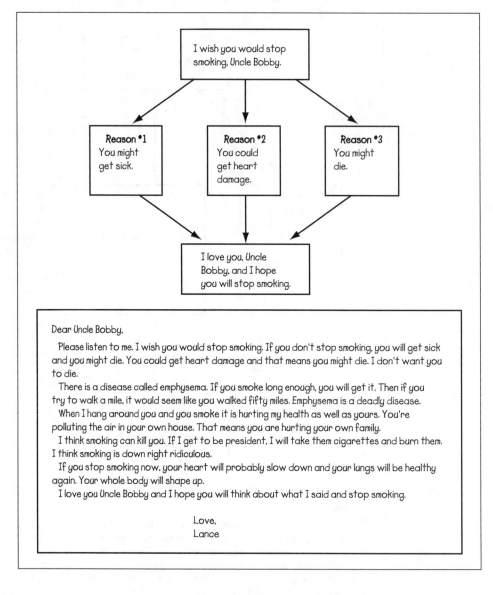

- Children make a final copy of their compositions.
- Children share their compositions with an appropriate audience.

A checklist can be developed from these steps and used in assessing children's compositions. This checklist should be distributed to children before beginning the project so they can keep track of their progress.

Teachers and children also make rubrics to assess the quality of children's letters and essays. They use the characteristics of persuasive writing to create the rubric. It's important to develop the rubric before children begin to write so they will know how they'll be assessed.

Step by Step: Writing Persuasive Letters and Essays

1. ***Identify a position.*** Children identify a position and plan their arguments using a graphic organizer. They include at least three reasons or pieces of evidence for their position; older children also identify counterarguments that they need to refute.

2. ***Write the rough draft.*** Children write rough drafts, one or more paragraphs in length, incorporating the information listed on the graphic organizer.

3. ***Revise and edit the rough draft.*** Children revise and edit their rough drafts using feedback from classmates and the teacher. In addition, children can use a "Writer's Revision Checklist," as shown in Figure 12–8, to revise their drafts. After completing the checklist, they make any needed changes before sharing their compositions in writing groups. Children can also ask their classmates to complete a "Reader's Revision Checklist," also shown in Figure 12–8. After classmates complete this form, writers compare their own responses with their classmates'. If readers' comments differ significantly from the writer's, then children should conclude that they are not communicating effectively and that additional revision is necessary. Then children proofread their essays, hunting for mechanical errors, and correct these errors.

4. ***Publish and share the composition.*** Children share their letters and essays with a real audience. Letters are sent to the people to whom they are addressed, and letters to the editor are submitted for possible publication in school and local newspapers. Persuasive essays can be read aloud from the author's chair or shared in some other way.

Figure 12–8 Revision Checklists for Persuasive Writing

Writer's Revision Checklist

Name _____   Yes   No

1. At the beginning, did you state your position clearly?   ☐   ☐

   Write your position here:

   _____
   _____
   _____

2. In the middle, did you present three pieces of evidence to
   support your position?   ☐   ☐

   Write your pieces of evidence here:
   1. _____
   2. _____
   3. _____

3. At the end, did you lead your readers to the conclusion?   ☐   ☐

   How did you lead them?
   ☐ Gave a personal statement.
   ☐ Made a prediction.
   ☐ Summarized the three main points.

Continued

Figure 12–8 *Continued*

Reader's Revision Checklist

Name _____   Yes   No

1. At the beginning, did the writer state his/her position clearly?   ☐   ☐

   Write the position here:

   _____
   _____
   _____

2. In the middle, did the writer present three pieces of evidence to support the position?   ☐   ☐

   Write the pieces of evidence here:
   1. _____
   2. _____
   3. _____

3. At the end, did the writer lead you to the conclusion?   ☐   ☐

   How did he/she lead you?
   ☐ Gave a personal statement.
   ☐ Made a prediction.
   ☐ Summarized the three main points.

ANSWERING TEACHERS' QUESTIONS ABOUT . . .

Persuasive Writing

You must be kidding. My primary graders can't write persuasively.

Even first and second graders use persuasion in their everyday talk. With guidance and encouragement, they can use the same kinds of persuasion in their writing. The Mother's Day letters that Mrs. Carson's second graders wrote are good examples of the kind of persuasive writing primary-grade students can do.

I'm confused. What's the difference between persuasion and propaganda?

That's a good question. People use both persuasion and propaganda to influence someone to do or believe something. In both, people use appeals to reason, character, and feelings. The difference is that propagandists may use deceptive language to distort, conceal, or exaggerate. The line between persuasion and propaganda is thin. Because it is so easy to cross back and forth between the two, children must learn to detect propaganda in order not to be swayed by it.

Can I tie persuasive writing to content areas?

Yes, children can write persuasively about topics they are learning in thematic units. For example, they can argue about historical events and even about contributions of various historical figures. They can investigate current issues about immigration quotas, English as the official language of the United States, or the rights of Native Americans. They can clarify positions on scientific concepts and consider topical issues such as nuclear energy, global warming, pollution, and conservation efforts.

References

Professional References

Allen, C. A. (2001). *The multigenre research paper: Voice, passion, and discovery in grades 4–6.* Portsmouth, NH: Heinemann.

Anderson, C. (2005). *Assessing writers.* Portsmouth, NH: Heinemann.

Anderson, J. (2005). *Mechanically inclined: Building grammar, usage, and style into writer's workshop.* Portland, ME: Stenhouse.

Angelillo, J. (2002). *A fresh approach to teaching punctuation.* New York: Scholastic.

Angelillo, J. (2005). *Writing to the prompt: When students don't have a choice.* Portsmouth, NH: Heinemann.

Applebee, A. N. (1978). *The child's concept of story: Ages 2 to 17.* Chicago: University of Chicago Press.

Applebee, A. N. (1980). Children's narratives: New directions. *The Reading Teacher, 34,* 137–142.

Applebee, A. N., Langer, J. A., & Mullis, I. V. (1986). *The writing report card: Writing achievement in American schools.* Princeton, NJ: Educational Testing Service.

Armbruster, B. B., McCarthey, S. J., & Cummins, S. (2005). Writing to learn in elementary classrooms. In R. Indrisano & J. R. Paratore (Eds.), *Learning to write, writing to learn: Theory and research in practice* (pp. 71–96). Newark, DE: International Reading Association.

Ashton-Warner, S. (1965). *Teacher.* New York: Simon & Schuster.

Atwell, N. (1998). *In the middle: New understandings about writing, reading, and learning* (2nd ed.). Portsmouth, NH: Heinemann.

Au, K. H. (1992). Constructing the theme of a story. *Language Arts, 69,* 106–111.

Barnes, D., Morgan, K., & Weinhold, K. (Eds.). (1997). *Writing process revisited: Sharing our stories.* Urbana, IL: National Council of Teachers of English.

Barone, D. (1990). The written responses of young children: Beyond comprehension to story understanding. *The New Advocate, 3,* 49–56.

Bereiter, C., & Scardamalia, M. (1982). From conversation to composition: The role of instruction in the developmental process. In R. Glaser (Ed.), *Advances in instructional psychology* (Vol. 2, pp. 1–64). Hillsdale, NJ: Erlbaum.

Bergman, J. L. (1992). SAIL—A way to success and independence for low-achieving readers. *The Reading Teacher, 45,* 598–602.

Berrill, D. P., & Gall, M. (2000). *Penpal programs in primary classrooms.* Markham, ON: Pembroke.

Berthoff, A. (1981). *The making of meaning.* Upper Montclair, NJ: Boynton/Cook.

Bode, B. A. (1989). Dialogue journal writing. *The Reading Teacher, 42,* 568–571.

Bottomley, D. M., Henk, W. A., & Melnick, S. A. (1998/1999). Assessing children's views about themselves as writers using the Writer Self-Perception Scale. *The Reading Teacher, 51,* 286–296.

Boyd, R. (1985). The message board: Language comes alive. In J. M. Newman (Ed.), *Whole language: Theory in use* (pp. 91–98). Portsmouth, NH: Heinemann.

Bratcher, S. (2004). *Evaluating children's writing: A handbook of communication choices for classroom teachers* (2nd ed.). Mahwah, NJ: Erlbaum.

Britton, J. (1970a). *Language and learning.* New York: Penguin Books.

Britton, J. (1970b). *Language and thought.* Harmondsworth: Penguin.

Britton, J., Burgess, T., Martin, N., McLeod, A., & Rosen, H. (1975). *The development of writing abilities* (11–18). London: Macmillan.

Bromley, K. D. (1996). *Webbing with literature: Creating story maps with children's books* (2nd ed.). Boston: Allyn & Bacon.

Button, K., Johnson, M. J., & Furgerson, P. (1996). Interactive writing in a primary classroom. *The Reading Teacher, 49,* 446–454.

Cahnmann, M. (2006). Reading, living, and writing bilingual poetry as scholARTistry in the language arts classroom. *Language Arts, 83,* 342–352.

Calkins, L. M. (1980). When children want to punctuate: Basic skills belong in context. *Language Arts, 57,* 567–573.

Calkins, L. M. (1991). *Living between the lines.* Portsmouth, NH: Heinemann.

Calkins, L. M. (1994). *The art of teaching writing* (new ed.). Portsmouth, NH: Heinemann.

Calkins, L., Hartman, A., & White, Z. (2005). *One to one: The art of conferring with young writers.* Portsmouth, NH: Heinemann.

Cappello, M. (2005, Winter). Supporting independent writing: A continuum of writing instruction. *The California Reader, 39*(2), 38–46.

Cecil, N. L. (1994). *For the love of poetry: Poetry for every learner.* Winnipeg, MB: Peguis.

Chandler-Olcott, K., & Mahar, D. (2001, September). A framework for choosing topics for, with, and by adolescent writers. *Voices From the Middle, 9*(1), 40–47.

Clay, M. M. (1991). *Becoming literate: The construction of inner control.* Portsmouth, NH: Heinemann.

Coggeshall, K., & Doherty, J. (2004). Technology that powers up learning. *Voices From the Middle, 11,* 23–29.

Cohle, D. M., & Towle, W. (2001). *Connecting reading and writing in the intermediate grades.* Newark, DE: International Reading Association.

Collins, J. L. (1998). *Strategies for struggling writers.* New York: Guilford Press.

Cordeiro, P., Giacobbe, M. E., & Cazden, C. (1983). Apostrophes, quotation marks, and periods: Learning punctuation in the first grade. *Language Arts, 60,* 323–332.

Coughlan, M. (1988). Let the students show us what they know. *Language Arts, 65,* 375–378.

Crowhurst, M. (1991). Interrelationships between reading and writing persuasive discourse. *Research in the Teaching of English, 25,* 314–338.

Crowhurst, M. (1992). Some effects of corresponding with an older audience. *Language Arts, 69,* 268–273.

Culham, R. (2003). *6 + 1 traits of writing: The complete guide, grades 3 and up.* New York: Scholastic.

Dahl, K. L., & Freppon, P. A. (1995). A comparison of inner-city children's interpretations of reading and writing instruction in the early grades in skills-based and whole language classrooms. *Reading Research Quarterly, 30,* 50–74.

D'Aoust, C. (1992). Portfolios: Process for students and teachers. In K. B. Yancey (Ed.), *Portfolios in the writing classroom: An introduction* (pp. 39–48). Urbana, IL: National Council of Teachers of English.

daSilva, K. E. (2001). Drawing on experience: Connecting art and language. *Primary Voices K–6, 10*(2), 2–8.

Davis, J., & Hill, S. (2003). *The no-nonsense guide to teaching writing.* Portsmouth, NH: Heinemann.

Dean, D. (2006). *Strategic writing.* Urbana, IL: National Council of Teachers of English.

de Beaugrande, R. (1980). *Text, discourse, and process.* Norwood, NJ: Ablex.

De Fina, A. A. (1992). *Portfolio assessment: Getting started.* New York: Scholastic.

Delpit, L. (1987). The silenced dialogue: Power and pedagogy in educating other people's children. *Harvard Educational Review, 58,* 280–298.

Delpit, L. (1991). A conversation with Lisa Delpit. *Language Arts, 68,* 541–547.

Devine, T. G. (1982). *Listening skills schoolwide: Activities and programs.* Urbana, IL: ERIC Clearinghouse on Reading and Communication Skills and the National Council of Teachers of English.

Dillon, D. (2005). *Practice with purpose: Literacy work stations for grades 3–6.* Portland, ME: Stenhouse.

Dix, S. (2006). I'll do it my way: Three writers and their revision practices. *The Reading Teacher, 59,* 566–573.

Donovan, C. A. (2001). Children's development and control of written story and informational genres: Insights from one elementary school. *Research in the Teaching of English, 35,* 394–447.

Dorn, L. J., & Soffos, C. (2001). *Scaffolding young writers: A writers' workshop approach.* Portland, ME: Stenhouse.

Dorotik, M., & Betzold, M. R. (1992). Expanding literacy for all. *The Reading Teacher, 45,* 574–578.

Dressel, J. H. (1990). The effects of listening to and discussing different qualities of children's literature on the narrative writing of fifth graders. *Research in the Teaching of English, 24,* 397–414.

Dudley-Marling, C. (1996). Explicit instruction within a whole language framework: Teaching struggling readers and writers. In E. McIntyre & M. Pressley (Eds.), *Balanced instruction: Strategies and skills in whole language* (pp. 23–38). Norwood, MA: Christopher-Gordon.

Dudley-Marling, C., & Dippo, D. (1991). The language of whole language. *Language Arts, 68,* 548–554.

Duffy, G. G., & Roehler, L. R. (1991). Teachers' instructional actions. In R. Barr, M. L. Kamil, P. B. Mosenthal, & P. D. Pearson (Eds.), *Handbook of reading research* (Vol. 2, pp. 861–884). New York: Longman.

Duke, N. K., & Bennett-Armistead, V. S. (2003). *Reading and writing informational text in the primary grades: Research-based practices.* New York: Scholastic.

Dworin, J. E. (2006). The Family Stories Project: Using funds of knowledge for writing. *The Reading Teacher, 59,* 510–520.

Dyson, A. H. (1993). *Social worlds of children learning to write in an urban primary school.* New York: Teachers College Press.

Edelsky, C. (1983). Segmentation and punctuation: Developmental data from young writers in a bilingual program. *Research in the Teaching of English, 17,* 135–136.

Elbow, P. (1998). *Writing without teachers* (2nd ed.). New York: Oxford University Press.

Elbow, P. (2002). Writing to publish is for every student. In C. Weber (Ed.), *Publishing with students: A comprehensive guide* (pp. 1–8). Portsmouth, NH: Heinemann.

Emig, J. (1971). *The composing processes of twelfth graders.* Champaign, IL: National Council of Teachers of English.

Emig, J. (1977). Writing as model of learning. *College Composition and Communication, 28*(2), 122–128.

Faigley, L., Cherry, R. D., Jolliffe, D. A., & Skinner, A. M. (1985). *Assessing writers' knowledge and processes of composing.* Norwood, NJ: Ablex.

Faigley, L., & Witte, S. (1981). Analyzing revision. *College Composition and Communication, 32,* 400–410.

Farr, R., & Tone, B. (1998). *Portfolio and performance assessment: Helping students evaluate their progress as readers and writers* (2nd ed.). Fort Worth, TX: Harcourt Brace.

Farris, P. J. (1991). Handwriting instruction should not become extinct. *Language Arts, 68,* 312–314.

Fearn, L., & Farnan, N. (1998). *Writing effectively: Helping children master the conventions of writing*. Boston: Allyn & Bacon.

Ferreiro, E., & Teberosky, A. (1982). *Literacy before schooling*. Portsmouth, NH: Heinemann.

Fine, E. S. (1987). Marbles lost, marbles found: Collaborative production of text. *Language Arts, 64*, 474–487.

Fleming, M. (1985). Writing assignments focusing on autobiographical and biographical topics. In M. Fleming & J. McGinnis (Eds.), *Portraits: Biography and autobiography in the secondary school* (pp. 95–97). Urbana, IL: National Council of Teachers of English.

Fleming, M., & McGinnis, J. (Eds.). (1985). *Portraits: Biography and autobiography in the secondary school*. Urbana, IL: National Council of Teachers of English.

Fletcher, R. (1996). *A writer's notebook: Unlocking the writer within*. New York: Camelot.

Fletcher, R., & Portalupi, J. (2001). *Writing workshop: The essential guide*. Portsmouth, NH: Heinemann.

Flower, L. S., & Hayes, J. R. (1977). Problem-solving strategies and the writing process. *College English, 39*, 449–461.

Flower, L. S., & Hayes, J. R. (1981). A cognitive process theory of writing. *College Composition and Communication, 32*, 365–387.

Fountas, I. C., & Pinnell, G. S. (1996). *Guided reading: Good first teaching for all children*. Portsmouth, NH: Heinemann.

Franklin, J. (2005). Finding the black ninja fish: Revision and writing groups in the first grade. *The Quarterly, 27*(1), 2–7.

Freppon, P. A., & Headings, L. (1996). Keeping it whole in whole language: A first grade teacher's phonics instruction in an urban whole language classroom. In E. McIntyre & M. Pressley (Eds.), *Balanced instruction: Strategies and skills in whole language* (pp. 65–80). Norwood, MA: Christopher-Gordon.

Fulwiler, T. (1987). *The journal book*. Portsmouth, NH: Boynton/Cook.

Geller, L. G. (1981). Riddling: A playful way to explore language. *Language Arts, 58*, 669–674.

Geller, L. G. (1985). *Wordplay and language learning for children*. Urbana, IL: National Council of Teachers of English.

Gibbons, P. (2002). *Scaffolding language, scaffolding learning*. Portsmouth, NH: Heinemann.

Goldberg, A., Russell, M., & Cook, A. (2003). The effects of computers on student writing: A meta-analysis of studies from 1992–2002. *Journal of Technology, Learning, and Assessment, 2*(1), 1–51.

Golden, J. M. (1984). Children's concept of story in reading and writing. *The Reading Teacher, 37*, 578–584.

Graves, D. H. (1975). An examination of the writing processes of seven-year-old children. *Research in the Teaching of English, 9*, 227–241.

Graves, D. H. (1976). Let's get rid of the welfare mess in the teaching of writing. *Language Arts, 53*, 645–651.

Graves, D. H. (1994). *A fresh look at writing*. Portsmouth, NH: Heinemann.

Graves, D. H. (2003). *Writing: Teachers and children at work* (20th anniversary ed.). Portsmouth, NH: Heinemann.

Graves, D. H., & Hansen, J. (1983). The author's chair. *Language Arts, 60*, 176–183.

Halliday, M. A. K. (1975). *Learning how to mean: Explorations in the development of language*. London: Edward Arnold.

Halliday, M. A. K. (1980). Three aspects of children's language development: Learning language, learning through language, learning about language. In Y. M. Goodman, M. M. Haussler, & D. S. Strickland (Eds.), *Oral and written language development research: Impact on the schools* (pp. 7–19). Proceedings from the 1979–1980 IMPACT Conferences sponsored by the International Reading Association and the National Council of Teachers of English.

Hancock, M. R. (1993). Exploring and extending personal response through literature journals. *The Reading Teacher, 46*, 466–474.

Hancock, M. R. (2004). *A celebration of literature and response: Children, books, and teachers in K–8 classrooms* (2nd ed.). Upper Saddle River, NJ: Merrill/Prentice Hall.

Harvey, S. (1998). *Nonfiction matters: Reading, writing, and research in grades 3–8*. Portland, ME: Stenhouse.

Harwayne, S. (2001). *Writing through childhood: Rethinking process and product*. Portsmouth, NH: Heinemann.

Hayes, J. R., & Flower, L. S. (1986). Writing research and the writer. *American Psychologist, 41*, 1106–1113.

Heard, G. (2002). *The revision toolbox: Teaching techniques that work*. Portsmouth, NH: Heinemann.

Heffernan, L. (2004). *Critical literacy and writer's workshop: Bringing purpose and passion to student writing*. Newark, DE: International Reading Association.

Hidi, S., & Hildyard, A. (1983). The comparison of oral and written productions in two discourse modes. *Discourse Processes, 6*, 91–105.

Hillocks, G., Jr. (2002). *The testing trap: How state writing assessments control learning*. New York: Teachers College Press.

Hodges, R. E. (2000). Mental processes and the conventions of writing: Spelling, punctuation, handwriting. In R. Indrisano & J. R. Squire (Eds.), *Perspectives on writing: Research, theory, and practice* (pp. 187–211). Newark, DE: International Reading Association.

Hoyt, L. (2000). *Snapshots: Literacy minilessons up close*. Portsmouth, NH: Heinemann.

Indrisano, R., & Paratore, J. R. (Eds.). (2005). *Learning to write, writing to learn: Theory and research in practice*. Newark, DE: International Reading Association.

Jenkins, C. B. (1996). *Inside the writing portfolio: What we need to know to assess children's writing*. Portsmouth, NH: Heinemann.

Kahn, J., & Freyd, P. (1990). Online: A whole language perspective on keyboarding. *Language Arts, 67*, 84–90.

Kamberelis, G. (1999). Genre development and learning: Children writing stories, science reports, and poems. *Research in the Teaching of English, 33*, 403–460.

Karelitz, E. B. (1988). Notewriting: A neglected genre. In T. Newkirk & N. Atwell (Eds.), *Understanding writing* (2nd ed.) (pp. 88–113). Portsmouth, NH: Heinemann.

Kiester, J. B. (2000). *Blowing away the state writing tests: Four steps to better scores for teachers of all levels*. New York: Maupin House.

Killgallon, D. (1997). *Sentence composing for middle school.* Portsmouth, NH: Heinemann.

Koch, K. (1990). *Rose, where did you get that red?* New York: Vintage.

Koch, K. (2000). *Wishes, lies, and dreams: Teaching children to write poetry.* New York: HarperPerennial.

Kroll, B. M. (1984). Audience adaptation in children's persuasive letters. *Written Communication, 1,* 407–427.

Kucer, S. B. (1991). Authenticity as the basis for instruction. *Language Arts, 68,* 532–540.

Kuhs, T. M., Johnson, R. L., Agruso, S. A., & Monrad, D. M. (2001). *Put to the test: Tools and techniques for classroom assessment.* Portsmouth, NH: Heinemann.

Kuroly, N. T. (2004). The power(point) of poetry. *Voices From the Middle, 11,* 30–33.

Lane, B. (1999). *Reviser's toolbox.* Shoreham, VT: Discover Writing Press.

Langer, J. A. (1985). Children's sense of genre. *Written Communication, 2,* 157–187.

Lehr, S. S. (1991). *The child's developing sense of theme: Responses to literature.* New York: Teachers College Press.

Lewin, L. (1992). Integrating reading and writing strategies using an alternating teacher-led, student-selected instructional pattern. *The Reading Teacher, 45,* 586–591.

Linaberger, M. (2004). Poetry top 10: A foolproof formula for teaching poetry. *The Reading Teacher, 58,* 366–372.

Lukens, R. J. (2006). *A critical handbook of children's literature* (8th ed.). New York: Longman.

Lutz, W. (1984). Notes toward a description of doublespeak. *Quarterly Review of Doublespeak, 10,* 1–2.

Lutz, W. (1999). *Doublespeak defined: Cut through the bull**** and get the point!* New York: HarperCollins.

Macon, J. M., Bewell, D., & Vogt, M. E. (1991). *Responses to literature, grades K–8.* Newark, DE: International Reading Association.

Macrorie, K. (1985). *Telling writing* (4th ed.). Upper Montclair, NJ: Boynton/Cook.

McGee, L. M., & Richgels, D. J. (2003). *Literacy's beginnings: Supporting young readers and writers* (4th ed.). Boston: Allyn & Bacon.

McIntyre, E. (1996). Strategies and skills in whole language: An introduction to balanced teaching. In E. McIntyre & M. Pressley (Eds.), *Balanced instruction: Strategies and skills in whole language* (pp. 23–38). Norwood, MA: Christopher-Gordon.

McIntyre, E., & Pressley, M. (Eds.). (1996). *Balanced instruction: Strategies and skills in whole language.* Norwood, MA: Christopher-Gordon.

McKenzie, G. R. (1979). Data charts: A crutch for helping pupils organize reports. *Language Arts, 56,* 784–788.

McKenzie, L., & Tompkins, G. E. (1984). Evaluating students' writing: A process approach. *Journal of Teaching Writing, 3,* 201–212.

Meyer, B. J., & Freedle, R. O. (1984). Effects of discourse type on recall. *American Educational Research Journal, 21,* 121–143.

Mohr, M. M. (1984). *Revision: The rhythm of meaning.* Upper Montclair, NJ: Boynton/Cook.

Moore, M. A. (1989). Computers can enhance transactions between readers and writers. *The Reading Teacher, 42,* 608–611.

Moore, M. A. (1991). Electronic dialoguing: An avenue to literacy. *The Reading Teacher, 45,* 280–286.

Morrow, L. M. (1992). The impact of a literature-based program on literacy achievement, use of literature, and attitudes of children from minority backgrounds. *Reading Research Quarterly, 27,* 251–275.

Murray, D. M. (1982). *Learning by teaching.* Montclair, NJ: Boynton/Cook.

Murray, D. M. (2004). *A writer teaches writing* (rev. 2nd ed.). Boston: Thomson/Heinle.

Murray, D. M. (2005). *Write to learn* (8th ed.). Boston: Thomson/Wadsworth.

Newkirk, T. (1989). *More than stories: The range of children's writing.* Portsmouth, NH: Heinemann.

Niday, D., & Campbell, M. (2000). You've got mail: "Near-peer" relationships in the middle. *Voices From the Middle, 7*(3), 55–61.

Noden, H. (1999). *Image grammar: Using grammatical structures to teach writing.* Portsmouth, NH: Boynton/Cook.

O'Donnell, R. C., Griffin, W. J., & Norris, R. C. (1967). *Syntax of kindergarten and elementary school children: A transformational analysis* (Research Report No. 8). Urbana, IL: National Council of Teachers of English.

Oldfather, P. (1995). Commentary: What's needed to maintain and extend motivation for literacy in the middle grades. *Journal of Reading, 38,* 420–422.

Overmeyer, M. (2005). *When writing workshop isn't working: Answers to ten tough questions, grades 2–5.* Portland, ME: Stenhouse.

Paris, S. G., & Jacobs, J. E. (1984). The benefits of informed instruction for children's reading awareness and comprehension skills. *Child Development, 55,* 2083–2093.

Paris, S. G., Wasik, B. A., & Turner, J. C. (1991). The development of strategic readers. In R. Barr, M. L. Kamil, P. B. Mosenthal, & P. D. Pearson (Eds.), *Handbook of reading research* (Vol. 2, pp. 609–640). New York: Longman.

Parsons, L. (2001). *Revising and editing.* Markham, ON: Pembroke.

Patterson, N. (2006). Computers and writing: The research says YES! *Voices From the Middle, 13*(4), 64–68.

Pearson, P. D., & Gallagher, M. C. (1983). The instruction of reading comprehension. *Contemporary Educational Psychology, 8,* 317–344.

Perl, S. (1994). The composing processes of unskilled college writers. In S. Perl (Ed.), *Landmark essays on the writing process* (pp. 39–62). Davis, CA: Hermagoras Press.

Peyton, J. K., & Seyoum, M. (1989). The effect of teacher strategies on students' interactive writing: The case of dialogue journals. *Research in the Teaching of English, 23,* 310–334.

Pitcher, E. G., & Prelinger, E. (1963). *Children tell stories: An analysis of fantasy.* New York: International Universities Press.

Pressley, M., Dolezal, S. E., Raphael, L. M., Mohan, L., Roehrig, A. D., & Bogner, K. (2003). *Motivating primary grade students.* New York: Guilford Press.

Ray, K. W. (2002). *What you know by heart: How to develop curriculum for your writing workshop.* Portsmouth, NH: Heinemann.

Readence, J. E., Baldwin, R. S., & Head, M. H. (1987). Teaching young readers to interpret metaphors. *The Reading Teacher, 40,* 430–443.

Reutzel, D. R., & Hollingsworth, P. M. (1991). Reading comprehension skills: Testing the skills distinctiveness hypothesis. *Reading Research and Instruction, 30,* 32–46.

Reyes, M. de la L. (1991). A process approach to literacy using dialogue journals and literature logs with second language learners. *Research in the Teaching of English, 25,* 291–313.

Rhodes, L. K., & Nathenson-Mejia, S. (1992). Anecdotal records: A powerful tool for ongoing literacy assessment. *The Reading Teacher, 45,* 502–509.

Rico, G. L. (2000). *Writing the natural way* (rev. ed.). Los Angeles: Tarcher.

Rief, L. (1992). *Seeking diversity: Language arts with adolescents.* Portsmouth, NH: Heinemann.

Rief, L. (2004). High tech, low tech: It's the thought that counts. *Voices From the Middle, 11,* 50–51.

Robb, L. (2003). *Teaching reading in social studies, science, and math: Practical ways to weave comprehension strategies into your content area teaching.* New York: Scholastic.

Robb, L. (2004). *Nonfiction writing: From the inside out.* New York: Scholastic.

Roblyer, M. D. (2006). *Integrating educational technology into teaching* (4th ed.). Upper Saddle River, NJ: Merrill/Prentice Hall.

Rogovin, P. (2001). *The research workshop: Bringing the world into your classroom.* Portsmouth, NH: Heinemann.

Romano, T. (1995). *Writing with passion: Life stories, multiple genres.* Portsmouth, NH: Heinemann/Boynton/Cook.

Romano, T. (2000). *Blending genre, altering style: Writing multigenre papers.* Portsmouth, NH: Heinemann/Boynton/Cook.

Rosen, H. (1986). The importance of story. *Language Arts, 63,* 226–237.

Routman, R. (2005). *Writing essentials: Raising expectations and results while simplifying teaching.* Portsmouth, NH: Heinemann.

Rubenstein, S. (1998). *Go public: Encouraging student writers to publish.* Urbana, IL: National Council of Teachers of English.

Saddler, B. (2003, December). "But teacher, I added a period!" Middle schoolers learn to revise. *Voices From the Middle, 11*(2), 20–26.

Scardamalia, M., & Bereiter, C. (1986). Written composition. In M. Wittrock (Ed.), *Handbook of research on teaching* (3rd ed., pp. 778–803). New York: Macmillan.

Schmitt, M. C. (1990). A questionnaire to measure children's awareness of strategic reading processes. *The Reading Teacher, 43,* 454–461.

Searle, D., & Dillon, D. (1980). Responding to student writing: What is said or how it is said. *Language Arts, 57,* 773–781.

Serafini, F. (2001). *The reading workshop: Creating space for readers.* Portsmouth, NH: Heinemann.

Simon, L. (2005). *Writing as an expert: Explicit teaching of genres.* Portsmouth, NH: Heinemann.

Smith, F. (1988). *Joining the literacy club: Further essays in education.* Portsmouth, NH: Heinemann.

Smith, F. (1994). *Writing and the writer* (2nd ed.). Hillsdale, NJ: Erlbaum.

Sommers, N. (1982). Responding to student writing. *College Composition and Communication, 33,* 148–156.

Sommers, N. (1994). Revision strategies of student writers and experienced writers. In S. Perl (Ed.), *Landmark essays on the writing process* (pp. 75–84). Davis, CA: Hermagoras Press.

Spandel, V. (2001). *Books, lessons, ideas for teaching the six traits: Writing in the elementary and middle grades.* Wilmington, MA: Great Source Education Group.

Spandel, V. (2004). *Creating young writers: Using the six traits to enrich writing process in primary classrooms.* Boston: Allyn & Bacon.

Spandel, V. (2005). *Creating writers through 6-trait writing assessment and instruction* (4th ed.). Boston: Allyn & Bacon.

Spandel, V., & Stiggens, R. J. (1997). *Creating writers: Linking writing assessment and instruction* (2nd ed.). New York: Longman.

Staton, J. (1987). The power of responding in dialogue journals. In Toby Fulwiler (Ed.), *The journal book* (pp. 47–63). Portsmouth, NH: Boynton/Cook.

Stead, T. (2002). *Is that a fact? Teaching nonfiction writing, K–3.* Portland, ME: Stenhouse.

Stein, N. L., & Glenn, C. G. (1979). An analysis of story comprehension in elementary school children. In R. O. Freedle (Ed.), *New directions in discourse processing* (pp. 53–120). Norwood, NJ: Ablex.

Steinberg, M. (1991). Personal narratives: Teaching and learning writing from the inside out. In R. Nathan (Ed.), *Writers in the classroom* (pp. 1–13). Norwood, MA: Christopher-Gordon.

Styslinger, M. E., & Whisenant, A. (2004, September). Crossing cultures with multi-voiced journals. *Voices From the Middle, 12*(1), 26–31.

Taylor, G. (2002/2003). Who's who? Engaging biography study. *The Reading Teacher, 56,* 342–344.

Temple, C., Nathan, R., Burris, N., & Temple, F. (1992). *The beginnings of writing* (3rd ed.). Boston: Allyn & Bacon.

Tiedt, I. (1970). *Exploring poetry patterns. Elementary English, 45,* 1082–1084.

Tierney, R., Carter, M., & Desai, L. (1991). *Portfolio assessment in the reading-writing classroom.* Norwood, MA: Christopher-Gordon.

Tompkins, G., & Zumwalt, S. (2005). Process posters: Making the writing process visible. In G. E. Tompkins & C. Blanchfield (Eds.), *50 ways to develop strategic writers* (pp. 92–94). Upper Saddle River, NJ: Merrill/Prentice Hall.

Topping, D., & McManus, R. (2002). *Real reading, real writing: Content-area strategies.* Portsmouth, NH: Heinemann.

Watson, J. J. (1991). An integral setting tells more than when and where. *The Reading Teacher, 44,* 638–646.

Watson, P. A., & Lacina, J. G. (2004). Lessons learned from integrating technology into a writer's workshop. *Voices From the Middle, 11,* 38–44.

Weaver, C. (1996). *Teaching grammar in context.* Portsmouth, NH: Heinemann.

Weaver, C. (Ed.). (1998). *Lessons to share: On teaching grammar in context.* Portsmouth, NH: Heinemann.

Weih, T. G. (2006). Literature autobiography bags. *The Reading Teacher, 59,* 472–479.

Wilde, S. (1992). *You kan red this! Spelling and punctuation for whole language classrooms, K–6.* Portsmouth, NH: Heinemann.

Wilkinson, A., Barnsley, G., Hanna, P., & Swan, M. (1980). *Assessing language development.* Oxford: Oxford University Press.

Wilson, L. (1994). *Write me a poem: Reading, writing, and performing poetry.* Portsmouth, NH: Heinemann.

Wollman-Bonilla, J. E. (2003). E-mail as genre: A beginning writer learns the conventions. *Language Arts, 81,* 126–134.

Zarnowski, M. (1988). The middle school student as biographer. *Middle School Journal, 19,* 25–27.

Children's Books

Adler, D. A. (1990). *A picture book of Helen Keller.* New York: Holiday House.

Ahlberg, J., & Ahlberg, G. (2001). *The jolly postman, or other people's letters.* Boston: Little, Brown.

Aliki. (1988). *A weed is a flower: The life of George Washington Carver.* New York: Simon & Schuster.

Avi. (1991). *Nothing but the truth: A documentary novel.* New York: Orchard Books.

Babbitt, N. (2000). *Tuck everlasting.* New York: Farrar, Straus & Giroux.

Barrett, J. (1978). *Cloudy with a chance of meatballs.* New York: Macmillan.

Bayer, J. (1992). *A my name is Alice.* New York: Dial Books.

Baylor, B. (1986). *The best town in the world.* New York: Aladdin Books.

Best, C. (2006). *Sally Jean, the bicycle queen.* New York: Farrar, Straus & Giroux.

Blume, J. (2003). *Tales of a fourth grade nothing.* New York: Puffin Books.

Brown, M. W. (1997). *The important book.* New York: HarperCollins.

Brown, R. (1996). *Toad.* New York: Puffin Books.

Bunting, E. (1991). *Fly away home.* New York: Clarion Books.

Bunting, E. (1998). *Your move.* San Diego: Harcourt Brace.

Byars, B. (1970). *Summer of the swans.* New York: Viking.

Carle, E. (1969). *The very hungry caterpillar.* New York: Philomel.

Chaikin, M. (2002). *Don't step on the sky: A handful of haiku.* New York: Henry Holt.

Ciardi, J. (1992). *The hopeful trout and other limericks.* Boston: Houghton Mifflin.

Cleary, B. (1981). *Ramona Quimby, age 8.* New York: Morrow.

Cleary, B. (1983). *Dear Mr. Henshaw.* New York: Morrow.

Cohen, B. (1983). *Molly's pilgrim.* New York: Lothrop, Lee & Shepard.

Cole, J. (1992). *The magic school bus on the ocean floor.* New York: Scholastic.

Cushman, K. (1994). *Catherine, called Birdy.* New York: HarperCollins.

Dahl, R. (1978). *The enormous crocodile.* New York: Knopf.

de Gasztold, C. B. (1992). *Prayers from the ark.* New York: Viking.

Delacre, L. (2000). *Salsa stories.* New York: Scholastic.

Demarest, C. L. (2005). *Alpha bravo charlie: The military alphabet.* New York: McElderry.

Edwards, P. D. (2001). *Slop goes the soup: A noisy warthog word book.* New York: Hyperion Books.

Ehlert, L. (1995). *Snowballs.* San Diego: Harcourt Brace.

Fitzhugh, L. (1964). *Harriet the spy.* New York: Harper & Row.

Fleischman, P. (1985). *I am phoenix: Poems for two voices.* New York: HarperCollins.

Fleischman, P. (1988). *Joyful noise: Poems for two voices.* New York: HarperCollins.

Fleischman, P. (1993). *Bull Run.* New York: HarperCollins.

Fleischman, P. (1997). Seedfolks. New York: HarperCollins.

Fleming, C. (2003). *Boxes for Katje.* New York: Farrar, Straus & Giroux.

Fogelin, A. (2000). *Crossing Jordan.* Atlanta: Peachtree.

Fox, H. (2004). *Eager.* New York: Wendy Lamb Books.

Fritz, J. (1973). *And then what happened, Paul Revere?* New York: Putnam.

George, J. C. (2003). *Julie of the wolves.* New York: HarperTrophy.

Gibbons, G. (1987). *Weather forecasting.* New York: Four Winds Press.

Goble, P. (1989). *Iktomi and the berries.* New York: Orchard Books.

Gollub, M. (1998). *Cool melons—turn to frogs!* New York: Lee & Low.

Gregory, K. (1999). *Cleopatra VII: Daughter of the Nile.* New York: Scholastic.

Hale, S. (2005). *Princess Academy.* New York: Bloomsbury.

Harter, P. (1994). *Shadow play: Night haiku.* New York: Simon & Schuster.

Hawes, J. (1997). *Ladybug, ladybug, fly away home.* New York: Crowell.

Henkes, K. (2004). *Kitten's first full moon.* New York: Greenwillow.

Henkes, K. (2005). *Olive's ocean.* New York: HarperCollins.

Hesse, K. (2001). *Witness.* New York: Scholastic.

Hines, A. G. (1996). *When we married Gary.* New York: Greenwillow.

Howe, D., & Howe, J. (1996). *Bunnicula: A rabbit-tale of mystery.* New York: Aladdin Books.

Hutchins, P. (1968). *Rosie's walk.* New York: Macmillan.

Janeczko, P. B. (1994). *Poetry from A to Z: A guide for young writers.* New York: Bradbury Press.

Kellogg, S. (1987). *Aster Aardvark's alphabet adventures.* New York: Morrow.

Kennedy, X. J., & Kennedy, D. M. (1999). *Knock at a star: A child's introduction to poetry* (rev. ed.). Boston: Little, Brown.

Kimmel, E. A. (2000). *The runaway tortilla.* Delray Beach, FL: Winslow Press.

Klise, K. (2005). *Regarding the trees: A splintered saga rooted in secrets.* San Diego: Harcourt Brace.

Kratter, P. (2004). *The living rain forest: An animal alphabet.* Watertown, MA: Charlesbridge.

Krensky, S. (2004). *There once was a very odd school.* New York: Dutton.

Kuskin, K. (2003). *Moon, have you met my mother?* New York: HarperCollins.

Lasky, K. (1996). *A journey to the new world: The diary of Remember Patience Whipple.* New York: Scholastic.

Lasky, K. (2000). *The journal of Augustus Pelletier: The Lewis and Clark expedition, 1804.* New York: Scholastic.

Lasky, K. (2002a). *Elizabeth I: Red rose of the House of Tudor.* New York: Scholastic.

Lasky, K. (2002b). *A time for courage: The suffragette diary of Kathleen Bowen.* New York: Scholastic.

Lear, E. (1995). *Daffy down dilly: Silly limericks by Edward Lear.* Honesdale, PA: Wordsong.

Lester, J. (1998). *To be a slave.* New York: Dial Books.

Look, L. (2004). *Ruby Lu, brave and true.* New York: Atheneum.

Love, D. A. (2003). *The puppeteer's apprentice.* New York: Aladdin Books.

Lowry, L. (1979). *Anastasia Krupnik.* Boston: Houghton Mifflin.

Lowry, L. (1989). *Number the stars.* Boston: Houghton Mifflin.

Lowry, L. (1993). *The giver.* Boston: Houghton Mifflin.

MacLachlan, P. (1985). *Sarah, plain and tall.* New York: Harper & Row.

Mammano, J. (1996). *Rhinos who surf.* San Francisco: Chronicle Books.

Mammano, J. (1999). *Rhinos who skateboard.* San Francisco: Chronicle Books.

Markle, S. (2005). *Chocolate: A sweet history.* New York: Grosset & Dunlap.

Marshall, J. (1993). *Red Riding Hood.* New York: Puffin Books.

Marshall, J. (2003). *Pocketful of nonsense.* Boston: Houghton Mifflin.

Martin, B., Jr., & Archambault, J. (1988). *The ghost-eye tree.* New York: Henry Holt.

Mayer, M. (1981). *Liverwurst is missing.* New York: Four Winds Press.

Mayer, M. (2003). *Frog goes to dinner.* New York: Dial Books.

McCloskey, R. (1999). *Make way for ducklings.* New York: Puffin Books.

McCord, D. (1999). *Every time I climb a tree.* Boston: Little, Brown.

McGill, A. (1999). *Molly Bannaky.* Boston: Houghton Mifflin.

McKissack, P. C. (1997). *A picture of freedom: The diary of Clotee, a slave girl.* New York: Scholastic.

Mora, P. (1999). *Confetti: Poems for children.* New York: Lee & Low.

Moss, M. (2006). *Amelia's notebook.* New York: Tricycle.

Myers, W. D. (2001). *The journal of Biddy Owens: The Negro leagues, 1948.* New York: Scholastic.

Noyes, A. (1999). *The highwayman.* New York: Oxford University Press.

O'Dell, S. (1990). *Island of the blue dolphins.* Boston: Houghton Mifflin.

O'Neill, M. (1989). *Hailstones and halibut bones: Adventures in color.* Garden City, NJ: Doubleday.

The Oregon Trail (CD-ROM simulation game). (1997). Cambridge, MA: The Learning Company.

Osborne, W., & Osborne, M. P. (2003). *Twisters and other terrible storms.* New York: Random House.

Paterson, K. (2005). *Bridge to Terabithia.* New York: HarperTrophy.

Pinkney, B. (2006). *Little Red Hen.* New York: Dial Books.

Podendorf, I. (1981). *Insects.* New York: Children's Press.

Polacco, P. (1990). *Thunder cake.* New York: Philomel.

Prelutsky, J. (1982). *The baby uggs are hatching.* New York: Mulberry Books.

Prelutsky, J. (1984). *The new kid on the block.* New York: Greenwillow.

Prelutsky, J. (1985). *My parents think I'm sleeping.* New York: Greenwillow.

Prelutsky, J. (1992). *The headless horseman rides tonight: More poems to trouble your sleep.* New York: HarperCollins.

Prelutsky, J. (1996). *A pizza the size of the sun: Poems by Jack Prelutsky.* New York: Greenwillow.

Prelutsky, J. (2000). *It's raining pigs and noodles.* New York: Greenwillow.

Provensen, A. (1995). *My fellow Americans: A family album.* San Diego: Browndeer Press.

Rash, A. (2004). *Agent A to Agent Z.* New York: Scholastic.

Rathmann, P. (1995). *Officer Buckle and Gloria.* New York: Putnam.

Russo, M. (1996). *Grandpa Abe.* New York: Greenwillow.

Rylant, C. (1985). *The relatives came.* New York: Bradbury Press.

Scieszka, J. (1989). *The true story of the 3 little pigs!* New York: Viking.

Scillian, D. (2001). *A is for America.* Farmington Hills, MI: Sleeping Bear Press.

Sendak, M. (1988). *Where the wild things are.* New York: Harper & Row.

Seuss, Dr. (1979). *Oh say can you say?* New York: Random House.

Simon, S. (2003). *Hurricanes.* New York: HarperCollins.

Snyder, Z. K. (1967). *The Egypt game.* Boston: Atheneum.

Soto, G. (1992). *Neighborhood odes.* San Diego: Harcourt Brace.

Soto, G. (1995). *Canto familiar.* San Diego: Harcourt Brace.

Soto, G. (1995). *Chato's kitchen.* New York: Putnam.

Speare, E. G. (1983). *The sign of the beaver.* Boston: Houghton Mifflin.

Speare, E. G. (2001). *The witch of Blackbird Pond.* Boston: Houghton Mifflin.

Spivak, D. (1997). *Grass sandals: The travels of Basho.* New York: Atheneum.

Stanley, D. (2000). *Michelangelo.* New York: HarperCollins.

Stevens, J. (1987). *The three billy goats Gruff.* San Diego: Harcourt Brace.

Teague, M. (2004). *Detective LaRue: Letters from the investigation.* New York: Scholastic.

Van Allsburg, C. (1981). *Jumanji.* Boston: Houghton Mifflin.

Van Allsburg, C. (1984). *The mysteries of Harris Burdick.* Boston: Houghton Mifflin.

Van Allsburg, C. (1987). *The Z was zapped*. Boston: Houghton Mifflin.

Van Allsburg, C. (1991). *The wretched stone*. Boston: Houghton Mifflin.

Ventura, P., & Ceserani, G. P. (1985). *In search of Tutankhamun*. Morristown, NJ: Silver Burdett.

Viorst, J. (1981). *If I were in charge of the world and other worries*. New York: Atheneum.

White, E. B. (1999). *Charlotte's web*. New York: HarperCollins.

White, E. E. (2002). *The journal of Patrick Seamus Flaherty: United States Marine Corps, Khe Sanh, Vietnam, 1968*. New York: Scholastic.

Williams, V. B. (1982). *A chair for my mother*. New York: Mulberry Books.

Wood, A. (1997). *Quick as a cricket*. London: Child's Play.

Wyeth, S. D. (2001). *Freedom's wings: Corey's Underground Railroad diary* (Book 1). New York: Scholastic.

Wyeth, S. D. (2002). *Flying free: Corey's Underground Railroad diary* (Book 2). New York: Scholastic.

Yolen, J. (1987). *Owl moon*. New York: Philomel.

Yolen, J. (1992). *Encounter*. Orlando: Harcourt Brace.

Yolen, J. (1993). *Weather report: Poems selected by Jane Yolen*. Honesdale, PA: Wordsong/Boyds Mills Press.

Author Index

Subject Index